THE IRISH HOUSE OF LORDS:

A COURT OF LAW

IN THE EIGHTEENTH CENTURY

The Irish House of Lords

A Court of Law in the Eighteenth Century

Andrew Lyall

PhD (London) LLD (London) FLS

Barrister of Gray's Inn

CLARUS
PRESS

Published by

Clarus Press Ltd,

Griffith Campus,

South Circular Road,

Dublin 8.

Typeset in LaTeX2e by

Andrew Lyall

With Additional Setting by

Deanta Global

Printed by

CPI Group (UK) Ltd, Croydon, CR0 4YY

ISBN

978-1-905536-56-6

A CIP catalogue record of this book is available from the British Library

for Victor

CONTENTS

Acknowledgements

I would like to express thanks to the following for their comments and suggestions: Professor James McGuire, formerly of the History Department, University College Dublin, Professor Geoffrey Hand, Dr Richard Humphreys, and Dr Nicholas Williams read early drafts, some years ago now. Professor Niall Osborough's knowledge of sources was helpful and generously shared. Professor Colum Kenny read the text when it had reached an advanced stage and made many useful comments. Jonathan Armstrong, the Librarian, King's Inns, Dublin and his staff, the Clerk of the Records and the staff at the House of Lords Record Office, Westminster, and Guy Holborn, the Librarian of Lincoln's Inn Library and his staff kindly and efficiently supplied my requests for material. I should also like to record my gratitude to Lord Normanton for his assistance.

Special thanks are due to Dr Michael Mackey of the Mathematics Department, University College Dublin for his expert guidance on LaTeX typesetting. I should also like to express my gratitude to David McCartney of Clarus Press who agreed to publish the book and for whom LaTeX was no deterrent. His enthusiastic support has been greatly encouraging. I am grateful to Dr Gavin Barrett for suggesting Clarus Press in the first place.

The publication of this work was made possible by grants from the Arthur Cox Foundation and the National University of Ireland whose support is much appreciated.

The Arthur Cox Foundation

Arthur Cox, solicitor, classical scholar and former president of the Incorporated Law Society of Ireland, was associated with the setting up of many Irish companies, not least the ESB. He was a specialist in company law and was a member of the Company Law Reform Committee which sat from 1951 and reported to the Government in 1958, ultimately giving rise to the Companies Act 1963. When he decided to retire from practice as a solicitor in 1961 a number of his clients, professional colleagues and other friends, in recognition of his outstanding contribution to Ireland and his profession, thought that a fund should be established as a tribute to him which fund would be used to encourage the writing and publication of legal text books. There was a generous response to this appeal.

After his retirement Arthur Cox studied for the priesthood and was ordained in 1963. He went to Zambia to do missionary work. He died there in 1965 as a result of a car accident.

The Foundation was established to honour Arthur Cox and was for many years administered by Mr. Justice John Kenny in conjunction with the Law Society. John Kenny was the encouraging force behind the publication of a number of Irish legal textbooks. Without his quiet drive and enthusiasm there would have been no Foundation. To both Arthur Cox and John Kenny we pay tribute.

The Foundation's funds have been used to assist the writing and publication of Irish legal textbooks and the development of electronic databases of Irish legal materials. The Foundation has recently inaugurated an annual prize for the best overall results in the business and corporate law modules of the Law Society's Professional Practice Courses.

The Law Society, as the continuing trustee of the Foundation, is pleased to have been able to assist in the publication of this book.

James B. McCourt
President
Law Society of Ireland

April 2013

Abbreviations

AG	attorney general (not conventionally hyphenated in Ireland)
B	baron of the Exchequer
CB	chief baron of the Exchequer
CP	Common Pleas
CJ	chief justice
DIB	Dictionary of Irish Biography
Cal. St. P. Ir.	Calendar of State Papers, Ireland
HEL	Holdsworth, *History of English Law*
HC	House of Commons
HL	House of Lords
HLRO	House of Lords Record Office, London
IMC	Irish Manuscripts Commission
Ir. Term Rep.	Ridgeway, Lapp and Schoales' Irish Term Reports, 1793–95
J. Eng. H.L.	Journals of the House of Lords, England
J. G.B. H.L.	Journals of the House of Lords, Great Britain
J. Ir. H.C.	Journal of the Irish House of Commons
J. Ir. H.L.	Journals of the House of Lords, Ireland
J	justice, judge
JCP	judge of the Common Pleas
JKB	judge of the King's Bench
KB	King's Bench
KI	King's Inns, Dublin
KI MS	King's Inns Manuscripts
L	Latin
LC	lord chancellor
LF	Law French
LK	lord keeper
NILQ	Northern Ireland Legal Quarterly
ODNB	Oxford Dictionary of National Biography
OED	Oxford English Dictionary
OHLE	*Oxford History of the Laws of England*
PIHL	Proceedings of the Irish House of Lords, 3 vols, IMC
Ridg. PC	Ridgeway's *Reports of Cases in the High Court of Parliament in Ireland* (Parliamentary Cases), 1784–96.
Seipp	An Index and Paraphrase of Printed Year Book Reports, 1268–1535 compiled by David J. Seipp (Seipp's Abridgement), at Boston University web site: [http://www.bu.edu/law//seipp/]
Seld. Soc.	Selden Society
St. P.	State Papers
St. Realm	Statutes of the Realm
St. Tr.	State Trials
UB	Upper Bench
Vern. & Scr.	Vernon & Scriven's Irish King's Bench Reports, 1789–1816

WHP	William Hewitt Papers, University of London Library, Senate House
Wal. by Lyn.	Wallis's Irish Chancery Reports temp. Lifford, ed. by Lyne, 1766–91 ('Wallis by Lyne')

Table of Illustrations

Illustrations appear between pages 102 and 103.

Table of Diagrams

Table of Cases

Year Books

Table of Statutes

The *Chronological Table of the Statutes* published by HMSO lists English and U.K. statutes by year, starting with the first calendar year of the regnal year. Thus, the Declaratory Act is listed under 1719 although it received the royal assent on 7 April 1720.

Introduction

In the summer of 1719 a squad of soldiers under the command of the gentleman usher of the Black Rod of the Irish House of Lords arrested Chief Baron Gilbert[1] and barons Pocklington and St Leger of the Court of Exchequer and confined them for three months, apparently under house arrest, for contempt of the Irish House. The period suggests that they were confined during the long vacation.[2] They were arrested for following the decision in the British House of Lords in *Annesley* v. *Sherlock*[3] instead of the decision of the Irish House of Lords in the same case. The British House of Lords had refused to recognise the Irish appeal in *Sherlock* v. *Annesley*.[4] It was a dispute over property and Maurice Annesley had won in the Irish Court of Exchequer. Hester Sherlock appealed to the Irish House (hence her name came first in the Irish appeal). Annesley appealed to the British House of Lords, who upheld the decision of the Irish Exchequer. The British House did not expressly deny the jurisdiction of the Irish House, but simply ignored it.

Gilbert's popularity in Ireland, at least among the tenant class, had risen to a great height after his decision in *Sweet* v. *Anderson*[5] only to plunge sharply after this incident. Ball[6] notes that Gilbert remained under restraint for three months and was 'treated afterwards with much disrespect'. He went to England and became a puisne baron of the Exchequer there and later chief baron.[7]

The incident in *Annesley* v. *Sherlock* must rate as one of the most extreme examples of a clash of jurisdictions on record. Why did it occur? The reason why the issue gave rise to such intense feeling and to such an extreme reaction was that the issue was a part of the wider political movement in Ireland in the

[1] Jeffrey (spelled variously Jeffray, or Geoffrey) Gilbert (1674–1726). Jeffrey Gilbert became chief baron in 1715 and resigned in 1722. After he resigned as CB in Ireland, on 18 May 1722, Gilbert became a serjeant in England on 7 June 1722 shortly before taking his seat as puisne baron of the English Exchequer on 9 June 1722. He became CB in 1725. F. Elrington Ball, *Judges in Ireland 1221–1921* (London, 1926, reprint by Round Hall, 1993), ii.191.

[2] (1719) 2 *J. Ir. H.L.* 627, 'Proceedings of the House of Lords in Ireland against Jeffery Gilbert, esq. Lord Chief Baron, John Pocklington, Esq. and Sir John St Leger, knt. Barons of the Exchequer there, for issuing Process in the Cause of Annesley and Sherlock, in opposition to an Order of that House: 5 George I. A. D. 1719', 15 St. Tr. 1301.

[3] (1718) 21 *J. G.B. H.L.* 55. See pages 45–45.

[4] (1716) 2 *J. Ir. H.L.* 541. The case is conventionally cited by the name used in the British appeal. Before the Union of the Parliaments of England and Scotland in 1707, the correct terminology for the body which sat at Westminster is the 'English' House of Lords and the citation will be 'J. Eng. H.L.'

[5] (1718) 2 Bro. P.C. 256, affirmed 430; 1 E.R. 927. He established an extensive right to renew leases for lives long after a life or lives had died. Below, pages 149–150.

[6] Elrington Ball, *Judges in Ireland 1221–1921*, ii.191; M. Macnair, 'Gilbert, Sir Jeffray (1674–1726)', ODNB, Oxford University Press, 2004 [http://www.oxforddnb.com/view/article/10688], accessed 21 February 2013; Michael Macnair, 'Sir Jeffrey Gilbert and his Treatises' (1994) 15 *Journal of Legal History* 252–268.

[7] Above note 1. A number of Gilbert's manuscripts, including books on uses and trusts, evidence and the history of the Court of Exchequer, were published after his death in 1726. He was very prolific and the manuscripts seems to have been part of a plan to produce a set of commentaries on the whole area of the law: Michael Macnair, 'Sir Jeffrey Gilbert and his Treatises' (1994) 15 *Journal of Legal History* 252–268. Gilbert was buried in Bath Abbey.

18th century. This movement sought to establish Ireland as a 'sister kingdom' to Great Britain, with autonomous institutions of its own. It reached its high point towards the end of the century in 'Grattan's Parliament', the Constitution of 1782 and changes following upon it. One object of that movement was to establish the Irish House of Lords as the final appeal court and to remove Irish cases from the jurisdiction of English courts. It did not achieve this object at the beginning of the century and the clash of jurisdictions in *Annesley* v. *Sherlock* in the short term was to put an end to this ambition, but it succeeded for a brief period from 1782 until the Union with Great Britain came into effect on 1 January 1801. This work is primarily concerned with the functioning of the Irish House of Lords as a judicial body during the latter period and is based mainly on the cases reported in Ridgeway's *Reports of Cases upon Appeals and Writs of Error in the High Court of Parliament in Ireland*. Ridgeway[8] expressed this connection between the jurisdiction and the political movement of the time in the introduction to his reports:[9]

> The appellate jurisdiction of this country has remained upwards of sixty years in the control of the British parliament, when the spirit of the Irish Nation demanded it should be restored to its natural and primitive tribunal and the more enlightened policy of the sister kingdom submitted to the claim.

As this quotation suggests, some of the material presented here is relevant to a wider constitutional debate, which was a live issue in the 18th century both in Ireland and in the American colonies. It has reappeared more recently as an academic issue in the United States. The debate is as to the legal validity of the claim of the English, and after the Union of the English and Scottish parliaments in 1707, the British parliament, to supremacy, that is, to legislate for the colonies even when they had legislatures of their own. In relation to Ireland, it is as well to point at this stage that this issue had a definite answer in that the English/British parliaments had indeed legislated for Ireland from an early period, although it came to be contested in Ireland from at least the 15th century.

This study however concentrates mainly on a related aspect of supremacy, which arose in the case of Ireland, namely, the claim that the British House of Lords had jurisdiction to hear appeals from cases originating in the Irish courts, either directly or via the Irish House of Lords. The controversy was resolved first in 1720 by the British parliament in the Declaratory Act[10] which declared that the Irish House had no appellate jurisdiction, after which appeals lay from the superior courts in Ireland to the British House of Lords. This remained the position until, as part of the constitutional changes of the 1780s, the Repealing Act[11] repealed the Declaratory Act and the Renunciation Act[12] renounced the

8 Paul O'Higgins, 'William Ridgeway (1765–1817) – Law Reporter' (1967) 18 NILQ 208–22.
9 1 Ridg. P.C. vii.
10 6 Geo. I, c. 5 (G.B.), 1720.
11 22 Geo. III, c. 53 (G.B.), 1782.
12 23 Geo. III, c. 28 (G.B.), 1783.

jurisdiction of the British House over Irish appeals, leaving the Irish House of Lords as the final court of appeal in Ireland until the Union of 1801. The latter part of this book is concerned with describing and analysing the work of the Irish House of Lords in that role.

CHAPTER 1

An Irish House

Tradition has it that the first parliament in Ireland was summoned by King Henry II in person.[1] Whatever the truth of that, the origin of the Irish House of Lords can be traced to the parliament at Castledermot summoned in 1264 by the justiciar, Richard of Rochelle.[2] It was probably a council of bishops, abbots and peers only.

The first parliament in Ireland to introduce the principle of representation was Wogan's Parliament of 1295. It was summoned by Sir John Wogan, Edward I's deputy[3] and was the origin of the Irish House of Commons. Representation was limited to the counties of Dublin, Louth, Kildare, Waterford, Tipperary, Cork, Limerick, Kerry, Roscommon and the liberties, i.e. the counties palatine of Meath, Kilkenny, and Ulster.[4]

Two knights from each county were to attend the assembly of bishops, abbots and peers then summoned. This followed the introduction of the same principle in England in 1254 with the summoning of the 'knights of the shire.' The principle of two representatives from each constituency continued into the 18th century when it formed the model in the constitution of the United States for the composition of the Senate. At first all members of the parliament sat together, but later divided into two houses. The time when this occurred in Ireland is unclear, but probably some time after a similar development in England which occurred about 1332.[5]

The first parliament in which Irish of Gaelic descent took part was that which sat in the thirty-third year of the reign of Henry VIII,[6] which was also

[1] W. Molyneux, *The Case of Ireland's Being Bound by Acts of Parliament in England, Stated* (London, 1698, 1720 edition), pp. 24–25. See also page 23.

[2] H. G. Richardson and G. O. Sayles, 'The Irish Parliaments of Edward I' *Papers of the Royal Irish Academy* 38 Sec. C. P. 129; R. P. Gadd, 'A Short Account of the Peerage of Ireland' (1986) *Coat of Arms* 42, 62.

[3] J. T. Ball, *Historical Review of the Legislative Systems Operative in Ireland* (London, 1889), p. 7.

[4] Black Book of Christ Church, Dublin, Ball, *Legislative Systems*, p. 7, appendix, note F.

[5] Ball, *Legislative Systems*, p. 11.

[6] Ball, *Legislative Systems*, p. 13 and Appendix, note L; St. P., Hen. VIII, iii.304–307. Deputy St Leger wrote to the king: 'The great O'Rayley, with many other Irish Captaines, attended.' A note against their names says: *isti nondum sunt de parliamento* (these are not yet out of parliament). See also *The Slane Peerage* (1835) 5 Cl. & F. 23 at 74, 7 E.R. 311 at 332, HL. The only peer of Gaelic descent

the parliament which passed the statute enacting that kings of England were to be kings of Ireland.[7] Up to that time the title used was 'Lord of Ireland', stemming from the authority given to Henry II by Pope Adrian IV to establish his authority in Ireland by the bull *Laudabiliter*.[8] The statute declaring the title of king can therefore be seen as a further rejection by Henry VIII of the authority of Rome.[9] Some Irish chiefs attended the parliament, although their function may have been more to give an appearance of legitimacy to the statute rather than to act as full members. One peer of Irish descent attended the parliament, Barnaby, or Bryan, Mac-Gilla-Patrick (or Fitzpatrick), Lord Upper Ossory.[10]

The doctrine of barony by tenure, i.e. in respect of tenure of certain lands, was accepted in 1377.[11] The first Irish peerage to be created by grant was that of Baron Trimelston in 1462, followed in 1478 by the creation of the first Irish viscount, Lord Gormanston, although his barony was much older, dating from about 1370.[12]

In 1489 Henry VII summoned fifteen Irish peers to Greenwich. Those summoned were the earls of Kildare, Ormond and Desmond, Viscount Gormanston, and Barons Trimelston, Buttevant, Fermoy, Athenry, Kinsale, Delvin, Slane, Killen, Howth, Dunsany and Kerry. The Earl of Desmond and Lord Kerry did not attend.[13] Thus, two earls and eleven other peers were present, and took their places by rank. The date of creation of the peerages of Lords Trimelston and Gormanston were known, and so the other nine peers became known as 'barons by prescription', i.e. by long usage, because their origin was unknown or the charters, if they ever existed, had been lost. This doctrine was peculiar to Irish peerage law.[14] In 1490 fifteen peers were summoned to the House of Lords in Dublin and met regularly from then on.

Catholics and Protestants

After the Reformation, James I increased the Irish peerage, but with the aim of increasing the number of Protestants. In 1613 there had been an early assertion of legislative independence when the Irish Lords rejected much of the legislation introduced from London. As a consequence it became a feature of Crown policy in the last years of James I's reign and the early years of that of Charles I to

seems to have been Lord Upper Ossery (Macgillapatrick, anglicised as FitzPatrick).

7 33 Hen. VIII, c. 1 (Ir.), 1542.

8 *A New History of Ireland: II - Medieval Ireland 1169–1534*, (Oxford, 1987).

9 Henry VIII had been made head of the Church of England by Act of parliament, but he maintained that his authority really came from God and the divinely-ordained nature of kingship. He also claimed to be head of the church in Ireland and, according to his theory, this mean that he also had to be King of Ireland, hence the statute.

10 *State Papers, Henry VIII* iii.304–307; Cokayne, *Complete Peerage* xii.182; Ball, *Legislative Systems*, appendix, note L, p. 265.

11 G. E. Cokayne, *The Complete Peerage*, vol. 11, Appendix A, p. 2.

12 Cokayne, *Complete Peerage*, vi.18.

13 Cokayne, *The Complete Peerage*, i.458, 462, Appendix A. R. P. Gadd, *Peerage Law* (Bristol, 1985), p. 88.

14 Cokayne, *Complete Peerage*, i.457, Appendix A; Gadd, *Peerage Law* p. 39.

create new peers most of whom would be Protestant.[15] Between 1603 and 1641 as many as eighty Irish peerages were created, sixty-one of them between 1621 and 1630. Only twenty of the new peers were Irish. In 1613 the House had been composed of twenty lords spiritual and twenty-five lords temporal.[16] Of the temporal lords, seventeen were Catholic and five were Protestant and three were minors. By 1634 the membership of the House had trebled to 123, with 24 lords spiritual and 99 lords temporal, most of whom were Protestant.[17]

In 1634 only two of the barons created since 1617 were Catholic: George Calvert, Lord Baltimore[18] and Theobald Bourke, Lord Bourke of Brittas.[19]

James II's Jacobite parliament of 1689 in Dublin was the last before the Union in which Catholics sat.[20] In fact, of the 230 members, six were Protestant, and there were five lay lords and four Protestant bishops.[21] On 12 February 1689, the Convention parliament in England declared that James had abdicated and the next day offered the Crown to William and Mary. The Scots parliament took similar action in May. James II had landed in Ireland in March 1689. His parliament sat from 7 May to 18 July of that year, that is after the English parliament had declared him to have abdicated. Hence, the statutes passed by James II's parliament were declared void in 1695 by the Irish parliament of William III.[22]

15 Cokayne, *Complete Peerage* iii.642, Appendix H, 'Profuse Creations and Promotions in the Irish Peerage', p. 642. Cokayne gives details for the year 1628 and the later creations at the end of the century.

16 Hugh F. Kearney, *Strafford in Ireland 1633–41: A Study in Absolutism* (Manchester, 1959), pp. 49–51.

17 *ibid.*, p. 49.

18 George Calvert (1578 or 1579–1632) obtained a grant of the province of Avalon, Newfoundland, but it had to be abandoned, due to the severity of the winter. He converted to Catholicism in February 1624/5 and since he had lands in Ireland, was created Baron Baltimore of Baltimore on 16 February 1624/5. Cokayne, *Complete Peerage*, i.393. Cokayne notes that no county was specified in the grant, according to Sir Bernard Burke, Ulster king of arms: 393, n. b. Cokayne also notes that Co. Longford is often cited, but there is no place of that name in Co. Longford, and never has been. There was the chartered town of Baltimore in Co. Cork, which was of importance at the time. On 20 June 1632 George Calvert obtained a grant from Charles I of Maryland, named after Queen Henrietta Maria. However, George Calvert died before the formal grant could be made out, and so the grant was made to his son and heir, Cecil Calvert, a few weeks after George Calvert's death. George Calvert's mother was Alice Crossland. The distinctive flag of the U.S. State of Maryland is the banner of Lord Baltimore, being, in heraldic terms, 'Calvert (paly of six Or and sable, a bend counterchanged) quartering Crossland (quarterly argent and gules, a cross botonny counterchanged)'.

19 Cokayne, *Complete Peerage*, ii.252.

20 Thomas Osborne Davis, *The Patriot Parliament of 1689. With its statutes, votes and proceedings* ... Edited with an introduction by the Hon. Sir Charles Gavan Duffy. (London, Dublin, New York, 1893).

21 S. J. Connolly, ed., *The Oxford Companion to Irish History* (Oxford, 2002).

22 By 7 Will. III, c. 3 (Ir.). The statute provided that all existing official copies should be taken to Dublin Castle and destroyed. However, a number of them survived and Ebenezer Rider published many of them in 1740: *The Acts of that short session of Parliament, held in Dublin, May 7, 1689* ... (Dublin, 1740). Davis (above, note 20) gives a list of thirty-five statutes, apparently complete, but did not reproduce all the ones which survived. The British Library has a volume containing many of them, but the pages from page 56 onward are missing, and has a separate copy of the Act of Supply. The volume is reproduced on-line in *Early English Books Online*. University College Dublin has a few printed copies and Trinity College Dublin has one. Marsh's Library, Dublin, contains MSS or drafts of some of them. The Irish Manuscripts Commission is shortly to publish an edition of the surviving

Nevertheless, James II's parliament of 1689 was the most representative assembly to sit in Ireland before 1922 and its statutes are worthy of historical study since they show the grievances felt in Ireland at that time, or at least those that were thought capable of being remedied by changes in the law. The parliament passed its own declaratory Act[23] which denied the right of the English parliament to legislate for Ireland and prohibited writs of error to remove a record from Irish courts to England, both from the King's Bench to the English King's Bench, and from the Irish Court of Chancery to the English House of Lords. Both of these issues were to be matters of contention in the early 18th century, and are considered in more detail below. King James, who still apparently hoped to regain the Crown of England, refused to consent to a statute to repeal Poynings' Law,[24] which would have meant the complete legislative independence of the Irish parliament.

Catholics Excluded

The Treaty of Limerick, 1691 had ended the siege of Limerick and concluded the war in Ireland between the forces of William III and James II. By Article 1 Catholics were to enjoy 'such privileges in the exercise of their religion as are consistent with the laws of Ireland, or as they did enjoy in the reign of King Charles the second', and further that 'their majesties, as soon as their affairs will permit them to summon a parliament in this kingdom, will endeavour to procure the said Roman Catholics such farther security in that particular, as may preserve them from any disturbance upon the account of their said religion.' The rights enjoyed by Catholics under Charles II included the right to sit and vote in parliament in Ireland.[25]

However, the rights secured by the Treaty were about to be eroded by the first Acts in what became known collectively as the Penal Laws. However piecemeal the legislation appeared, the more recent view is that there lay behind it a fairly consistent long-term political aim of converting the Irish to Protestantism.[26] Such legislation was by no means unique in Europe and reflected a widespread notion at the time that there was a necessary connection between citizenship and religious conformity. Catholic states had such legislation aimed against the Protestant minorities.[27] The difference in Ireland was that the legislation discriminated against the majority of the population.

An English Act in 1691[28] made it compulsory for all persons in Ireland to make a declaration and take oaths before taking seats in either house of

statutes, edited by Dr John Bergin of Queen's University Belfast and the present author.

23 Davis (above, note 20), p. 43. The statute is reproduced in Appendix F at page 221.

24 See below, page 18.

25 Although not in England: 30 Cha. II, st. 2, c.1 (Eng.), 1678, required a declaration against the doctrine of transubstantiation before sitting and voting in parliament, but exempted James, then Duke of York. See J. P. Kenyon, *The Stuart Constitution, 1603–1688: Documents and Commentary* (Cambridge, 1986).

26 Ian McBride, *Eighteenth-Century Ireland: The Isle of Slaves* (Dublin, 2008), chapter 5, 'What Were the Penal Laws For?'.

27 *ibid.*, pp. 194–195, 202–203.

28 3 Will. & Mar., c. 2, (Eng.), 1691. Colum Kenny, 'The Exclusion of Catholics from the Legal

parliament or practising as doctors or at the Bar. Catholics had to make a declaration against the doctrine of transubstantiation, which required Catholics to renounce their faith.[29] The oaths were of allegiance to the Crown and of abhorrence and abjuration, denying that the Pope had power to depose monarchs and that excommunicated rulers could be 'deposed or murdered by their subjects'[30] and denying that any foreign person, ruler or ecclesiastical authority had any authority within the realm. However, an exception in the English Act allowed those within the Articles of Limerick and who had sworn allegiance to the king to continue to practise law or medicine.[31] The Act posed a certain dilemma for the members of the Irish parliament, since many members refused to recognise that the English parliament could legislate for Ireland, but it was implemented in Ireland.[32]

In 1695 the Irish parliament enacted 7 Will. III, c. 4 (Ir.) against foreign education, which was aimed against Catholics and in breach of the Treaty and another statute, 9 Will. III, c. 2 (Ir.), 1697, while it purported to 'confirm' the Treaty, did nothing to re-establish the rights guaranteed by it and which had already been taken away by the same parliament. Catholics continued to be denied the right to sit in parliament and were excluded from any official office until the end of the 18th century.[33]

The next blow against Catholics came with the Sacramental Test Act of 1703.[34] Any person holding a civil or military office under the Crown had not only to make the declaration and take the oaths, but also had to produce a certificate within three months of appointment stating that they had received the sacrament of The Lord's Supper 'according to the usage of the church of Ireland'[35] in a public church on a Sunday. Any person failing to do so was '*ipso facto*

Profession in Ireland, 1537–1829', (1987) 25 *Irish Historical Studies*, 337–57; John Bergin, 'The Irish Catholic interest at the London inns of court, 1674–1800' (2009) 24 *Eighteenth-Century Ireland* 37–62.

[29] The declaration contained in section 5 of 3 Will. & Mar., c. 2, (Eng.), 1691 renounced the doctrine of transubstantiation of bread and wine, the invocation of the Virgin Mary or any other saints and the sacrifice of the mass and denounced them as superstitious and idolatrous. The declaration was to be made 'without any Evasion, Equivocation, or mental Reservation whatsoever', a phrase used subsequently in many prescribed declarations and oaths. The oaths of the Vice President of the United States and members of Congress states that it is taken 'freely, without any mental reservation or purpose of evasion'; See also Henry Parnell, *A History of the Penal Laws Against the Irish Catholics* (Dublin, 1808); Ian McBride, *Eighteenth-Century Ireland: The Isle of Slaves* (Dublin, 2008); John Bergin, (et al. eds), *New Perspectives on the Penal Laws: Eighteenth-Century Ireland* Special issue No. 1 (Dublin, 2011).

[30] The latter oath had existed since the time of James I, in the aftermath of the Gunpowder Plot, was included in the Bill of Rights, 1 Wm. & Mar., sess. 2, c. 2 (Eng.), 1689 and was still included in the Catholic Relief Act, 1829, 10 Geo. IV, c. 7 (G.B.).

[31] Section 11.

[32] Interestingly, Henry Parnell in his *A History of the Penal Laws Against the Irish Catholics* (1808), p. 26, still argued that the English Act did not apply in Ireland 'according to the constitution of Ireland, as granted by Henry 2nd, and confirmed in 1782...'

[33] See below page 13.

[34] 'An Act to prevent the further Growth of Popery', 2 Ann., c. 6 (Ir.), 1703, s. 16.

[35] The word 'church' in 'church of Ireland' in s. 16 is spelled with a small 'c'. 'Church of Ireland' with a capital 'C' was not the normal usage at the time, although the expression referred to the established episcopal church.

adjudged incapable and disabled in law' from occupying the offices specified. The test clause had been added in England.

The Irish parliament went even further in 1715 when it denied Catholics the right to vote, again by the requirement of oaths.[36]

By the early 18th century there were 120 members of the Irish Lords, of whom 22 were bishops of the established church, a larger proportion than the bishops who sat in the English or British House of Lords.[37] Bishops were appointed for life by the Crown on the nomination of administrations, and so office holders at any time would have been nominated by administrations of varying political bias.[38]

Protestant dissenters, such as Presbyterians, fared better than Catholics. In 1715 there was alarm at the prospect of an invasion by the 'Old Pretender', Prince James Francis Edward Stuart, and a rebellion by his Catholic supporters in Ireland. It was felt that the army would be weakened if dissenting officers were forced to resign, and this led to the passing of the Toleration Act in 1719.[39] Although the test remained until 1779, Protestant dissenters were relieved of various penalties if they took the oath of allegiance and an oath of abjuration of the pretender. Bizarrely, they also had to take an oath of abjuration of the papal power to depose sovereigns and a declaration against transubstantiation and other Catholic doctrines. Presumably this was in case they were secretly Catholics. Quakers, who objected to taking oaths of any kind, could make a declaration in similar terms.[40] If dissenters took the oaths, then they were no longer liable to the penalties for non-attendance at parish churches under the Elizabethan Act of Uniformity, and they could not be prosecuted for mere non-conformity.[41] The Test Act did not apply to membership of parliament (Catholics being excluded under other legislation, as has been seen) and the Toleration Act also meant that Protestant dissenters could sit in parliament, and there seem to have been a few in the House of Commons in the 18th century, although their influence was slight.[42]

Catholics were excluded from practice at the bar or as attorneys in England in 1696[43] by requiring the declaration against transubstantiation and the oaths of allegiance and of abhorrence and abjuration. A small number of barristers and

36 2 Geo. I, c. 19, (Ir.), 1715, s. 7. The 1715 Act may have been ineffective, because the provision was repeated in 1727 by 1 Geo. II, c. 9, 1727 (Ir.), s. 7.

37 In the English Lords there were 26 out of 190: Francis James, *Lords of the Ascendancy* (Dublin, Irish Academic Press, 1995), pp. 131; J.L. McCracken in T. W. Moody, W.E. Vaughan (eds.) *New History of Ireland* (Oxford, 1986), iv.71–72.

38 Francis James, *Lords of the Ascendancy* (Dublin, 1995), pp. 131–132.

39 6 Geo. I, c. 5 (Ir.).

40 Section 17.

41 A long series of indemnity Acts from 1719 onwards laid down additional time limits within which to comply with the test. See J. C. Beckett, *Protestant Dissent in Ireland 1687–1780* (London, 1948), pp. 43–46. The appendix to ch. 7 contains a list of the indemnity Acts.

42 In 1723 Grafton spoke of the 'chiefs of the Presbyterians in this country who are members of the House of Commons', Beckett, *ibid.*, p. 140, Grafton to —, 14 December 1723, Transcriptions of state papers of Ireland in the Public record Office of Northern Ireland.

43 By 7 & 8 William III, c. 24, 1696..

attorneys had immunity under the Articles of Limerick and some barristers who did not fall within the immunity continued in 'chambers practice', giving advice and drafting wills and deeds without actually practising as barristers.[44]

In 1727 an Irish statute of George II[45] went further than the English Act of 1691 and was in breach of the Treaty. It required the oaths prescribed by the 1703 statute for anyone applying from 1728 onwards for admission as a barrister, a six clerk,[46] solicitor,[47] attorney,[48] or court officer. They were also required to educated their children as members of the Church of Ireland. It contained an exception in favour of solicitors within the Articles of Limerick, but not for barristers, nor attorneys, nor the other offices.[49] The Act was therefore in breach of the Treaty, unlike the English Act of 1691, but the British government cannot be absolved from blame, assuming that the Irish statute had gone through the procedure in Poynings' Law.

The main purpose of the Irish Act of 1727 was evidently to bar from practice ostensible converts who had in reality reverted to being Catholic, by requiring such converts to prove, on applying to practise law, before the lord chancellor or two judges, with witnesses, that they had continued to be Protestants for two years previously. This suggests that in Ireland in the 36 years between the English Act of 1691 and the 1727 Act that some converts may have reverted to Catholic religious practice while remaining in legal practice in Ireland. After 1727, they may also have continued to practise as advisers and conveyancers, as an equivalent of the English 'chambers practice'.[50]

Writs of Acceleration

By a writ of acceleration the heir apparent of a peer with multiple titles could be admitted under one of his father's subsidiary titles.[51] Cokayne[52] lists nine

[44] John Bergin and Liam Chambers (eds), 'The library of Dennis Molony (1650–1726), an Irish Catholic lawyer in London', in *Analecta Hibernica*, no. 41 (2009), pp. 83–132.

[45] 1 Geo. II, c. 20 (Ir.), s. 1.

[46] i.e. one of the six clerks of Chancery. The term came to be used as a generic term.

[47] Solicitors had been required to take oaths of allegiance under 10 Will. III, c. 13 (Ir.), 1698, reinforced by 6 Ann., c. 6. (Ir.), 1707.

[48] Solicitors practised before the Court of Chancery, attorneys before the common law courts. The Judicature Acts in England and Ireland at the end of the 19th century merged the courts into a single High Court and provided that in cases where there was a 'conflict or variance' between the rules of the common law and the principles of equity, equity was to prevail. It also prevailed as to the terminology, since all attorneys from then on became known as solicitors.

[49] s. 5.

[50] John Bergin, 'The Irish Catholic interest at the London inns of court, 1674–1800' (2009) 24 *Eighteenth-Century Ireland* 37–62.

[51] M. MacDonagh, 'The Old Irish Parliament' (1916) 8 *Irish Ecclesiastical Record* 99 at p. 112, refers the practice in the Irish House of Lords of allowing 'the sons of peers' to attend. Jonah Barrington, *Personal Sketches*, 3rd edn. pp. 108–9 refers to the practice of allowing 'eldest sons' to attend: below page 196. Presumably this was a form of training in anticipation of their succeeding to their father's peerage. As such they would merely be there as spectators, but this is to be distinguished from attendance under a writ of acceleration which would give the right to participate in debates and vote.

[52] Cokayne, *Complete Peerage*, vol. 1, appendix G.

instances of the eldest sons of Irish peers being summoned to the Irish House of Lords in one of their fathers' titles, including the son of the Duke of Ormonde in 1662 as Earl of Ossery, the son of the Earl of Clancarty, also in 1662, as Viscount Muskerry, the son of the Earl of Cork, in 1663, as Viscount Dungarvan and the son of Viscount Strabane in 1736 as Baron Mountcastle.[53] Normally a writ of acceleration wa used when the father was old and unable to attend sittings of the House.

Reform of the Franchise

The prohibition as to legal practice was repealed in Ireland by Langrishe's Act 1792[54] and in England by 31 George III, c. 32, 1791.

At the end of the century the Penal Laws were modified as part of the constitutional changes at that time. The test was repealed as to Protestant dissenters by 19 & 20 Geo. III, c. 6 (Ir.), 1779. The property aspects of the Penal Laws had already been relaxed by the Catholic Relief Act 1778.[55] All 'forty shilling freeholders' (i.e. those who owned or held land by a lease for lives, as opposed to a term of years, worth 40 shillings per annum after payment of rent and other charges), were given the right to vote by the Catholic Relief Act 1793,[56] part of the price that William Pitt, the prime minister, exacted for the concessions to the Protestant interest.[57]

It was also in this year that the speech from the throne, in effect from the lord lieutenant, Lord Westmorland, stated that 'his Majesty trusts that the situation of his Majesty's Catholic subjects will engage your serious attention, and in the consideration of this subject he relies on the wisdom and liberality of his parliament'.[58] One is tempted to comment that if he was relying on that, then he was in serious trouble. However, the flattering phrase masked the realities of political

[53] The last time a writ of acceleration was used as to the British House of Lords was after the 1992 general election, when John Major made use of it to make Robert Michael James Gascoyne–Cecil a member of the Lords in one of his father's junior baronies, his father being 6th Marquess of Salisbury. He was summoned as Baron Cecil of Essendon, his father's most junior title, although he continued to be known by his courtesy title of Viscount Cranborne. He succeeded his father in 2003.

[54] 32 George III, c. 21 (Ir.); *A New History of Ireland*. viii.286. Named after Sir Hercules Langrishe, (1731–1811), 1st baronet, politician, the eldest surviving son of Robert Langrishe (c.1696–1770) of Knocktopher, Co. Kilkenny, gentleman usher of the black rod, and his wife, Anne Langrishe (née Whitby). He was a friend of Henry Flood and a supporter of Catholic concessions, although not of enfranchisement. He wrote a letter to Edmund Burke for advice on the subject in 1791, eliciting Burke's famous response of sixty printed pages, the *Letter to Sir Hercules Langrishe* (1792). The letter was a powerful analysis of the necessity for removing the remaining civil restrictions on Catholics: Patrick M. Geoghegan, 'Langrishe, Sir Hercules', DIB James McGuire, James Quinn (eds.). Cambridge, 2009. [http://dib.cambridge.org/viewReadPage.do?articleId=a4671], accessed 31 January 2011.

[55] 17 & 18 Geo. III, c. 49 (Ir.), 1778. See page 166.

[56] 33 Geo. III, c. 21 (Ir.), 1793. See also 37 Geo. III, c. 47 (Ir.), 1797, s. 19.

[57] The franchise qualification for the Union parliament was raised to ten pounds, thus excluding many previous voters, both Catholic and Protestant, in county seats in Ireland. The forty shilling qualification continued after 1829 in Irish boroughs ('county of a city or county of a town'), which had the status of a corporate county, an example being Cork City: Representation of the People (Ireland) Act 1832, ss. 3, 5, 6, 64.

[58] *Parliamentary Register*, 10 January 1793, p. 3.

power. It was generally accepted that the phrase 'his Majesty's Catholic subjects' had been deliberately chosen to indicate that the offensive term 'papist' was now officially deprecated and no longer to be used in official documents or communications. According to MacDonagh the term 'papist' had generally fallen into disuse, at least in official circles, by about 1778.[59]

The Act of 1793, by section 9, retained the oaths for Catholics for the right to sit or vote in parliament and for the offices of lord lieutenant, lord chancellor or lord keeper, chancellor of the Exchequer, the chief justices of the Common Pleas and King's Bench and the chief baron of the Exchequer, puisne judges of those courts, the serjeants, the attorney and solicitor general, members of the Irish Privy Council and various other posts.

Catholics had to take an oath of allegiance, but not the other oaths, before voting for an MP. Voting in Ireland was for members of the Irish House of Commons, since the Irish House of Lords remained an unelected chamber. A clause in the bill of 1793 to admit Catholics to sit in parliament had been moved, but was opposed by the government. The chief speaker against the clause for the government was a young man by the name of Arthur Wesley. By 1829 he had changed both his name and his opinion and as Arthur Wellesley, Duke of Wellington and prime minister, he carried the Catholic Emancipation Bill through the British parliament.[60]

Even where the vote was exercised after 1793 it was still restricted, in the case of both Protestants and Catholics, to male freeholders who held land of the value of forty shillings, the 'forty shilling freeholders'.[61] In a country of four or five million, of whom perhaps 800,000 were non-Catholics, the reform of the franchise, it was estimated,[62] tripled the electorate but still left it somewhere between 3.6 and 4.5 percent of the total population. Nevertheless, this estimate, if correct, implies that Catholics were then the majority of the electorate. Catholics were still excluded from the right to sit in either house of parliament.

A contemporary manuscript[63] records that in 1782 there were seven peers who were Catholic: The Earl of Waterford and Wexford, Viscount Netterville

59 M. MacDonagh, 'Catholics under the Irish Parliament' (1914) 4 *Irish Ecclesiastical Record*, 5th series, pp. 342–43.

60 *ibid.*, p. 344. The duke's support of Catholic emancipation was the cause of one of the last duels to be fought in England, and certainly the last by a serving prime minister. The Earl of Winchelsea had supported the foundation of King's College London and had donated money, as others had done, because it was supposed to further the Anglican religion. Wellington had also supported the foundation, but when Catholic emancipation became an issue he supported that also. Winchelsea accused him of being a traitor, immoral and betraying the Protestant State. The duke challenged him to a duel. When it took place, the duke fired wide and Winchelsea shot into the air. Winchelsea's second then handed the duke's second a note of apology. The whole incident caused an outcry in the newspapers. Outrage was expressed at the idea that the prime minister could risk his life in such a way.

61 See 37 Geo. III c. 47 (Ir), 1797 s. 2; Ingram, *A History of the Legislative Union of Great Britain and Ireland*, (1887), p. 23. For an account of the effect of the 1793 Act see M. MacDonagh, 'Catholics under the Irish Parliament' (1914) 4 *Irish Ecclesiastical Record*, 5th series, pp. 337–46.

62 MacDonagh, *ibid.*, p. 345; see also T. D. Ingram, *A History of the Legislative Union of Great Britain and Ireland* (London, 1887), pp. 23 et seq.

63 G.O. Sayles, 'Contemporary Sketches of Members of the Irish Parliament in 1782' (1954) 56 PRIA sect C. 227 at 273.

(only 'supposed to be' and never took his seat), Viscount Taaff ('in the German service' and whose father had sold their land in Ireland), Viscount Fairfax (described as 'absent'), Viscount Barnewall of Kingsland (who was under age), Viscount Southwell (who had converted to Catholicism and was also absent), and Baron Caher. As peers, they were entitled to receive a writ of summons but they could not take their seats without taking the oaths.[64]

The Parliament House

The chamber of the Irish House of Lords still survives largely intact within the magnificent Parliament House in College Green, opposite Trinity College Dublin. At present the building is owned by the Bank of Ireland. The House of Lords chamber is open to the public during normal banking hours.

The Irish parliament had settled in Chichester House, College Green, in the 17th century, but by the early 18th century it had become decayed. In 1727 £6,000 was voted for the building of a new parliament house. The architect was Sir Edward Lovett Pearce,[65] who was a member of parliament and a protégé of the speaker of the House of Commons, William Connolly of Castletown.

On 3 February 1729 Lord Chancellor Wyndham laid the foundation stone of the new building which was completed in 1731.[66] The building is thought to have the distinction of being the first in the world designed to house a bicameral legislature. The Royal Arms are carved into the tympanum above the grand portico and above are statues representing Hibernia, Fidelity and Commerce. A distinctive feature of the main front are the two arches on either side leading into two colonnades whose columns face into the central quadrangle. The colonnades turn at right angles to form the colonnade along the front of the building. The observer thus has the impression of looking into two chambers simultaneously. The colonnaded main entrance was used as a model for the British Museum building, and aspects of the design, particularly the ceilings of the old Commons chamber, were used in the design for the United States Capitol.

The portico in Westmoreland Street, known as 'the House of Lords entrance', and the curved wall connecting it to Pearce's building were added during later extension work and were designed by James Gandon in 1785.[67] The pediment

64 A number of Catholic peers, including Baron Kingston, were summoned to attend the Irish House on 25 September 1695, since they were entitled to a writ, but did not take the oaths: G. E. Cokayne, *The Complete Peerage*, vii.297.

65 (d. 1733); Edward McParland, 'Pearce, Sir Edward Lovett'. DIB online. [http://dib.cambridge.org/ viewReadPage.do?articleId=a7245], accessed 10 March 2013.

66 F. Elrington Ball, *The Judges in Ireland 1221-1921* (1926); reprinted 1993). For a description of the building see C.P. Curran and M. J. Craig, *The Irish Parliament House*, a pamphlet prepared by for the Public Relations Department of the Bank of Ireland and J. O'Brien and G. Guinness *Dublin: A Grand Tour* (London, 1994). Ball gives the year of the laying of the foundation stone as 1729 without a date: ii.197; Curran and Craig give the year as 1728, without a date, while O'Brien and Guinness give the date as 3 February 1729, op. cit. p. 64. The explanation is probably that until 1752 the legal year 1728 did not end until 25 March: page 122. In modern style the year was 1729.

67 Irish Architectural Archive, 'Gandon, James' *Dictionary of Irish Architects 1720–1940*, online database, accessed 15 February 2011; Frederick O'Dwyer, 'Gandon, James (1742–1823)', ODNB online. [http://www.oxforddnb.com/view/article/10332], accessed 15 February 2011.

on the portico is adorned with statues of Wisdom, Justice and Liberty by Edward Smyth. The columns on the main building, and the pilasters on the later curved wall, are in Ionic style, while those on the portico are Corinthian. When asked why he had introduced a different style for the portico, Gandon replied that he was 'working to the order of the House of Lords'. The taller proportions of the Corinthian columns take up the fall in the ground level in Westmorland Street. They also mirror the style of Trinity College on the other side of the street. Gandon is noted for his other work in Dublin, principally the Custom House, the Four Courts and King's Inns.

A curved wall and portico were added later on the other side of the building and are the work of Robert Parke. The portico in the quieter surroundings of Foster Place known as the House of Commons Entrance, is smaller than the House of Lords Entrance and the pillars are in Ionic style, matching the main building.

The original Commons chamber was octagonal with a large dome above it. The chamber burned down in a fire in 1796 and was replaced, only four years before the Union, by a new chamber, but the dome was not replaced. Wheatley's famous painting[68] of Grattan's parliament in session shows the Commons chamber before the fire.

Shortly after the Union took place the parliament building was sold to the Bank of Ireland[69] and it remains at present the main branch of the bank. One of the conditions of the sale was that the interior of the building be altered so as to obliterate the memory of it as the home of the Irish parliament. This act of cultural vandalism was, regrettably, carried out in the case of the Commons chamber but fortunately was ignored as to the House of Lords, hence its survival to the present day. The Commons chamber, the scene of 'Grattan's parliament', occupied the space which is now the banking hall of the Bank of Ireland.

As to the House of Lords chamber, the tapestries that hang within it were commissioned for the chamber in 1728 from Thomas Baillie of Dublin and woven by Jan (or John) van Beaver. They were designed by Johann van der Hagen, a landscape and marine painter. They depict the Siege of Derry and the Battle of the Boyne. The choice of subjects reflects the fact that although membership of the Irish parliament at the time was confined to members of the Church of Ireland by the Penal Laws, such membership also extended to the whole island of Ireland.

The chandelier, consisting of 1,233 pieces of glass, was made in 1788 especially for the room. It was probably made at the Chebsey's glass-houses near Ballybough Bridge.

A long-case clock by Joseph Donisthorpe of Birmingham stands near the entrance to the chamber. It is contemporary with the building and was probably bought or commissioned for the chamber.[70]

[68] Francis Wheatley (1747–1801), 'The Irish House of Commons'. Gascoigne Collection, Leeds City Art Gallery.

[69] 42 Geo. III c. 87 (U.K.), 1802..

[70] A similar clock, known as 'The Speakers Clock', which is thought to have stood in the Irish

The oak mantelpiece was designed by Inigo Jones and finished, though not necessarily carved in its entirety, by Thomas Oldham of Dublin in 1748 or 1749.

In the chamber of the Irish House of Lords is also displayed the mace of the Irish House of Commons. It was made in England in 1765. The last speaker, Foster, took custody of it at the Union, considering that the House had committed it to his 'safe-keeping and in my charge it will remain until demanded of me by the authority which placed it in my custody.' His descendants sold the mace and it was bought by the Bank of Ireland at a sale at Christie's in 1937. The mace of the House of Lords was displayed in the Four Courts until 1921 or 1922 and survived the fire. It is now held by the National Museum of Ireland which also has Fitzgibbon's robe, featured in the Stuart portrait.[71] The mace is of silver gilt with a large crown on top, although the orb and cross are missing. It bears the cypher 'GR III' and the Dublin hallmarks for c. 1760–70. and the maker's mark, 'WT', for William Townsend. The Irish House of Commons Journal[72] records that Isaac D'Olier, silversmith was paid £286.9.4$\frac{3}{4}$ for a silver mace for the House of Lords, so it seems to have made by one and supplied by the other. It was deposited in the Museum by the Executive Council of Ireland.

A large table which stood in the middle of the chamber was removed at the Union to the Royal Irish Academy and is reputedly the one in the library. The speaker's chair of the House of Lords was also removed to the Royal Irish Academy at that time. The Royal Irish Academy also received the benches of the Irish House of Commons and they now furnish the lecture hall of the Academy.[73]

In 2011 in the wake of the banking crisis the government proposed that the Bank of Ireland should hand over the building on College Green to the state for cultural purposes, but this was resisted by the Bank of Ireland on the ground of its value to the bank's shareholders.[74]

Commons chamber, later passed into the possession of the architect Francis Johnston and in 2006 was given on loan to the state by an anonymous benefactor. It was placed in Leinster House, in the Oireachtas chamber of the Irish parliament. *Irish Times*, 15 April, 6 May and 26 August 2006.

[71] *Irish Independent*, 27 May 1927, p.8.

[72] 22 Dec. 1766, xiv.365.

[73] See Curran, C. P. 'The Architecture of the Bank: 1. The Parliament House 1728–1800', in F. G. Hall *The Bank of Ireland 1783–1946* (Dublin, Hodges Figgis, 1949).

[74] *Irish Times*, 14 May, 17 June, and 12 July 2011. The *Irish Times* of 14 May 2011 reported that: 'Five years ago, former Green Party minister Eamon Ryan met the bank's chief executive and chairman about his proposal to turn [the building] into an electronic library but he was rebuffed.'

CHAPTER 2

The Constitutional Position

The Constitutional Debate

The main focus of this work is the role of the Irish House of Lords as an appellate court at the end of the 18th century and the struggle to establish that role. The government and parliament of Great Britain at first prevented the Irish House of Lords exercising appellate jurisdiction by legislation but later, towards the end of the century, conceded it as one of the reforms of the Constitution of 1782. It is therefore relevant to give some account of the position of the parliament of Great Britain in relation to Ireland. To give a proper account one should first deal with the restrictions on the power of the Irish parliament contained in Poynings' Law, 1495. Poynings' Law was an Act of the Irish parliament, and so it might appear that these restrictions were self-imposed, but this relates to the other question, namely the extent to which the Irish parliament was subordinate to the British parliament. We shall then turn to the debate on that other question, recently revived, in the United States, namely, the issue of the legality of the colonists' claim that the parliament of England, or Great Britain, had no power to legislate for the American colonies. That debate has obvious relevance to the similar claim made by the Irish Protestant 'patriots' in 18th century Ireland. Indeed, the American colonists' argument was informed by the debate in Ireland earlier in the 18th century.

Poynings' Law, 1495

Confusingly, there were two statutes of the Irish parliament commonly known in Ireland as 'Poynings' Law', both enacted when Sir Edward Poynings[1] was lord deputy under Henry VII. The statute 10 Hen. VII c. 22 (Ir.), 1495, applied English statutes 'late made' in England 'concerning or belonging to the common and publique weal' to Ireland,[2] hereinafter referred to as 'Poynings' Law, 1495 (English statutes)'. However, it is the other statute known as Poynings' Law that

[1] See Steven G. Ellis, 'Poynings, Sir Edward (1459–1521)', ODNB, [http://www.oxforddnb.com/view/article/22683], accessed 13 March 2013; David Beresford, 'Poynings, Sir Edward', DIB online, [http://dib.cambridge.org/viewReadPage.do?articleId=a7470], accessed 13 March 2013.

[2] The *Statutes at Large* of the Irish parliament give the year as 1495, and also *The Irish Statutes: Revised Edition, 3 Edward II to the Union AD 1310–1800* (Dublin, 1885, reprint 1995), although some

concerns us here. Under 10 Hen. VII c. 4 (Ir.), 1495, hereinafter referred to as 'Poynings' Law, 1495 (Irish parliament)', no parliament could be held in Ireland until the 'king's lieutenant' and council, that is, the Irish Privy Council, certified under the great seal of Ireland a list of proposed legislation. Only when this had been approved by the king and the English/British council would the king grant a licence, under the great seal of England, to hold a parliament in Ireland.

Taken literally, the statute would have meant that bills could not be initiated after a session of parliament had begun, and also that the Irish parliament had no role in initiating legislation itself, since the the statute was based on the premise that an Irish parliament did not exist until the licence, with its list of bills, had been granted in the first place.[3] An Act of 1556[4] overcame this defect, by providing that legislation could be proposed by the lord lieutenant and council while the parliament was in session. However, this may not have become a regular practice until after Lord Strafford's[5] time as lord deputy.[6]

Routledge[7] pointed out that in the 1580s Poynings' Law was welcomed by the Irish parliament which saw it as a safeguard against oppression by an unscrupulous king's deputy. At that time, only the king's deputy could initiate legislation, and Poynings' Law required him to obtain the British Privy Council's approval. Nevertheless, it would also have to pass the Irish parliament which could vote against it, but perhaps there was a fear that pressure of various kinds could be put upon the members, and at least the requirement of British consent erected a preliminary hurdle in the deputy's way. However, when the Irish 'patriots' and their parliament began to assert themselves from the end of the 17th century, they came to see Poynings' Law as an obstacle to their own ambitions. It was not until that time that the Irish parliament won the right to initiate bills itself. A faction of the Irish parliament had demanded the sole right to initiate legislation.[8] Under the Capell compromise of 1695, brought about

sources give it as 1494. On the meaning of these somewhat vague phrases, see D. B. Quinn, 'The Early Interpretation of Poynings' Law, 1494–1534' (1941) 2:7 *Irish Historical Studies* 241–254; A. G. Donaldson, 'The Application in Ireland of English and British Legislation made before 1801', (PhD. 2 vols. Appendix of statutes. Queen's University, Belfast. 1952), pp. 174–84. Donaldson's work contains an appendix listing English statutes, 1236–1800, and their applicability to Ireland.

3 See generally, James Kelly, *Poynings' Law and the Making of Law in Ireland, 1660–1800* (Four Courts, and Irish Legal History Society, 2007). Kelly's work is an outstandingly-researched and detailed account of the operation of Poynings' Law, 1495 (Irish parliament) and the history of Irish bills in the period.

4 3 & 4 Ph. & Mar. c. 4 (Ir.), 1556; Madden & Fieldhouse, p. 109.

5 Thomas Wentworth, Earl of Strafford (1593–1641).

6 Kelly, *Poynings' Law*, p. 45, above, note 3.

7 F. T. Routledge, 'Journal of the Irish House of Lords in Sir John Perrot's Parliament (3 May 1585–13 May 1586)' (1914) 29 *English Historical Review* 104–117. The surviving journal is reproduced at pp. 111–117. Routledge transcribed the journal from the Carte MS 61 in the Bodleian Library, of which it forms the first nine leaves, although the first leaf was missing. He also notes that the earliest document extant which could possibly be described as a journal of the Irish parliament is a diary of John Hooker, *alias* Vowell, an Exeter antiquary, who recorded daily proceedings of Sir Henry Sidney's parliament of 1568/9: p. 104. He also notes that the diary is printed in C. Litton Falkiner, *Essays relating to Ireland* (London, 1909), p. 210, Appendix C. The printed series of *Journals of the Irish House of Lords* begins in 1634, and that of the Commons in 1613.

8 Kelly, *Poynings' Law*, p. 64. The faction was led by Alan Broderick (1656–1728), then MP for

principally by Henry Capell (or Capel), the lord lieutenant,[9] the Irish parliament was to have the right to initiate draft legislation, including money bills, but not the sole right. The term 'bills' came to be used for bills initiated by the lord lieutenant and the Irish council. Draft legislation initiated by the Irish parliament itself came to be known as 'heads of bills', an expression still used in Ireland today to refer to draft legislation.[10]

Heads of bills required the approval of both the Irish and the British councils and the seal of Great Britain. The Irish parliament could then either pass them unamended, or reject the bills outright. The British Privy Council might also submit a bill to the British attorney general for advice, who might suggest amendments. Often the bill would be sent to a barrister who would be employed to advise and suggest amendments. Such barristers would often be tempted to suggest amendments because they were paid by the length of their opinions. Lord Pery in *Magrath* v. *Lord Muskerry* specifically mentions this in relation to the Tenantry Act 1780:[11]

> It was usual in England to refer our bills to the attorney and solicitor general and some of those attorneys and solicitors general have given them over to a lower class of people, who made a practice of deriving profit to themselves by altering them.

Originally the English Privy Council affixed the great seal of England to bills and returned them to Ireland. After 1707 it was the British Privy Council and it affixed the great seal of Great Britain. In Ireland the bill had to pass through three readings in both Houses, but no alteration could be made to a bill once the great seal had been affixed. This left the Irish legislature at the mercy of the British Privy Council and a British Attorney General who might have little or no knowledge of Ireland and yet who might be tempted, because he had the power of amendment, to exercise the power.

In the 18th century, before the constitutional changes brought about by Yelverton's Act,[12] heads of bills were regularly proposed by the Irish parliament and went through the process of amendment or rejection by the Irish and British councils.

Cork. He was appointed chief justice of the Queen's Bench in 1710, but was replaced in 1711 when the Tory Ormonde became lord lieutenant. After the accession of George I in 1714 he was appointed lord chancellor, in 1715, created Baron Broderick in the same year, and Viscount Midleton in 1717: Johnston-Liik, Edith Mary, ed., *Hist. Ir. Parlt.* (no. 0237) Broderick, Alan. (Belfast, 2002).

9 1st Baron Capell of Tewkesbury, appointed one of the lords justices of Ireland in June 1693, appointed lord deputy by William III in 1695; Cokayne, *Complete Peerage*, iii.6, 'Capell of Tewkesbury'; C. Ivar McGrath, 'Capel (Capell), Sir Henry, Baron Capel of Tewkesbury', DIB [http://dib.cambridge.org/ viewReadPage.do?articleId=a1455], accessed 19 February 2011; Thomas Doyle, 'Capel, Henry, Baron Capel of Tewkesbury (bap. 1638, d. 1696)', ODNB online. [http://www.oxforddnb.com/ view/article/4585], accessed 3 August 2009.

10 e.g. Dáil Debates, Tuesday, 23 November 2004: 'The Taoiseach: The Office of the Attorney General believes there is merit in the heads of Bills being drafted by people with legal qualifications in the various Departments.'

11 1 Ridg. PC at 505–6.

12 Below, page 37.

The Debate in the United States

In 1923, Charles McIlwain[13] argued that the English parliament had never legislated outside the realm of England until well after the colonies had been settled, that subsequent imperial legislation constituted an innovation without colonial consent, and that colonists like John Adams were legally justified in resisting interference by the British parliament in their affairs. Shortly after McIlwain's thesis appeared Robert Livingston Schuyler[14] attacked it and apparently demolished it. He cited one statute after another to show that the English parliament had legislated for the dominions outside England since the 14th century at least.

Schuyler's view prevailed until the 1970s when Barbara A. Black[15] and others[16] challenged what by then had become the orthodox view, that the imperial jurisdiction of the British Parliament was well-established by the late 18th century and therefore that the American colonists had a weak legal case on this point.[17]

Black developed a point made by Schuyler and turned it against his argument. Schuyler had observed that parliament in the Middle Ages made laws not as a representative body but as the king's council. The conflict between Crown and parliament in the 17th century established parliament as a representative assembly.[18] Black argued that McIlwain had ignored the centuries of imperial statutes not because he was unaware of them, but because they were irrelevant to his argument.[19] Schuyler had falsely attributed to its legislative capacity actions of parliament which were in reality exercises of its capacity as the royal council.[20] McIlwain's view, Black argued, was that if any body had inherited this imperial supremacy, it was not the legislature of the later centuries, but the 'nominal' descendant of the king's council, the Privy Council.

Black's arguments, or rather McIlwain's arguments as represented by Black, do not fully take account of the reality of the changing English constitution. In the medieval period the *curia regis* incorportated, as we would see it today, executive, judicial and legislative functions, but at the time they were not clearly seen as distinct and they only became distinct over time.[21] The *curia regis* or king's council evolved into a body consulting the Commons and then incorporating

13 C. McIlwain *The American Revolution: A Constitutional Interpretation* (1923) 186–98.

14 R. Schuyler, *Parliament and the British Empire* (New York, 1929).

15 Barbara A. Black, 'The Constitution of Empire: The Case for the Colonists' (1976) 124 *U. Pa. L. Rev.* 1157, 1179–81, 1186.

16 T. C. Grey, 'Origins of the Unwritten Constitution: Fundamental Law in American Revolutionary Thought' (1978) 30 *Stan. L. Rev.* 843, 857–58; J. P. Reid, 'In Legitimate Stirps: The Concept of "Arbitrary," the Supremacy of Parliament, and the Coming of the American Revolution' (1977) 5 *Hofstra L. Rev.* 459, 476–99. Greene, 'From the Perspective of Law: Context and Legitimacy in the Origins of the American Revolution' (1986) 85 *S. Atl. Q.* 56, 56–77.

17 Black, pp. 1170–72, note 34.

18 *ibid.*, at 1169.

19 Black, note 34, at 1170–72.

20 *ibid.*, at 1171.

21 Baker, *Introduction*, pp. 205–206; A. F. Pollard, *The Evolution of Parliament* (London, 1920), p. 70, cited in Donaldson, 'The Application in Ireland of English and British Legislation made before 1801', (PhD, Queen's University, Belfast, 1952), i.5–6.

it later into a distinct parliament. The definition of the law-making body was changing with the growing role of the House of Commons and was transformed fundamentally in the 17th century. The English Civil War had been fought precisely on the issue of whether the king could legislate without parliament, as Charles I had attempted to do, or whether parliament was supreme over the monarch. The king had chosen to resort to arms to settle the matter, and had lost. The final resolution of the conflict was the Revolution of 1688/9 which established, if had not been established earlier, that the law-making body was 'the king in parliament'. It was, and is, true that orders-in-council made formally by the monarch and Privy Council are used as a form of secondary legislation within the United Kingdom and primary legislation outside Great Britain or the United Kingdom, but whether that applied at the time to the American colonies, is beyond the scope of this work to examine, as is the related issue of whether orders-in-council could be overridden by the British parliament in relation to the colonies at the time, as they can be within the United Kingdom at the present time. Black was on surer ground when she pointed out that when the early colonists first established themselves in America, the English parliament, or the king in parliament, had not yet emerged as the sovereign legislative body.

Nevertheless, as far as Ireland was concerned, the historical record shows that from the earliest times the English Parliament, however then defined, claimed the power to make law for Ireland, and exercised it from time to time. An early example was the statute of 1293 which was made, presumably by the king in council, and 'sent' to Ireland, creating special provisions as to the application of the English statute *Quia Emptores* 1290 in Ireland.[22] Donaldson[23] also cited many medieval statutes applied to Ireland by writ. It is also true that from the earliest times many members of the Irish parliament, however then defined, denied the legitimacy of such a power, or claimed that English statutes required to be confirmed by an Irish statute, but in practice the power was acquiesced in, or not successfully opposed, and they were in any case 'confirmed' by Poynings' Law, 1485, a statute of the Irish parliament, discussed above. We shall also deal below with the British legislation under William III which applied to Ireland.[24]

The leading example[25] of the British parliament legislating for Ireland for the purpose of the present study is the Declaratory Act 1720 which also resolved the conflict over the claim of the Irish House of Lords to appellate jurisdiction. There are complex issues of jurisprudence and legitimacy here which can only be touched on in the present study. On the one hand, the claim of the English/British parliament did not of course depend upon acquiescence by the

[22] 21 Edw. I c. 2 (Ir.); Lyall, *Land Law in Ireland* (3rd edition, 2010), pp. 104–109; Lyall, 'Quia Emptores in Ireland' in *Liber memorialis: Professor James C. Brady*. (Dublin, 2001), pp. 275–294.

[23] A. G. Donaldson, 'The Application in Ireland of English and British Legislation made before 1801'. (PhD. 2 vols. Queen's University, Belfast. 1952).

[24] Below, page 31.

[25] Other examples were 3 Will. & Mar., c. 2, 1691, s. 4, preventing Catholics from practising at the bar, or as attorneys, etc., although it was 'confirmed' by a statute of the Irish parliament, 1 Geo. II, c. 20 (Ir.), s. 1., and 24 Geo. II, c. 23, 1750 (also known as Chesterfield's Act) changing the calendar from Julian to Gregorian.

Irish parliament, if it could be sustained by resort to other sources of legitimacy. Also, a successful resistance to it by the Irish parliament, accepted by the British parliament, would only have occurred if there had been, on the level of political or indeed military power, a successful assertion of the complete independence of Irish institutions by the Protestant patriots. The leaders of the American colonists were able to mobilise military power, with the assistance of France, to win independence by force, after which the issue as to their original legal claim to independence became moot. The leaders of the Irish parliament were never in that position, since they were a religiously-defined minority in a predominantly Catholic nation, and were ultimately dependent upon the support of the British government for maintaining that position, as the compromise of the 1780s demonstrated.

Molyneux's Arguments

Black's argument, and Schuyler's observation, can be traced to the argument of William Molyneux, an Irish protagonist of the constitutional debate at the time when it was a live issue.[26] Molyneux was one of the first people to apply Locke's social contract theory to practical political issues, long before the theorists of the French and American revolutions.

One issue addressed by Molyneux was the practice of issuing writs of error from the Irish King's Bench to the English King's Bench. There was in fact considerable evidence of this. Hand[27] found examples in the reign of Henry III in the 1250s, 83 cases in the reign of Edward I and 15 in the reign of Edward II.[28] Newark[29] mentions that this procedure was 'reiterated in 1633[30] and never questioned until 1641'. The practice was referred to in the time of Charles I in the 1633 'Notes of some particular instances of the hearing of Causes that have their beginning in Ireland before His Majesty in his courts in England':[31]

> The common laws are in force there, and an appeal lies there from the Ecclesiastical Courts to the Delegates in England.[32] By common law a writ of error lies out of the King's Bench here for an error committed on the King's Bench there.

In the 18th century examples of writs of error from the Irish King's Bench to the English King's Bench are *Strong* v. *Teatt*[33] and *Massey* v. *Rice*[34] The last such appeal was apparently *Barry* v. *Nugent*[35] in 1782.[36]

[26] W. Molyneux, *The Case of Ireland's Being Bound by Acts of Parliament in England, Stated* (1698, 1720 ed.)
[27] *English Law in Ireland 1290–1324* (Cambridge, 1967), pp. 14–19, 140–43.
[28] *ibid.*, p. 140; see also pp. 168–71, 184–85.
[29] F. H. Newark *Notes on Irish Legal History* (1960) in *Elegantia Juris.*
[30] Citing *Cal. St. P. Ir.*, 1647–1660, Addenda, 1633, p. 181.
[31] *Cal. St. P. Ir.* 1647–60, p. 181.
[32] See below, page 66.
[33] (1760) 1 Black. W. 201, 96 E.R. 109, Hilary Term, 33 Geo. II. K.B.
[34] (1775) 1 Cowp. 346, 98 E.R. 1122.
[35] (1782) 3 Dougl. 180, 99 E.R. 60.
[36] Below, page 47.

Molyneux argued[37] that the system of appeals from the Irish to the English King's Bench did not imply subordination of the Irish parliament to the British parliament. Molyneux reasoned that the King's Bench derived its authority from the Crown. The King of Ireland, he argued, could allow appeals from the Irish King's Bench into the English King's Bench if he wished. The system of appeals derived not from any subordination but was an act of the King of Ireland in a sovereign capacity. This implied that the King of Ireland could change his mind at any time, and revoke the practice. Molyneux further argued that the English parliament could not assert supremacy over the Irish parliament because, among other reasons, Ireland sent no representatives to Westminster. This latter argument was also to be used by the American colonists. The argument essentially ran as follows: the British parliament by the 18th century could hardly claim to be a manifestation of the King's Council, since it had fought a war on the denial of the proposition that the King with or without his council, could rule alone. The 17th century constitutional settlement had at its heart the assertion of parliamentary supremacy over the King in England and that proposition had been reasserted in the Revolution of 1688. Therefore, if the British parliament asserted supremacy over colonial parliaments, it could plausibly do so only as the representative body which it had by then become. This argument was essentially based on the democratic principle that the right to rule derives from the people. Supremacy, if it were legitimate, had to be based on the consent of the ruled. In this context that meant that the consent of the colonists was necessary to the supremacy of the imperial parliament. In principle the argument might diverge here into different versions on the issue of how the consent could be expressed. One version might assert that the consent could be by general acquiescence. Another version might be that an act of their own colonial parliament, where it existed, would be required. Finally, another version, the one apparently supported by Molyneux, asserted that the colony must at least have had representatives sitting in the British parliament. Ireland had no such representatives.

The latter democratic argument was a dangerous one for the Irish Protestants to use, although not for the Americans, for two reasons. First, it drew attention to the unrepresentative and undemocratic nature of the Irish parliament itself. The majority of the Irish population, who were excluded by the Penal Laws, had no representation in the Irish parliament, let alone the British one. Secondly, it could have been used as an argument in favour of union with Great Britain, rather than greater independence for the Irish Protestant Ascendancy. If the objection to the application of British legislation to Ireland was the lack of Irish representation at Westminster, then the answer could be to grant such representation, and to grant it in lieu of the Irish parliament.

The argument based on historic precedent, i.e. that, whatever the democratic argument, the English parliament had in fact exercised an unchallenged

37 W. Molyneux, *The Case of Ireland's Being Bound by Acts of Parliament in England, Stated* (London, 1720 edn.) pp. 125–26. See also W. Atwood, *The History, and Reasons, of the Dependency of Ireland upon the Imperial Crown of the Kingdom of England, Rectifying Mr. Molyneux's State of the Case of Ireland's Being Bound by Acts of Parliament in England* (London, 1698) pp. 129–31.

supremacy over a long period and therefore in doing so had the sanction of law by long usage, or prescription, was also challenged by Molyneux. The distinction between the parliament as the king's council and parliament as a representative body is not evident in Molyneux's argument here, but it is not important to his argument, since Molyneux set out to show that the supposed power had never, or hardly ever, gone unchallenged. On the question of statutes, the English parliament had attempted to legislate for Ireland, but usually such statutes had been confirmed by statutes of the Irish parliament.[38] One such Irish statute[39] in 1468 had declared in the preamble that 'the learned people of this land are of different opinions whether the said statute should be in force in this land without confirmation'. The motive behind Poynings' Law, 1495 (English statutes)[40] may have been not so much to apply new law to Ireland but to re-affirm the application of English statutes whose legitimacy had been doubted in Ireland in the absence of confirming Irish statutes.

One of the most cogent precedents cited by Molyneux's was the opinion of all the English common law judges sitting in the Court of Exchequer Chamber in 1484, the *Merchants of Waterford's Case*.[41] The case concerned the Staple Act 1423, 2 Hen. VI c. 4, of the English parliament. The Act purported to apply also to Ireland. In that case the merchants of Waterford shipped wool to Flanders, but due to bad weather their vessel put in at Calais, then part of the dominions of the king of England. Sir Thomas Thwaits, Treasurer of Calais, seized the wool as forfeit under the statute:[42]

> *Et ibi* [in the Exchequer Chamber] *quoad Primam Questionem dicebant quod Terr. Hibern. inter se habent Parliament. et omnimodo Cur. prout in Anl. et pei idem Parliamentum faciunt Leges et mutant Leges et non obligantur per Statuta in Anglia, quia non hic habent Milites Parliamenti sed hoc intelligitur de terris et rebus in terris illis tantum efficiendo; sed personæeorum sunt subject. Regis et tanquam subjecti erunt obligati ad aliquam rem extra Terram illam faciend. contra Statut. sicut habitantes in Calesia, Gascoignte, Guien, etc., dum fuere subjecti; et obedientes erunt sub Admiral. Angl. de re fact. super altum mare; et similit. Brev. de Errore de Judicio reddit. in Hibern. in Banco Reg. hic in Angl.*
>
> And there (in the Exchequer Chamber) they declared, that in the kingdom of Ireland they have parliaments and courts in every respect as in England; and by their own parliament they make and change laws, and are not bound by statutes made in England; because

38 See G. J. Hand, *English Law in Ireland 1290–1324* (Cambridge, 1967).

39 8 Edw. IV c. 1 (Ir.), 1468, enacted by the parliament of Drogheda, Madden & Fieldhouse, p. 80. The Act concerned the English statute on rape, cited in the Act as 6 Ric. II c. 6, but in *Chronological Table of the Statutes*, HMSO, as 6 Ric. II st. 1, 1382.

40 10 Hen. VII c. 22 (Ir.), 1495.

41 Y.B. 2 Ric. III f. 11b pl. 26, Seipp No. 1484.026; Y.B. Mich. 1 Hen. VII f. 2 pl. 2b–3a, Seipp No. 1485.002.

42 Quoted in Molyneux, *The Case of Ireland...* 1892 p. 66.

> they have not Knights of parliament here but this is to be understood only concerning the affecting of lands and property in that kingdom; for their persons are the king's subjects; and as subjects they shall be bound, when out of that territory, not to do anything contrary to the statutes [of England], like the inhabitants of Calais, Gascoign, Guienne, &c., whilst they were subjects; and they shall be obedient to the Admiralty of England, as touching any thing committed on the high seas; and in like manner, there shall be a writ of error from a judgment given in Ireland, to the King's Bench here in England.[43]

The phrase 'because they have not Knights of parliament here' is striking. Here is an instance of all the common law judges of England at the time of Richard III accepting the principle of 'no legislation without representation'. The case is recorded as having come before the judges in Exchequer Chamber a second time[44] and this time the chief justice of the King's Bench, Huse (or Hussey), declared that statutes enacted in England should be binding in Ireland 'which was not much gain-said by the other judges.' Molyneux comments that 'how the presence and opinion of the chief justice came to influence them now, I leave the reader to judge.' Molyneux also notes that Brooke in his *Abridgement*[45] comments that Ireland was a kingdom by itself and had parliaments of its own, indicating that he did not agree with the opinion of the chief justice.[46]

There are some objections to Molyneux's arguments. One concerns the question of writs of error to the English King's Bench. Writs of error in England lay from the English King's Bench to the English House of Lords. It would seem logical to conclude that a writ of error could be taken from the King's Bench in Ireland to the King's Bench in England and then a further writ of error to the English House of Lords, although there is no known example.[47] Nevertheless, this would suggest that the English Lords in some sense had supremacy over Irish institutions and that there was a potential conflict, although in support of Molyneux's view, it would not necessarily follow that they had a jurisdiction overriding that of the Irish House of Lords. Nor would it imply any legislative supremacy of the English Lords, even less of the English parliament, of which the Lords were only a part.

In the *Prior of Llanthony's Case*,[48] discussed later,[49] an appeal was taken to the English Lords, but the record does not indicate whether they took any decision. It could therefore be questioned whether such a power ever existed, or to use Molyneux's turn of phrase, whether it was ever the will of the King of Ireland

[43] Translation in Molyneux *The Case of Ireland...*, (1892) p. 66 n. 58.

[44] Y.B. Mich. 1 Hen. VII f. 2b–3a pl. 2, Seipp No. 1485.002.

[45] Title: 'Parliament', section 90.

[46] See also *Polehill, qui tam* v. *Sandborne* (1627) *Robert Paynell's Reports (1627–1631)*, W. H. Bryson, ed., case No. 34, p. 57: Bankes, for the defendant: 'And where Ireland is not named in any statute, it is not bound by it.'

[47] See Flaherty, below, page 32 note 80.

[48] Sir Matthew Hale, *Prerogatives of the King* (D. E. C. Yale, ed.) 92 Seld. Soc. (for 1975) p. 39 n. 2,, see below, note 53.

[49] Below, pp. 41–42.

that such appeals could be taken.

Another objection concerns the capacity in which the English king acted in Ireland. From the time of King John until the time of Henry VIII the monarchs of England asserted rule in Ireland as Lord of Ireland.[50] Henry VIII was the first monarch to claim the title 'King of Ireland', a claim given legal form by a statute of the Irish parliament in 1542.[51] However, as the preamble to the Act asserted that English kings had been kings of Ireland in all but name, with royal sovereignty, power and authority, so it might be argued that there was no essential difference.

Another objection was Poynings' Law, 1495 (Irish parliament)[52] which subjected the Irish parliament to the English Council in the matter of legislation. However, in support of Molyneux, that was not the same as subjecting the Irish parliament to the British parliament, or the Irish courts to the British House of Lords.

Sir Matthew Hale

Sir Matthew Hale (1609–1676) referred to the constitutional position of Ireland in a number of his works. In *The Prerogatives of the King*,[53] which was unpublished in his lifetime,[54] he asserted:

> (i) That an act of the English parliament doth not regularly extend to Ireland, and of the country of Ireland, unless Ireland be specially named, because they having a parliament of their own, and no knights nor peers here, it is not to be presumed that the parliament of England intended to include them by general words, unless specially named...
>
> (ii) But if Ireland or the Irish be particularly named, they were bound by the acts of English parliaments, though they have neither peers (unless specially summoned) knights nor burgesses here. And they have no reason to trouble at it, for Wales and counties palatine and ancient demesnes, if specially named, were at common law bound by acts of parliament and yet at common law had no members that

[50] Henry II at the Oxford parliament in May 1177 had appointed John, his younger son, to be Lord of Ireland. He had wanted John to be crowned King of Ireland in 1185, but Pope Lucius III refused permission. The tile was only conferred after Lucius's death when Henry obtained consent from Pope Urban III. When John became King of England on the death of his elder brothers, the title Lord of Ireland became united with that of the English Crown. *A New History of Ireland: II - Medieval Ireland 1169–1534*, (Oxford, 1987) p. 126.

[51] 33 Hen. VIII c. 1. (Ir.).

[52] Above, page 18, and for the distinction between the two statutes Poynings' Law, 1495 (Irish parliament) and Poynings' Law, 1495 (English statutes).

[53] 92 Seld. Soc. (for 1975) (D. E. C. Yale, ed.) p. 38.

[54] An autograph MS belonged to Francis Hargrave who donated it to Lincoln's Inn library and had it copied. It now LI MS Hargrave 1. A further copy is in the British Library where it is Hargrave 94. 92 Seld. Soc. ix–x. Yale dates the MS to sometime after 1660, based on internal evidence.

> sat in parliament for them or elected by them. 20 H. 6, 8;[55] 2 R 3, 11;[56] 1 H 7, 2;[57] 7 Rep. Calvin's Case.[58] And this was accordingly frequently practiced in reference to Ireland. Rot. Parl. 3 R. 2, n. 42,[59] against absentees. Rot. Parl. 4 H. 5, n. [21],[60] against preferment of the Irish. Rot. Parl. 5 H 4, n 53,[61] restitution upon attainder. It is true that the Irish [48] procured an act of parliament, 10 Hen. 4, but not enrolled,[62] that statutes made in England should not bind Ireland unless enacted there. But this law thus made in Ireland could not bind the superintendence of the English parliament without consent of the English parliament.

Hale does not here necessarily assume the legislative 'superintendence' of the English parliament over Ireland, but rather makes the point that no statute of the Irish parliament could bind the English parliament without the latter's consent. He also notes that the statute was not enrolled, suggesting that it was of dubious validity.

In another text, *The Rights of the Crown*,[63] which Yale dates from the 1640s and before *The Prerogatives of the King*,[64] Hale commented on this Irish statute as follows:[65]

> But clearly this act, if admitted, cannot exclude the power of the English parliament, unless it had been here enacted. That power which originally was in the parliament here cannot be taken away by an act *inter alios actum*. Though both here and there the efficacy riseth from the king's consent, yet I take it no acts here can bind the Irish in point of subsidies or common taxes, because our parliament here by introducing a parliament there, and those acts or laws which prohibit

55 Y.B. Mich. 20 Hen. VI f. 8a–9a pl. 18 (Ireland, prescription). See Seipp, No. 1441.073: 'Plaintiff brought Scire facias to revoke the king's letters patent granting an office in Ireland to defendant which the king had previously granted to plaintiff... Portyngton said that the land of Ireland could not prescribe in things that were prejudicial to the king, because they would make a statute there that one of his enemies should have a vill there, which was a king, that would not bind the king, no more could they defeat the patents of the king; Sjt Fortescue said that this prescription was not in any person in Ireland, but it was in the king, because as I (Sjt Fortescue) understood it, no tenant at will could prescribe, and yet a tenant at will of the king could prescribe, since his prescription was in the king; because the Chancellor of England could prescribe as to a presentment to the church, under a certain value, and yet he held his office only at will.'

56 Y.B. Mich. 2 Ric. III f. 11b pl. 26, (Waterford), Seipp No. 1484.026; 64 Seld. Soc. (for 1945) p. 94.

57 Y.B. Mich. 1 Hen. VII f. 2 pl. 2b–3a, 1485 (Waterford), Seipp No. 1485.002.

58 (1609) 7 Co. Rep. 1a.

59 RP iii.85b–86a.

60 RP vi.102a, b.

61 RP iii.537a, b.

62 The statute is not listed in the *The Statutes at Large*, vol. 1, Dublin, 1786–1804, nor in the *Chronological Table of the Statutes*, published by HMSO.

63 The full title of the MS is *Preparatory Notes touching the Rights of the Crown*, which Yale in 92 Seld. Soc. abbreviates to *The Rights of the Crown*. LI MS Hargrave 9, Lincoln's Inn library; 92 Seld. ix, Introduction by D. E. C. Yale.

64 92 Seld. Soc., Introduction, pp. xxiii, xxv.

65 92 Seld. Soc. (for 1975) p. 38 n. 14.

> common charges without consent of parliament, have implicitly as to that point excluded their own power, the which is the stronger, for that it was never practiced to my knowledge. Yet it is a considerable point.

However, in *The Prerogatives of the King*[66] he seems to have had some doubts as to his earlier opinion, or at least that the opinion was not based on precedent:

> But how far English parliaments might repeal the laws made in Ireland or impose taxes upon the Irish without their consent in their parliament, I shall not proceed to determine, because I find no practice yet thereof to lead me.

Hale was a puritan, but also, unusually, a royalist and some of his points on constitutional law, not unnaturally, were influenced by his political sympathies. In the earlier text he accepted the principle, which had emerged from the English Revolution, that the king could not raise taxes without the consent of parliament. He went further in his assertion that the English parliament had implicitly accepted that this was also so in relation to Ireland. In other words, that the English parliament had implicitly accepted that it could not impose taxes on Ireland without the consent of the Irish parliament, nor could the king, whether as king or England or king of Ireland, or, to put it more succinctly, 'no taxation without representation' applied in Ireland as well as England. If so, then the Irish parliament was in a stronger position than the assemblies of the North American colonies. It also raises the interesting question as to why the parliament of Great Britain did not take the same view as to those colonial legislatures. Possibly it was because the taxation in the American case was intended to be a contribution to the cost of British troops sent to North America to protect the colonists from the French and their Indian allies.

Hale had also written a text on the jurisdiction of the English House of Lords, in which he maintained that its jurisdiction to hear writs of error from the Court of King's Bench derived from the king's consent, rather than from any inherent power.[67] Holdsworth[68] comments that this was one of his ideas which did not prevail. In second passage quoted above, Hale expresses a similar view in relation to the legislative power of both parliaments. Yet it is odd that he asserts that the Irish parliament had been established by the English parliament. According to tradition, the Irish parliament was originally established by the king, i.e. Henry II.[69] Perhaps Hale was thinking of a re-establishment by the English parliament of the 17th century.

Hale's rejection, in the first quoted passage, of the argument that Ireland could not be bound by English statutes since the Irish had no representation in the English parliament, rested on the dubious analogy with Wales and with

66 *ibid.*, p. 39.

67 Sir Matthew Hale, *Jurisdiction of the Lord's House* (London, 1796), see Holdsworth, *Some Makers of English Law: The Tagore Lectures* (Cambridge, 1966) p. 140.

68 *ibid.*, p. 140.

69 Above, page 5.

counties palatine in England. In this context the argument ignores, or rejects, the notion that legitimacy stemmed from democratic principle, which is not an anachronistic criticism, since it was an idea present in Hale's own time. His view seems to be that legitimacy stems from the king, but a king whose prerogatives had been, legitimately, limited by parliament. It is the compromise of 'the king in parliament' which emerged from the constitutional conflict of the 17th century. He pointed out that the English parliament had passed statutes applying to Ireland, but does not mention that the practice was in any way contentious. He asserted that Ireland was bound by such Acts 'at common law'. Hale seems to have regarded the common law as eternal and unchanging, at least in this respect, and as having been unaffected, the taxation issue aside, by the constitutional principles which were emerging in his own time and indeed earlier. On the issue of English legislative supremacy, Hale seems somewhat equivocal. It was limited, but only by the limitations which the English parliament had imposed on itself.

One might note that he does not mention a later Irish statute which had asserted Irish legislative independence, namely the statute of the parliament of Drogheda in 1460, 38 Hen. VI, c. 6 (Ir.),[70] and was probably right not to do so. The parliament was held by Richard, Duke of York while ostensibly acting as 'lieutenant' of Henry VI in Ireland, but it was in the period of the Wars of the Roses and Richard seems to have had ambitions of his own, and to establish an fiefdom in Ireland in opposition to the king. The statute virtually proclaimed independence. The validity of the statutes of the parliament was therefore contentious. The statute is not reproduced in the *Statutes at Large* (Dublin, 1786–1804), probably because its validity was doubted.[71]

Francis Hargrave

Francis Hargrave,[72] the Chancery practitioner and legal writer, in his preface to *A Collection of Tracts relative to the Law of England*[73] said that he had planned to write an opinion on the claim of the English/British parliament to supremacy over Ireland, and had mapped out the various sections it was to contain. However, the passing of the Renunciation Act made it redundant, and he abandoned the scheme.

Hargrave had come to national prominence through his argument as counsel for James Somerset in the famous case of *Somerset* v. *Stewart*[74] in which habeas corpus was granted by Lord Mansfield on behalf of Somerset who had been

[70] See Appendix A, page 209.

[71] On the other hand, 38 Hen. VI, c. 1, which dealt with the 'minister' or 'official' fiction in the Exchequer, and was not contentious, seems to have been regarded by the 18th century Irish parliament as valid. Below, page 55.

[72] J. H. Baker, 'Hargrave, Francis (1740/41–1821)', ODNB [http://www.oxforddnb.com/view/article/12313], accessed 1 August 2009. He devilled for Edward Thurlow, when Thurlow was attorney general, advised him after he became lord chancellor and also advised Charles Jenkinson, later 1st Earl of Liverpool.

[73] (Dublin, 1787).

[74] (1772) Lofft 1, 98 E.R. 499, 20 St. Tr. 1.

purchased as a slave on the African coast and had been held as a slave by Stewart in Virginia.[75]

As to his planned opinion on the claim of the English/British parliament to supremacy over Ireland, from what he says of its intended contents in his preface, it is perhaps as well that he did abandon it. His legal research was as usual conscientious and thorough, and he honestly acknowledged that his conclusions might be partial, but his appreciation of the political system in Ireland and judgment on such matters display what may be called 'blind spots' that were often evident on the part of English commentators. It is worth quoting at length:

> ...I became curious to investigate the subject, and to consider the principal arguments on each side. The result was favourable to the English side of the question: though I am far from supposing that this might not be owing to prejudices, such as may be expected to operate naturally, insensibly, and forcibly, upon the mind of a person born in England. ...I meant to have arranged my proofs of a subordination, under the three great divisions of power *executive*, power *legislative*, and power *judicial*. On the first of these heads I should have particularly considered, how the connection of our kings grew with Ireland: and how the government there was founded on a colony from England; which having been begun in the reign of Henry the second, and being at first restricted within narrow limits, gradually increased, till what was called the *English pale* spread over the whole island; by the final completion of which enlargement, after violent struggles and various revolutions, the Englishry and Irishry, in the reign of our James the first, became consolidated into one people, and quite associated under one government... On the second head I should have assembled all the instances of an exercise of legislative power by England over Ireland, by arranging them under various heads; and I should have inferred much from those English statutes, under which many Protestants in Ireland are understood to hold their lands against the ancient Irish Roman Catholic proprietors, for the sake of showing, that at least the former could not consistently deny the force of English statutes in Ireland. With respect to the third head, I should have endeavoured to have proved a subordinate judicature in Ireland from the infancy of the English colony there; and more particularly, that an appellant jurisdiction over Ireland by writ of error had been uniformly exercised immediately in the King's Bench of England, and finally in the English parliament, as far back at least as the reign of Edward the first. In respect also to the late commencement of English appellate jurisdiction, as exercised by the English House of Lords over Ireland in equity causes, I should have explained, that it was to be accounted for in a great measure from

[75] 'Argument in the Negro case, before the King's Bench in 1772; made to evince the Absolute Illegality of judicially reviving Domestic Slavery in England', in *Jurisconsult exercitations*, i.1–62.

> the late adjustment of the appellate jurisdiction from from our own courts having original jurisdiction in equity; it being well known, that the appellant jurisdiction of our House of Lords was questioned by an English House of Commons, as lately as the reign of queen Anne. ... that however force and oppression might anciently have operated; yet finally the subordination of Ireland to England in a certain qualified way, was sanctioned by the consent of those over whom it is claimed; what passed between the two islands amounting to impliedly to a sort of contract between them, that subordination of Ireland should be taken by England as the price for such an entire communication of its government laws and liberties, as should consolidate the inhabitants of the two islands into one nation.

An example of a blind spot is his naïve description of the Irish population as 'consolidated into one people' while at the same time recognising that the titles of Protestants to ownership of land derived from an expropriation of the former Catholic owners. Another example is that, although he is generally honest in attempting an objective assessment, he refers to the 'force and oppression' which 'might anciently have operated', apparently oblivious to the fact that it did indeed operate, that the Penal Laws had been introduced in the reign of William and Mary and strengthened under Queen Anne, continued in force for most of the 18th century and were still in force at the time that he wrote. Yet it is also true that at the end of the quoted passage he seems to recognise that this project of 'consolidation' remained to be achieved, and that an obligation remained on England to establish full liberties for the Irish population as a whole. He seems unclear whether he is addressing the issue in relation to the whole population or merely as to the small minority of Protestants in the Irish parliament. As to them, his point, that it would be inconsistent for them to assert independence from British legislation, given that the titles to their land depended on English or British statutes, is also questionable, since the Settlement of Ireland Acts were principally statutes of the Irish parliament.[76]

Nevertheless, the point is more a political or debating one than legal. If the 'patriots' in the Irish parliament had been willing to forego their landed titles for the sake of independence, that would be a matter for them. In reality, of course, they had no intention of doing so, and presumably the Irish 'patriots' would have taken the first opportunity to pass Irish legislation confirming their titles.

[76] i.e. the Settlement of Ireland Acts: 10 Cha. I, sess. 3, cc. 2, 3 (Ir.), 1634; 15 Cha. I, sess. 2, c. 6 (Ir.), 1639; 14 & 15 Cha. II, c. 2 (Ir.), 1662; 17 & 18 Cha. II, c. 2 (Ir.), 1665; 7 Will. III, c. 3 (Ir.), 1695; 10 Will. III, c. 7 (Ir.), 1698 (Act of Settlement and Explanation). The English Act, 'An Act for the reducing the Rebels in Ireland to their Obedience to his Majesty and the Crown of England', 16 Cha. I, c. 33 (Eng.), 1640, had expired and was replaced by the Irish Acts of 1662 and 1698. The exception was the statutes relating to the sale of James II's forfeited estates. 11 Will. III, c. 2. (Eng.), 1698 (11 & 12 Will. III in Ruffhead), variously called the Resumption Act, the Trustee Act, or the Statute of Trustees, William III had distributed the estates among his followers, but the British parliament did not countenance this exercise of royal patronage and vested them in the commissioners and forfeited estates, the sales being required to be to Protestants. 1 Ann., c. 6 (Eng.), 1702, ss. 133–34; 1 Ann., st. 2, c. 18 (Eng.), 1702 (c. 21 in Ruffhead). Catholic proprietors who had not sided with James II had a limited right to challenge the forfeiture and to recover their land.

It is worth noting that in a remarkable speech, FitzGibbon, who was nothing if not honest about the realities of power, expressed much the same political point as Hargrave but with none of Hargrave's self-deception:[77]

> Sir, the ancient nobility and gentry of this kingdom have been hardly treated. That act by which most of us hold our estates was an act of violence, an act palpably subverting the first principles of the common law of England and Ireland. I speak of the Act of Settlement passed in this country immediately after the Restoration,[78] which vests the estate of every man who had been dispossessed during the rebellion of 1641 absolutely in the Crown, and puts the old proprietors to the necessity of proving that they had not been guilty of high treason, in order to avoid the penalties of confiscation, which by the sacred and fundamental principles of the common law can be incurred only upon conviction and attainder...So that I trust the gentlemen whom I see upon the opposite benches, will deem it a subject worthy of their consideration, how far it may be prudent to pursue the successive claims of dignified and unequivocal independence made for Ireland by the right honourable gentleman.

Hargrave also notes that the assumption of appellate jurisdiction in equity appeals by the British House of Lords was of recent origin and that its assumption, even as to England, had been challenged by the British House of Commons in the time of Queen Anne. He also noted the more ancient origin of writs of error from the Irish King's Bench to the English King's Bench, but there seems no evidence for his assertion that there were examples of further writs of error to the English 'parliament'.[79]

Conclusion as to Ireland

Flaherty[80] argued that the doctrine of imperial parliamentary supremacy, the very heart of the colonies' conflict with Britain, emerged between 1717 and 1720, when the Irish and British Houses of Lords clashed over appellate jurisdiction in the case of *Annesley* v. *Sherlock*. The result of that conflict, as we shall see, was the establishment of British parliamentary (appellate) supremacy in Ireland in 1720 by a British Act of parliament. As Flaherty points out, John Adams was aware of developments in Ireland, but regarded the assertion of the authority as so recent as to amount to a usurpation of power. Hargrave also considered it to be of recent origin.

77 Speech, (as attorney general), 20 February 1789, on Grattan's motion to the Prince of Wales, in Fleming and Malcomson, eds., *A Volley of Execrations*, p. 83.

78 i.e. 14 & 15 Cha. II, c. 2 (Ir.), 1662 (Settlement of Ireland).

79 Above, page 25.

80 M. S. Flaherty, 'The Empire Strikes Back: Annesley v. Sherlock and the Triumph of Imperial parliamentary Supremacy' (1987) 87 *Colum. L. Rev.* 593.

In fact, a claim by the English parliament to supremacy over Ireland as to judicature was made in 1641 in the trial of Thomas Wentworth, the Earl of Strafford, some sixty years before *Annesley* v. *Sherlock*, but it arose in the context of the original criminal jurisdiction, out of a question concerning the trial of peers by the Irish House. The case is discussed in more detail below.[81] Then there were a number of direct appeals in the 1670s from Ireland to the English Lords, which was either novel or at least unusual in number. However, the Irish parliament was suspended between 1666 and 1692, so there was nowhere else to appeal. It certainly created a precedent, but arguably limited to when the Irish House was suspended, and not when the Irish House was in existence.

This is followed by a few appeals going to the Irish Lords in the 1690s and being challenged by the English House. One can therefore argue that the controversy over appeals which came to a head in the *Derry* and *Meath* cases and finally in *Annesley* v. *Sherlock* had its origins in the earlier controversy in the 1640s over the original jurisdiction of the Irish House of Lords and the assertion of supremacy by the English parliament of that time over Irish institutions. It is also true, however, that there were a number of instances of writs of error to the Irish Lords in 1644, 1661 and 1663[82] and equity appeals from 1661 to 1695,[83] prior to the *Bishop of Derry's Case*.[84]

If any conclusion can be drawn about the constitutional arguments with respect to Ireland it seems to be as follows. As to English legislation applying to Ireland, the English king in council certainly legislated for Ireland on occasion in the medieval period. Irish statutes were often passed to confirm the English ones, but that does not indicate an assertion of legislative independence. The Irish parliament certainly complained against English legislation applying to Ireland, but whether this had any effect is difficult to judge. It is true that when Henry VIII proclaimed himself king of Ireland, it was done by an Irish Act. The English parliament did not begin to assert a general claim to parliamentary supremacy over Ireland until it emerged as a distinct body in the 17th century, and the Revolution of 1688/9 saw some direct English legislation. The claim was therefore recent, from the point of view of 1719. Nevertheless, it could be argued, in relation to legislation at least, that the English parliament had succeeded to the legislative powers of the king, or the king in council, that being the effect of the constitutional changes in that century. The claim was immediately challenged by the Irish parliament, but there was no overall forum to resolve the legal issue. The picture is a somewhat confusing one. It should also not be forgotten that there are examples dating back to just after Poynings' Law and later of the courts in Ireland on occasion, when there was a gap in Irish legislation

[81] See 'Original Criminal Jurisdiction.'

[82] 1 *J. Ir. H.L.* 204, 205, 237, 378. *Verschoyle* v. *Hunt*, at p.205, failed, but not because the Irish House of Lords refused jurisdiction. In 1662 in the case of *Parke* v. *O'Hara et uxor.* directions are given as to the bringing in of the record, Baron Santry CJKB, having declared he was commanded by a writ of error to produce it to the Lords, at p. 362. Further general directions as to writs of error were given in 1692, at pp. 474, 475.

[83] 1 *J. Ir. H.L.*, Index, 'Appeal'; e. g. *Viscount Loftus of Ely* v. *Heirs of Manwaring* (1662) at 371;

[84] Below, page 43.

on a non-politically sensitive matter, treating English legislation as applicable to Ireland.[85]

So far as judicature was concerned, the claim of the British House of Lords to hear appeals from Ireland was on much weaker ground, especially when the Irish House was in session, and the denial by the British House of Lords of the appellate jurisdiction of the Irish House had little basis at all, especially as to civil appeals and writs of error. The claim seems to have been generated in the 17th century as to cases of alleged treason. This perceived danger had clearly abated by the early 18th century, not least because the Penal Laws had concentrated power, both legislative and judicial, in local Protestant hands.

The Irish House of Lords recovered its jurisdiction in 1782 as part of the constitutional changes at that time[86] and the British parliament did not thereafter attempt to legislate for Ireland until the Union of 1801, when all such arguments became irrelevant.

Yelverton's Act, 1782

The other constitutional issue towards the end of the 18th century concerned the control that Poynings' Law exerted over the Irish parliament and the demand of the Protestant leaders legislative independence. This would mean either the repeal of Poynings' Law or its modification.

One preliminary legal issue is perhaps worth mentioning although it has not attracted much attention. Since Poynings' Law was an a Act of the Irish parliament, it could be repealed by the Irish parliament, but in doing so would the Irish parliament have to comply with Poynings' Law?' It was, and is, a principle of British constitutional law, following from its 'unwritten' constitution, that parliament cannot bind itself. Legislation is made by a bill passing the legislative stages in both Houses and then receiving the royal assent, and can be repealed by the same method. Was there such a principle underlying the Irish constitution at the time? If so, then the Irish parliament could have repealed Poynings' Law by the same procedure. The lord lieutenant might still have insisted that the repeal statute itself comply with Poynings' Law and referred it to the Privy Council in London, which would no doubt have advised against consent. Or, even if the lord lieutenant had accepted that it was not subject to Poynings' Law, such a bill would still require the royal assent after it passed through both Irish Houses, and that could also have been refused. To complicate matters further, a statute of the Irish parliament at the time of Queen Elizabeth[87] had provided that no bill could be certified into England to repeal or suspension of Poynings' Law without the consent of a majority of both House of the Irish parliament. This was a response to the experiment of Sir Henry Sidney, the lord lieutenant who had

85 *Irish Exchequer Reports 1716–1734* (Andrew Lyall, ed.), 125 Seld. Soc. (for 2008), Introduction, pp. cli–clii. For example, the Pauper Act, 11 Hen. VII, c. 12 (Eng.), 1495, enacted just after Poynings' Law; 34 & 35 Hen. VIII, c. 4 (Eng.), 1542 (Statute of Bankrupts); 27 Eliz. I, c. 8 (Eng.), 1585 (error from Queen's Bench); 16 Cha. I, c. 10 (Eng.), 1640 (abolition of Star Chamber).

86 Flaherty states on page 619 that 'the Irish Lords never heard another appeal after George [I] granted the royal assent [to the Declaratory Act]'. Perhaps he was referring to the early 18th century.

87 11 Eliz. I, sess. 3, c. 8 (Ir.), 1569.

secured the enactment of a statute[88] suspending Poynings' law, brought about at his own request. The statute nevertheless assumed that a bill passed by both Houses would still have to be comply with Poynings' Act. But the argument is still circular, if the Irish parliament could not bind itself. To make the point again, there was no neutral forum in which such legal issues could be resolved. In fact, the issue was not put to the test, since the bill which modified Poynings' Law and became Yelverton's Act, discussed below, was certified into England in the usual way.[89]

Towards the end of the 18th century the political power of the Irish Protestant 'patriots' had increased relative to Great Britain. The arguments of the American colonists had encouraged them to make similar demands. The engagement of British forces in North America meant that the British were militarily weaker at home and politically weaker after the surrender at Yorktown. The Irish Protestants underlined the position by raising and arming regiments of Volunteers. Nevertheless, the dilemma of the Protestant patriots was that their position was not comparable to that of the American colonists. The American colonists had substantial support among the general population within the colonies, although there were also a substantial number of loyalists,[90] whereas the Irish Protestants were a small minority in an overwhelmingly Catholic country and their privileged position of Protestants in public life was only maintainable with the ultimate support of the British government. In fact, Pocklington, one of the barons of the Irish Court of Exchequer, had remarked long before in 1719 that '...whatever the Lords do here or on your side of the water, I think it will not be in the power of any designing men to make this Nation forget their duty and true interest so much as to run them into rebellion'.[91]

It should also not be forgotten that for all the patriotic rhetoric and talk of freedoms and rights, the 'patriots', apart from the most extreme, who were also the most sincere, sought at base to pursue the narrow interests of their class and of those who supported them. A principal grievance of the 'patriots' in parliament at the time was the discrimination against Irish trade and commerce contained in the Navigation Acts.[92] The Acts forbade the import directly into Ireland of products of the British colonies and required such commodities to be landed first in ports in Great Britain before re-export to Ireland, which considerably increased their cost. The restrictions were removed in 1780[93] but issues

[88] 11 Eliz. I, sess. 2, c. 1 (Ir.), 1569.

[89] James Kelly, *Poynings' Law*, p. 336, n. 74.

[90] At the battle of King's Mountain it was said that there was only one person present who was not born in North America, and that was the commander on the loyalist side, Major Patrick Ferguson of the 71st Foot: Hugh Bicheno, *Rebels and Redcoats* (London, 2004), p. 191.

[91] Christ Church, Oxford, Wake MSS xiii, f. 104, Baron Pocklington to Wake, 1 September 1719; cited by Victory, 'The Making of the 1720 Declaratory Act', pp. 21–22, in Gerard O'Brien ed., *Parliament, Politics and People: Essays in Eighteenth-Century Irish History*. (Dublin, 1989).

[92] The legislation, originally aimed at encouraging the growth of a British merchant navy, and against the Dutch, applied to Ireland from 1670: 22 & 23 Cha. II, c. 26 (Eng.), 1670 (plantation trade). See 125 Seld. Soc. (for 2008), Introduction, pp. cxliii–cxlviii for a description of the Acts as they applied to Ireland.

[93] 20 Geo. III, c. 10. (G.B.), 1780 (trade).

remained as to the adjustment of duties between Great Britain and Ireland, particularly regarding sugar from the West Indies. A sugar refining industry had developed in Ireland and the ban on free trade with the West Indies had badly affecting the sugar refiners. Yelverton, in 1781, in proposing the amendment of Poynings' Law, gave an impassioned speech in which he actually linked his efforts to amend the law to the remaining issue of duties on the import of sugar:[94]

> Mr. *Yelverton* now rose, and declared that he was determined to profit by the excellent advice the *Speaker* had given the House. He gave notice, that immediately after the recess, he would move the House for leave to bring in heads of a bill to regulate the transmission of bills from this kingdom to England – at the present OUR CONSTITUTION was the CONSTITUTION OF ENGLAND INVERTED.– Bills originated with the British Minister, and with this House it only remained to REGISTER or REJECT them. This was the miserable fate of Ireland, and in this Fate it would remain as long as a MONSTER unknown to the constitution! a BRITISH ATTORNEY-GENERAL, through the influence of a law of Poynings, had power to alter our bills. This, he said, was so generally admitted by every Member of the House, that last session, when he moved for a modification of Poynings Law, gentlemen urged, that though this power lay in the hands of the English Attorney-General, yet it was never exercised to any bad purpose; but the declaration was scarcely made, when an altered Sugar Bill annihilated our trade to the West-Indies – annihilate might be thought too strong an expression, but surely it injured it in a very high degree. To prevent, therefore, such an abuse in future, and to relieve the constitution from this oppression, he would again move for the bill he had mentioned. The House adjourned to the 29th instant.

Neither his passion, nor his indignation, nor that of the other parliamentary 'patriots', was aroused by the consideration that all sugar at the time was the product of slave labour. Many abolitionists refused to use sugar for that reason.[95] Thomas Clarkson estimated that by the 1790s as many as 300,000 people had given up using sugar.[96] Dr Johnson's jibe at the American colonists, 'How is it that we hear the loudest yelps for liberty among the drivers of negroes?'[97] could have been applied almost as aptly to the 'patriots' in the Irish parliament.

94 Thursday, 11 October 1781, 1 *Parliamentary Register* 15; Nini Rogers, 'Ireland and the Black Atlantic in the Eighteenth Century.' (2000) 32 *Irish Historical Studies* 174–192.

95 William Hague, *William Wilberforce: the Life of the Great Anti-Slave Trade Campaigner* (London, 2007), p. 228.

96 Thomas Clarkson, *The History of the Rise, Progress and Accomplishment of the Abolition of the African Slave-Trade by the British Parliament* (London, 1839) ii.349–50.

97 Samuel Johnson, *Taxation No Tyranny* (1775, Yale ed., vol. 10), p. 454. See also Johnson, 'Milton', in *Lives of the Poets*: 'They who most loudly clamour for liberty do not most liberally grant it.'

Among the leaders in parliament there developed a radical wing, led by Henry Flood,[98] and a more moderate wing led by Grattan, FitzGibbon and Yelverton, and both reflected in different ways their own approach to this dilemma.

Henry Flood called for the complete repeal of Poynings' Law, and the renunciation of any claim by the British to legislate for Ireland, to amend laws passed by the Irish parliament, and an end to writs of error from Irish to British courts.[99] Yet at the same time, Flood aggressively sought political office through the patronage of the lord lieutenant.[100]

Flood was to succeed in his arguments over renunciation, as we shall see.[101] However, despite his four-hour speech, described as a *tour de force*,[102] the arguments of Yelverton prevailed as to the modification of Poynings' Law.

Yelverton's Act, 1782[103] provided that:

> 'the lord lieutenant, or other chief governor or governors and council of this kingdom, for the time being, do and shall certify all such bills, and none other, as both Houses of Parliament shall judge expedient to be enacted in this kingdom, to his Majesty, his heirs and successors, under the great seal of this kingdom, without addition, diminution, or alteration.'

This provision re-enacted the royal assent for Irish bills, originally contained in Poynings' Law (Irish parliament). As to the royal assent in relation to British bills, the last occasion on which the royal assent had been refused was by Queen Anne in 1708 when she refused assent to a bill to raise a militia in Scotland, for the reason that she considered it dangerous to arm the Scots. George I did not speak English and the early Hanoverians lacked political influence and the convention developed that the royal assent would not in future be refused in Great Britain to legislation passed by both houses of parliament. Yelverton's Act, on the other hand, by re-enacting the royal assent for Ireland, implied that it was distinct from the royal assent as to British bills and therefore possibly that it was not subject to a similar constitutional convention. There was no express provision in the Act seeking to limit the power to refuse the royal assent. Although Irish bills could not henceforth be amended, the royal assent could have been refused.[104]

Independence was qualified in other ways, some formal and some practical. The executive power still lay in the hands of the lord lieutenant, appointed by the British government and therefore answerable to them. The Irish parliament

98 James Kelly, *Henry Flood: Patriots and Politics in Eighteenth-Century Ireland* (Dublin, 1998); James Kelly, 'Flood, Henry (1732–1791)', ODNB online. [http://www.oxforddnb.com/view/article/9755], accessed 23 May 2009.

99 Kelly, *Henry Flood*, pp. 311–36.

100 Flood sought the chancellorship of the Exchequer but reluctantly accepted a vice-treasureship instead: *ibid.*, chapter 5, especially pp. 178–99, 214–15.

101 Below, page 48.

102 Kelly, *Henry Flood*, 290.

103 21 & 22 Geo.. III c. 47 (Ir.), 1782. Appendix O.

104 J. C. Beckett, *The Making of Modern Ireland, 1603–1923* (London, 1966) p. 225.

could not dismiss the lord lieutenant.[105] The executive was thus free of control by the Irish parliament and this could have negated the restriction on the power of the Privy Council in either country, because the king, in deciding whether to assent to bills, could have taken their advice. In theory the Irish parliament could have passed legislation to make the executive accountable, but this again could have provoked a refusal of the royal assent. An alternative might have been to deny the executive supply, i.e. by refusing to pass finance bills. However, in these hypothetical circumstances the British parliament might have passed an Act granting supply to the Irish executive, which would have raised the issue already dealt with. At any rate, neither the Irish 'patriots' nor the British government put these issues to the test.

Tenure of Judges

Irish judges had no security of tenure until 1781.[106] First, they held office only during the king's pleasure, by an Irish statute of 1495,[107] and secondly, their commissions ended on a demise of the Crown. The exception as to barons specifically did not apply in Ireland under the statute of 1495.[108]

Judges in Ireland could thus be removed at will and there were several examples from the early 18th century, when there was a change of administration. They were generally removed because of their political views, rather than professional failings. James Macartney (1651–1727), appointed second justice of the King's Bench in 1701, was removed in 1711 with the change of administration, at the same time that Alan Broderick (1656–1728), later Lord Midleton, was removed as chief justice of the Queen's Bench by the Tory lord lieutenant, the Duke of Ormonde.[109] Sir Henry Echlin,[110] a judge of the King's Bench and later baron of the Exchequer, was removed on the accession of George I,[111] as was the

[105] *ibid.*

[106] Before 1700 English judges had generally lacked security of tenure. See Baker, *Introduction*, at pp. 167–68. One exception was the chief baron of the Exchequer, and the other barons, Coke Inst., iv.117. This practice as to barons in England was not guaranteed by statute, but the majority of them were given such tenure from 1450 until the reign of Charles I: Baker, *Introduction*, at p. 167. William III had appointed all his judges in England during good behaviour and this was guaranteed by the Act of Settlement, 1700, which required that judges' patents so appoint them: 12 & 13 Will. III, c. 2 (Eng.). Thereafter they could be removed only on an address to both Houses of parliament: s. 3; Lemmings, 'The Independence of the Judiciary in Eighteenth-Century England' in P. Birks, ed., *Life of the Law: Proceedings of the Tenth British Legal History Conference* (London, 1993). Even so, English judges' tenure ceased automatically on a demise of the Crown until a statute of 1760: 1 Geo. III, c. 23 (Eng.).

[107] See 10 Hen. VII, c. 2 (Ir.), 1495, including the lord chancellor, the chief and second baron of the Exchequer, and the master and clerk of the rolls (in the case of the master of the rolls, only if he had been granted the judicial power).

[108] The fact that they were replaced in practice is shown by the cases of Rochfort and Echlin mentioned below.

[109] James Butler, 2nd Duke of Ormonde, (1665–1745), lord lieutenant, 1703–1707, 1710–1713, Cokayne, *Complete Peerage*, x.157; Stuart Handley, 'Butler, James, second Duke of Ormond (1665–1745)', ODNB online. [http://www.oxforddnb.com/view/article/4193], accessed 14 July 2008.

[110] Sir Henry Echlin (1652–1725) was the second son of Robert Echlin of Ardquin in Co. Down, was B. of the Exchequer in 1690, J.K.B. in 1692, reappointed to the Exchequer in 1693.

[111] Ball, *Judges in Ireland*, ii.56–57.

chief baron of the Exchequer, Rochfort,[112] when the Tory administration gave way to the Whigs. Sir Constantine Phipps (1656–1723), who was suspected of being a Jacobite, was removed as lord chancellor at the same time.[113]

Maintaining the insecurity of the Irish judiciary was one of the ways in which Ireland was subordinated to the control of the British government and that was also the case with the judges in North America, which was one of the grievances set out by Jefferson in the *Declaration of Independence* of 1776: 'He [George III] has made judges dependent on his Will alone, for the tenure of their offices, and the amount and payment of their salaries.'

The first judicial officer in Ireland to be appointed 'during good behaviour' was the recorder of Dublin in 1759.[114] Up to that time he had been elected by the city corporation, and held office at the pleasure of the city. There had been great agitation in the years before 1759 at the state of law and order in the city, and the failure of the City corporation to control it. This in turn was attributed to the constitution of the corporation which allowed a small group of people to elect the officers of the City, including the recorder, thus weakening the authority of the magistrates.[115] The recorder was appointed by the city corporation and so from 1759 he was removable, by the city, on failure of good behaviour and also on promotion to the bench of the superior courts.

Irish judges of the superior courts came to be appointed 'during good behaviour' in 1781,[116] and removable only on an address to both houses of the Irish parliament. Thereafter their commissions did not end on a demise of the Crown either. Thurlow, as British attorney general, had reported against the change, on the ground that the resolution would not be subject to the procedure under Poynings' Law.[117] The change was nevertheless made.

112 Ball, *Judges in Ireland* ii.69. He was appointed CB in 1707 and removed in 1714.

113 *ibid.*, ii.71.

114 33 Geo. II, c. 16 (Ir.), 1759, s. 20.

115 See Irish parliament, Commons, 'Heads of a Bill for better Regulating the Elections of the Lord Mayor, Aldermen, Sheriffs, Commons and other Officers of the City of Dublin, and for Preserving Peace, Order and Good Government in the said City' (Dublin, 1759), and an earlier version, 1758. See generally J. R. Hill, *From Patriots to Unionists: Dublin Civic Politics and Irish Protestant Patriotism, 1660–1840*, (Oxford, 1997). Appendix C is a list of recorders of Dublin from 1660 to 1841.

116 21 & 22 Geo. III, c. 50 (Ir.), 1781–82, s. 1; William Dwyer Ferguson, *A Treatise on the Practice of the Queen's Bench, Common Pleas, and Exchequer of Pleas, in Ireland, in Personal Actions and Ejectments* (Dublin, 1841), i.16.

117 'Report of the Attorney and Solicitor General on an Irish bill, the Judges' Commission Bill', 28 Feb. 1776, PRO PC 1/11/9. See Appendix K, below, page 239.

CHAPTER 3

Loss and Recovery

Early Examples of the Appellate Jurisdiction

A manuscript[1] in Marsh's Library Dublin gives a number of examples of appeals or other legal proceedings heard by the Irish House of Lords before 1700. The manuscript is a single undated sheet, but probably dates from the period of the *Derry* and *Meath* cases, discussed below, in the 1690s. The two earliest examples are both from the time of Edward IV and are cases concerning Michael, Archbishop of Dublin in 1463 and John, also Archbishop of Dublin, in 1476. Then there was a case concerning Nicholas Husse, Baron of Galtrym [i.e. Galtrim, Co. Meath] who had been imprisoned in Dublin Castle by the Earl of Shrewsbury in 1447 or 1448.

There is one example in 1420 of a writ of error from the Irish King's Bench to the Irish House of Lords. This was the *Prior of Llanthony's Case*.[2] The case is mentioned by Molyneux.[3] The Prior of Llanthony in Wales brought an action in the Common Pleas of Ireland against the 'Prior of Mollingar' (Mullingar), for the arrears of an annuity. Judgment went against the Prior of Mollingar, who then brought a writ of error in the Irish King's Bench. The King's Bench affirmed the judgment of the Common Pleas. The Prior of Mollingar then appealed to the parliament of Ireland held in 1427 (5 Henry VI) before James Butler, 4th Earl of Ormond. The Irish parliament - we are not told whether it was the House of Lords alone - reversed both judgments and held in favour of the Prior of Mollingar. The Prior of Llanthony applied to the King's Bench in England but that court refused to intermeddle as having 'no power over what had passed in the parliament of Ireland.' The Prior of Llanthony then appealed to the English

[1] Below, Appendix E, page 219.

[2] Prynne on 4 Inst. pp. 313–14, Serjeant [Sir Samuel] Mayart in answer to Sir Richard Bolton, Harris' *Hibernica* pt. 2 p. 180. Sir Matthew Hale, *Prerogatives of the King* (D. E. C. Yale, ed.) 92 Seld. Soc. (for 1975), p. 39 n. 2. See also 3 St. Tr. 1504: 'until 29 Edw. III erroneous judgments given in Ireland were determinable no where but in England, no, not in the parliament of Ireland', 'Close Rolls of the Tower', 29 Edw. III, memb. 12, *Prior of Lentham's Case* (1429) 8 Hen. VI no. 70.

[3] Molyneux, *The Case of Ireland's being bound by Acts of Parliament made in England Stated* (1782 edn.), p. 46. Molyneux cites 'Mr Pryn against the 4th Inst [Coke's] ch. 76 p. 313.' See also Newark op. cit. note 128, p. 16.

parliament. However, it seems from the parliament roll[4] that nothing was done about the appeal. The petition appears at the end of the roll, but nothing follows it. As an authority for or against the acceptance by the English of the appellate jurisdiction of the Irish House of Lords it is inconclusive.

Sir Matthew Hale mentions the case in his *Prerogatives of the King*:[5]

> Now consider the lords' house in parliament as a court of justice. And as we find the King's Bench of Ireland subject or subordinate to the King's Bench here, and the parliament there to the parliament here, so the lords' house in parliament of Ireland, though not subordinate to the King's Bench of England because not in the same rank of constitution, yet it was subordinate to the lords house of parliament here as a court or judicatory. It appears, Rot. Parl. 8 H. 6, n. 70, the prior of Lanthony recovered in a writ of annuity in the Common Pleas of Ireland against the prior of Mullingar. Upon a writ of error in the King's Bench of Ireland that judgment affirmed. Then it was brought by writ of error into the lords house in the parliament of Ireland and that judgment reversed. A writ of error brought upon that judgment in the king's bench of England. *Et pur ceo que les justices as plees tener devant vous en votre banck en Engleterre n'ont my poer de terminer ne d'adjudger par le ley ce que fuit fait en votre dit parlement d'Ireland,*[6] it is desired that the record might be removed out of the King's Bench into the parliament here, though it appears [49] not what was done thereupon.

The comment that 'the lords' house in parliament of Ireland, though not subordinate to the King's Bench of England because not in the same rank of constitution, yet it was subordinate to the lords' house of parliament here as a court or judicatory' is interesting in that it does not deny the jurisdiction of the Irish Lords, merely asserting that it was subordinate to that of the English House. The *Prior of Llanthony's Case*, as Hale seems to concede, does not support his main contention, that the Irish house, in its appellate capacity, was subordinate to the English lords. If the case proves anything it shows that the Irish parliament — possibly the House of Lords alone, but perhaps not - exercised appellate jurisdiction in the 15th century, that the English King's Bench deferred to this jurisdiction and that the English parliament seemingly took no action either to quash it or to assert its own jurisdiction.

4 Roll, parliament, 8 Hen. VI in ult.

5 Hale, (D. E. C. Yale, ed.) 92 Seld. Soc. (for 1975), p. 39.

6 LF. And in as much as the justices to the pleas held before you in your [King's] bench in England have not the power to determine nor to judge with respect to the law which was made in your said parliament of Ireland...

The *Derry* and *Meath* Cases

The appellate jurisdiction emerged as an issue at the end of the 17th century in two cases, the *Bishop of Derry's Case*[7] and the *Earl of Meath's Case*[8] in the 1690s.

In the *Bishop of Derry's Case* the London Society sought an injunction in the Irish Court of Chancery against William King, bishop of Derry, over property in Derry/Londonderry. The bishop appealed to the Irish House of Lords, which quashed the injunction.[9] The society then appealed to the English House of Lords. The English House ruled that the Irish Chancery should disregard the Irish House of Lords because it was *coram non iudice*.[10] A committee of the Irish privy council, judges and others appointed by the lords justices[11] then examined the matter and reported: 'we do find that the lords spiritual and temporal in parliament assembled are in possession of a Supreme judicature over inferior courts and particularly over the Chancery here.'[12] Strengthened by this support, the Irish Lords then arrested the sheriff of Derry for enforcing the injunction despite their reversal of the Irish Chancery. The English lords mounted their own investigation and collected precedents. In May 1698 they reaffirmed their original decision and in November 1699 the London Society gained control of the premises.[13] The Irish House of Lords accepted defeat in the case at hand, but did not accept that it had settled the question of its claim to appellate jurisdiction. A sub-committee of the Irish parliament consisting of the Bishop of Clogher and William Molyneaux, MP for Trinity College, drew up a list of early statutes to show the independence of the Irish parliament.

The Meath case was also a dispute about land. The Earl and Countess of Meath petitioned the Irish House of Lords to set aside a decision of the chancellor of the palatine court of Tipperary who had awarded the land to Baron Ward, an English peer and his associates. The Irish Lords allowed the appeal, and ordered the sheriff to return the land to them. Lord Ward then appealed to the Irish house to rescind the earlier order on the ground that it violated his privilege as a peer of the British House of Lords. The Irish Lords held against him, by a vote of 34 to 4. In the meantime, Ward had regained possession of his property, but the Derry case had also been decided by the Irish peers and Molyneaux had written his treatise arguing for Irish parliamentary independence. The Meaths again applied to the Irish House and this time there was no dissenting voice.[14] The House ordered the property to be returned to the earl and countess. However, an intervention by the lord lieutenant, by which the earl was induced to accept a

[7] *Society of Governor and Assistants, London* v. *Bishop of Derry* (1698) 16 *J. Eng. H.L.* 292.

[8] *Ward* v. *Earl of Meath* (1699) 16 *J. Eng. H.L.* 457.

[9] 2 *J. Ir. H.L.* 637, 706.

[10] L. 'before one who is not a judge', i.e. without jurisdiction.

[11] The lords justices performed the functions of the lord lieutenant in his absence.

[12] *Report of the Committee of the Privy Council, Judges and others appointed by the Lords Justices and the Privy Council to inspect the Journals of the House of Lords, Records and other Papers*, Marsh's Library, Dublin, pp. 277–87; see James (1995) 69.

[13] HMC, House of Lords, MSS, n. s. III, 16–56.79.

[14] Francis James, *Lords of the Ascendancy* (Dublin, 1995), p. 69.

financial composition, prevented further conflict between the two parliaments, but the issue was merely postponed rather than resolved.[15]

In 1703, as a result of the *Derry Case*[16] and the *Earl of Meath's Case*,[17] the Irish Lords reinforced the 1641 joint resolution with a resolution of their own declaring that 'her Majesty hath an undoubted jurisdiction and prerogative of judging in her high Court of Parliament, in all appeals and causes within this her Majesty's realm of Ireland.'[18] Further resolutions declared that the judgments of the Irish Lords were 'final and conclusive and cannot be reversed or set aside by any other court whatsoever' and denounced anyone who attempted to 'remove a cause' from the Irish Lords as 'betrayers of her Majesty's prerogative and jurisdiction and the undoubted rights and privileges of this House.'[19] It is noticeable that the resolutions, while rejecting the doctrine of supremacy of the British parliament, affirmed the supremacy of the Crown and moreover used the one doctrine against the other. The argument was that the English parliament was usurping the prerogatives of Queen Anne as Queen of Ireland and in particular the prerogative of justice which, the Irish Lords impliedly asserted, had been delegated to them. The Irish Lords continued to hear appeals until the final clash in *Annesley* v. *Sherlock*. It is interesting to note that the statute passed by James II's Jacobite parliament in Dublin in 1689[20] had both noted that 'of late times' several persons had brought appeals before the English House of Lords to reverse decisions in the Irish Chancery, provided that any such appeals were to be void and moreover that any attempt to bring such an appeal was to be 'a high misdemeanour' and subject to a fine or imprisonment at the discretion of the Irish court.[21] The Jacobite statute predates the *Derry* and *Meath* cases and so the reference to appeals to the English House of Lords brought 'of late times' suggests that there were examples of such appeals prior to those cases. It is possible that they arose from the proceedings in the Irish House of Lords listed in the manuscript in Marsh's Library and reproduced in Appendix E.[22]

[15] D. W. Hayton, 'The Stanhope/Sunderland Ministry and the Repudiation of Irish Parliamentary Independence'. *English Historical Review* (1998) 113 No. 452, 610–636, p. 611; Isolde Victory, 'The Making of the 1720 Declaratory Act', in Gerard O'Brien ed., *Parliament, Politics and People: Essays in Eighteenth-Century Irish History*. (Dublin, 1989), pp. 12–13; F. G. James, *Ireland in the Empire, 1688–1770* (Cambridge, 1973), pp. 100–1; HMC, House of Lords MSS, n.s., iii. 31, 297–9; Calendar of State Papers, Domestic, 1703–4, pp. 226–7, 491, 492–3, 499–500, 531; HMC, Ormonde MSS, n.s., viii.53, 56.

[16] *Society of Governor and Assistants, London* v. *Bishop of Derry* (1698) 16 *J. Eng. H.L.* 292; above, page 43 .

[17] *Ward* v. *Earl of Meath* (1699) 16 *J. Eng. H.L.* 457.

[18] (1703) 2 *J. Ir. H.L.* 52.

[19] *ibid.*

[20] Section 7, see Appendix F, page 223.

[21] Section 8, page 223. It contained similar provisions as to attempts to produce writs of error obtained in England in the Irish King's Bench returnable to the King's Bench in England.

[22] Below, page 219.

The Loss of Jurisdiction (*Annesley's Case*)

In *Annesley* v. *Sherlock*[23] Maurice Annesley reclaimed lands in Ireland from Hester Sherlock. Annesley won a verdict in his favour in the Irish Court of Exchequer, but Sherlock appealed to the Irish House of Lords who on 19 June 1716 reversed the judgment of the Exchequer. The High Sheriff of County Kildare, Alexander Burrowes, was instructed to see that Hester obtained the title to the lands. Annesley appealed to the British House of Lords on 7 May 1717. In fact, he did not 'complain of the want of jurisdiction in the house of lords in Ireland, but only that he is aggrieved by the decree made by their lordships.'[24] On 31 May 1717 the committee of the British Lords reported that resolutions of their House in May 1698 in the *Bishop of Derry's Case*[25] had instructed the Irish Court of Chancery to disregard appeals to the Irish Lords and ensure that appeals should lie to the House of Lords in England. Since Annesley had not denied the jurisdiction of the Irish House, but claimed only error, the British House did not entertain his appeal. Hester Sherlock refused to answer in the British Lords and appealed again to the Irish Lords. On 1 February 1718 the British Lords held that the land should be restored to Annesley.[26] The Irish Court of Exchequer under Chief Baron Gilbert, an Englishman, declined to follow the decision of the Irish House of Lords and attempted to follow the British Lords instead. The sheriff, Alexander Burrowes, refused to execute the order and the court imposed a fine on him for his refusal. The matter came to the attention of the Irish lords who ordered the arrest of the Exchequer judges.[27]

The immediate result of the conflict of jurisdictions which came to a head in 1720 was the passing by the British parliament in that year of the statute 6 Geo. I c. 5, known as the Declaratory Act, or at the time as 'the Sixth of George the First'.[28] The background to the political debates is dealt with in detail by a number of historians.[29] Hayton[30] calls the statute the 'keystone of the eighteenth-century Irish constitution' until 1782 and points out that it asserted the supremacy of the British parliament over the Irish one, and therefore legislatively as well as judicially, although he also asserts that the British house

[23] (1718) 21 *J. G.B. H.L.* 55, reversing *Sherlock* v. *Annesley* (1716) 2 *J. Ir. H.L.* 541. Before the Union of the parliaments of England and Scotland, the correct terminology for the body which sat at Westminster is the 'English' House of Lords, and the citation will be 'J. Eng. H.L.'

[24] 20 *J. G.B. H.L.* 484.

[25] Above page 43.

[26] 20 *J. G.B H.L.* 594.

[27] 2 *J. Ir. H.L.* 624. Above, page 1.

[28] See Appendix I, page 231.

[29] D. W. Hayton, 'The Stanhope/Sunderland Ministry and the Repudiation of Irish Parliamentary Independence' (1998) *The English Historical Review* 113, No. 452 (Jun., 1998), pp. 610–636; Isolde Victory, 'The Making of the 1720 Declaratory Act'; Isolde L. Victory, 'Colonial Nationalism in Ireland, 1692–1725: From Common Law to Natural Right' (Trinity College, Dublin, Ph.D. thesis, 1984). The regnal year 6 Geo. I lasted from 1 August 1719 to 31 July 1720. The *Chronological Table of the Statutes* published by HMSO lists statutes by year, starting with the first calendar year of the regnal year and the Declaratory Act is therefore listed under 1719. The Declaratory Act passed its second reading on 26 March 1720, Victory, 'The Making of the 1720 Declaratory Act', p. 27, J. G.B. H.C. xix. 293, 321, and received the royal assent on 7 April 1720, 21 *J. G.B. H.L.* 296.

[30] Hayton, 'The Stanhope/Sunderland Ministry...' p. 610.

used its asserted power to legislate for Ireland only sparingly in the 18th century. Hayton also says that the British were not confident that it had settled the issue for all time, and quotes Robert Walpole's remark at the time of the furore against Wood's Halfpence, that 'the Irish had a mind to be independent', and Hayton comments, 'almost as if reciting a law of nature'.[31] Victory[32] shows that the 'patriots' of the Irish parliament were more concerned with claiming greater control over legislation, but realizing that this was unlikely to succeed, attempted to establish judicial control as a sort of second best, but were unable to succeed in that either. Hayton's assertion that the political crisis had the appearance of a 'phoney war' is addressed no doubt as to the legislative issue. This study, however, is not concerned with the political background as such but rather with the aspect of judicial appeals. As far as judicial appeals were concerned, the effect of the Act was to prevent the Irish Lords from hearing any appeals or writs of error for the rest of the century until the changes in 1782.

After reciting the claim of the Irish House to hear appeals from Irish courts the statute declared that Ireland was and 'of right ought to be' subordinate to the 'Imperial Crown of Great Britain' and provided that in future the British parliament was to have 'full power and authority to make laws and statutes of sufficient force and validity to bind the Kingdom and people of Ireland.' It thus attempted to resolve not only the conflict over judicature but also the age-old struggle over the claim of the English legislature to legislate for Ireland. The 'patriots' in Ireland were horrified that the statute was not limited to the immediate issue at hand and went further to make this imperial claim.[33] It is also interesting to note that the Act was to be used in 1766 as the model for the statute[34] making a similar declaration in relation to the newly-assertive colonial legislatures in America. Although the statute arose specifically out of an Irish demand, it could be seen in the wider context as one of the earliest examples of Britain's perceived need to retain control over its growing empire.

Jonathan Swift was among those who denounced the Act. An English correspondent, Charles Ford, had expressed some sympathy for the measure on the ground that the Irish Lords had shown themselves to be incompetent in dealing with legal appeals. Showing a grasp of the political priorities, as well as his customary prejudice against the Scots, Swift wrote in reply:[35]

> I believe myself not guilty of too much veneration for the Irish H. of Lds, but differ from you in politicks, the question is whether people ought to be slaves or no...You fetter a man for seven years, then let him loose to shew his skill in dancing, and because he does it

[31] Hayton, 'The Stanhope/Sunderland Ministry...'p. 619; E. C. Hawtrey (ed.), *The Private Diary of William, First Earl Cowper* (Eton, 1833), p. 37; William Coxe, *Memoirs of the Life and Administration of Sir Robert Walpole...* (3 vols., London, 1798), ii.350.

[32] Victory, 'Colonial Nationalism in Ireland, 1692–1725...', pp. 142–8; Hayton, 'The Stanhope/Sunderland Ministry...' p. 615.

[33] Hayton, 'The Stanhope/Sunderland Ministry...'p. 614.

[34] 6 Geo. III c. 12 (G.B.), 1766.

[35] Swift to Ford, 4 April 1720, Williams ed., *The Correspondence of Jonathan Swift* (Oxford, Clarendon Press, 1963), ii.342–43.

> awkwardly, you say he ought to be fettered for life. Scotland is poorer and more northward than this Island, yet [they] were satisfied with their own legislature till they were united on their conditions, which though I think too good for them, yet they are proud enough to be ashamed of. I do assure you I never saw so universall a discontent as there is among the highest most virulent and antichurch Whigs against that Bill and every author or abetter of it without exception.

From the date of the royal assent to the Declaratory Act, i.e. 7 April 1720 until 1782 it was accepted that the Irish House of Lords had no appellate jurisdiction. In 1782, as we shall see, the Irish House recovered its jurisdiction and remained the final appeal court in Ireland until the Union. By the end of that period they were as nimble at dancing a legal minuet or a sarabande as their British counterparts.

The Sixth of George the First, since it was an Act of the British parliament, was in itself an assertion of the power of the British parliament to legislate for Ireland. It was accepted in Ireland by the Irish House of Lords and other institutions in Ireland at the time and this, one might argue, gave it legitimacy by consent. There was, of course, no neutral forum where the legal issues between the parties could be decided, and so the arguments remained part of a diplomatic dialogue and power play between the parties. The leaders of the Irish parliament did not have the realistic alternative of a unilateral declaration of independence followed by revolution to which the American colonists had resorted.

The Restoration of Jurisdiction

The Repealing Act

In 1782 the Act 22 Geo. III, c. 53 (G.B.), the 'Repealing Act', repealed the Declaratory Act of 1720.[36] Henry Grattan had been foremost in procuring its enactment. However, it became clear almost at once that it had failed to settle the issue. The repeal of the Declaratory Act left the law in the state it was in before 1720. The Repealing Act did not expressly renounce British jurisdiction and so only had the effect of resurrecting the old controversy over jurisdiction. Fuel was added to the fire in 1782 by *Barry* v. *Nugent*[37] in which Lord Mansfield heard a writ of error in the English King's Bench from the Irish King's Bench. This procedure was supported by precedent, but it was significant in the context of struggle over the jurisdiction, because a further writ of error could be taken from the English King's Bench to the British House of Lords. The case itself was of little significance: an action over a lease. Nugent claimed that he had a valid lease granted to him by Barry. Barry's father, James, Earl of Barrymore, had granted a lease

36 See Appendix N, page 249.

37 (1782) 3 Dougl. 180, 99 E.R. 60. P. Jupp, 'Earl Temple's Viceroyalty and the Question of Renunciation, 1782–3' 17 *Irish Historical Studies* 499 at p. 511; R. B. McDowell, *Ireland in the Age of Imperialism and Revolution* (Oxford, 1979) p. 287, mentions a case he refers to as *Holland* v. *Barry*, but without citation, in the same context. It may be the same case as *Barry* v. *Nugent*.

over the land in 1751 for a term of 21 years. At the end of the lease the tenant, O'Hea, refused to give up possession, claiming he held the fee simple. For reasons that are not made clear by the report, O'Hea remained, or was allowed to remain, in possession until 1779, at which time O'Hea released any claims to the land and gave up possession in return for £500 from Barry. Nugent produced a lease for 21 years granted to him in 1751 by Barry, stated to be a present demise, to take effect after Barry should recover the land from O'Hea. Nugent claimed now to be entitled to enter under the lease, while Barry maintained that it was not a present demise but merely preparatory to a valid lease. The Irish court held for Nugent, on precedents, and in a short judgment in the English King's Bench, Lord Mansfield agreed. The importance of the case, however, was that it gave further ammunition to Henry Flood's attack on the dependence of the Irish courts on the English courts.[38]

The concern over the incident was increased by the allegation that Mansfield was known to be personally opposed to further concessions to the Irish. The appeal had been lodged before the Repealing Act came into force, but Flood's argument was that the mere repeal of the Declaratory Act was insufficient and had left the issue of English jurisdiction over Irish law unclear. The existing practice of the English King's Bench hearing writs of error from the Irish King's Bench had not been affected by the repeal. *Barry* v. *Nugent* merely gave prominence to his point. Nevertheless, it was unfair to blame Mansfield who was bound on the basis of existing practice to hear the case. As to his personal attitudes, Mansfield favoured religious toleration. He had upheld the right of Quakers to give evidence by affirmation rather than oath[39] and his direction to a jury in a case in which a Catholic priest had been charged with saying mass, which was then still against the law under statutes of Elizabeth I and William III, amounted to an invitation to acquit, which it duly did.[40] This made him extremely unpopular in England in certain quarters. He supported the British Catholic Relief Act 1778[41] and indeed paid a heavy price for doing so. His house in London was attacked during the subsequent Gordon Riots and his library destroyed.[42] Mansfield's support for Catholic emancipation may therefore have made him reluctant to make further concessions to the Irish Protestants, but there is no evidence that his personal attitudes played any part in the conduct of the appeal.

The Renunciation Act

Flood's radical stand in opposition to 'simple repeal' gained widespread support and made him the most popular politician in Ireland in the summer of 1782. He had eclipsed Grattan on the issue. In 1783 the 'Renunciation Act'[43] as it became

38 Kelly, *Henry Flood*, p. 337.

39 *Atcheson* v. *Everett* (1775) 1 Cowp. 382, 98 E.R. 1142. Quakers in Ireland had been permitted to give evidence by affirmation by 1 Geo. II, c. 5 (Ir.), 1727. *Irish Exchequer Reports 1716–1734* (Lyall, ed.) 125 Seld. Soc. (for 2008) at p. cxli.

40 Campbell, *Lives of the Chief Justices of England*, ii.514–16.

41 18 Geo. III c. 60 (G.B.), 1778.

42 Campbell, *Lives of the Chief Justices of England*, ii.524.

43 23 Geo. III c. 28 (G.B.), 1783,; see Appendix Q, page 255.

known, was passed by the British parliament. It renounced the supremacy of the British parliament over Ireland and declared that all actions at law or in equity should be decided exclusively by Irish courts and that no writs of error or appeal should lie to England:

> the said Right claimed by the People of Ireland to be bound only by laws enacted by His Majesty and the parliament of that Kingdom, in all cases whatever and to have all actions and suits at law or in equity which may be instituted in that kingdom decided in His Majesty's courts therein finally and without appeal from thence.

Interestingly, the measure had been anticipated in Ireland by the statute 21 & 22 Geo. III c. 49 (Ir.), 1781–82[44] which indicates that official opinion in Great Britain had already accepted the constitutional change.

The wording of the Renunciation Act was deliberately chosen not to offend sensibilities on either side of the Irish Sea.[45] It pointedly referred to the right 'claimed' by the people of Ireland to be bound only by statutes enacted by the Irish parliament, and so neither conceded its validity nor asserted the validity of the supremacy of the British parliament. Nor did it express a view as to whether appeals to the British House of Lords had ever been supported by constitutional doctrine. Furthermore, it neither asserted, nor denied, that the Irish House of Lords was the ultimate appeal court in Ireland. Was the Irish House of Lords one of 'His Majesty's courts therein'? This ambiguity has been seen by some as casting doubt on the jurisdiction of the Irish Lords as the ultimate appeal court in Ireland and on whether that jurisdiction had ever properly been conferred. This, however, is to misunderstand the nature of the Irish and British constitutions of the time and the consequent nuances involved in British legislation as to Ireland. If the British statute had purported *to confer* jurisdiction on the Irish House, that in itself would have been a re-assertion of British parliamentary supremacy over Ireland. The Irish Protestants did not accept that the British parliament had the power to confer jurisdiction on the Irish Lords. Their position was that the Irish House derived its authority directly from the Crown, from the prerogative of justice of the Crown of Ireland. We have noted that the words of the statute were deliberately chosen and this seems clearly to be another instance. The British legislators simply left it to the Irish to decide what court should be the final appeal court.

The criticism that the Renunciation Act did not purport to confer jurisdiction on the Irish House of Lords also misunderstands the nature of the British constitution in another respect. It is often described as 'unwritten'. More correctly, it was composed then, as now, of common law and statute, and more specifically, not in single written document which could be amended only by a special procedure. It is not too fanciful to suggest that those who drafted the Renunciation Act accepted the conventions of the 'unwritten' constitutions.

[44] Below, page 77.

[45] Peter Jupp, 'Earl Temple's Viceroyalty and the Question of Renunciation, 1782–83' 17 *Irish Historical Studies* 499 at 514–16.

By renouncing jurisdiction without attempting expressly to confer it on the Irish Lords, the British legislators necessarily accepted that the matter of appeals was to be left to the Irish. As to the system of appeals in Great Britain, the custom of the British House of Lords of hearing appeals from Scottish courts was simply adopted by that House after the Union with Scotland. It was not prescribed by statute law.[46] There was no provision in the treaty of Union between Scotland and England providing for appeals from Scottish courts to the British House of Lords. In Scotland it had remained a moot point as to whether, before the union of the parliaments, appeals had lain from the Scots courts to the Scottish parliament.[47] As it turned out, the Irish patriots were not content to leave it to the practice of the courts or the Irish House of Lords itself to decide. The statute of the Irish parliament, 21 & 22 Geo. III c. 49 (Ir.), 1781–82 expressly conferred jurisdiction on the Irish House, and any doubts as to the legitimacy of the judicial role of the Irish House of Lords must be discounted by the fact that statute had obviously obtained the royal assent.[48]

The first case reported by Ridgeway after the restoration of the appellate jurisdiction is *Davis* v. *Oliver*,[49] concerning fraud in equity, the hearing being reported as taking place on 15 March 1784. The *Freeman's Journal*, on the other hand, reported the first case as the more significant *Hume* v. *Burton*,[50] concerning the mental capacity of the Earl of Ely, the date of the proceedings being given as 27 February 1784.[51] *Hume* v. *Burton* appears in Ridgeway as the second case, the arguments and speeches being dated 24 March 1784.

In fact, Ridgeway is correct, although the dates are not exactly as he gives them in his reports. The chronology is as follows. *Davis* v. *Oliver* was the first petition to be read by the lords, given in the *Journals of the Irish House of Lords* as on 14 November 1783.[52] The answer and further affidavits then followed,[53] and the appeal was dismissed on 15 March 1784.[54] On the other hand, the *Journals* show that in *Hume* the judges attached their seals to the bill of exceptions, the first step in the proceedings on the writ of error in the House of Lords, on 23 November 1783, and the petition was read on 2 December.[55] Counsel for the plaintiff was heard on 27 February 1784, for the defendant on 1 March, the common law

[46] D. M. Walker, *The Scottish Legal System* (Edinburgh, 1981) p. 127–128.

[47] In 1707/8 the British House accepted jurisdiction in an appeal by the Earl of Rosebery and in 1711 an appeal was taken in the case of James Greenshields a clergyman accused of using the Anglican form of service. See Malcolm, 'The House of Lords and Appeals from Scotland' (1910) 22 *Juridical Review* 295. Criminal appeals did not lie from Scottish courts to the British House of Lords, nor will they lie to the new Supreme Court of the United Kingdom, except those dealing with devolution issues: Constitutional Reform Act 2005 (U.K.), s. 40(3). See 'Final Appellate Jurisdiction in the Scottish Legal System', [http://www.scotland.gov.uk/ Publications/2010/01/19154813/0], accessed 22 March 2013.

[48] Below, page 81.

[49] 1 Ridg. PC 1.

[50] *ibid.*, p. 16.

[51] PIHL, iii.181.

[52] *J. Ir. H.L.*, v. 395.

[53] *ibid.*, v. 409, 415, 447, 448, 449.

[54] *ibid.*, v. 452.

[55] *ibid.*, v. 399, 408.

judges opinions were given on 17 March and the debate and decision on the motion took place on 24 March 1784.[56] As to *Hume* v. *Burton*, which excited much more public attention than *Davis* v. *Oliver*, the *Freeman's Journal* described the scene on 27 February in florid language:

> This was a day much to be remembered in the annals of Ireland, on which the grand tribunal of the nation sat to do business in their judicial capacity, for the first time [*sic*] since their legal powers were wrested from them by a foreign legislature. The resumption of this inestimable privilege cannot but fill the hearts of Irishmen with the most lively gratitude for those who have, in any degree, contributed to the restoration of those rights, which must highly conduce to the advantage of every man who may hereafter be obliged to contend for his liberty or property through the means of those ministers of distributive justice, in the *dernier resort*.[57]
>
> The assembly was so solemnly grand, as its object was novel; and the importance of the cause which their lordships had to try, contributed not a little to complete the awful picture.
>
> The lord chancellor and the twelve judges were at the table, amongst whom, of course, were those who were supposed, or from error in judgment, to have deprived an heir of his birthright, and who will now, in the face of the surrounding nobility, and their country, have an opportunity of accounting for the error or errors, if any – a satisfaction which the judges of Ireland never could have, and their decrees and judgments were liable to be investigated by a foreign judicature.

Practical considerations also supported the notion that the Irish Lords should be the ultimate appeal court in Ireland. Statutes passed by the newly-active Irish legislature would be more appropriately interpreted by Irish courts. It is true that this argument was more likely to commend itself to opinion in Ireland than Great Britain, but clearly there was no effective opposition to the notion in 1781–82. The courts in Ireland had developed doctrines which were not understood by the British House of Lords. One of these was the equity to renew leases for lives, which we shall consider shortly. The reversal by the British House of Lords of the decisions of Irish courts[58] had already impelled the Irish parliament to pass the Tenantry Act, 1780[59] in order to restore what had been the legal position in Ireland before those reversals. This particular experience may well have been one of the reasons for the Renunciation Act: what had happened before could happen again in some other context and at any time.

[56] *ibid.*, v. 442, 443, 454, 465.

[57] LF. last resort, i.e. a final appellate court.

[58] *Kane* v. *Hamilton* (1784) 1 Ridg. PC 180 at 185, see page 152, and *Bateman* v. *Murray* (1779) 1 Ridg. PC 187 at 201. Both are discussed in *Boyle* v. *Lysaght* (1787) 1 Ridg. PC 384.

[59] Below, page 155.

As we have seen, the Irish House of Lords assumed jurisdiction and continued to act as the highest appeal court in Ireland until the Act of Union came into force on 1 January 1801.[60] On that date both the Irish House of Commons and the Irish House of Lords ceased to exist. As to the British House of Lords, its judicial role was brought to an end by the Constitutional Reform Act 2005, which transferred its functions to the new Supreme Court of the United Kingdom in 2009.

60 39 & 40 Geo. III, c. 67 (G.B.), 1800. 1 January 1801 was the first day of the 19th century, according to the Gregorian calendar.

CHAPTER 4

Jurisdiction of the Superior Courts

Before dealing with the procedure on writs of error and appeals, it is necessary to explain something of the jurisdiction of the superior courts in Ireland in the 18th century. It is not possible to explain that without describing some features of the system by which actions were begun. By the 18th century that system was a complex one, the product both of the survival of the medieval writ system and of the methods which had developed to avoid the technicalities of the medieval system.[1]

In the middle ages an action was begun by an original writ issued from the common law side of Chancery. Original writs were in Latin and developed a law of their own, with many technical points of pleading. Failure to comply with some technical requirement could mean that the plaintiff failed in his or her action without ever getting to trial. In order to overcome this problem, by the 18th century courts had developed ways to dispense with original writs in certain cases. Another factor driving the development of the procedure of the courts was the fact that they sought to increase their own business, which also led to jurisdictions overlapping. Judges were paid salaries, but their clerks and other officers of the court often relied on fees, and the judges were willing to accommodate the officers of their own court, or the parties to an action who, for various reasons, wished to bring an action in a particular court. Fictions played a large part in this development. Judges could not simply announce a change in the common law, but they could allow a fact to be pleaded which was not true, and then not permit that fact to be contradicted (traversed, in the language of pleading) by the other side. It was not a satisfactory method to reform the legal system, but the judges used the only techniques that were available to them, and they were effective, although at the cost of making the law appear absurd and of tolerating untruths, which is what fictions were. These two factors, the need to avoid original writs, and the extension of jurisdictions, were sometimes interrelated in ways which the following account will, hopefully, make clear.

[1] See generally, Baker, *Introduction*, esp. Chapter 4 'Forms of Action'; F. W. Maitland, *The Forms of Action at Common Law* (Cambridge, 1st edn., 1909, reprint 1968).

The Court of Exchequer

The Court of Exchequer, or the Exchequer of Pleas, had developed from the administrative department of the Exchequer which dealt with the king's revenue and so originally the jurisdiction of the court was confined to matters concerning the revenue. It did not therefore originally entertain actions by private persons at all. However, in the course of time it began to allow accountants and then debtors of the king to bring actions of debt, and other similar actions, in the court. Clearly, if a person who collected money on behalf of the king, or actually owed money to the king, was himself owed money by a third party, who had not paid his debt, then, it was reasoned, the king was interested in the matter. This extension of its jurisdiction was greatly increased later by the fiction of *quo minus*, whereby the court began to allow private persons to bring actions 'on the mere surmise' that because the defendant owed them money, they were *thereby the less* (*quo minus*) able to pay the king the debt they owed to him.[2] The plea of *quo minus* had been known since the early to mid-14th century[3] but it only seems to have become a fully-formed fiction possibly from the time of Queen Mary I[4] but more likely from the time of Charles I or the Commonwealth.[5]

The clerks on the common law side of Chancery had never issued original writs to begin actions in the Exchequer, since private persons had not originally brought actions there at all, and so the Court of Exchequer itself found a way to permit such actions. In any court, if a defendant failed to appear in response to an action, the next step was for the court itself to issue a writ, called a judicial writ, usually a *capias*,[6] requiring the defendant to attend or be arrested, etc. The Court of Exchequer adopted the practice of allowing private persons to *start* an action by a *capias*. It might be preceded by a bill, or declaration (the common law term for a bill) stating briefly the facts, but the *capias* was the essential step to require the defendant to attend and answer.[7] What in other courts would

2 As to England, see: Sheppard, *Grand Abridgement* (1675), p. 126; Harold Wurzel, 'The Origin and Development of Quo Minus', (1939) 49 *Yale Law Journal* 39–64, at 42–47; Baker, OHEL, vol. 6, p. 167; W. H. Bryson, *The Equity Side of Exchequer* (Cambridge, 1975), p. 25. As to Ireland: Ferguson, *Treatise*, i.12; *Irish Exchequer Reports 1716–1734* (Andrew Lyall, ed.), 125 Seld. Soc. (for 2008), Introduction, pp. lxix–lxx.

3 Wurzel, *ibid.*, at 42–47.

4 R. M. Ball, 'Exchequer of Pleas, Bills and Writs' (1988) *Journal of Legal History* 308, at p. 317; Baker, OHEL, vi.167.

5 Bryson, *The Equity Side of Exchequer*, p. 25. As to Ireland, the earliest example discovered to date of a refusal to allow a traverse of the assertion that the plaintiff was a debtor of the king comes from a manuscript in King's Inns, Dublin, 'Notes of cases', KI MS No. 108 in 1637: *Irish Exchequer Reports 1716–1734* 125 Seld. Soc. pp. lxx–lxxi. I am grateful to Prof. Sir John Baker for reference to this source.

6 L. 'you may take, seize', sing. A writ or process commanding the officer to take the body of the person named in it, that is, to arrest him. Writs of capias were of various kinds; *capias ad respondendum*, to enforce attendance at court, the form dealt with here; *capias ad satisfaciendum*, after judgment, to imprison the defendant, until the plaintiff's claim was satisfied; *capias utlagatum*, to arrest an outlawed person and *capias in withernam*, to distrain in reprisal the cattle or goods of someone who had made an unlawful distraint.

7 Ferguson, *Treatise*, i.124, said that in Ireland in 1841 the proper course was to insert the *quo minus* clause in the declaration. Nevertheless, in the earlier case of *Higgins* v. *McClenaghan* (1794) Ir.

originally have been the second step in requiring the defendant to attend, became the first step in the case of the Exchequer.

There is evidence in Ireland that actions in the Irish Exchequer had been begun by *capias* before the 1350s. A statute in that year of the parliament of Drogheda[8] recited that an earlier writ of 1356 had apparently been ignored and that 'men of the liberty of [Meath]' had been subjected to writs of *capias* and distress issued by the Irish Exchequer at the suit of persons claiming to be 'yeomen or ministers' of the court, but who were not so in fact. The statute prohibited, under penalty, the beginning of any action by *capias* or distress from the Exchequer to answer any plea of trespass, contract, debt, or account at the suit of persons who were not ministers of the Exchequer.[9] If it was necessary to prohibit the practice, obviously that is because it had been going on before the prohibition. The statute of 1460, and the earlier writ, concerned what may have begun as a corrupt practice and had become a more general fiction, that certain persons were 'ministers' or officials of the court. This fiction seems to have been suppressed, and was replaced by the fiction of *quo minus*. The king may not have been too pleased at people claiming to be his servants, who were not, but had little or no objection to people claiming to be his debtors.

There was one consequence of starting an action by *capias*: civil outlawry could only be obtained in any case if the action had been started by an original writ, and since no action in the Exchequer was begun by such a writ, no outlawry could be obtained in the Exchequer.[10]

Civil outlawry could arise when an original writ[11] had been issued and the defendant either had failed to appear in answer (outlawry in mesne process) or had failed to satisfy a judgment (outlawry in final process). Civil outlawry meant that the outlaw was incapably of bringing, or defending, actions,[12] could be imprisoned, and forfeited his personal and real property: personal property immediately upon outlawry and his leaseholds and the profits of real property when found by inquisition.[13] Civil outlawry did not necessarily result in a permanent forfeiture of real property, but the profits vested in the Crown while

Term Rep. 253, Yelverton CB dismissed a demurrer objecting to the absence of a *quo minus* clause in the plaintiff's declaration with the one sentence: 'That is a great objection to be sure!' King's Inns manuscript, KI MS No. 108, contains a note of an order of 21 May 1637 indicating that in a specific case the *capias* was preceded by a bill: above, page 54 note 5.

8 38 Hen. VI, c. 1 (Ir.), 1460. The statute is reproduced in *The Statutes at Large* of Ireland, 1310–1800. 22 vols. (Dublin, printed by George Grierson, 1786–1804). Ferguson, *Treatise*. i.12.

9 Ferguson, *Treatise*. i.12. In England the Statute of Rutland, 1281, 12 Edw. I (10 Edw. I in Ruffhead), 1281 (Eng.) provided that no plea should be held in the Exchequer unless it specially concerned the king or his ministers.

10 Gorges Edmond Howard, *A Compendious Treatise of the Rules and Practice of the Pleas Side of the Exchequer in Ireland* (Dublin, 1759. 2d ed., Dublin, 1793), pp. 2–3: 'nor are there any original writs in it [the Exchequer]; neither is any process of outlawry sued forth here upon any actions.'; *Irish Exchequer Reports 1716–1734* (Andrew Lyall, ed.), 125 Seld. Soc. (for 2008) lxxiii.

11 i.e. in the courts of Common Pleas or King's Bench.

12 *Wallis* v. *Scott*, KI MS No. 50, p. 55 (Chancery: defendant pleaded the outlawry of plaintiff, and swore that person named in the *capias utlagatum* was the same person who preferred the bill); *Aldridge* v. *Buller* (1837) 2 M. & W. 412, 150 E.R. 818.

13 Jacob, *Law Dictionary*, 'outlawry I'; Ferguson, *Treatise*, iii.1045.

the outlawry was in force.[14] Outlawry could be reversed by writ of error, on motion, or by Act of parliament[15] If a civil outlawry was reversed, the former outlaw recovered his land, but lost the profits which had accrued in the meantime, unless it was by Act of parliament and the statute provided otherwise. Howard,[16] writing in the middle of the 18th century, strongly criticised civil outlawry as far too drastic a remedy, since those who held mortgages and other securities over the land of the outlaw would lose their rights on its becoming vested in the Crown. Innocent third parties were injured by it, and commerce damaged. Civil outlawry was curtailed in Ireland in 1840[17] and it was finally abolished throughout the then United Kingdom by the Civil Procedure Acts Repeal Act, 1879.[18]

On the common law side of Exchequer the development of the *quo minus* jurisdiction meant that the jurisdiction of the court overlapped with that of the other common law courts. By the early 18th century rules had developed which, while they did not eliminate the problem, allocated certain causes of action among the different courts. Howard[19] says of the Exchequer that:

> this court has greatly enlarged its jurisdiction and power, most actions being now allowed to be brought therein; as *debt, detinue, trover and conversion, trespass, covenant, case, ejectment, waste, prohibition, actions on penal statutes, &c.*[20]

'Case', or trespass on the special case, also called an action on the case, included *assumpsit*, the prolific form of case which increasingly replaced the action of debt and gave rise to the law of contract and tort.[21]

The remarkable inclusion of prohibition, normally a prerogative writ, was the result of the case of *Carey* against a judge of the consistory court of Cloyne and Forster, 19 and 20 June 1750, cited in Howard.[22] It was decided in the Exchequer after full debate that an order of prohibition could 'issue from the court'. Howard adds that 'this jurisdiction is taken up by the court, under the notion or surmise that the party is debtor to the king'.[23]

At an earlier period there was an advantage in bringing debt in the Exchequer rather than in Common Pleas, in that wager of law was not allowed in *quo minus*, although this had probably ceased be a factor by the end of the 18th century.

14 Ferguson, *Treatise*, iii.1045.

15 Jacob, *Law Dictionary*, 'outlawry V'; The outlaw had to appear in person. The statute 4 & 5 Will. & Mar., c. 18 (Eng.) (appearance by attorney), allowing, by section 9, appearance by attorney, except in cases of treason and felony, did not apply to Ireland: Ferguson, *Treatise*, iii.1054.

16 *Treatise*, Introduction.

17 3 & 4 Vict., c. 105 (Ir.), 1840; Ferguson, *Treatise*, iii.1047.

18 42 & 43 Vict., c. 59. (G.B.), s. 3.

19 *Pleas Side*, i.1–2.

20 KI MS No. 82, p. 97, on the pleas side, states that the actions were: 'Actions of debt, trover and conversion, ejectment, trespasses, actions on penal statutes and covenants, etc.'

21 See for example, *Anonymous* v. *Administrators of Cogan*, 125 Seld. Soc. (for 2008) cvii, 12. and *Hind* v. *Lynch*, 125 Seld. Soc. (for 2008) 72.

22 *Pleas Side*, i.3.

23 *ibid.*

Any action which involved the king's revenue or property had also to brought in the Exchequer, or if started elsewhere, it had to be removed to the Exchequer. So if someone had been outlawed in a civil action and his lands forfeited to the Crown, but a third party then claimed that some of the lands were in fact his and had wrongfully been included in the forfeiture, the third party had to bring his action in the Exchequer.[24] It seems from what Howard says that the 'revenue side' of the Court of Exchequer exercised either common law or equity jurisdiction depending on the issues raised.[25]

Howard says that: 'actions in *replevin, dower, quare impedit*,[26] etc. and all real actions' were excluded from the Exchequer.[27] KI MS No. 82 adds that 'all other writs issued out of Chancery and returnable into a court of common law cannot be returnable into this court'.[28] It has been mentioned that no outlawry could be obtained in an action in the Exchequer. For this reason the Exchequer remedy against someone who was in contempt by failure to appear, or resisting enforcement of decrees, was attachment (arrest by the sheriff or bail) and commission of rebellion.[29]

The jurisdiction of the equity side of the Exchequer in England was in theory just as extensive as that of the Court of Chancery[30] and the same was true in Ireland. Indeed, in so far as the Exchequer dealt with equity disputes involving the king's revenue, it was more extensive.

The judges of the equity side of the Exchequer were originally the lord treasurer, the lord chancellor and the barons of the Exchequer.[31] On the common law side the barons alone were judges, although the treasurer may have been present, as keeper of the records.[32] Of the court of law, Coke says that:[33] 'All judiciall proceedings according to law in the Exchequer, are *coram baronibus*, and not *coram thesaurario et baronibus*: but the court of equity holden in the Exchequer Chamber [meaning, the equity side of Exchequer] is holden before the lord treasurer, chancellor, and barons.' However, the presence of the lord treasurer on the equity side had long since ceased to be necessary in England or in Ireland

[24] Howard, *Treatise*, i.4.

[25] Howard, *Pleas Side*, i.224, cites the case of *Attorney General* v. *Dillon*, Michaelmas Term 1751 'in the pleas office of the revenue side'. In his *A Treatise on the rules and practice of the Equity Side of the Exchequer in Ireland* (Nelson, 1760), i.4, he cites the case of *Attorney General* v. *Carden, Gilborne and others*, Trinity Term, 1759, 'on an information for a forfeited estate in the nature of an English bill'.

[26] L. 'why he hinders'. An action by which a person whose right to a benefice had been obstructed recovered the presentation, and also an action to try a disputed title to an advowson.

[27] Howard, *Pleas Side*, i.1–2; Ferguson, *Treatise*, i.12; KI MS No. 82, 'Proceedings in the Chancery side of the Exchequer', p. 98.

[28] At p. 98.

[29] 125 Seld. Soc. (for 2008) lxxiv–lxxv, xcvi–xcvii. Commissioners of rebellion were generally four private persons (Howard, *Equity Side*, ii.764) appointed by the court to apprehend the recalcitrant party and bring him to court, using force if necessary and able to call upon other persons to assist them. They could also grant bail.

[30] Inst., iv. 118; Bryson, *The Equity Side of Exchequer*, at p. 11.

[31] Inst., iv. 118.

[32] Inst., iv. 105.

[33] *ibid.*, iv. 109

by the mid 18th century.[34] Procedure was by English bill.[35]

The question as to why, by the 18th century, there were two superior courts with equity jurisdiction, is probably answered by the fact that in Chancery the only judge was the lord chancellor and with the growth of equity suits up to the end of the 17th century there was simply a need for additional capacity.

The available evidence shows a full range of equity issues before the court in Ireland, although with a certain financial flavour in many cases.[36] Examples of bills and issues before the Irish court in the early part of the century include: bills for redemption of a mortgage with an account for sums due, and for foreclosure with account, for account of various other kinds, including for sums due by a tenant holding over, for interest due, and account in a partition action by tenants in common. Other actions include a bill against an executor for discovery of assets; the enforcement in equity of a conditional bond; the enforcement of an equitable charge; specific performance of an agreement for a lease; part performance of a contract of sale of land; bills to set aside a conveyance of land for misrepresentation; bills to compel a tenant to execute a counterpart of a lease; consideration in equity; notice in equity; whether interest on interest was allowable, in the case of a portion; and an injunction to restrain repeated common law actions.

The Court of Common Pleas

Real actions, that is, the writ of right, the possessory assizes of novel disseisin, mort d'ancestor, etc., and writs of entry, were in England within the exclusive jurisdiction of the Court of Common Pleas, as were fines and recoveries,[37] and the same was true of the Irish Court of Common Pleas.[38]

The common law real actions were the actions by which freeholders had recovered their land, but it is doubtful whether they were of much significance by the 18th century. The action of ejectment was the means by which leaseholders and their grantors enforced their titles to land, and since it was a more recent action, it was not attended by the complexities and expense of the real actions at common law. Moreover, the ancient rule which reserved jurisdiction in the real actions to the Court of Common Pleas did not apply to ejectment, which could be brought also in the Exchequer. Ejectment was permitted in the Exchequer because a small amount of damages for trespass was claimed, and therefore satisfied the *quo minus* requirement.

In Ireland ejectment took two main forms, ejectment on title, in which the plaintiff claimed a superior title to the defendant, and ejectment for non-payment of rent, in which a landlord sought to eject a tenant who had failed to pay the rent.[39]

34 Howard, *Treatise*, i.3.

35 i.e. in the English language, as opposed to Latin. Howard, *Treatise*, i.3; *Equity Side*, i.205; *Sir Thomas Cecil's Case* (1597) 7 Co. Rep. 18b, 77 E.R. 440.

36 *Irish Exchequer Reports 1716–1734* (Andrew Lyall, ed.), 125 Seld. Soc. (for 2008) lxxvii–lxxviii.

37 Inst., iv.99.

38 Ferguson, *Treatise*, i.11.

39 Howard, *Pleas Side*, ii.41.

Freeholders naturally wished to avail themselves of the action. In England a fictitious form of the action was invented to enable them to do so. This involved the imaginary plaintiff John Doe.[40] The principal fiction was that the freeholder had granted a lease to John Doe, who was the fictitious plaintiff. No actual lease was granted. The sole purpose was to test the title of the defendant.[41] As Howard explains it:[42]

> The party who claims the title, feigns a lease and in the name of the feigned lessee, delivers a declaration to the tenant in possession, in the name of the casual ejector, who is also now some feigned person.

In other words, if A wished to claim that his land was wrongfully occupied by B, who was in possession as a freeholder, A would bring the action in ejectment in the name of a fictitious person, to whom he was supposed to have granted a lease. The action would be brought against an equally fictitious person to whom B had allegedly also granted a lease, the 'casual ejector', who was supposed to have ejected A's fictitious lessee. B was not allowed to deny the existence of either lease.[43] Since A controlled the fictions, he was also permitted to have the casual ejector enter an appearance. A's attorney then wrote a letter to B — known as the summons — in the name of the fictitious defendant, informing B that an action had been commenced against him and inviting him to come an defend his title.[44] The 'casual ejector' was fictitious, but notice was still given to the 'tenant in possession', i.e. the defendant/'lessor', so that his title was then in issue. It was a rule of court in ejectment that notice had to be given to the defendant/lessor in order that he should not lose his right to possession without an opportunity to defend it.[45]

The name 'John Doe' was not in fact used in Ireland, where the phrase 'The Lessee of [A]' was used instead. In England the name of the fictitious defendant was often given as 'Richard Roe', or 'William Stiles', or even Shamtitle[46] but in Ireland the name usually given in the pleadings was 'John Thrustout'[47] and in the name of the case as 'the Casual Ejector'. On at least one occasion a name was chosen that was fictional as well as fictitious.[48]

40 The fiction has been attributed to the ingenuity of Chief Justice Rolle, CJ of the Upper Bench during the Commonwealth: Jacob, *Law Dictionary*, 'Ejectment'; *HEL*, vii.10, although by about 1565–70 freeholders may have granted nominal leases to friends in order to bring the action: Baker, *Introduction*, 301.

41 Jacob, *Law Dictionary*, 'Ejectment'.

42 *Pleas Side*, ii.36, and generally see *Pleas Side*, ii.36–59. Howard cites rules of court in 1663 and 1665.

43 If the person in possession was actually a lessee, then the second fiction was not required. Below, note 48.

44 Baker, *Introduction*, p. 302; Howard, *Pleas Side*, ii.37 gives the precedent of a summons, signed by 'John Thrustout'.

45 Howard, *Pleas Side*, ii.33–34.

46 Baker, *Introduction*, p. 302.

47 Howard, *Pleas Side*, ii.37.

48 *Barnaby Rudge, Lessee of Hull* v. *McCarthy* (1841) 4 Ir. L. R. 157. Dickens published his novel, *Barnaby Rudge*, in weekly parts in his serial *Master Humphrey's Clock* between February and November 1841. The ejectment action was begun in the names of the plaintiffs on 3 May 1841.

The Court of King's or Queen's Bench

The King's Bench had originally been the premier common law court. It had grown out of the *Curia Regis*, the king's court, in which the king presided surrounded by his advisers. It had jurisdiction to preserve the king's peace, which meant that it had jurisdiction over criminal cases, or as they were anciently known, pleas of the Crown and the civil action of trespass *vi et armis* (with force and arms), i.e. a trespass to the person or property with the use of force which threatened the king's peace.[49] The King's Bench also had a supervisory role over other jurisdictions, including public corporations and the judiciary generally, and included the prerogative writs of habeas corpus,[50] quo warranto,[51] prohibition, certiorari[52] and mandamus.[53] Its supervisory role also meant that it had jurisdiction to hear writs of error from other courts and correct errors of fact and law, not merely in pleas of the Crown but also in the real actions, which it did not deal with at first instance.[54] The real actions and other civil pleas were within the jurisdiction of the Court of Common Pleas, and so from an early period writs of error lay from the Court of Common Pleas to the King's Bench.

In the course of time, the King's Bench developed a fiction both to extend its jurisdiction and to avoid the inconvenience to litigants of an original writ issued by Chancery. When the medieval itinerant justices in eyre or, later, the King's Bench, sat in a county, the sheriff of the county personally attended and there was no need to apply to the Chancery for a writ ordering the sheriff to initiate proceedings.[55] Proceedings could be started by bill, which was a petition addressed to the court requesting it to initiate the action. Bill procedure remained available when the King's Bench settled in England at Westminster[56] and the same seems to have been true in Ireland from when the King's Bench sat in Dublin. Bills could also be used by the King's Bench and the other superior courts to begin actions against their own officers or prisoners in their

49 It is interesting to note that in *Maingay* v. *Gahan* (1793) Ir. Term Rep. 1, noted in 1 Ridg. PC at p. 43, see page 85, trespass *vi et armis* was brought in the Court of Exchequer, in a case challenging the seizure of goods by revenue commissioners, which is no doubt why it was thought appropriate to bring it in that court.

50 L. 'You may have the body'. The writ whereby a person who is detained in custody, or any person on their behalf, may require the person who is detaining them to produce them in court and justify their detention. The writ existed at common law but was also regulated by statute. In the Republic of Ireland the provisions as to habeas corpus are contained in Art. 40. 4. 3° of the Constitution. See Kevin Costello, *The Law of Habeas Corpus in Ireland* (Dublin, Four Courts, 2006).

51 L. 'by what warrant?' A writ which required the person to whom it was addressed to show by what authority he exercised some right, power or franchise. In Ireland, although the writ no longer exists, such a claim would be a cause of action and the remedy is an injunction.

52 Originally, a writ issued to bring the record of an inferior court into the King's Bench for review, or to bring indictments for trial into the King's Bench. It has since been developed into a general remedy to bring decisions of an inferior court or tribunal or public authority before a superior court for review so that the court can determine whether such decisions should be quashed.

53 Latin, 'we command'. A writ issued by a superior court to compel a lower court, a government officer, or someone else performing otherwise lawful functions, to perform them correctly.

54 Ferguson, *Treatise*, i.10.

55 Baker, *Introduction*, pp. 41–2.

56 *ibid.*

custody, that is, in the case of the King's Bench, the custody of the marshal of the Marshalsea prison. The fictional action by which the King's Bench extended its jurisdiction proceeded as follows. The plaintiff was allowed to start a feigned action of trespass, although in reality the plaintiff was claiming a debt. At first a writ from Chancery would be obtained in order to commit the defendant to the Marshalsea.[57] The marshal could allow him bail, but technically he was still a prisoner of the marshal. 'Bail' was not a sum of money or a bond to pay it, as it is thought of today in criminal bail, but referred to the people appointed to take the prisoner into their custody and produce him when required. A 'prisoner' was deemed already to be present in court, and so no additional process was necessary to start an action against him. With one final refinement, the fiction dispensed with the need for a writ from Chancery to start the action. Since the action of trespass was a fiction, the plaintiff merely had to embellish it by alleging a trespass in Middlesex and he could then proceed by a bill of trespass. Since the defendant was now in custody, the action of trespass would then be waived, and a bill could be filed against the defendant for debt. The court would not enquire how the defendant came to be in custody in the first place[58] and regarded him as amendable to the authority of the court in any other personal action whatever.[59]

In England, the fiction was called the bill of Middlesex, since the trespass fictionally had taken place in that county, which was where the courts in Westminster Hall were situated. Ferguson,[60] writing of Ireland in 1841, described a similar fiction, although it does not seem to have been given a specific name.[61]

One further complication was overcome. In the normal case of a writ of *capias* addressed to the sheriff of the county to arrest the defendant, the sheriff might return that the defendant 'is not found' (*non est inventus*) in the county (of Middlesex).[62] In that case the plaintiff had to inform the court that the defendant 'lurks and roams about' (*latitat et discurrit*) in the county where he actually lived. The court then issued a writ called a *latitat* to the sheriff of that county to arrest the defendant.[63] It was by these elaborate fictions that the King's Bench extended its jurisdiction far beyond its original bounds and so increased its own business while providing greater convenience to individual litigants.[64]

Starting an action by bill and *capias*,[65] while necessary in the Exchequer, became the alternative to the issue of original writs in the King's Bench and

[57] Baker, OHLE, vol. 6, p. 152.

[58] Baker, *Introduction*, p. 42 and n. 24, shows that this point may be traced to decisions of Fortescue CJ about 1450.

[59] Baker, *ibid.*, p. 42.

[60] *Treatise*, i.11.

[61] Ferguson, *ibid.*, does not mention any specific county.

[62] Baker, OHLE, vol. 6, p. 153.

[63] Baker, *Introduction*, p. 42; Ferguson does not mention a writ of *latitat* in Ireland. It is possible that by the 1840s actions were started by bill in Ireland without fictitious allegations.

[64] The bill procedure may not have been less expensive for litigants: Baker, *OHLE*, vol. 6, p. 152 n. 59.

[65] The bill initiated the action, the *capias* was the means to enforce attendance by the defendant. Baker, *OHLE*, vol. 6, p. 153.

Common Pleas in many cases, as, for example, when the plaintiff did not wish to proceed to outlawry or simply wished to avoid the inconvenience of an original writ. Jacob,[66] citing Stephen[67] on the Common Pleas, says that starting an action by *capias* was not possible in real or mixed actions, and that an original writ was still necessary in some personal actions where *capias* did not lie, as as where the defendant was privileged against arrest. An original writ was also still necessary in actions on the case. These were developments of the law of trespass by the clerks in Chancery issuing writs on facts not previously recognised as a cause of action. It was necessary to specify the precise facts on which the action was to lie, for a statement of facts which, if proved, would entitle the litigant to a remedy constituted the substantive law, and the requirement in original writs of a precise statement of the facts meant that the development of the law in that respect was in the control of the clerks in Chancery. The Irish House of Lords in *Hamilton* v. *Marquess of Donegall*[68] had to consider whether a particular set of facts was actionable as an action on the case, since it did not strictly constitute a trespass.[69]

The Court of Chancery

The common law courts generally took account only of the rules of the common law and their application, regardless of issues of conscience or general morality. In the reigns of Edward II and Edward III many petitions were presented to the king by litigants who claimed they had not received justice in the common law courts. After the time of Edward III they were regularly referred to the chancellor, one of the King's ministers. The chancellor was usually a cleric. For this reason the jurisdiction of his department, the Chancery, was often exercised on moral grounds, taking into account the conscience of the plaintiff or defendant. In the time of Elizabeth I the post was secularised and the Chancellor became 'the keeper of the Queen's conscience'. The Court of Chancery, in which the lord chancellor presided, developed a supplementary body of law, called equity, to mitigate the rigours of the common law. At first, decisions of the chancellor were not reported, since chancellors wished to maintain a wide discretion. In the next phase of its development, equity in England under Lord Ellesmere (1596–1617)[70] and particularly Lord Nottingham (1673–82)[71] became a distinct body of

66 *Law Dictionary*, 'Capias.' Holdsworth, *HEL*, ix. 251.

67 H. J. Stephen, *A Treatise on the Principles of Pleading in Civil Actions* (London, 1824), at p. 27.

68 (1795) 3 Ridg. PC 267.

69 Below, page 170.

70 Egerton, Thomas, Baron Ellesmere, 1st Viscount Brackley (1540–1617), lord chancellor, was born on 23 January 1540, the illegitimate son of Sir Richard Egerton, landowner, of Ridley, Cheshire, and a servant girl called Alice Sparke. Lord keeper, 1596–1603, lord chancellor 1603–1617. On the accession of James I, Egerton was reappointed lord keeper and created Baron Ellesmere, of Ellesmere in Shropshire in 1603. In the same year Egerton was appointed lord chancellor, relinquishing his position as lord keeper. On 7 November 1616, he was created Viscount Brackley, and four months later he resigned on health grounds.

71 Heneage Finch, 1st Earl of Nottingham (1621–1682). On the Restoration of 1660 he became solicitor general. He became lord keeper on 9 November 1673. The following January he received a peerage as Baron Finch of Daventry. He was appointed lord chancellor in 1675 and created Earl of

principles embodied in law reports, aided by the recording of equity decisions.[72]

The Irish Chancery began in 1232 when Henry III granted the English Chancellor, Ralph Neville, Bishop of Chichester, the Chancery of Ireland for life.[73] Neville nominated a deputy to execute the office in his place and it is likely therefore that the Irish Chancery was in fact established by Neville's deputy, Geoffrey de Turville. However, the Irish Chancery seems to have been largely administrative at first and did not emerge as a court until the 1470s.[74] In England Cardinal Wolsey (*c.* 1475–1530) was the last of the English medieval ecclesiastical chancellors and Sir Thomas More (1478–1535)[75] was the first of the chancellors not to hold a position within the church. In Ireland, clerics continued to be appointed until much later. Adam Loftus (1533/4–1605),[76] Church of Ireland archbishop of Armagh, was appointed lord keeper in 1573 and again in 1577, 1579 and lord chancellor in 1581.[77] Whether this had any effect on equity jurisdiction in Ireland is a matter of speculation. The Court of Exchequer had also developed an equity side and in Ireland this jurisdiction may have been more significant than in England.[78]

Equity developed new remedies and new rights. Its most characteristic invention was the trust. If the common law owner of land held it subject to an obligation to apply the benefits of ownership, the rent and profits, to another, the Chancery would in certain circumstances enforce the obligation as a trust. Equitable principles also gave rise to what today is called proprietary estoppel and as lord chancellor, FitzGibbon made a notable contribution in this respect, which is considered in detail below.[79] The beneficiary under the trust, or cestui que trust in the Law French term, had a kind of ownership recognised by the chancellor, which the chancellor would enforce, not against everyone, as a common law estate would be enforced, but against those whom he recognised as affected 'in conscience', such as an heir to the common law estate, and by the 18th century, against all except a purchaser of the common law estate who took without notice of the equitable interest affecting it. In Ireland, equity also developed an equity to renew a leases for life renewable forever which was more extensive than in England, where such interests were less common. This equity became of major importance in Ireland in the 18th century and saw a conflict between the Irish and British courts over the extent of the equity which will be

Nottingham in 1681.

[72] L. A. Knafla, *Law and Politics in Jacobean England: the Tracts of Lord Chancellor Ellesmere* (Cambridge, 1977); *Lord Nottingham's Chancery Cases* vols. 1 & 2. (D. E. C. Yale, ed.), 73 & 79 Seld. Soc. (for 1954, 1961-62).

[73] Ball, *Judges in Ireland* i.6-10; Otway-Ruthven, *Medieval Ireland*, p. 154 et seq.

[74] *ibid.*, p. 154.

[75] He was a canonised by Pope Pius XI in 1935. Seymour Baker House, 'More, Sir Thomas (1478–1535)', ODNB online. [http://www.oxforddnb.com/ view/article/19191], accessed 15 March 2013.

[76] James Murray, 'Loftus, Adam', DIB online. [http://dib.cambridge.org/ viewReadPage.do? articleId=a4867], accessed 15 March 2013.

[77] Ball, *Judges in Ireland*, i.155–56, 215–17.

[78] A. J. Otway-Ruthven, *A History of Medieval Ireland* (London, 1968) pp. 154–55; Hand, *English Law in Ireland 1290–1324*, pp. 99–103.

[79] *Kenney* v. *Browne* (1796) 3 Ridg. PC 462, below, page 166.

dealt with in detail later.[80]

One Irish lord chancellor of note before Lifford and FitzGibbon was Richard West,[81] although his tenure was brief. He was active in the British parliament before coming to Ireland and was one of the managers of the trial of Thomas Parker, first Earl of Macclesfield, LC, in 1725. Ball,[82] describes him as giving a 'masterly' speech on 11 May. He summed up the case for impeachment 'with great skill and vigour', and was scathing in his condemnation of the lord chancellor's 'corruption and avarice'.[83] West was appointed lord chancellor of Ireland, receiving his patent on 23 July 1725. West had been in office for less than a year and a half when he succumbed to 'a fever of the most malignant type.'[84] After twelve days' illness he died in Dublin on 3 December 1726. West's death gave rise to suspicion and there were rumours that his wife, having taken West's secretary John Williams as her lover, had poisoned her husband. The rumours were never substantiated. Williams in fact went on to marry West's daughter.[85]

West may have been the origin of the infamous concept of 'constructive papist', used by judges to extend the effect of the Penal Laws to those who had conformed to the Church of Ireland, where there was evidence, or even mere suspicion, that their conversion was only an outward appearance, or for the purpose of defeating a (genuine) Protestant discoveror.[86] In *Leamore* v. *Burke*[87] he apparently[88] held that:

> [the] Protestant who marries a Popish wife is a more odious Papist than a real and actual Papist in profession and principle... the Acts against the growth of Popery, expressing *every Papist or person professing the Popish religion*, &c., take in and regard *constructive*, as well as *actual*, Papists.

West was the author of the book *A Discourse Concerning Treasons, and Bills of Attainder*,[89] in which he defended the use of acts of attainder in some circumstances.

80 Below, pages 143–154.

81 Nathan Wells, 'West, Richard (*c.* 1691–1726)', ODNB online. [http://www.oxforddnb.com/view/article/29094], accessed 23 Feb 2013.

82 Ball, *Judges in Ireland*, ii.102.

83 St. Tr., xvi.1057–80.

84 Oliver J. Burke, *The History of the Lord Chancellors of Ireland from AD 1186 to AD 1874* (Dublin, 1879), p. 119, *The Making of Modern Law*, online. 2009, accessed 1 November 2009.

85 Nathan Wells, West, Richard (*c.* 1691–1726), ODNB online. [http://www.oxforddnb.com/view/article/29094], accessed 23 February 2013.

86 Below, page 164; 125 Seld. Soc. (for 2008), Introduction, pp. cxxxvi–cxxvii.

87 Howard, *Equity Side*, i.261.

88 Howard cites the case at p. 261, as a case in Chancery and the quotation below appears to be in Howard's words, but he does not state that it is a decision of West and gives no date. The case is cited sub. nom. *Leymore* v. *Burke* and the attribution to West is given in O'Flanagan, *Lord Chancellors of Ireland*, ii.43, although it is not clear how he attributed it to him. Nathan Wells, 'West, Richard (*c.* 1691–1726)', ODNB online. [http://www.oxforddnb.com/view/article/29094], accessed 23 February 2013, repeats O'Flanagan's attribution.

89 (London, 1716); Nathan Wells, 'West, Richard (*c.* 1691–1726)', ODNB.

The Court of Delegates

Before the Reformation, appeals from ecclesiastical courts went ultimately to the Pope, but at the time of the Reformation an Act of 1533[90] provided that in future petitions seeking an appeal from decisions of archbishops could be addressed to 'the King's Majesty in the King's Court of Chancery', that is, to the lord chancellor.[91] An appeal in ecclesiastical matters was not as of right, but *ex debito justitiæ*, that is, if, in the opinion of the lord chancellor, justice required it.[92] The lord chancellor had a discretion whether to grant an appeal. There was no provision in the statute for any appeal from his decision, and according to Duncan, there was no instance in England of an attempt to question it.[93]

If the petition was granted, a commission was issued under the Great Seal appointing delegates to hear the petition. The Crown had a complete discretion as to whom to appoint, but by the 18th century in England it was unusual to appoint bishops.[94]

'The court of law before the King in Chancery',[95] or 'the Crown in Chancery', was more usually called the Court of Delegates, although it would probably be more accurate to refer to 'a' Court of Delegates in a particular case, since the court had no permanent existence and no permanent judges. The Court of Delgates was composed of the lord chancellor and whoever else the the lord chancellor chose to appoint, so that the composition of the court varied in each case.[96] The court could therefore be composed of lay people, that is, non-ecclesiastics and in England increasingly was so. In England there would be civilians drawn from Doctors' Commons, but the position in Ireland is less clear. There was no equivalent of Doctors' Commons in Ireland and it would probably have been too expensive and cumbersome to bring civilians over from England, so it may be that in Ireland the other members were ecclesiastics with qualifications in civil law.

A new court was constituted for each appeal. The decision of the English court was said to be final,[97] so there was no further writ of error or appeal to the English House of Lords. Nevertheless, there was nothing to prevent the presentations of petitions for review or rehearing which the king on the advice of the Privy Council, in effect on the advice of the lord chancellor, was free to grant.

90 25 Hen. VIII, c. 19 (Eng.), 1533, repealed, 1 & 2 Ph. & Mar. c. 8, (Eng.) 1554, revived, 1 Eliz. I, c. 1, (Eng.), 1559, with saving for certain pending appeals to the Pope.

91 Holdsworth, *HEL*, i.375, 604; G. I. O. Duncan, *The High Court of Delegates* (Cambridge, 1971).

92 Duncan, *High Court of Delegates*, p. 54–55.

93 *ibid.*, p. 54.

94 R. M. Helmholz, OHLE, i.211.

95 The phrase is used in Ireland in the statute 40 Geo. III, c. 39, (Ir.), 1800: see Appendix R, page 257.

96 Duncan, *The High Court of Delegates*, p. 54.

97 Act of 1533, s. 4; 8 Eliz. I, c. 5, 1566. Holdsworth, *HEL*, i.375, 604; R. M. Helmholz, OHLE i.211.

In Ireland a Court of Delegates was established by 28 Hen. VIII, c. 6 (Ir.), 1537.[98] Petitions for appeals were to be addressed to 'the King of England and lord of Ireland'[99] or to his 'lieutenant, deputie, justice or other governour' of Ireland 'to his court...of chauncerie within the same realm of England or land of Ireland.' On a petition to the king, if it were granted, the chancellor of England, or keeper of the great seal, was to grant 'a commission or delegacy to some discreet and well learned persons of this land of Ireland, or else in the realm of England, for final determination of all causes and griefs' set out in the appeal. On an appeal made to the lieutenant or deputy, if it were granted, the chancellor of Ireland, with the assent of the chief justices of the King's Bench, Common Pleas, master of the rolls and 'underthesaurer' (under- treasurer) of Ireland, or any two of them, the under-treasurer being one, were to grant a commission to 'some discreet and well learned persons' in Ireland 'for final determination of all causes and griefs' contained in the appeal, and moreover the commissioners were to have 'the like power and authority in all manner of things' as commissioners assigned in appeals made to the king in England.

The interesting point here is that the statute clearly contemplated that while ecclesiastical appeals from ecclesiastical courts in Ireland could be made *either* to the king in England *or* to his deputy in Ireland, in either case the decision of a commission was to be the final determination of the case. Nevertheless, it appears from the case of *Loftus* v. *Callage*[100] that a convention had been adopted from at least the 1760s that appeals from ecclesiastical courts in Ireland should normally be granted to delegates in Ireland rather than to delegates in England. That case was an action in the Consistory Court of Dublin brought by the Rev. Smyth Loftus, vicar of Coolock, against Peter Callage, a farmer in his parish for subtraction of tithes,[101] in other words, alleging that Callage had failed to render the tithe due to him. William Wynne, a member of Doctors' Commons, stated in his opinion[102] that while the king under 25 Hen. VIII, c. 19 (Eng.), s. 4 could name persons to hear appeals from any archbishop's court within Great Britain or Ireland or any of his dominions, there were a number of cases in which it was stated that an appeal from ecclesiastical courts in Ireland should always be granted to delegates in Ireland unless there were special circumstances which required an English commission. Those circumstances would be that

98 Section 2. The statute of 1537 was repealed by 3 & 4 Ph. & Mar. c. 8 (Ir.), 1556, and revived by 2 Eliz. I, c. 1 (Ir.), 1560.

99 Henry had not at that time declared himself King of Ireland, which he did in 1542. Above, page 6. In *Lady Dillon* v. *Hussy et Uxr. et Al.* (1734) 125 Seld. Soc. 335, at 336 the case concerned the will of Lady Tyrconnel. She had made a will in 1704. A second will was made in 1726 was proved before the Prerogatve court of Canterbury, but this later will was alleged to have consisted only of notes which the deceased had no intent to execute as a will. The case was instituted in the Prerogative Court in Ireland which found in favour of the will, but that 'she [the plaintiff] had appealed from this sentence... to the Delegates in England.'

100 *A Report of the Case, which some time since depended in the Consistorial Court of Dublin between the late Rev. Smyth Loftus, Vicar of Coolock, and Peter Callage, one of his parishioners, for subtraction of tithes;...* (Dublin, 1787). I am obliged to Prof. Nial Osborough for reference to this source.

101 Under the statute 7 Geo. III, c. 21 (Ir.), 1767.

102 *ibid.*, pp. 61–62.

the decision would have considerable consequences in England, or that witnesses in England would have to be examined. He could only recall one case in which Lord Northington LC had granted a commission in England from an Irish ecclesiastical court and that was *Countess of Anglesey* v. *Simpson* (1762)[103] and the reason there being that it had brought into question the right to an English peerage. In five other cases an English commission had been refused.[104] It may also be noted that in the case mentioned earlier, *Lady Dillon* v. *Hussy et Uxr. et Al.* (1734)[105] there was an English element in that the second will had been proved in Canterbury. In *Loftus* v. *Callage* Callage had tendered tithes in grass mown and collected together in stoops or bundles on the field. Loftus maintained that they should have been made into hay. The consistory court held against Callage. He appealed to the English lord chancellor, having been advised that such a tender had been held legal in England, but the English Privy Council and civilians gave the above opinions, as a result of which he then petitioned for an appeal to delegates in Ireland instead, which was granted. However, it proved difficult to assemble a court of suitably qualified members in Ireland. Loftus then died and the case died with him, so the issue as to tithe was never resolved, but the case does make clear the convention that had developed.

There seems never at any stage to have been any suggestion in Ireland of an appeal from delegates to the Irish House of Lords.

The Irish Court of Delegates was reformed by a statute of George III in 1788.[106] Appeals were to be addressed, in future, to the king in the Irish Court of Chancery and a commission was to be directed under the great seal of Ireland to 'such persons as shall be named' by the king 'in his court of Chancery... to hear and definitely determine such appeals' and the decision of the court was to be 'good and effectual, and also definitive' and no further appeals were to be allowed. This appears on the face of it to have put an end to any appeals to delegates in England. Nevertheless, one perhaps should not exclude the possibility that there may have been instances where a litigant who had lost in an Irish Court of Delegates had then petitioned for a separate appeal to England, despite the statute.

Although there was no appeal from a Court of Delegates to another court, the decision of the delegates was not necessarily final in that a petition for a bill of review could be presented to the King in Council. It was usual for the petition to be referred to the lord chancellor for his report advising on whether a review should be granted.[107] The grant of a petition of review was not *ex debito justitiæ* but a matter of grace.[108] A commission of review could reverse the decision of the delegates.

This system continued until 1800 when the Irish Act reforming the Irish

[103] No citation given.

[104] *Thompson* v. *Thompson* (1765), *Jones and Doile* v. *Spann* (1767). *Lady Trollop and Onslow* v. *Lord Conyngham* (1769), per Lord Camden LC, *Shea* v. *Shea* (1771), *Homan* v. *Phipps* (1772).

[105] 125 Seld. Soc. 335, at 336, above page 66.

[106] 28 Geo. III, c. 32 (Ir.), 1788, s. 2.

[107] Duncan, *High Court of Delegates*, p. 62; Stein, (1972A) Camb. L. J. 348.

[108] Duncan, *High Court of Delegates*, p. 62.

Court of Exchequer Chamber[109] provided that in future writs of error from the Court of Delegates should lie to the newly-constituted Exchequer Chamber in Ireland.

One of the many anomalous, and indeed absurd, aspects of the ecclesiastical courts was that until 1858 their jurisdiction extended over the estates of all deceased persons, not only members of the Church of Ireland, but also Catholics, who in Ireland were of course the majority of the population, and also dissenters and Jews.[110] A Consistory Court in each diocese was responsible for granting probate and conferring on executors the power to administer the estate of the deceased. This court also dealt with those situations in which the deceased had died intestate, and issued letters of administration. However, if the deceased had property valued at more than £5 in another diocese, then the responsibility for the will passed to the Prerogative Court under the authority of the archbishop.

There is at least one instance, in the period between 1788 and 1800, of a decision of an ecclesiastical court and the Court of Delegates being the subject of a report on a bill of review by the lord chancellor, FitzGibbon, who recommended a review. *Goodwin* v. *Giesler*[111] concerned the validity of the will of James Goodwin, who had died unmarried in August 1788 when he was more than eighty years of age. He had lived for some years with a near relative and when the relative died, with the relative's widow. In May 1788 he had gone to dinner at the invitation of Giesler and never returned, continuing to live at Giesler's house until his death. During the time he lived with the widow he had never been charged for bed or board and seemed content with the arrangement. Shortly after his moving into Giesler's house, Giesler prevailed upon Goodwin to lend him £450 without independent advice on the security of Giesler's house, which security was evidently insufficient. The will was challenged by Goodwin's nephews as next of kin. The will was executed only a few hours before Goodwin died and had been prepared by a relation of Giesler's wife. Giesler was named as executor and residuary legatee.

The procedure in the Prerogative Court was civilian, evidence being taken in the form of written depositions.[112] Interrogatories were then drawn up which posed questions about the evidence in the depositions. The witnesses were examined in private and in separate rooms on the interrogatories. The private examination of witnesses was a basic feature of the civilian procedure and was seen as protection against the 'abuse' of public cross-examination. The judge examined them a second time on the depositions and interrogatories, to determine whether they wished to alter their testimony in any way. They then signed their depositions. So far, all this was as it should have been. However, after

[109] 40 Geo. III c. 39 (Ir.), 1800, and see page 137, Appendix R, page 257.

[110] [http://www.nationalarchives.ie/genealogy/testamentary.html]; [http://www.from-ireland.net/genealogy/Wills-%26-Deeds-Explanation], accessed 9 April 2011. Ecclesiastical jurisdiction, apart from Church matters, was transferred to the secular courts in 1857: 18 & 19 Vict., c. 41, 1855 (defamation jurisdiction abolished); 20 & 21 Vict., c. 77, 1857 and c. 85, 1857 (family law and probate). Baker, *Introduction*, p. 132.

[111] (1794) Ir. Term Rep. 371; Fleming and Malcomson, eds., *A Volley of Execrations* pp. 200–205.

[112] *ibid.*, p. 378.

several days of hearing, the judge granted motions brought by the respondent's proctor to re-examine the witnesses orally and the witnesses were then examined and cross-examined by the advocates for both sides in open court. It was this a later oral hearing that was the subject of appeal to the delegates and the objection was to be upheld by FitzGibbon's report. The judge then found in favour of the will and granted probate.

The petitioner appealed against this finding and a commission was issued under the great seal to delegates to hear the appeal.[113] When the Court of Delegates met they called on the advocates for the petitioner to support the appeal. His advocates asked for time to prepare printed cases, but the delegates refused. They also refused to allow the advocates for the petitioner time to prepare oral arguments. The judges then proceeded immediately to examine the depositions and held in favour of the Prerogative Court.

A petition was presented for review of the decision of the delegates and on the advice of the Privy Council an order was made referring the matter to the lord chancellor[114] who recommended that a commission of review should be granted to rehear the case and review the original sentence of the judge. We are not told the ultimate result of this. FitzGibbon strongly disapproved of the action of the judge in allowing oral examination after the presentation of depositions and held that he had no authority to do so.[115] He also considered that the delegates had acted improperly in not allowing sufficient opportunity to the petitioner to prepare his case. He further commented that 'In making this report, I have to lament deeply, that I must detail a proceeding which will not reflect credit upon the jurisprudence of this country.'[116]

113 *ibid.*, p. 375.

114 *ibid.*, p. 376.

115 *ibid.*, pp. 381–384; Fleming and Malcomson, eds., *A Volley of Execrations* pp. 200–205, [257] FitzGibbon to the lord chancellor of England [Lord Loughborough], 6 January 1795, [258] Report to the King's Most Excellent Majesty in Council', 3 January 1795.

116 *ibid.*, p. 384.

CHAPTER 5

Writs of Error and Appeals

Writs of Error

A writ of error of law[1] lay where the judges had made an error of law on the face of the record. It consisted of a certiorari to remove the record, or a transcript, to the higher court. A writ of error in theory was a separate action.[2] Hence, the person bringing it was called the 'plaintiff in error', rather than 'the appellant', the latter being the term used in an equity appeal. This also meant, among other things, that until the early 18th century there was no set time within which a writ of error had to be brought.[3]

A writ of error lay only if an error appeared on the face of the record of the court below, so that, if the plaintiff had made an oral submission which was overruled by the judge, this could not be 'assigned for error', since it did not appear on the record.[4] For that reason the Statute of Westminster II, 1285[5] provided that either party could submit 'exceptions', (as in 'taking exception to...') that is, objections, in writing before the judge who tried the case and signed by counsel for both parties. A bill of exceptions would then be drawn up and the judge was to put his seal to it. If a writ of error was brought, the bill of exceptions was part of the record to be removed to the higher court.

An intriguing reference to a bill of exceptions occurs in *Hume* v. *Burton*,[6] the case concerning the mental capacity of the Earl of Ely. Procedural issues in legal history are often particularly difficult to unravel, not only because of the complexity but also because the practitioners at the time understood them and found no reason to explain them at length to each other. What follows is an attempt to explain the main points.

The writ of error had been brought to reverse a judgment of the court of King's Bench, affirming a judgment of the Court of Common Pleas in a common

[1] Writs of error of fact are not considered here. For those, see *Irish Exchequer Reports 1716–1734* (Lyall ed.), 125 Seld. Soc. (for 2008) p. cx.

[2] Until 1852 in England: Common Law Procedure Amendment Act, 1852 (Eng.), s. 148. and until 1853 in Ireland: Common Law Procedure Amendment Act (Ireland), 1853, s. 169.

[3] 6 Geo. I, c. 6 (Ir.), 1719 s. 3 laid down a generous 20 years. See also 5 Geo. I, c. 13 (Eng.), 1718.

[4] 2 Inst. 426; Jacob, *Law Dictionary*, 'Bill of exceptions.'

[5] 13 Edw. I, c. 31.

[6] (1785) 1 Ridg. PC 204, at 219–222., and see below, page 88.

recovery. The writ of error was based on a bill of exceptions taken to an opinion of the King's Bench on the issue of whether the earl had the mental capacity to be a party to the common recovery brought to free his estates from a settlement and thereby to vest the powers of dealing with the estate into the hands of other members of the family.

The case had been before the Lords previously, on the issue as to whether a warrant appearing in the body of the record removed to the King's Bench contained evidence which precluded the plaintiff from going into parol evidence as to the mental state of the earl. A new trial in King's Bench had been ordered. In the King's Bench counsel for the plaintiff, who sought to impeach the recovery, offered to give evidence to prove that, at the time of the warrant of attorney given by the earl, the earl was of unsound mind.

Counsel for the defendant argued that such evidence should not be given because the recital in the record of the inquisition[7] was conclusive evidence in favour of the capacity of the earl. If so, this would preclude oral evidence to be given on that point and therefore the issue should not have been included in the bill of exceptions. King's Bench held that the inquisition was not conclusive evidence on the issue, but that the warrant stated on the record *was* conclusive as to the earl's sanity and refused to allow the plaintiff to give oral evidence on the point. The jury then found that the earl was of sound mind at the time and King's Bench then affirmed the judgment of Common Pleas.

FitzGibbon, then attorney general, appeared for the defendant before Lifford LC. He argued that the judgment of the King's Bench should be affirmed, and that the inquisition, finding that the earl was of sound mind, was conclusive evidence of his sanity, the fact in issue. Mr Wolfe for the plaintiff, argued that FitzGibbon should not be allowed to address the issue of the inquisition, because the *defendant* did not take a bill of exceptions to the judgment of King's Bench, since it was otherwise in his favour. FitzGibbon continued:[8]

> I should make a pretty figure at you lordships bar with a writ of error in my hand from a judgment pronounced in my favour, because that judgment may be supported upon a different ground from that which was stated by the learned judges in the court below. But I understand this manoeuvre completely:– it is a pretence of counsel to avoid stating his objections to this inquisition until he comes to reply, in order to deprive me of an opportunity to answer him. But I hope your lordships will call upon him to state his objections to this inquisition as evidence now, or that you will not suffer him to say one word on the subject when he is called upon to reply.–

[7] The jurisdiction of Chancery over the care of 'idiots' and 'lunatics' came from the royal prerogative. The lord chancellor could order an inquisition into the person's mental condition and if necessary appoint committees to conduct the affairs of a person found incapable. 'Idiots' were those born with a mental disability, while 'lunatics' were those who developed a mental illness after their birth. See Siobhán Ní Chúlacháin, 'Wardship of Adults in Ireland', LLM thesis, University College Dublin, 1997.

[8] 1 Ridg. PC at 221.

FitzGibbon then in a somewhat theatrical gesture, simply sat down. Lifford LC responded mildly: 'Mr Attorney, you had better go on.' FitzGibbon then continued by remarking that he was then 'under the necessity to conjecture what will be objected on this head, and to conjecture what my learned friend will say...'

FitzGibbon would hardly have brought a bill of exceptions to a judgment the conclusion of which was *in favour* of his client, but Wolfe's point was that, since that was so, FitzGibbon should not be allowed to address the issue in his speech, but that Wolfe, who had put in a bill of exceptions, could address the point in his. Lifford LC was nevertheless prepared to allow FitzGibbon to address the point in his speech, but FitzGibbon would still be at the disadvantage of having to think in advance of what objections Wolfe might raise to the inquisition without actually knowing what they would turn out to be. The incident illustrates that Lifford LC, at least by allowing FitzGibbon address the issue, was prepared to allow a partial departure from the strict logic of the system of writs of error and bills of exceptions in the interests of fairness. Nevertheless, the partial departure from the strict logic of the writ system still left the other side at a disadvantage and shows how procedure could prevent what today is called 'equality of arms', that both sides should be in an equal position to address the issues.

Appeals in Equity

In equity, matters were much simpler. An appeal in equity was in the form of a petition[9] and equity appeals were not confined to the record.

As to Chancery, and the equity side of Exchequer, appeals lay directly to the House of Lords, of England until 1782[10] and to the Irish House of Lords from 1782 to the Union.[11]

The Court of Exchequer Chamber

Coke, writing of England, said there were seven different courts held in the Exchequer.[12] Three[13] of these were concerned with writs of error or references on matters of law and have been called 'Exchequer Chamber' from time to time:

1. the assembly of all the judges of England for settling matters of law;
2. the court for errors in the Court of Exchequer, under 31 Edw. III, st. 1, c. 12 (Eng.), 1357[14] and 31 Eliz. I, c. 1 (Eng.), 1588, properly called the Court of Council Chamber;
3. the court for errors in the King's Bench, under 27 Eliz. I, c. 8, (Eng.), 1584 and 31 Eliz. I, c. 1 (Eng.), 1588.

[9] 'Rules and Orders to be Observed in the Upper House of Parliament upon Writs of Error and Appeals', (Dublin, 1784), rule 84, 85. The Rules and Orders are reproduced in 1 Ridg. PC xix,.

[10] See below, note 40.

[11] Jacob, *Law Dictionary*, 'Chancery' p. 435. 'Rules and Orders to be Observed in the Upper House of Parliament upon Writs of Error and Appeals', 1 Ridg. PC xix.

[12] Inst., iv. 119. The first three he mentions, the court of pleas, the court of accounts and the court of receipt, were all forms of the Court of Exchequer. See *Irish Exchequer Reports 1716–1734* (Andrew Lyall ed.) 125 Seld. Soc. (for 2008) p. lxxxii.

[13] The 'Court of equity in the Exchequer Chamber', as Coke calls it, is synonymous with what later became known as the equity side of Exchequer.

[14] c. 8 in Coke.

The Assembly of all the Judges

This court in England was apparently the most ancient and grew up as a matter of practice.[15] It can hardly be termed a court at all, since proceedings were not started by writ, nor by the parties. If a difficult point of law arose in one of the common law courts it became the practice to adjourn proceedings and wait until the common law judges assembled in a room near the Exchequer, and had expressed their opinions on the point. The common law court in which the issue had arisen would then give judgment on the case. In theory the assembly was purely advisory, and so it was unlike a court in this respect also.

The common law judges in Ireland, unlike those in England, actually had to attend the sittings of the Irish House of Lords, but could not speak unless and until called upon to give their opinion on a point of law. The procedure was provided for in standing orders of the House adopted in 1692.[16] Examples of the procedure are discussed below.[17]

The Court of Council Chamber

The court for errors in the Court of Exchequer, more usually known as the Court of Exchequer Chamber, was strictly 'the chamber of Council' or the 'Court of Council Chamber'. It was a court in the true sense, in that proceedings were begun by writ of error.

The court was established in 1357 by the statute 31 Edw. III, st. 1, c. 12 (Eng.).[18] The statute is not listed by Donaldson[19] as having been expressly applied to Ireland, but it would have applied through Poynings' Law, 1495[20] in any case.

The statute of 1357 provided:

> That in all cases touching the King, or other persons, where a man complaineth of error made in process in the Exchequer the chancellor and treasurer shall cause to come before them in any chamber of council nigh the Exchequer the record of process out of the Exchequer taking to them the justices and other sage persons such as to them seemeth to be taken ... and if any error be found they shall correct and amend the rolls.

In England, by the statute 5 Eliz. I, c. 18 in 1562, the lord keeper was given the same powers as the lord chancellor. In fact, under the statute of 1562, the title was merely an alternative and the offices of lord chancellor and lord keeper

15 *Select Cases in the Exchequer Chamber* (M. Hemmant, ed.) 51 Seld. Soc. (for 1933), p. xix.

16 'Rules and Orders of the Upper House' (1692) *Ir. Lords J.* p. 470, 'Concerning the Judges'. *Irish Exchequer Reports 1716–1734* (Andrew Lyall ed.) 125 Seld. Soc. (for 2008) p. lxxxii.

17 Below, page 96.

18 St. Realm i.351–352.

19 A. G. Donaldson, 'The Application in Ireland of English and British Legislation Made Before 1801', (unpublished Ph.D. thesis, Queen's University, Belfast, 1952).

20 Above, page 17.

could not be held by different people at the same time.[21] There are only two instances of a lord keeper being appointed in Ireland, both in the 16th century. Ball[22] identifies these two as Thomas Cusake in 1546 and Adam Loftus, archbishop,[23] in 1573 and again in 1577, 1579 and 1581. Loftus was appointed lord chancellor in 1581.

In England a statute of 1588[24] first recited that the lord chancellor and lord treasurer, 'being great officers of the realm', were often suddenly called away, causing a discontinuance in the Court of Council Chamber, and then, to prevent such a thing happening in future, provided that if either one of them, or if both chief justices, were present, there should be no discontinuance. However, no judgment could be given unless both the lord chancellor and the lord treasurer were present. In 1668 the vacancy in the office of lord treasurer made it necessary to enact that the judgment of the court could be given by either the lord chancellor or the lord keeper.[25] It was this provision that persuaded the court in *The Banker's Case, The King* v. *Hornby*[26] that the other judges present were merely 'assistants' and so in that case that Lord Keeper Somers could reverse the Court of Exchequer contrary to the opinion of the majority of the judges.

In Ireland the composition of the Court of Exchequer Chamber was amended in 1639[27] by adding the vice-treasurer as an alternative to the lord treasurer and by providing that if one of the three (lord chancellor, lord treasurer, or vice-treasurer), or both chief justices, appeared on the day of adjournment, it would prevent a discontinuance. It also provided that judgment was to be given by the lord chancellor and lord treasurer 'in the presence and by advice of both the chief justices'. A further amendment in 1727[28] provided that the lord chancellor, in the absence of the treasurer and vice-treasurer, could give judgment, 'in the presence and by the advice of both or either of the said chief justices'. There was no mention of a lord keeper.

The Court for Errors in the King's Bench

This court was created in England by 27 Eliz. I, c. 8, 1584 and 31 Eliz. I, c. 1, 1588. No corresponding statutes were passed in Ireland and, as we have seen, in so far as there were writs of error from King's or Queen's Bench in Ireland, they lay to the King's or Queen's Bench in England.

[21] Jacob, *Dictionary*, 'Chancellor' maintains that there were instances before this of the offices being vested in different people at the same time, citing Coke. Inst., iv. 88. Coke relates that a doubt had arisen on this point since King Henry V had two great seals made, one of gold and one of silver, and had given the gold one to the bishop of Durham, making him chancellor, and the silver one to the bishop of London 'to keep'. He gives no other example. There were four lord keepers in England in the 18th century, the last being Sir Robert Henley LK, afterwards 1st Earl of Northington who became LC in 1761 having been LK since 1757.

[22] *Judges in Ireland*, i.155.

[23] *ibid.*, i.155–56, 215–17.

[24] 31 Eliz. I, c. 1 (Eng.), 4 St. Realm 799 (1547-1624); and see also 16 Cha. II, c. 2 (Eng.), 1664.

[25] 19 & 20 Cha. II, c. 9 (Eng.), 1668; *HEL*, i.244. The statute actually says 'lord keeper', but necessarily implied by then that it included lord chancellor if there was one.

[26] (1695) 5 Mod. 29, 87 E.R. 500; 14 St.Tr. 1 at 105.

[27] 15 Cha. I, c. 5 (Ir.).

[28] 1 Geo. II, c. 17 (Ir.).

The English statute of 1584 had provided for a special writ in Chancery to be issued to bring the record into the Exchequer Chamber before such judges of the other two courts, the Common Pleas and Exchequer, as were serjeants or any six of them, who were to have power to reverse or affirm the judgment.[29] A further writ of error was to lie to the House of Lords.[30] Nevertheless, the statute of 1584 only applied to the actions of debt, detinue, covenant, account, actions on the case, ejectment, and trespass 'first commenced or to be first commenced there',[31] and so in other actions, the writ of error still lay directly to the House of Lords. Furthermore, it did not apply to actions started by original writ, because they did not begin in King's Bench, but in Chancery, by issue of the original there.[32] At common law writs of error had lain from the King's Bench directly to the House of Lords and so continued to do so if started by original writ.[33] Hence, the writs of error which were to go from King's Bench to Exchequer Chamber were those listed, if started by bill. By the end of the 18th century, bill would be the normal method in such cases.

It was one of the provisions of the statute of James II's Jacobite parliament that in future writs of error from the Irish King's Bench should go to the Court of Exchequer Chamber in Ireland.[34] Its provisions were almost identical to the English statute of 1584[35] except that it required only four or more of the judges of the Common Pleas and barons of the Exchequer to be present. Neither the statute of Elizabeth nor the Irish Jacobite statute proposed to alter the existing system in Ireland and England, whereby writs of error lay from the Court of Common Pleas to the King's Bench. This left something of an anomaly, in that the Court of Common Pleas had been, and remained, to that extent inferior to the King's Bench, and yet if a case had started in the Common Pleas, a writ of error would now lie to the King's Bench, and a further writ of error to the Exchequer Chamber, where it would be heard again by judges of the Common Pleas. The logical solution to removing the appellate jurisdiction of the English King's Bench over the Irish King's Bench, would be to deal with the issue of writs of error from all three common law courts, and to provide that they would all lie directly to a reconstituted Court of Exchequer Chamber, but that reform was not to happen until 1800, as we discuss below.[36]

The Jacobite statute, and all other statutes of James II's parliament, were declared void by the parliament of William III,[37] and so the change did not take effect, except possibly while James II remained in Ireland. Although some of the reforms provided for in the statutes of James II's parliament were later enacted

[29] Section 1.

[30] Section 2.

[31] Section 1.

[32] Tidd's *Practice*, 5th ed. 1812, p. 1101.

[33] Tidd's *Practice*, 5th ed. 1812, pp. 1099–1101; Ferguson, *Treatise*, i.11.

[34] Below, page 221.

[35] It also contained the limitation as to the types of actions within the statute and included the phrase 'first commenced or to be first commenced there': s. 3.

[36] Chapter 13, 'The Later History of Exchequer Chamber', below, page 137.

[37] 7 Will. III, c. 3 (Ir.), 1695. See above 7, note 22.

by the parliament of William III, where they were not politically controversial,[38] the ending of writs of error from the Irish King's Bench to the English King's Bench was not one of them. That was not to happen until 1782. The English presumably wished to retain that control over the Irish King's Bench, which heard cases of treason.

We have seen that there are examples of writs of error to the English King's Bench in 1775 and 1782.[39] The statute 21 & 22 Geo. III, c. 49, 1781–82[40] then provided that 'from henceforth all such [erroneous] judgments, orders, and decrees, shall be finally examined and reformed in the high Court of parliament in this kingdom only'. The only further change to this came in 1800 with the extension to the jurisdiction of the Irish Exchequer Chamber, interposing that court between the (briefly Irish, then British) House of Lords and the courts of King's Bench and Common Pleas.[41]

Appeals to the House of Lords

Printed Pleadings

In the case of writs of error and equity appeals[42] to the House of Lords, both Irish and British, written pleadings or statements of the case, often referred to simply as 'cases', were submitted by each party. The 'Rules and Orders to be Observed in the Upper House of Parliament upon Writs of Error and Appeals',[43] rule 87, in relation to equity appeals, specified that they be 'engrossed on parchment', but by the 18th century they were usually printed, and the printed pleadings survive in various collections, including King's Inns, Dublin and Trinity College Dublin[44]

Reports

Reports of the appeals heard by the Irish House of Lords since the Repealing Act were published in three volumes as Ridgeway's *Reports of Cases upon Appeals and Writs of Error in the High Court of Parliament in Ireland, since the Restoration of Appellate Jurisdiction* (Dublin, 1795), often referred to as 'Ridgeway's Parliamentary Cases' and usually abbreviated to 'Ridg. PC.' or 'Ridg. App.', covering the

38 See Davis, *The Patriot Parliament of 1689*. Davis includes *inter alia* a transcription of the statute he lists as Chapter 17, *An Act for Relief and Release of poor distressed Prisoners for Debt*. 10 Will. III, c. 1 (Ir.), 1695 adopted several of its provisions and had a similar aim.

39 Above, page 22 *Massey* v. *Rice* (1775) 1 Cowp. 346, 98 E.R. 1122. *Barry* v. *Nugent* (1782) 3 Dougl. 180, 99 E.R. 60.

40 Below, page 81 and Appendix P, page 253.

41 Below, page 137.

42 From now on, for the sake of brevity, the word 'appeal' or 'appeals' will be used to include writs of error unless the context otherwise requires.

43 They are reproduced in Ridgeway: 1 Ridg. PC xix.

44 Colum Kenny, *King's Inns and the Battle of the Books, 1972* (Dublin, 2002), p. 37 describes the 97 volumes of printed appeals as 'one of the richest veins for unique Irish historical information which I have come across for many years.' See 'Bibliography', page 262 and below, page 79. The parchment petition and appeal of Stephen Sweet to the British House of Lords in the case of *Sweet* v. *Anderson* (1722) at 430; 1 E.R. 927, survives and is to be found at: HLRO, large parchments, HL/PO/JO/10/3/214/46.

years 1784 to 1796.[45] Some judgments of the court are also to be found in Vernon and Scriven's *Irish Reports; or, Reports of Cases determined in the King's Courts, Dublin; with Select Cases in the House of Lords of Ireland* (Dublin, 1790) ('Vern. & Scr.') and Ridgeway, Lapp and Schoales' *Irish Term Reports* ('Ridg. L. & S.', or Ir. Term. Rep.). Ridgeway's reports are not reproduced in the English Reports, nor are Vernon and Scriven's reports, nor Ridgeway, Lapp and Schoales, which is understandable.[46] Some Irish appeals to the British House of Lords are published in Brown's Parliamentary Cases ('Bro. PC'), reproduced in volumes 1, 2 and 3 of the English Reports. Both Ridgeway's Parliamentary Cases, Vernon and Scriven's Reports, and Ridgeway, Lapp and Schoales are now available in an online version through the subscription database, *Eighteenth Century Collections Online*[47] The available law reports have now been supplemented as as source to some extent by the publication by the Irish Manuscripts Commission in 2008 of the *Proceedings of the Irish House of Lords* (PIHL) in three volumes ably edited, and with an informative introduction, by James Kelly. These volumes consist mainly of accounts of the proceedings in the Irish House of Lords as reported in newspapers of the time, such as the *Freeman's Journal*, the *Hibernian Journal*, etc. While these accounts provide interesting background to some of the cases, and statutes, they are no substitute for the law reports, since they rarely give a full account of the legal judgments. In the case of *Kenny* v. *Browne*, discussed elsewhere in this work,[48] for example, the *Proceedings* report[49] that the Earl of Clare LC 'accurately stated the whole of the proceedings in this business from beginning to end...and concluded with observing that he considered the conduct of the appellant...a premeditated system of the greatest fraud...' and that Lord Yelverton spoke for about half an hour in which he 'made several acute observations', etc., whereas Ridgeway reports, apparently verbatim, what both of them actually said, including their important statements on estoppel in equity, which are significant contributions to the development of the law, but were apparently of little interest to general readers of the newspapers.

As to Ridgeway's own attitude to the restoration of the appellate jurisdiction to the Irish House of Lords, the passage quoted above on page 2, indicates that he approved of it and he refers to the 'enlightened policy' which had that as one of its results.[50]

45 O'Higgins, 'William Ridgeway (1765-1817) – Law Reporter' (1967) 18 NILQ 208–22; see *Guide to Law Reports and Statutes* (London, Sweet and Maxwell, 4th. edn. 1962).

46 The English Reports do, somewhat inconsistently, reproduce Davies' Reports in 80 E.R., the first published Irish law reports, but which have been described as largely works of fiction, designed to discredit Brehon law: Hans Pawlisch 'The Cases of Gavelkind and Tanistry: Legal Imperialism in Ireland, 1603–1610' in *Sir John Davies and the Conquest of Ireland* (Cambridge, 2002); Paul Brand, 'Sir John Davies: Law Reporter or Self-Publicist?' (2008) 43(1) Ir. Jur. 1–20.

47 [ECCO], Gale publishers.

48 Below, page 166.

49 PIHL, iii.17, Friday, 19 February 1796.

50 O'Higgins, 'William Ridgeway (1765–1817) – Law Reporter' (1967) 18 NILQ 208–22, at p. 210 n. 138, comments that Ridgeway was 'careful in the preface to avoid committing himself as to the wisdom of the restoration of its appellate jurisdiction to the House of Lords in 1783', but Ridgeway's words do not seem to support that. On the contrary, his view seems to accord with that of the

The Irish House of Lords followed the practice of the British house in requiring pleadings in appeals to their house to be printed[51] and copies exist in the Library of King's Inns, Dublin and elsewhere.[52] The Kings' Inns collection is part of a long series of volumes of pleadings before the 'House of Lords' from 1699 into the 19th century, totalling some fifty volumes up to the end of the 18th century. For much of the 18th century, from 1720 to 1782, the 'House of Lords' refers to the British House of Lords, to whom appeals and writs of error lay from the Declaratory Act until the Repealing Act. Neither the volumes nor the pleadings in particular cases specify whether they refer to the Irish house or the British house and a researcher has to work this out from the name of the case and the date. Each case therefore normally has two printed pleadings, one for each side of the case on appeal. They usually contain an exhaustive statement of the facts, more detailed than is found in Ridgeway's reports and which should be of interest to social as well as legal historians. They also contain a statement of the argument of counsel on the appeal. The decision of the court is sometimes noted on the printed pleading, just as it would be on an ordinary brief by the barrister appearing in the case. Ridgeway himself used 'a large collection of the printed cases, with the decisions',[53] collected by an Irish judge at whose suggestion Ridgeway prepared the reports, as well as his own notes from what he witnessed himself at sittings of the House.

There are several references to the printed pleadings in the reports of cases in the Irish House of Lords. In *Crowe* v. *Halliday (No. 2)*[54] the existence of printed pleadings is mentioned and in that case it is said that they relieved counsel from the necessity of arguing the case orally. Lord Yelverton in *Kenney* v. *Browne*[55] says that he formed his opinion in the case on reading the printed pleadings.

In *Redington* v. *Redington*[56] FitzGibbon, the lord chancellor, mentions that one of the parties had committed a contempt of the House by distributing copies of the printed pleadings outside the House in order to influence opinion in his favour:[57]

> The chancellor then observed, that he considered it to be his duty to state a circumstance, which appeared to him to be highly reprehensible on the part of the appellants:– He said he had the best reason to know, that for some days past they have been busily employed in distributing their printed cases, and copies of opinions taken by them of very eminent counsel in another kingdom upon the merits of their cause... He said he mentioned this aggression on the part of the appellants for the purpose only of preventing a repetition

'patriots' in parliament, namely, enthusiastic support for the restoration of the Lords' appellate role.

51 Above, page 77.

52 See Bibliography, page 262.

53 O'Higgins, 'William Ridgeway', p. 210, n. 138.

54 (1788) 2 Ridg. PC 58.

55 (1796) 3 Ridg. PC 462 at 528.

56 (1794) 3 Ridg. PC 201. See below page 165.

57 *ibid.*, at pp. 201–2.

> of it. He said it was on their part a canvass for clamour to drown the voice of justice; that they had been busily employed in distributing their printed cases and laying the opinions of their counsel before many Members of both houses of parliament, since this appeal was preferred, and if it had been an appeal from the court of Exchequer, he would certainly have have complained of this proceeding as a high contempt of the House of Lords. That he mentioned it now with a view only to prevent the repetition of such an aggression, because if the practice should be suffered to prevail, it must inevitably tend to corrupt the forces of justice – and therefore, if he should again detect any suitor of this High Court of Judicature in such a proceeding, he would without regard to the court from whence the appeal was preferred, infallibly bring him forward to answer for the contempt.

His comment seems to have been a form of reprimand and there is no indication of any further action being taken.

Ridgeway reports some 68 appeals, of which equity appeals are by far the most numerous. Of the appeals which can be classified as common law or equity, there are some 38 equity appeals and 16 common law, a ratio of about three to one. Among the common law appeals, none is criminal. One is from Exchequer Chamber.[58] Most cases concern property. Of the equity appeals, about two-thirds are from Chancery, and one third from the Exchequer.

From Exchequer Chamber

The destination of appeals from the Irish Exchequer Chamber (the Court of Council Chamber, errors from the Exchequer) was open to doubt before 1782. The original English statute of 1357[59] spoke of appeal to 'parliament.' In Ireland that might reasonably have been interpreted to refer to the Irish parliament. From this it could have been argued that the Irish House of Lords had appellate jurisdiction from the Irish Court of Exchequer Chamber since 1357, but no such argument prevailed. The issue is subsumed within the general issue of the jurisdiction of the Irish House of Lords which has already been discussed.

From Chancery

There was no appeal from the Irish Chancery to Exchequer Chamber, which heard writs of error from the Exchequer and, in Ireland from 1800, from the other common law courts also. In England, appeals from the Court of Chancery lay to the English House of Lords.

The suspension of the Irish parliament in the latter half of the 17th century meant that there was no Irish House of Lords to which appeals could be made and this period consequently saw a number of appeals from the Irish Chancery to the English House of Lords, the first of these being *Nugent* v. *Talbot*

58 *Hamilton* v. *Marquess of Donegall* (1795) 3 Ridg. PC 267.

59 31 Edw. III, st. 1, c. 12 (Eng.). St. Realm i.351. Above, page 74.

in 1670,[60] which may also have been the first instance of a direct appeal from the Irish courts to the English Lords. Appeals from the Irish Chancery to the English/British House of Lords are therefore of late date, immediately preceding the clash over *Annesley* v. *Sherlock*.

Writs of Error: a Matter of Right?

In 1644 the lord chancellor informed the Irish House of Lords that he had consulted precedents for the bringing of writs of error in the parliament and that they were to the effect that 'writs of error to parliament must be awarded by virtue of the king's warrant, under hand upon the writ'. The judge should then bring the record and the royal warrant and leave a transcript. A writ of *scire facias*[61] would then issue to the plaintiff to 'assign his errors', i.e. to state the errors on the record. If he did so, then a *scire facias* would issue to the defendant to respond. The lord chancellor then proposed a declaration that the writ of error in the case of *Verschoyle* v. *Hunt*[62] was void, since the king's writ had not been procured. However, the journals show that the writ had already been disallowed because the plaintiff failed to assign errors.[63] Writs of error, as has been mentioned, were common law proceedings and the journal of the House of Lords is not clear as to the procedure to be followed in the case of equity appeals.

The procedure was not given statutory form until the jurisdiction of the Irish House of Lords was restored in 1782.[64] *An Act for the Redress of erroneous Judgments, Orders and Decrees* specifically provided that 'from henceforth all... judgments, orders and decrees shall be finally examined and reformed in the High Court of Parliament in this kingdom only'. This was not to invalidate any judgment, order or decree given in Great Britain before the 1 June 1782.[65] The lord lieutenant was empowered to grant warrants to seal writs of error 'returnable into parliament'.[66] 'Judgments' was the common law term while 'decrees' was the term in Chancery, so it appears that both required the warrant of the Crown. The lord lieutenant acted on the advice of the attorney general.

Despite the 1644 statement of the lord chancellor in Ireland, there was considerable support for the view that at common law a writ of error was a matter of right, especially in criminal cases, and an Irish lord chancellor, Hart LC, certainly said so in 1828.

[60] (1670) 16 *J. Eng. H.L.* 195, (1698) 80; Flaherty, 'The Empire Strikes Back', p. 605 n. 79. Newark, *Elegantia Juris*, p. 16, refers to the same date, without giving the name of the case. Flaherty lists the case among seven appeals from the Irish Chancery to the English Lords in the late 17th century: p. 605 n. 79. He also mentions that in the years 1712, 1713 and 1714 ten appeals from Ireland were heard by the British House of Lords: six from the Chancery and four from the Exchequer.

[61] L. 'that you make known'. A judicial writ ordering the party to whom it was addressed to produce a record or documents.

[62] (1644) 1 *J. Ir. H.L.* 205, 13 April 644.

[63] *ibid.*, pp. 202, 204.

[64] 21 & 22 Geo. III c. 49 (Ir.), 1781–82, s. 1; see Appendix P.

[65] s. 2.

[66] s. 3.

In *King* v. *Rowe*[67] the case concerned a misdemeanour and the attorney general had refused to issue his certificate since it was his opinion that it was not necessary in such a case. As a result, the intending plaintiff in error had been unable to obtain the writ. Hart LC held that the attorney general's fiat could be dispensed with. The lord chancellor expressed the opinion, contrary to the view of his predecessor in 1644, that writs of error were as of right at common law. He went on to say that before 1800 the practice was that a person applying for a writ of error to the Irish Lords would present a petition to the lord lieutenant, which he referred to the attorney general, whose certificate was granted as a matter of course unless the Crown was directly involved, as opposed to merely being named as a party. Hart LC considered that it was not the intention of the statute 21 & 22 Geo. III c. 49 (Ir.) to alter the common law.

In England, the issue as to whether writs of error in criminal cases were a matter of right or discretion was the subject of an opinion by Francis Hargrave, on behalf of an undisclosed client, which he published in *Juridical Arguments*.[68] His conclusions, with added commentary and notes by the present author, were as follows:[69]

1. Long before the reign of Queen Anne there were opinions in favour of considering writs of error even in treason and felony as writs of right. Lord Chief Justice Wray expressed this opinion in *Hurlston's Case*[70] in the King's Bench in the reign of Queen Elizabeth, Coke approved of Wray's opinion.[71] Wray said that 'an outlawry may be reversed by bringing a writ of error without suing petition to the king.'[72]

In 1683 when North was lord keeper there were two cases in Chancery in which he denied that writs of error in criminal cases were as of right.[73]

In 1689 the issue was the subject of a debate in the English House of Commons on the case of Sir Thomas Armstrong. Armstrong had been proceeded against in 1684 in the reign of Charles II on an outlawry for high treason. He pleaded that he had the benefit of the statute 5 & 6 Edw. VI, c. 11 (Eng.), 1551, which gave a year for such persons who were beyond the seas at the time the outlawry was pronounced to surrender, bring a writ of error and assign errors. Although he had done so within the year, the notorious Chief Justice Jeffreys and the other judges of the King's Bench refused the plea, on the ground that since he was already a prisoner, his surrender to the court was not within the intent of the Act. Lady Armstrong on behalf of her husband delivered a paper[74] to Lord Keeper North, Jeffreys and Sir Robert Sawyer, the attorney general, claiming that

67 (1828) 2 Molloy 27, per Hart LC.

68 'Concerning Writs of Error in Criminal Cases', Francis Hargrave, *Juridical Arguments and Collections* (London, 1797–99). i.403–10.

69 Hargrave, *Juridical Arguments*, i.409–410.

70 (1587) 2 Leon. 194, 3 Leon. 160, 4 Inst. 194.

71 4 Inst. 194.

72 (1686) 3 Leon. 160, 74 E.R. 605.

73 *Crawle* v. *Crawle* (1683) 1 Vern. 170; *The Rioter's Case* (1680-1687) 1 Vern. 175, 23 E.R. 396.

74 10 St. Tr. 106, at p. 119.

a writ of error was a matter of right at common law, citing *Menville's Case* from Coke's Institutes[75] in support, but the application failed and Armstrong was executed.[76]

After the Revolution in 1689 the House of Commons declared that the plea should have been allowed, that Armstrong's execution had been illegal and passed the following resolution:[77]

> Resolved, That the House doth agree with the Committee, That a Writ of Error for the reversal of a judgment in felony, or treason, is the right of the subject; and ought to be granted at his desire; and is not an act of grace or favour, which may be denied or granted at pleasure.

In the debate, the solicitor general, John Hawles,[78] said: 'A writ of error is a writ of right, and I am sorry it was left out in the Bill of Rights.'[79] On the day following, 20 November 1689, Sir Robert Sawyer was expelled from the English House of Commons for his part in the illegal proceedings against Armstrong.

2. The idea that writs of error in any criminal case were as of right was not novel at the time and the contrary view was a mistake due to ignorance of the history of the subject.

3. In 1703, in the controversy associated with the great constitutional case of *Ashby* v. *White*[80] there was a resolution of ten judges, including Holt CJKB, out of twelve delivered in parliament, declaring the absolute right to a writ of error in all criminal cases, except treason and felony.[81]

75 1 & 2 Ph. & Mar., 1554, 3 Inst. 215; 4 Inst. 21.

76 10 St. Tr. 106.

77 Resolution, English House of Commons, 19 November 1689; 10 *J. Eng. H.C.*, 1688–1693, pp. 289–290.

78 He attended Winchester College, matriculated at Queen's College, Oxford, on 15 May 1662, and entered Lincoln's Inn on 10 February 1664, being called to the bar on 10 February 1670. John Aubrey described him as 'an exceeding ingenious young man' (*Brief Lives*, 305). Stuart Handley, 'Hawles, Sir John (bap. 1645, d. 1716), ODNB online. [http://www.oxforddnb.com/view/article/12694,], accessed 4 August 2009. He published *The English-man's Right. A dialogue between a Barrister at Law, and a Jury-man ... setting forth the antiquity ... use ... office, and ... priviledges of Juries by the laws of England.* (London, 1680.) According to Cohen's *Bibliography*, (Morris L. Cohen, *Bibliography of Early American Law.* Buffalo: William S. Hein, 1998–2003. 7 vol. with CD-ROM) it was probably the first English law book reprinted in the American colonies.

79 *Grey's Debates of the House of Commons*, vol. 9, 1690, January 10th–18th, pp. 510–529.

80 (1703) 1 Bro. PC 62, 1 E.R. 417; (1705) 14 St. Tr. 695. See the comments on the case by Lord Bingham of Cornhill in *Watkins* v. *Home Office* [2006] UKHL 17, at paragraph 13. Holt CJ had originally characterised the right to vote as 'a personal right' (1 *Smith's Leading Cases* (13th ed, 1929) 253, p. 270) but also (p. 276) 'a matter of property' and regarded the plaintiff as entitled to the benefit of a franchise vested in the corporation (p. 271), but also that it was (p. 273) 'a thing of the highest importance.' Lord Bingham points out that Holt revised his judgment before the case went to the House of Lords (p. 283), where his dissent was upheld by a large majority (50 to 16) of lay peers (p. 278), on grounds which he is said to have drafted.

81 Hargrave, *Juridical Arguments*, i.407.

The other two were of the opinion that the subject did not have an absolute right to a writ of error in any criminal case. The House of Lords went further, in an address to the queen subsequent to the case, and expressed the view that a writ of error was a matter of right even in cases of felony and treason.

Ashby, a poor cobbler, had been denied the right to vote at an election, on the ground that he was not a 'settled inhabitant', by a constable acting for the returning officer for the election. Ashby sued the mayor and the constable in an action on the case and on trial of the issue obtained damages. The defendants moved in arrest of judgment and the Court of Queen's Bench, Holt CJ dissenting, held that no action lay. The House of Commons asserted that any matter concerning elections to that House were outside the jurisdiction of the common law courts and exclusively within their own. Several persons were committed for contempt, but habeas corpus was brought in Queen's Bench, and Holt CJ held the committal illegal, but the other two judges disagreed, and the prisoners were remanded.[82] A writ of error was then brought in the Lords, and the judges were asked for their opinions, as to whether a writ of error was as of right in such a case, or any other, or only *ex gratia*. The above-mentioned opinion was then given, and a resolution passed by the Lords:[83]

> that a writ of error is not a writ of grace, but of right, and ought not to be denied to the subject when duly applied for, though at the request of either house of parliament, the denial thereof being an obstruction of justice contrary to Magna Carta.

The Lords sent an address to the queen, to grant the petition for the writ of error. The writ of error was granted and the Lords upheld the judgment in favour of the plaintiff. In the address they stated;

> We are sure that the House of Commons in 1689 were of opinion, that a writ of error, even in cases of felony and treason, is the right of the subject, and ought to be granted at his desire, and is not an act of grace and favour, which may be denied or granted at pleasure.

4. Since the reign of Queen Anne, the right of the subject to a writ of error in treason and felony had been recognised in Westminster Hall by some judges, without contradiction from the rest.[84]

5. Lord Mansfield qualified the right to a writ of error in misdemeanours, by explaining the writ not to be *absolutely of course*, but only claimable as a right on *probable* error shown.[85]

6. Whether Lord Mansfield's qualification of the right to a writ of error in misdemeanours was adopted by other judges, or was Mansfield's personal opinion,

[82] *Regina* v. *Paty* (1703) 2 Ld. Raym. 1105, 92 E.R. 232; Holt KB 526, 90 E.R. 1189.
[83] Hargrave, *Juridical Arguments*, i.409; (1704) *J. Eng. H.L.* 706.
[84] Hargrave, *Juridical Arguments*, i.409.
[85] Hargrave, *Juridical Arguments*, i.409.

was 'not discoverable at present'.[86]

System of Appeals from 1782 to 1800

The system of appeals in Ireland from 1782 until the reform of the Irish Court of Exchequer Chamber in 1800 shortly before the Union was as follows.[87] Writs of error lay from the the Court of Common Pleas to the Court of King's Bench. Error from King's Bench apparently lay directly to the Irish House of Lords between 1782 and 1800[88] when the Irish Court of Exchequer Chamber was re-constituted and was interposed between the Irish Lords and the King's Bench. Error from the common law side of Exchequer lay to Exchequer Chamber. Equity appeals, whether from Chancery or from the equity side of Exchequer, went directly to the Irish Lords, as did appeals from the revenue side of Exchequer in its equity jurisdiction.[89]

The Court of Chancery also had a common law side, which was largely but not entirely administrative. Original writs to begin actions between subject and subject issued out of the Hanaper Office, so-called because in the medieval period they had been stored in hampers, or hanapers. Prerogative writs and writs in which the Crown was a party issued out of the Petty Bag office, so-called because in the past the writs had been stored in small bags.[90] The Hanaper and Petty Bag offices together were sometimes referred to as the common law side of Chancery. The lord chancellor could hear pleas of *scire facias*, challenging the validity of a record and in so doing he was exercising a common law jurisdiction, known as his Petty Bag jurisdiction. When an issue was joined the record was delivered to the King's Bench for trial before a jury.[91]

[86] Hargrave, *Juridical Arguments*, i.410.

[87] The system is illustrated by the diagram at the end of this chapter, page 86. What follows is based on evidence from Ridgeway's reports, the statute 21 & 22 Geo. III, c. 49 (Ir.), 1781–82, providing for writs of error to the Irish Lords and the statute 40 Geo. III, c. 39 (Ir.), 1800 reforming the Irish Court of Exchequer Chamber. The changes to the system brought about by the act of 1800, which only lasted until the Union took effect on 1 January 1801, are discussed below, page 137.

[88] This follows from the words of 21 & 22 Geo. III, c. 49 (Ir.), 1781–82 giving the Irish Lords power to hear all writs of error and confirmed by the words in 40 Geo. III c. 39 (Ir.), 1800, s. 1: 'or to sue any writ of error returnable directly to parliament to reverse any judgment of the Court of King's Bench', implying that it was possible to do so immediately before the statute.

[89] In *Dillon* v. *Burton* (1794) 3 Ridg. PC 80 there was an appeal from the revenue side of Exchequer directly to the Lords. The Lords held that there was no appeal from the revenue side of Exchequer to the equity side of the same court. In *Maingay* v. *Gahan* (1793) Ir. Term Rep. 1 on the interpretation of statute law there was a writ of error to Exchequer Chamber. See page 134.

[90] Bl. Com., iii.49; Jacob, *Law Dictionary*, 'Writ'; Brown, *Law Dictionary*, 'Hanaper', 'Petty Bag Office'.

[91] Ferguson, *Treatise*, i.16, writing of Ireland in 1841, says: 'The petty bag jurisdiction of the lord chancellor to hold pleas of *scire facias*, is a common law authority, in which, when an issue is joined, the record is delivered into the King's Bench by mittimus, [L. 'We send'] to be tried by a jury at the sittings or at bar ... and when tried, the record is returned to the chancellor, who may then give judgment and award execution; and the Court of law may do so also. But in exercising this jurisdiction, the chancellor acts entirely in analogy to the rules and principles of the common law courts.' In *Rex* v. *Dolphin* (1828) 1 Molloy 392, Hart LC noted that although the technicality of common law pleading was preserved on the Petty Bag side, he allowed considerable latitude where it was not strictly complied with.

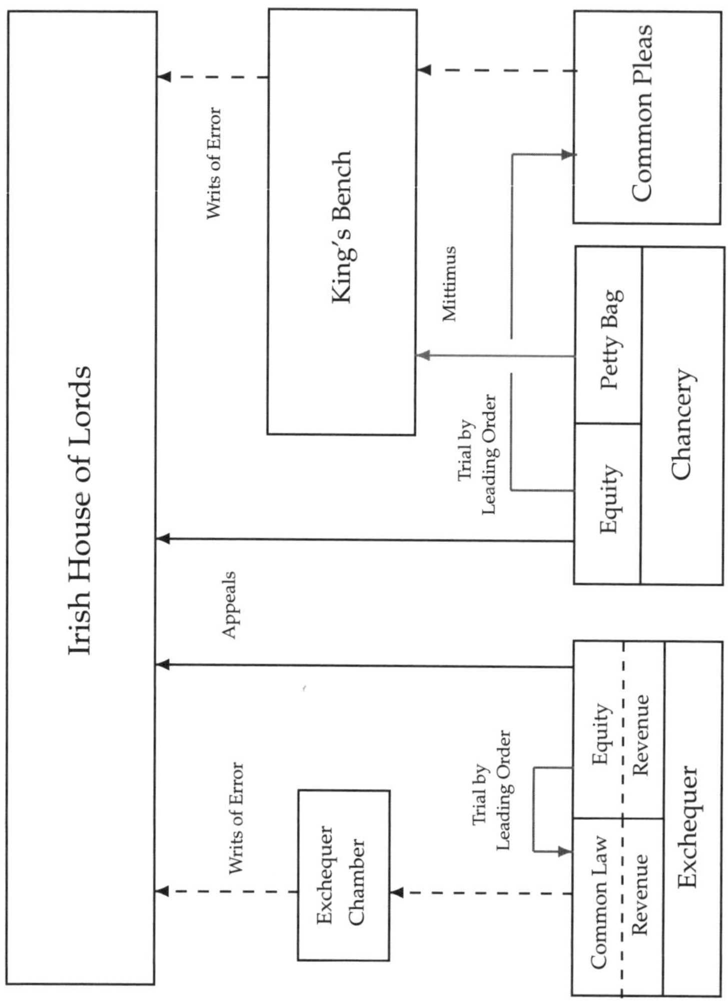

The Irish Legal System 1782–1800

CHAPTER 6

Procedure in the Lords

There were many peculiarities of procedure in the Irish House of Lords. From the opening of the new parliament building in 1731 the House of Commons had admitted members of the public to a gallery to watch debates, but the House of Lords never tolerated such an intrusion.[1] However, the procedure we are concerned with in this chapter is that adopted by the members of the Irish House of Lords when deciding appeals and writs of error. From examining Ridgeway's *Reports* it can be seen that the procedure of deciding appeals evolved throughout the period, from that of a debating chamber, to that of a court.

The most significant convention to be adopted in the period was to confine participation in appeals to legally-qualified members, and the Irish House of Lords seems to have reached this point before its British counterpart.

There are broadly three discernible periods.

Procedural Periods

The Early 'Debating Chamber' Period

The early period covers about the first seven years from the restoration of appellate jurisdiction in 1782. In this period the only professional judge in the Lords was the lord chancellor, Lord Lifford, who had held the office since 1768.[2] In 1784 he was joined by John Scott, as Baron Earlsfort, later Earl of Clonmell. Scott had been made chief justice of the King's Bench in the same year and thus sat as a common law judge as well as in the Lords. However, although a principal part of his expertise was in criminal law and there are no reports of writs of error in criminal cases in the Lords, according to accounts he was widely knowledgeable on law and made several contributions in debate.

In civil common law appeals the House usually called for the opinion of the common law judges who attended the sittings of the House for the purpose.[3] Judgments were not given by members of the House of Lords, even the lord

[1] Although they apparently permitted sons of peers to attend debates. This is to be distinguished from attendance of *eldest* sons under writs of acceleration. Above, page 11.

[2] James Hewitt, Viscount Lifford. See below, page 122. He died in 1789 and John FitzGibbon then became lord chancellor, as Baron FitzGibbon, below, page 113.

[3] Below, page 96.

chancellor. The procedure was more that of a debating chamber than a court, particularly since cases were normally decided by a vote of all the members present.

Hume v. *Burton*,[4] a common law writ of error on an entail in 1785, is an illustration of the early procedure. It was part of the lengthy litigation concerning the mental competence of Nicholas Hume-Loftus, Earl of Ely.[5] This writ of error concerned the validity of a common recovery to bar an entail. The Earl of Ely had made a warrant of attorney giving authority to make the recovery on his behalf. He had since died. The common recovery was brought in the Court of Common Pleas, which had exclusive jurisdiction over recoveries.[6] A commission had been issued in the Court of Chancery in 1776 which found in 1767 that Nicholas was not of unsound mind.[7] The Court of Common Pleas had therefore allowed the recovery. A writ of error was taken from Common Pleas to the Court of King's Bench by Gustavus Hume to impeach it, on the ground that the commission was not conclusive of Nicholas' sanity. The judges in the King's Bench told the jury, which had been impanelled to try the issue, that evidence to impeach the finding of the commission was inadmissible, and that the commission's finding was conclusive. The jury duly found that Nicholas was of sound mind.[8] The present writ of error to the Lords was for a new trial, on the ground that the direction of the judges to the jury was in error and that evidence should have been allowed.

The arguments of counsel are reported at great length, including that of FitzGibbon as attorney general,[9] and the opinion of the judges was obtained. Their opinions are also reproduced in full.[10] A motion was then made to reverse the judgment of the King's Bench, to set aside the verdict in that court and for a new trial in the issue. The report then states that 'a long debate arose thereupon', which is not reported. Thirty one members took part in the vote. The result was contents 16, not-contents 15, and there is then a note in the report that Lord Lifford LC agreed with the majority of the judges. This suggests that it was Lifford's vote which decided the issue.[11] The Rules and Orders of

4 (1785) 1 Ridg. PC 16.

5 Nicholas Hume-Loftus, 2nd Earl of Ely (1738–1769), Cokayne, *Complete Peerage*, v.65. The title refers to Ely in County Wicklow, Ireland, not to Ely in Cambridgeshire, England. The second syllable is pronounced to rhyme with "lie" rather than "lee", as in the personal name 'Eli'.

6 The court had exclusive jurisdiction in the real actions, both in England and Ireland: above, page 58.

7 1 Ridg. PC at 205.

8 1 Ridg. PC at 23.

9 *ibid.*, at p. 35. FitzGibbon's argument is reproduced in D. A. Fleming and A.P.W. Malcomson [eds.]. *'A Volley of Execrations': the letters and papers of John FitzGibbon, Earl of Clare 1772–1802* (Dublin, IMC, 2005), pp. 24–26.

10 Kelly J., at p. 93; Hellen J. at 95; Metge B. at 98; Power B. at 105; Yelverton CB at 110; Paterson CJ at 113.

11 The Duke of Rutland in a letter to Lord Sydney, 24 March 1784, HMS Rutland MSS, 1894, iii.83, appears to refer to the same litigation when he says, referring to 'Loftus' (the Ely family name), that 'he has lost his great cause with Mr Rochford [*sic*], the judgment of King's Bench being this day being set aside in the House of Lords by the casting voice of the Chancellor.' See *Rochfort* v. *Ely* (1768) 1 Ridg. PC 528, Appendix 3, setting out Lifford LC's argument on a motion for a new trial. Rochford's

the House of Lords[12] are not explicit on the point, but presumably, in a division of the House, the peers present voted, with the exception of the lord chancellor who, as speaker,[13] remained in place until the result of the vote had been reported to him. It appears that in this instance the vote of the peers other than the lord chancellor was tied, 15 to 15, and Lifford LC then used his casting vote, in favour of the judges' opinion. It was then 'ordered and adjudged' that the judgment in the King's Bench be reversed and that there should be a new trial. Thus, although the majority of judges were in favour of a new trial, the result in the Lords was only reached by a majority of one out of 31 who participated, most of whom must have been lay members.

Further proceedings in the Lords followed the new trial.[14] At the new trial, the same issue arose, as to whether evidence contradicting the commission could be presented. The jury was directed that the commission was not conclusive, but that the documents constituting the fine and recovery and the warrant of attorney were conclusive. The jury again found, as directed, that Nicholas was of sound mind at the time. The issue was again brought before the Lords. The opinion of the judges was taken. They agreed that the commission alone was not conclusive, but disagreed as to whether the documents were conclusive or not. The opinions of the judges are reported, but no speeches by members of the Lords. A motion was put to reverse the judgment of the King's Bench, but was lost by contents 11, not-contents 21. On this occasion there were 32 members present, the overwhelming majority of whom were obviously lay members. It was ordered that the judgment of the King's Bench be affirmed.

On the substantive issue of the earl's competence, it seems an extraordinary result to find that he was of sound mind, given the evidence of his condition set out in great detail in earlier proceedings before the British House of Lords:[15]

> His person and looks were extraordinary and different from those of other children; his looks were vacant and foolish; he hung his under-jaw... He had a great stoop forwards, his arms hung as if disjointed, his knees bent forwards, his hands dangling forwards bent at the wrists, his toes turned in; he almost at all times looked straight forward, with his eyes motionless or fixed to the first object which struck him, and he seldom or never turned his head to assist his sight – he

wife Alice was entitled to the next remainder after an estate tail limited to Lord Ely by the settlement of Sir Gustavus Hume.

12 Ireland, Parliament, House of Lords, *Rules and Orders to be Observed in the Upper House of Parliament upon Writs of Error and Appeals*, Dublin, Printed by W. Sleater, 1784. Lord Mountmorres relates that the rules were the work of a committee which sat for three months, and that the work was done mainly by himself and the Archbishop of Cashel: Hervey Redmond Morres, Viscount Mountmorres of Castlemorres, *An historical dissertation upon the origin, suspension, and revival, of the judicature and independency of the Irish parliament. With a narrative of the transactions in 1719, relative to the celebrated declaratory law*, (London, 1795), p. 59.

13 Rules and Orders, rules 8, 14.

14 Reported at 1 Ridg. PC 204.

15 'Appeal Cases and Writs of Error, 1775–76', HL/PO/JU/4/3/19, *Gustavus Hume, a minor, by George Rochford, his father and next friend, and George Rochford as administrator of Alice, his late wife* v. *Henry, Earl of Ely*, Appellant's case, f. 25.

> first began to speak, or attempted to speak, at the age of about six or seven years or later, nor could he then articulate or pronounce words in the usual manner, but only attempted to utter a sort of jargon, as *Nonona Boy, Aunty, Dood Boy, Unky, Chocke*, and *Aunty Cha*, which were all the words he attempted to pronounce, and, when he began, he went on repeating them several times over till he was stopped...He was... continually running with violence towards the fire, without seeming apprehension of any danger, to the great terror of his grandmother, who often used to run between him and the fire, and to extend her arms to prevent his running or falling into it... he could neither feed nor dress himself... nor could he ever be taught to read or write...

The reliance on lay peers, the absence of judgments in the House itself and decision simply by vote meant that the procedure resembled that of a jury. Juries do not give reasons for their decisions and so on occasion can set aside the law in favour of their own instinct of what is just. It may be that at the time that was thought to be an advantage in the procedure. The earl was clearly unable to manage his affairs. The result of the finding that the earl was of sound mind was that the recovery was valid and so presumably the estate could then be put in competent hands. If the recovery had been held invalid because of the earl's capacity, then a committee of guardians would have to be appointed to manage his affairs, but why this was less desirable is unclear. It appears that the facts were essentially ignored in order to produce a result acceptable to the parties.

There are instances of equity appeals, in which the lord chancellor, who was the only equity judge in the Lords at that point, did not make a speech, and neither does there seem to have been any debate. The lord chancellor would in any case be hearing appeals from himself in the Court of Chancery, but arguments of counsel are simply followed by the decision of the Lords without any indication by whom they were taken. There may have been a vote, but none is reported. The first case reported in Ridgeway, *Davis* v. *Oliver*[16] was an appeal from Lord Lifford LC concerning fraud. Arguments of counsel are reported, John FitzGibbon and Hugh Carleton appearing for the appellants, and John Scott and Charles O'Neil for the respondents, at the end of which the report simply states that 'it was ordered and adjudged' that the appeal should be dismissed.

The same is true in *Lord Doneraile* v. *Chartres*,[17] Lord Lifford had decreed in favour of a renewal of a lease for lives, where three lives had to be renewed and there had been delay, provided the fines payable under the lease were duly paid. Lord Doneraile appealed, and again after the reported arguments of counsel, it was ordered that the appeal be dismissed. It is not stated in either case in the report that any debate took place.

In *O'Neil* v. *Jones*[18] the respondent claimed to be entitled to renew a lease for lives renewable forever. This property interest is described more fully below.

16 (1784) 1 Ridg. PC 1.
17 (1784) 1 Ridg. PC 122.
18 (1785) 1 Ridg. PC 170.

It was quite common in 18th century Ireland. It was a kind of estate pur autre vie in which three lives were specified as the measure of the duration of the estate. The tenant paid a rent, which was why it was called a 'lease', although the tenure was freehold. It was also a commercial interest, as opposed to an interest arising under a family settlement. When any of the lives died the tenant had the right to renew the life on payment of a fine, i.e. a lump sum. It was common to specify in the lease that a life should be renewed within a definite period of time. The courts of equity in Ireland had ensured that the interest was virtually perpetual by developing an equity to renew even after the period specified in the lease and after any amount of delay, provided there was not actual fraud. When the Irish House of Lords lost its appellate jurisdiction after 1720 the British House of Lords refused to recognise the Irish equity as being as extensive as the Irish courts had held it to be. In 1780 the Irish parliament took the opportunity of restoring the position with the Tenantry Act. This was still before the passing of Yelverton's Act and so the old procedure of submitting the bill to the British Privy Council for possible amendment had to be followed. This resulted in an amendment to the bill. The Act was not to apply where a judgment or decree had already been obtained. In *O'Neil* the lessor had brought an action of ejectment and issue had been joined at law before the respondent issued his bill. The appellant had also obtained judgment by consent at common law before the Tenantry Act became law.

The case came before Lord Lifford LC in equity in November 1782 and he held the lessee entitled to a renewal. If the Tenantry Act, as seemed clear, did not apply, because judgment at law had been obtained, then, equally clearly, the law before the Act applied. But what was that law? The English lawyers who amended the Act may well have assumed that the law was the more restricted equity applied by the British House of Lords since 1720. The lessor in O'Neil had made repeated demands to the tenant for renewal and so there seems little doubt that the renewal would have been refused by the British House of Lords. Lord Lifford, however, seems to have applied the Irish understanding of the equity. The Tenantry Act 1780 had already come into force, so perhaps he was emboldened by the consideration that any appeal from his judgment would go to the Irish Lords.[19] The fact that judgment at law had been obtained did not affect the jurisdiction in equity. The jurisdiction of equity was precisely to give relief against a judgment at common law. Delay in itself would not, in the Irish courts, have prevented the lessee obtaining a renewal in equity. Nor, before the Tenantry Act, it seems, would demands for renewal by the lessor.

[19] Ridgeway appends a note at the end of the case of the decisions in the British House of Lords of *Kane* v. *Hamilton* and *Bateman* v. *Murray* in which the British House of Lords had taken a more restrictive view of the equity. It is the only contemporary report of the decisions. Ridgeway sayd that he had obtained notes of the opinions from 'a very ingenious gentleman of the profession in England' (1 Ridg. PC at 179). These cases are discussed as to the substantive issues below, page 151 et seq. It is possible, but seems unlikely, that Lifford was unaware of them when *O'Neil* came before him in Chancery on 11 November 1782 (1 Ridge. PC at 173). *Kane* was an appeal from the Irish Exchequer, but *Bateman* was an appeal from his own decision in Chancery. It was decided by the British Lords on 18 February 1779.

The lessor appealed from the lord chancellor's decision to the Irish House of Lords, but failed. There are no judgments and the House voted in favour of renewal. There was therefore no decision as to what the law was before the Tenantry Act. On the face of it, it should have been the more restricted equity applied by the British House of Lords before the Tenantry Act. Since, however, the Irish Lords did not give reasons for their decision, there was no need to address these issues. Their instinct, or preference, for the Irish solution could be applied without the need to justify it.

The 'debating chamber' procedure therefore had its advantages, but only in the rather specific context of cases instituted before the Tenantry Act came into force. In the long term the stronger impulse was the need to establish the legitimacy of the Irish House of Lords as an appeal court and that meant developing a more rational procedure, basing decisions on reasoned judgments delivered by legally-qualified members.

The Transitional Period

There then followed a transitional period of about two years in which judgments were given by members of the House, principally Lord Chancellor Lifford assisted, apart from Baron Earlsfort, by members who had legal expertise but little or no previous judicial experience. One of these was, for example, Lord Pery, who had been a barrister and who was for most of his career the Speaker of the Irish House of Commons. Another was Lord Farnham. We shall consider their biographies in more detail later.

The transitional period saw the first judgments delivered by members of the House themselves, despite, in some instances, by those without previous experience as judges.

Magrath v. *Lord Muskerry*[20] in 1784 seems to exhibit this transitional stage in the development towards a professional court. The plaintiff had applied to the Court of Chancery to renew a lease for lives. Lifford LC had refused an order to that effect, on the basis that the landlord came within the proviso to the Tenantry Act 1780, having already succeeded in ejectment at law. So far, the situation was the same as *O'Neil* v. *Jones*. But now Lifford's speech is reported. Lifford explained that he felt bound to apply the law as it stood immediately before the Act,[21] as it had been laid down by the British House of Lords in *Bateman* v. *Murray*.[22] That case had restricted the Irish equity to an extent that caused consternation in Ireland and led to the passing of the 1780 Act. Lifford LC in the Lords spoke first, explaining why he had he had felt bound to follow the law as laid down by the British House of Lords, although he also expressed the view that the tenant on the facts of the case would not have obtained relief in Ireland in any case. Lord Pery then spoke. He took a radical position, refusing

[20] (1784) 1 Ridg. PC 469.

[21] Lord Lifford LC, *ibid.*, at 481.

[22] Initially reported as a note: *Bateman* v. *Murray* (1779) 1 Ridg. PC 187 note. The Irish Chancery decision is reported as *Murray* v. *Bateman, Lady Rosse, his wife* (1776) Wal. by L. 181. The British House of Lords decision is reported at (1779) 5 Brown 20, 2 E.R. 506.

to accept that an English lord chancellor could overturn numerous Irish cases on the equity. Despite the participation of these 'legal' members, a motion in the usual form was put to reverse the Chancery. The result was contents 4, not-contents 5, and it was ordered that the appeal be dismissed.

The following day the appellant, with some temerity, then petitioned the Lords to rehear the appeal on the ground they had not properly considered the merits on the first occasion. The Earl of Carhampton[23] moved that the petition be supported. Lord Pery proposed an amendment: the judges should be asked their opinion.[24] This was opposed and both the motion and amendment were rejected without a division. A motion was then put to reject the petition. The report says that a debate then took place, but the speeches are not reported, although Ridgeway reported in a note[25] that Lord Mountmorres, a lay peer, published his speech on the appeal.[26] Lifford spoke, as did Lord Farnham and Baron Earlsfort (John Scott), and several lay peers: Charles Agar, Archbishop of Cashel, earls Hillsborough and Bellamont and viscounts Mountgarrett[27] and Mountmorres. The prevailing view was that the House should not, in general, rehear appeals. The petition was rejected without a division. Thus, although legal members took part, their opinions were not regarded as conclusive.

The early procedure seems to have been necessitated by a shortage of legally qualified members of the House.

The 'Professional Court' Period

The third and final period lasted from about 1787–89 until the Union. It can be seen as the period in which the Irish Lords began to function as a professional court. There is also one instance in 1791 of the House dividing and a vote being taken, the last reported occasion of this happening. In *Chandos (Duchess) v. Brownlow*[28] the unanimous opinion of the judges was delivered by Yelverton CB. The lord chancellor then gave a long speech urging reversal of the Court of Exchequer, but the issue was then put to the vote. The result was contents 3, not-contents 6 and the appeal was therefore dismissed.

23 Simon Luttrell, 1st Earl of Carhampton (1713–1787). He was the son of Major General Henry Luttrell of Luttrellstown, 'whose desertion of the cause of James II is said to have caused the fatal defeat at Aughrim, a piece of treachery which "excited the abhorrence of the Catholic population" in Ireland, by one of whom, finally, he was assassinated in Dublin, 22 Oct. 1717, aged 63.' Cokayne, *Complete Peerage*, iii.23, n. a. Cokayne also notes that the Luttrellstown estate had been owned by the Luttrells from the time of Henry VI until the early 19th century when it was sold to Luke White, the bookseller, and father of the John Gore, 1st Baron Annaly CJKB. *ibid.*, iii.23, n. b.

24 This would have been their opinion on the Tenantry Act, 1780. See below, page 155 for a discussion of the substantive point.

25 (1784) 1 Ridg. PC, p. 509 n. a, at 510.

26 See page 97.

27 Edmund Butler, 11th Viscount Mountgarret (1745–1793), Cokayne, *Complete Peerage*, ix. 327: 'He died at the age of 49 after three days' sickness occasioned by a meal of strawberries and cider.' His obituary in the *Gentleman's Magazine* said: 'he was an excellent scholar, a man of strong intellect, of a violent disposition…an excellent parliamentary speaker…had been for several years a staunch and dauntless patriot, but at length died in the religion of the court.'

28 (1791) 2 Ridg. PC 383.

On writs of error, that is, in common law 'appeals', the court normally asked the common law judges for their opinion, and if it was unanimous, followed it. Where it was not so, and in equity appeals, the decision rested with, and judgments were delivered by, a small body of Irish professional lawyers with previous judicial experience. These professionals were principally FitzGibbon, Carleton, Yelverton and Scott. Lord Lifford, Fitzgibbon's predecessor as lord chancellor, played some part, but died in 1789. Since no criminal writs of error were heard, Scott might have been expected to play a minor role, but in fact he was hardly less active than the others. Nevertheless, even in this period, judgments were sometimes also delivered by peers who were legally-qualified but did not have judicial experience, and who may be described as 'semi-professionals', namely Lord Pery and Lord Farnham. On three occasions, lay peers made speeches expressing their opinions on cases and these are reported in Ridgeway: Lord Mountmorres, Charles Agar, Archbishop of Cashel and George Frederick Nugent, Earl of Westmeath.

The first reported case in which the decision was arrived at by legal members alone was *Haire* v. *Lloyd*[29] in March 1787.[30] This was some fifty 50 years before the British House of Lords adopted the same practice.[31]

The case was an action of replevin brought by the plaintiffs in the King's Bench, for return of goods seized in distress for rent. The defendant had levied a distress for rent against the plaintiff, and the plaintiff demurred on a technical ground of pleading, as to the validity of the avowry and cognisance. The Court of King's Bench overruled the demurrer and gave judgment for the defendant.

In the Lords, after hearing counsel for both sides, Lifford LC, made a speech expressing his opinion as to what questions should be put to the judges. Lifford noted the dangers of a landlord relying on distress at common law, as there were many technical pitfalls. The landlord, in order to justify a distress, had to show privity between him and the tenant. This would mean proving the original lease and how the interests of landlord and tenant had passed to the present parties. It was usually a wiser course to bring ejectment for non-payment of rent, but that would mean the loss of possibly an otherwise good tenant. For that reason 25 Geo. II, c. 13[32] was passed which did away with the need for the landlord to state by whom the original lease had been made or all the intermediate transfers of title. The English and Irish Acts were to the same effect. The statute required an avowry[33] to state only that the tenant held under a demise, and not by what title, or the nature of it. As Lifford noted, the landlord still had to prove the lease at trial and that he was the person entitled to the rent under it. In the present case the landlord had not stated in the avowry by whom the lease had been made and the issue was as to whether he had complied with the statute.

29 (1787) 1 Ridg. PC 341.

30 From pages 341 to 352 the pages in Ridgeway are marked 1787, but from pages 353 to 358, the last page of the judgment, they are marked 1786, the latter presumably in error.

31 See 'Lay Peers' below.

32 25 Geo. II, c. 13 (Ir.), 1751, s. 4.

33 A plea by a person taking a distress for rent showing cause why he or she took it.

Sullivan v. *Stradling*[34] had been cited in argument. The landlord in that case had complied with the statute precisely. Despite that, the tenant tried to take advantage of some alleged defect in the landlord's title. The landlord demurred and the court upheld the demurrer, holding that the tenant's plea was bad, and if allowed, would have brought back all the old defects of the common law. Lifford mentions that he had forgotten the case until it was cited in argument, but then recalled that he had appeared in it in England as counsel. He then makes the following comment, showing some sensitivity to differences in Irish and English law:[35]

> I have no difficulty concerning this matter in my own mind; but it is right that your Lordships having the judges of the land to direct you, should not be bound by those of England, or any faint recollection of mine.– I think you should therefore take the opinion of you own judges, and by that means you will always preserve the laws of your country uniform.

Lifford formulated two questions, the second of which was whether the avowry of the landlord was good in law, under 25 Geo. II, c. 13 (Ir.).

The report then says 'it was agreed' that the second question alone would be sufficient. The opinions of Lords Pery and Earlsfort (John Scott) are reported. The lord chief baron, who was present with the other judges, conferred with them, and reported that they all agreed the avowry was good in law. Pery then gave his opinion, which was that he accepted the judges opinion although it was contrary to his own private opinion. Earlsfort, from whose court, the King's Bench, the writ of error had been taken, declared that:[36]

> upon as clear grounds as I ever formed an opinion, I am satisfied with that now delivered by the judges. I did not think myself at all bound by the decision of my court, or by what was then my opinion, but was as much open to a consideration of the question as if it never had been argued.

In view of Earlsfort's character,[37] this is perhaps straining credulity somewhat. The report then states that it was 'ordered and adjudged' that the judgment of the Court of King's Bench should be affirmed. There is no mention of a debate or a vote. It is the first case in which only legally-qualified members apparently took part in the deliberations, although they show considerable deference to the unanimous opinion of the common law judges.

Even in the third period there is no indication of a judicial committee, or panel, of the House. The decision remained formally that of the whole House and it was only a convention that the House decided according to the opinion

[34] (1764) Wils. K.B. 208, 95 E.R. 769.
[35] 1 Ridg. PC 356.
[36] 1 Ridg. PC 358.
[37] Below, page 128.

of the legal members. On the other hand, although there was a panel[38] in the British House of Lords, the same remained true of that body also. It was only a convention, resting on *Daniel O'Connell's Case* in 1844,[39] that lay members did not take part in appeals.[40]

In the Irish House of Lords, although there did emerge the convention that legal judgments were delivered by legally-qualified members, and at an earlier period than was the case with the British House of Lords,[41] on the common law side much reliance was placed on framing questions to be submitted to the common law judges for their opinion, and then considering their answers, sometimes followed by speeches of legal members. On the equity side, as might be expected, speeches were almost exclusively confined to the lord chancellor, John FitzGibbon, the Earl of Clare LC, with some contributions by Yelverton, who as, chief baron of the Exchequer, also exercised equity jurisdiction.

Opinions of the Common Law Judges

The practice of seeking the opinions of the judges continued into the third period. In the early period the opinions of the common law judges were frequently sought and often actually reported.[42]

The common law judges in Ireland, unlike those in Great Britain, actually had to attend the sittings of the Irish House, but could not speak unless and until called upon to give their opinion on a point of law. The procedure was provided for in standing orders of the House adopted in 1692.[43]

There is one instance of the judges being asked for their opinion on an appeal from Chancery, in *Hayden* v. *Carroll*,[44] but that was on a question of statutory interpretation.[45]

If the judges agreed then it was customary for the House to accept their decision.[46] If the judges disagreed, a vote was taken. The motion was always

38 The phrase 'judicial committee' in the United Kingdom refers to the judicial committee of the Privy Council, which, although it is in fact composed of lords of appeal who are also members of the House of Lords, is a distinct body.

39 Below, page 100.

40 Under the Appellate Jurisdiction Act 1876, an appeal could not be heard and determined by the House of Lords unless there were present at the hearing not less than three of the following persons: the lord chancellor, the lords of appeal in ordinary appointed under the Act, or peers of parliament who had held high judicial office, as defined by the Act. But the Act did not formally disqualify other peers.

41 Below, page 104.

42 *Hume* v. *Burton* (1785) 1 Ridg. PC 204. The opinions of the judges are reported at 1 Ridg. PC 77. *Haire* v. *Lloyd* (1787) 1 Ridg. PC 341 at 358; *Westby* v. *Carroll* (1787) 1 Ridg. PC 361; *Atkinson* v. *Pillsworth* (1787) 1 Ridg. PC 449. *Fauconberg (Lord)* v. *Birch* (1790) 2 Ridg. PC 158 at 175. In *Fauconberg (Lord)* v. *Birch* the Lords on an appeal from the King's Bench took the opinion of the judges of the Common Pleas and the Exchequer and then reversed the King's Bench.

43 'Rules and Orders of the Upper House' (1692) *J. Ir. H.L.* p. 470, 'Concerning the Judges'.

44 (1796) 3 Ridg. PC 545.

45 The Banker's Act, 33 Geo. II, c. 14 (Ir), s. 8.

46 *Gay* v. *Cox* (1784) 1 Ridg. PC 165; *Hume* v. *Burton* (1785) 1 Ridg. PC 204 (vote taken only as to the issue on which the judges disagreed); *Westby* v. *Carroll* (1787) 1 Ridg. PC 361. In *Gay* v. *Cox* the judges' answers are reported. As to the English practice, see *Select Cases in the Exchequer Chamber* (M. Hemmant, ed.) 51 Seld. Soc. (for 1933), at p. xxxvi.

put in the form that the House would reverse the decision of the lower court, for if there were an equality of votes the lower court decision would stand.[47] This procedure was adapted from the procedure on debates, whereby a motion which received an equality of votes was considered not to have been carried.

Re-Hearings

After the decision in *Magrath* v. *Lord Muskerry*[48] the unsuccessful appellant petitioned the Irish Lords for a re-hearing. The petition merely alleged that the merits of the appellant's case had not been sufficiently laid before the House. The Earl of Carhampton moved the motion to grant the petition. He was supported in the debate[49] only by Viscount Pery, who recognised the obvious dangers of allowing re-hearings, but argued, as noted above, that the petition in the present case should be allowed solely for the purpose of taking the opinion of the common law judges on the effect of the Tenantry Act. The motion to deny the petition was passed without a division. The following lay peers gave speeches, against the petition to re-hear, as previously noted: Charles Agar, Archbishop of Cashel, earls Hillsborough and Bellamont and viscounts Mountgarrett and Mountmorres.

Viscount Mountmorres[50] was against re-hearing an appeal, and the House so decided, but whether they were influenced by his speech, Ridgeway says he was 'unable to learn'.[51] Ridgeway comments on the speech:[52]

> I confess his Lordship's argument, though extremely ingenious, and displaying profound parliamentary knowledge, has not wrought perfect conviction in my mind.

Lord Mountmorres published his speech in his *The History of the Principal Transactions of the Irish Parliament, from the year 1634 to 1666*.[53] His argument was based on standing order 79:[54]

> 79. No petition which relates to the re-hearing of any cause, or part of a cause, formerly heard in the House, shall be read the same day it is offered, but shall lie upon the table, and a future day be appointed for the reading thereof.

Mountmorres asserted it was based on two principles: 1. that cases were not originally heard by the English Lords, but by select committees of that House, and he inferred from that that the order might refer to re-hearing a case before the whole House which had been previously heard in select committee, and

47 'Rules and Orders of the Upper House' (1692) Ir. Lords J. p. 475:
48 (1787) Vern. & Scr. 166 at 172. Above, page 19.
49 On 21 May 1787. The debate is noted in Vern. & Scr. at pages 192–93.
50 Hervey Redmond Morres, 2nd Viscount Mountmorres (*c.* 1743–1797). Below, page 126.
51 1 Ridg. PC 509, note a, at 510.
52 *ibid.*
53 2 vols. (London, 1792), ii.201.
54 Ridgeway notes that he refers to it as the 60th order: 1 Ridg. PC at 510.

2. that judicial matters continued from one session of parliament to another and were not lost by prorogation or dissolution, and were taken from the point where they left off, so that the order might apply to the House hearing in a succeeding session the remainder of a case which had been partly heard in a previous session.

As to the first point, Ridgeway responded that select committees referred to committees to redress delays in the common law courts, and not to appeals before the Lords' House.[55] On the second point, Ridgeway commented that a rehearing implied hearing the whole of an appeal again, whereas the order seemed rather to refer to continuing a hearing from the point where it left off, as Lord Mountmorres in fact recognised.

Those who spoke against the earlier motion to grant the petition did so not only on the ground that the petition lacked merit in itself, but also on the ground that it was undesirable as a matter of principle. Vernon and Scriven, in their account of the debate,[56] add a footnote referring to the comment of Blackstone, in his introduction to his *Commentaries*, on the jurisdiction of the Lords, in which he says: 'Their sentence is final decisive, irrecoverable; no appeal, no correction, not even a review can be had: and to their determination, whatever it be, the inferior Courts of Justice must conform; otherwise the rule of property would no longer be uniform and steady.' Blackstone was referring to the British Lords, but his reason would as well apply to the Irish House. There is little doubt that the concern as to property law and the need for it to be stable and reliable were present to the minds of the Irish peers.

Procedure in Equity Appeals

The peculiarity of appeals from the Court of Chancery was that the lord chancellor sat in the House as well as in the Court of Chancery and thus could hear appeals from himself. The chief baron of the Court of Exchequer, Barry Yelverton joined the lord chancellor in the Lords in 1783. He was created Baron Avonmore in 1795. The Court of Exchequer, as we have seen, had its own equity jurisdiction. There are certainly many cases in the early period in which the reports simply state that the House was addressed by counsel for both sides and that it was then 'ordered and adjudged' that the decree of the Court of Chancery be affirmed.[57]

The anomaly of the Lord Chancellor participating in appeals from his own decisions was compounded by the power of the Lords to order lower courts

55 1 Ridg. PC 510–11.

56 Vern. & Scr. 193.

57 *Davis* v. *Oliver* (1784) 1 Ridg. PC 1; *Doneraile* v. *Chartres* (1784) 1 Ridg. PC 122; *Conner* v. *Browne* (1784) 1 Ridg. PC 139; *Stratford* v. *Aldborough (Earl)* (1786) 1 Ridg. PC 281; *Wrixon* v. *Cotter* (1786) 1 Ridg. PC 295; *Gill* v. *Fleming* (1787) 1 Ridg. PC 420 (equity side of Exchequer); *Crafford* v. *Oliver* (1786) 1 Ridg. PC 315; *Whittingham* v. *Mitchell* (1787) 1 Ridg. PC 448 (original decree affirmed, with variations). In *Freeman* v. *Boyle* (1780) 2 Ridg. PC 69, 76, however, the House reversed Chancery, allowing the renewal of a lease for lives. This case is discussed below.

to rehear a case.[58] The result was a procedure which might have met with the approval of the Queen of Hearts in *Alice's Adventures in Wonderland* but would hardly commend itself to anyone else. In *Blundell* v. *Macartney*[59] the lord chancellor, FitzGibbon, advised his brother peers that they could, if they so wished, order him to retry the case in Chancery. He had already tried it once, of course, and the present appeal was from his judgment. He nevertheless made it clear that if he was to re-hear the case in the court of Chancery, he would come to the same decision:[60]

> therefore [the appellants] desire of your Lordships to direct a re-hearing of the case in the Court of Chancery, or that you will rescind that part of the leading order,[61] which was made at their express desire, and was founded upon the consent of all parties signified in open court. Such an application, I suppose was never before made to a court of justice. ... Your Lordships certainly may direct me to re-hear the cause, if you shall think fit. Such a direction was once given by the House of Lords of Great Britain in the case of *Lord Fingal* v. *Lord Glerawly*,[62] upon an appeal brought from a decree made by Lord Lifford. But if I am to re-hear the cause in the Court of Chancery, I shall most assuredly, as I am at present advised, affirm the leading order of that court. I am bound to administer justice to rich and poor according to the laws and usage.

Not surprisingly, perhaps, the Lords declined to take this course of action. Nor did they decide to reverse the order themselves. The appeal was dismissed.

In 1787 Lord Lifford LC in the Chancery appeal in *Magrath* v. *Lord Muskerry*[63] had indicated that he placed a limit on his own role in speaking in the Lords on such appeals:

> My Lords, I rise rather to furnish your lordships with the principles which governed me in making my decree, than to offer any arguments to induce you to affirm it. It is perfectly indifferent to me which way you decide. I am not at all anxious about the fate of any appeal from a decision of mine. On the contrary, it is a great consolation to me, when sitting on the bench, to reflect, that if I decide

58 They ordered the Court of Exchequer to rehear a case in *Johnston* v. *Johnston* (1790) 1 Ridg. PC 176 at 191; and the Court of Common Pleas in *Sherborne (Lord)* v. *Naper* (1790) 1 Ridg. PC 224 at 250.

59 (1793) 2 Ridg. PC 557 at 589. See also *Macartney* v. *Blundell* (1789) 2 Ridg. PC 112 (action at law).

60 (1793) 2 Ridg. PC 557 at 589–90.

61 If an issue of fact arose in the Court of Chancery, where there was no jury, the court would order the issue to be tried before a jury in the Court of Common Pleas. On the equity side of Exchequer, the order issued to the common law side. In Ireland this was known as a 'trial by leading order'. The same procedure occurred in England, but the phrase 'leading order' seems to have been peculiar to Ireland. See also *Irish Exchequer Reports 1716–1734* 125 Seld. Soc. (for 2008), pp. ciii–civ.

62 No citation is given. The case is neither in E.R. nor in Bridgman's Index. Glerawly is, correctly, Glenawley. William Annesley was created Viscount Glerawly in 1766. Cokayne, *Complete Peerage*, v.682. The error in the grant was made by a clerk, who wrote 'r' instead of 'n' and omitted the 'e': *ibid.*, i.169, note c.

63 (1787) Vern. & Scr. 166 at 172.

> wrong, there is this House to rectify my mistake. The wisdom of this House is superior to that of any individual though sitting in his judicial capacity, and therefore ought to be exerted without any influence from the opinion of such individual.

FitzGibbon in *Blundell* v. *Macartney* clearly felt that he saw no other result that could be justified, but the contrast between FitzGibbon and Lifford in the two cases also seems to illustrate FitzGibbon's more confident and less deferential approach to his colleagues.

Lay Peers

Since there was no formal distinction between professional and lay members of the House, it was possible for lay members to give judgment on appeals, as was also the case with the British Peers at this time.[64] All judgments remained technically speeches, whether delivered by professionals or lay members.

The last British case in which *only* lay peers took part was in 1834, considerably later than in the Irish House.[65] In the British Lords it was not until 1844, in the case of Daniel O'Connell, that it became recognised that legal appeals should be decided only by legally-qualified members.[66]

The Irish House, on the other hand, had accepted by about 1795 the convention that at least it was undesirable for lay members to give judgment in legal cases. There are three instances[67] from Ridgeway's *Reports* of lay peers giving speeches on appeals which are reported. The first was by Lord Mountmorres[68] in *McGrath* v. *Lord Muskerry*[69] on the petition praying a re-hearing of an appeal. The following lay peers also made speeches in the case against the petition to re-hear, although they are not reported by Ridgeway:[70] Lord Farnham

[64] On lay peers in the British House of Lords, see R.E. Megarry, 'Lay Peers in Appeals to the House of Lords' (1949) 65 *LQR* 22; Robert Stevens, *The House of Lords as a Judicial Body, 1800-1976* (London, 1979); H. Twiss, *The Public and Private Life of Lord Chancellor Eldon* (London, 1844), pp. 232-33. The common law judges were summoned to give their advice on the question as to whether lay peers should take part. Lord Eldon objected to the procedure and there was a general feeling that it should not happen again.

[65] Stevens, *House of Lords*, p. 29; Holdsworth, *HEL*, i.377; Twiss, *Life of Eldon*, iii.232–33. Twiss says that the judges were to deliver their opinions that day, but does not say in what matter.

[66] Daniel O'Connell was tried and convicted of conspiracy by the Queen's Bench in Dublin. Proceedings by writ of error were taken to the British House of Lords (the Irish House having been abolished at the time of the Union.) The common law judges were summoned to give advice and the majority denied error. Five law lords then gave judgment. The majority, consisting of Lords Denman, Cottenham and Campbell were in favour of upholding the writ of error, while the minority, consisting of Lords Brougham and Lyndhurst, were in favour of upholding the conviction. Various lay peers then tried to participate in the vote, on the side of the minority of the law lords, in order to uphold the conviction. Lord Wharncliffe, a senior cabinet member, was dispatched to the House to give the view, evidently of the cabinet, that the participation of lay peers would undermine the authority of the House as a court of law. The lay peers then withdrew.

[67] Barry Maxwell, the Earl of Farnham, might be considered a fourth, although he held the office of prothonotary of the Court of Common Pleas. His contributions are mentioned below, page 126.

[68] Below, page 126.

[69] (1784) 1 Ridg. PC 469.

[70] See also page 93.

(semi-professional), Charles Agar, Archbishop of Cashel, earls Hillsborough and Bellamont and Viscount Mountgarrett but their speeches are not reported by Ridgeway.

The second was by George Nugent, Earl of Westmeath, in *Barton* v. *Massey*.[71] Barton, the defendant in the court below, had been ordered to lodge in court the huge sum of £24,000. When he failed to do so, an order of sequestration was made. He had chosen instead to flee the jurisdiction of the court and go to Holyhead and from there to France. Later, he made an application to set aside the the order, which was refused. A decree was then made against him in Chancery – Ridgeway is not more explicit – and he then entered an appeal to reverse it. FitzGibbon notes that he had fled the jurisdiction to evade the order, as FitzGibbon put it:[72]

> he has withdrawn himself from the jurisdiction of his King and Country, from his allegiance due to his lawful Sovereign, and departs the kingdom to evade the process of the law. After this proof, not only of disobedience, but of contumacy, it rests with your Lordships whether you will hear his appeal or not. If you are inclined to do so, I shall not object to it, but I thought it my duty to submit this matter to the House, feeling, as I do, that the appellant did not deserve any favour.

While making it abundantly clear what he expected the decision to be, FitzGibbon on this occasion is full of reasonableness and deference to his colleagues, something which Fleming and Malcomson[73] also note in FitzGibbon's attitude to other members of the Lords. It explains his dominance: he does not patronise, he sets out his view and defers to their judgment, which was somewhat flattering since it must have been clear to them that he had greater expertise in equity matters than they did. Not surprisingly, Lords Carleton, Westmeath, and Clonmell all agreed. Lord Westmeath's speech was as follows:[74]

> My Lords, it would be degrading the dignity of this House to hear the appeal under these circumstances. We ought not, particularly at this time, to encourage men who disobey the laws of the country, and I trust this House will always lend its assistance to enforce obedience to the laws.

FitzGibbon then moved that the appeal should be postponed until further order. It is not clear why Nugent, the Earl of Westmeath, participates. He had married a niece of FitzGibbon, so perhaps his presence that day was due to this personal connection.

The third instance of an intervention by a lay peer was at a later date when one would have expected the practice to have become obsolete, given the precocity of the Irish Lords in this respect. Charles Agar, then Archbishop of

[71] (1793) 2 Ridg. PC 553.
[72] 2 Ridge. PC 554.
[73] *'A Volley of Execrations'*, p. xxvii.
[74] 2 Ridg. PC at 555.

Cashel, gave a speech in the case of *Mandeville* v. *Lord Carrick*.[75] The explanation lies in Agar's idiosyncrasies as an archbishop. He was notorious for meddling in almost everything. As a Church of Ireland archbishop he had been appointed to the See by the government. He had also amassed a large fortune while occupying that position. According to a contemporary description, his ambitions were more of a secular than spiritual kind: he wanted to be a government minister in the House of Lords and was said to be 'very active in business'.[76] On the other hand, the case concerned the construction of wills, involving matters of intention and conscience, so he may have felt justified in intervening on that ground.[77] This seems a more likely explaination of his intervention. He probably did not consider himself 'lay' in the technical legal sense, as he was not in the more general sense.

In fact, the case concerned the highly technical Rule in *Shelley's Case*[78] in its application to wills. The testator had left property 'to EM for life only, remainder to the lawful issue male [of EM] and the lawful issue male of such heirs, the eldest of such sons always to be preferred...' On failure of such issue there was an ultimate remainder to Lord Carrick in tail male. On the testator's death in 1788 EM purported to bar the entail by suffering a recovery. EM died two years later leaving a wife and daughter. If, under the Rule in *Shelley's Case*, EM had obtained under the will not a life estate but a fee tail, and if he had successfully barred the entail, that would also have destroyed the contingent remainder to Lord Carrick. EM would have obtained, by virtue of the recovery, a fee simple estate in the land. Such an estate could pass to daughters as well as sons, and so EM's daughter would have been his heir at law and would take the land. If *Shelley's Case* did not apply, then EM would have had only a life estate and the contingent remainder to Lord Carrick would not have been destroyed. Lord Carrick claimed the land.

The rule in *Shelley's Case* laid down[79] that if an estate of freehold was given by a deed to a person and in the same deed there was a further gift to that person's 'heirs', then the heirs did not take any interest in the land. Instead, the words in the later gift operated as 'words of limitation' defining the estate given to the first-named person. Thus, the person named in the will took a fee simple or, if other words were added to 'heirs', such as 'of the body', indicating that it was restricted to descendants, the named person took a fee tail. At the end of the 18th century even an expression such as 'issue', if contained in a will, could function as a word of limitation and give rise to a fee tail.

75 (1795) 3 Ridg PC 366 at 372.

76 G. O. Sayles, 'Contemporary Sketches of Members of the Irish Parliament in 1782' (1954) 56 *PRIA*, section C 227, at p. 273.

77 Ecclesiastical courts had long had jurisdiction over capacity to make wills, probate and succession to personal property and retained it into the 19th century, Baker, *Introduction*, 126–134, 387; R.H. Helmholz, *The Canon Law and Ecclesiastical Jurisdiction from 597 to the 1640s*. OHLE vol.1. The present case, however, concerned real property.

78 (1581) 1 Co. Rep. 88b. The judges in *Mandeville* v. *Lord Carrick* do not refer to the Rule by that name, or indeed by any name at all.

79 The rule in Ireland remained in force until the enactment of the Land Law and Conveyancing Law Reform Act 2009, s. 67(3), Lyall, *Land Law in Ireland*, (3rd edn. Round Hall, 2010), p, 191–197.

John Fitzgibbon, Baron Fitzgibbon, lord chancellor, c. 1789.
(later Earl of Clare) By Gilbert Stuart.
Cleveland Museum of Art, Cleveland, Ohio, USA

Charles Agar, Archbishop of Cashel.
Mezzotint by William Say, 1803, after Stuart, c. 1790.
Courtesy of A.P.W. Malcomson.

Under the Rule as it applied to wills, everything depended upon what the testator intended by the expression 'heirs' or 'issue' or whatever words were used in the remainder clause. If the testator had meant to refer to the whole succession of heirs as a class, the rule applied and the first devisee took a fee tail. If he or she meant by that expression to refer to a specific person or persons, then the first devisee took only a life estate and the specific person or persons took a fee tail in remainder. *Shelley's Case* had originally been a strict rule of law independent of any intention, which probably shows that its purpose was to impose a feudal policy on the parties regardless of their intention. Lord Clare, LC in *Mandeville's Case*[80] sheds some light on this obscure subject:

> ...It was originally founded in the principles of the feudal law, to prevent conveyances in fraud of the tenure; because if by such a limitation the issue could take an estate tail in remainder, as purchasers, it would at any time be in the power of the ancestor to defeat the contingent remainder to his issue and thus acquire a dominion over the estate. Or if he did not defeat the remainder, to transmit the remainder to his issue exonerated from the duties to which the lord was entitled from his tenant coming in by descent.[81]

By the 18th century the strictness of the rule had been mitigated in its application to wills to the extent that the testator's *intention* was allowed to enter into the question of the meaning of 'issue', or whatever expression had been used in the remainder clause, but to that extent only. The rule never fully became a rule of construction, but it had become partially disguised as such out of an excessive respect for precedent and certainty on the one hand and an attempt at mitigation on the other.

It will be recalled that if, under *Shelley's Case*, the effect of the will had been to vest in EM an entail, which had then been barred, EM would then have died possessed of a fee simple and his daughter, being the heir at law, would have been entitled to the land. On the other hand, if *Shelley's Case* did not apply, EM only had a life estate at his death. Since he had no male issue the fees tail male would not take effect and Lord Carrick would be entitled to the land under the ultimate remainder.

The Irish House of Lords, upholding the King's Bench, held that *Shelley's Case* did not apply and that consequently Lord Carrick was entitled to the land. The lord chancellor, FitzGibbon, first gave a short speech, pointing out that the opinion of the judges had been sought,[82] that he agreed with them and that *Shelley* did not apply in the case at hand. The will was essentially a settlement,

[80] (1795) 3 Ridg. PC 352 at p. 369.

[81] This latter point seems to be the explanation based on 'principles of feudal' law, i.e. that the limitation was intended to avoid feudal dues which would only arise if the heir took 'by descent' i.e. under the common law rules of descent, and that the rule therefore defeated that intention. The point that the rule was intended to defeat the ability of the ancestor to destroy contingent remainders is less clear, since the remainder was normally not contingent, but also, if it was, then contingent remainders were not recognized until about the 14th century.

[82] Yelverton CB delivered the agreed opinions of the common law judges at 3 Ridg. PC 363–368.

giving a life estate to the father and successive entails to possible sons. Then the archbishop spoke. All the subtleties of *Shelley's Case* were of no consequence to him. To him it was obvious that if a testator left land to someone 'for life only' that meant a life estate. As far as he was concerned, it was common sense. And so he opened his speech:[83]

> My lords it would be improper for me to enter into this question, was it a legal one, which I conceive it is not.

It is significant that even at this relatively early date it was thought 'improper' in the Irish House for a lay peer to give judgment, at least where a technical legal point was involved.

Agar's intervention was a breach of a convention already established, as his comment indicates, although he was not deterred by it. Agar also felt bold enough to venture an opinion on costs, saying that it was wasting the time of the court for the unsuccessful defendant even to appeal such an obvious point, and proposed that the court should award 'the largest costs we can give' against the defendant.

The Lord Chancellor then spoke again, which suggests a certain informality in the proceedings. He did not know of a case on a writ of error in which more than 'common and ordinary costs' had been awarded, although the house had a discretion.

Finally, Lord Carleton spoke. The archbishop's comments could well have produced apoplexy in a real property lawyer of the period, but the judge adopted a restrained approach:[84]

> I beg leave to assure my most Reverend Friend, that there is more difficulty attending the construction of wills, upon which this species of question has arisen, than he is aware of; and if the greater number of the wills upon which these questions arose had been submitted to men of untechnical understanding, almost every one of them would have received a different decision from that which the judges have given, finding themselves bound by strict rules of law.

The judge evidently regarded this as an argument against submitting such problems to the opinion of laymen.[85] He also rejected the archbishop's views on costs. The defendant's appeal was dismissed and no special costs were awarded. The archbishop was therefore in the majority on the main issue, but was outvoted on the issue of costs.

[83] 3 Ridg. PC 366 at 372.
[84] 3 Ridg. PC. 373.
[85] Carleton's concern for predictability in property law is mentioned below, page 112.

CHAPTER 7

Biographical Details

Introduction

In the 18th century there was no formal distinction between legally-qualified and lay members of the House, with the exception of the lord chancellor. Other legally qualified members would include former lord chancellors and judges on whom peerages had been conferred. In the later period those peers who regularly delivered judgment on appeals, and who could therefore be described as the professionals of the court, were a very small number of career lawyers promoted from the bar to the bench and later to the House. The following are short biographies of those who gave judgment on appeals, including lay peers and 'semi-professionals', and whose judgments are reported in Ridgeway.[1] In these brief accounts particular attention will be paid to aspects of their lives, characters and work that relate to the decisions of the Irish House of Lords as court of law and will attempt to assess their contribution to it. Where titles are given in headings they are those used during the period of this study.

Charles Agar (1736–1809), Archbishop of Cashel

Charles Agar[2] was born in Dublin in 1736, the third son of Henry Agar of Gowran Castle, Co. Kilkenny and of Anne, daughter of Welbore Ellis, Bishop of Meath. Charles attended Westminster School and graduated BA from Christ Church, Oxford, in 1759. He graduated MA in 1762 and DCL in 1765. He took holy orders and was chaplain to the Duke of Northumberland, lord lieutenant of Ireland, in 1763. He became Dean of Kilmore in 1765. He married Jane, the daughter of William Benson of Downpatrick, Co. Down, formerly a merchant in Dublin. Agar became Bishop of Cloyne in 1768 and was sworn of the Privy Council in 1779. He became Archbishop of Cashel in 1779 and was created Baron

[1] The information is taken from F. E. Ball, *The Judges in Ireland 1221-1921*. 2 vols. (London, 1927; reprint, Dublin, 1993), G. E. Cokayne, *The Complete Peerage* (London, 1926) the ODNB and the DIB unless otherwise indicated.

[2] A. P. W. Malcomson, *Archbishop Charles Agar: churchmanship and politics in Ireland, 1760–1810* (Dublin, 2002); Peter MacDonagh, 'Agar, Charles 1st Earl of Normanton Baron Somerton Viscount Somerton'. DIB online. [http://dib.cambridge.org/viewReadPage.do?articleId=a0054], accessed 26 February 2013.

Somerton of Somerton, Co. Kilkenny in 1795. After the Union he became Archbishop of Dublin, from 1801 to 1809. He was created Viscount Somerton (Ir.) in 1800, and Earl of Normanton[3] (Ir.) in 1806. He died in 1809 and was buried in Westminster Abbey.

Charles Agar was a notoriously ambitious and, according to the traditional view, corrupt or at least venal, cleric. He amassed a huge fortune and acquired three temporal peerages, one of them shortly before the Union. It is said that when Archbishop of Cashel he completed the destruction 'of the magnificent old Cathedral on the Rock of Cashel',[4] but this is certainly untrue.[5] It was his predecessor, Archbishop Price who vandalised it by having the roof removed and part of it dismantled. Agar, on the other hand, had plans to restore it and in fact rescued the oldest part, the Romanesque chapel put up by Cormac MacCarthaigh, king of Cashel, in 1127. As to the main part, the walls were in a dangerous state and Agar abandoned the idea. Malcomson,[6] has recently published a lengthy biography of Agar in which he argues that his reputation for corruption or venality is not entirely deserved. Nevertheless, in his time as Archbishop of Cashel he became enormously rich. This may have come in some part from the sale of many of the valuable objects in the old cathedral, although the major part of his wealth came from the income of leases of ecclesiastical land.

Ecclesiastical leases were long a source of income for bishops of the Church of Ireland, but became a scandal at the time, not only because the bishops grew rich from them and used various strategies to increase their income at the expense of the tenants, but also because many leases had been granted in violation of statute law. The statute 10 & 11 Cha. I, c. 3 (Ir.), 1635 had restricted ecclesiastics to granting leases for no more than 21 years, or, in the case of property in a corporate or market town, 40 years and also required the land to be let at not less than half its annual value at the time of making the lease.[7] Despite this, is seems that the statute had been widely ignored. Leases for lives had been granted and at lower values than that authorised by the statute. John Scott, Earl of Clonmell, had ventured the opinion, as Agar himself reported, that 'at present no tenant to any archbishop or bishop had a legal lease, and their only security depended on the perjury of juries'.[8] The statute 17 & 18 Cha. II, c. 2 (Ir.), 1665, had permitted augmentation lands to be let for 21 years or three lives at not less than half the improved rent.[9] Augmentation lands were impropriate church lands (lands relating to a benefice or its revenues) which had been forfeited by their owners in the 1640s or 1650s and which had been granted at the Restoration to eight southern bishoprics of which, in practice, only five including Cashel had

[3] The full title was Earl of Normanton of Co. Kilkenny despite the fact that, although there are several Normantons, there is none in Co. Kilkenny: Cokayne, *Complete Peerage*, ix.642.

[4] Cokayne, *Complete Peerage*, ix. 641 n. a.

[5] Malcomson, *Archbishop Agar*, pp. 305–307.

[6] *ibid.*

[7] Malcomson, *Archbishop Agar*, pp. 393–94, 399.

[8] *ibid.*, p. 398 n. 61, Agar's 'state' of the diocese of Cashel, 1779–1801, and p. 399.

[9] Section 29.

come into possession of such lands intended for them.[10] Finally, the statute 12 Geo. I, c. 10 (Ir.), 1726,[11] empowered bishops to let 'bog or fenny land' for 60 years at a low rent to encourage tenants to reclaim them.[12]

Thus, although there were cases where leases for lives would have been valid, there were others where the had been granted in ignorance, or disregard, of the statutory restrictions.[13] Various attempts had been made between 1735 and 1793 to remedy the situation but with no result. It was to be Agar who was instrumental in bringing about the change. In the Lords, he opposed a bill drawn up and passed by the Commons which would have allowed bishops and other ecclesiastical persons to grant leases for 21 years or three lives, whichever should last the longest, reserving a rent greater than the present reserved rent. Its tendency, according to Agar, was 'to mend the situation of the immediate lessees, without any benefit to the terre-tenants, and to the injury of all succeeding archbishops and bishops, etc. to the destruction of the patronage of the Crown.' It was strenuously supported in the Lords by Lord Clonmell, who 'holds most valuable possessions under [the church]'.[14] Agar introduced his own bill which he had apparently drafted himself.[15] It rather disingenuously recited that 'doubts' had arisen as to the validity of leases made under the Act of 1635. The draft was more favourable to the church and also validated existing ecclesiastical leases.[16] In an eloquent speech, Agar persuaded members of the Lords to vote for it, some despite their initial opposition. What became known as 'the Archbishop of Cashel's Act'[17] became law on 5 June 1795.

Agar's position in relation to church leases was conflicted: he was both a landlord and a tenant of other church lands. Malcomson,[18] concluded that it would be wrong to infer that Agar's motive was simply to protect or augment his own income in Cashel. Nevertheless, his motive may have been a more subtle political one. Although the immediate effect of the Act may not have been to his benefit, and have even been to his disadvantage, it seems to have been to the advantage of the bishops and archbishops in general, for which they might well have felt an obligation to him. Agar was ambitious for further preferment, and obtained it later when he was appointed Archbishop of Dublin.

The way the Act dealt with other abuses of the system of ecclesiastical leases nevertheless gives an insight into Agar's motives and character. The system of letting bishops' land for lives by incumbents was motivated in general by the narrow desire on the part of the current incumbent to maximise his income from

[10] Malcomson, *Archbishop Agar*, p. 400, n. 69.

[11] Sections 13 and 16.

[12] Malcomson, *Archbishop Agar*, p. 400.

[13] The tenancies might have been valid between the parties by the doctrine of estoppel, but that would not assist those who were not parties to the estoppel.

[14] *ibid.*, pp. 397–98; Agar's 'state' of the diocese of Cashel, 1779–1801.

[15] *ibid.*, p. 399: A draft of it in Agar's handwriting is among his papers: Normanton Papers, Hampshire Record Office, Winchester, 21 M 57/B19/6.

[16] Section 2.

[17] 35 Geo. III, c. 23 (Ir.), 1795.

[18] *Archbishop Agar*, p. 411.

renewal fines, rather than to promote the long-term interest of the cultivation of the land.[19] As to leases for years, the practice had been adopted of 'renewing' what were typically 21-year leases every two or three years in return for a substantial fine. Technically, this involved the surrender of the old lease by the tenant and acceptance of a new grant of a 21-year term by the bishop, or other ecclesiastical person. The churchmen would accept a surrender of the existing lease and grant a new one for 21 years, in order to gain from the 'renewal' fines. If this was done shortly before the incumbent moved to a new living, or better bishopric, he would deprive the new incumbent of income.[20]

Renewals of both leases for lives, and 'renewals' of leases for years, were also methods by which churchmen sought to take advantage of the rising rents received by their tenants, who were also landlords in their turn. In the case of leases for lives, fines on renewals were an unpredictable windfall, whereas in the case of leases for years, the above practice of renewals every two or three years provided a reliable boost to income. This practice had, according to Wakefield,[21] been held illegal in England by the Court of Chancery [22] but was considered legal in Ireland.

Agar's Act declared it lawful for archbishops, bishops, deans, etc., to accept surrenders of leases and to grant new leases of church lands even if the rent reserved was less than half the annual value, provided they were let at the same rent as had been received for them for the previous 20 years.[23] It also allowed land to be let by separate leases where previously it had been let under a single lease.[24] Even more importantly, it validated, on the same conditions, existing leases made in breach of the earlier Acts.[25] It therefore allowed what had been prohibited by the Act of 1635, and went beyond what the Act of Charles II[26] had permitted for augmentation lands, in that it allowed the rent to be below half the full value.

As to the renewal of ecclesiastical leases for lives, Agar had been less successful some years earlier when he opposed the Tenantry Bill in the Irish House of Lords. Lord Buckinghamshire,[27] who disliked Agar, reported in October 1780 that Agar had attacked the bill with 'uncontrolled fury'.[28] However, a protest

19 Malcomson, *Archbishop Agar*, p.403.

20 Malcomson, *Archbishop Agar*, p. 404, mentions the instance of Charles Dodgson, outgoing Bishop of Ossery, of whom his successor, William Newcome, complained that he had 'exhausted' the see 'on his removal by taking fines to the amount of more than £2,600 a fortnight after his name was in the Gazette for Elphin.'

21 Edward Wakefield, *An Account of Ireland statistical and political* (London, 1812), ii.469–70.

22 Wakefield does not give a citation.

23 35 Geo. III, c. 23, 1795, s. 1..

24 *ibid.*, s. 3.

25 Section 2.

26 Above, page 106.

27 John Hobart, 2nd Earl of Buckinghamshire, lord lieutenant of Ireland, 1776–80. James Kelly, 'Hobart, John, 2nd Earl of Buckinghamshire (1723–1793)', ODNB online. [http://www.oxforddnb.com/view/article/13394], accessed 21 June 2009.

28 Malcomson, *Archbishop Agar*, p. 394; Buckinghamshire to Hotham Thompson, 11 Oct 1789, PRONI T/3429/1/68.

of a dissident minority of peers who opposed the bill, as reported in the Lords *Journals*, and which may have been Agar's work, did present reasoned arguments.[29] Agar was apparently convinced that the bill extended the power of tenants to renew leases for lives renewable forever in violation of stipulations in the leases. He found it unacceptable that the bill, in his view, increased the power of tenants and largely removed the ability of bishops to refuse renewals and then grant new leases on more favourable terms to themselves. The bill[30] did indeed allow tenants to renew the lives despite covenants in the leases, but in doing so it was merely re-instating the old Irish equity as it was known earlier in the century, before the British House of Lords appeals in *Kane* v. *Hamilton* and *Murray* v. *Bateman*.[31] Although it may be true that Agar had considerable knowledge of ecclesiastical statute law, he did not demonstrate the same grasp of the Irish equity to renew leases for lives renewable forever.

Malcomson,[32] puts the issue of ecclesiastical leases and Agar's activities concerning them into the wider context:

> due allowance had not been made for all the drawbacks and distractions of their situation... – an invidious and inefficient system of pay and promotion, an absence of any arrangement for retirement on grounds of age or ill-health, the requirement that bishops run huge and complex see estates, the bishops' individual liability for the sometimes daunting cost of episcopal palaces, and the responsibility imposed on some of them for the political management of parliamentary boroughs. All these things consumed time and energy... [and] did not conduce to spirituality or a concentration on pastoral activity.

The Church of Ireland in this period does not seem to have paid much regard, in other words, to the precept in Matthew 6.19–21: 'Lay not up for yourselves treasures upon earth, where moth and rust doth corrupt, and where thieves break through and steal: But lay up for yourselves treasures in heaven, where neither moth nor rust doth corrupt, and where thieves do not break through nor steal: for where your treasure is, there will your heart be also.'

Other members of Agar's family acquired four peerages between them, a remarkable haul. His elder brother James, born 1734, was created Baron Clifden of Gowran in 1776, and Viscount Clifden of Gowran in 1781.[33] His aunt, Ellis, was created Countess of Brandon in 1758.[34] A cousin, George Agar, the son of James Agar of Ringwood, a brother of Henry Agar of Gowran, was created Baron Callan of Callan in 1790.[35] The Church of Ireland primacy fell vacant

[29] *ibid.*, p. 395

[30] Below, page 155, and Appendix M, page 246.

[31] Below, page 152.

[32] *Archbishop Agar*, p. 615.

[33] Cokayne, *Complete Peerage* iii.287–88.

[34] *ibid.*, ii.487.

[35] *ibid.*, ii.487–88.

while the Union debates were going on, and Cornwallis[36] tried, without success, to have an Irishman appointed.[37] Both Lord Clifden and Lord Callan intervened on Agar's behalf in an attempt to secure his appointment. In 1799 Agar had been opposed to the Union, but was 'persuaded' to alter his opinion by Cornwallis who agreed to his demand for the see of Dublin.[38] Cornwallis also promised him a seat in the British House of Lords 'for life.'[39] This can hardly have been a promise of a British peerage, since they could not be granted for life only and it could hardly have been a reference to what became Irish representative peers, since they were chosen by vote of the Irish peers.[40] At any rate, Agar did not get a British peerage.[41] However, as Archbishop of Dublin he qualified as an Irish spiritual peer and under the terms of the Union sat in rotation by session with four other Irish bishops.[42]

Apart from his legislative activities, Agar delivered one of the two reported judgments by non-legal members of the Irish House of Lords in *Mandeville* v. *Lord Carrick*,[43] a case involving the highly technical rule in *Shelley's Case*,[44] which must have seemed an impertinence to the legal members of the House. Possibly, since it concerned a gift in a will, he may have thought it was an area with which he was familiar with from ecclesiastical law.

Hugh Carleton (1739–1826), Viscount Carleton CJCP

Hugh Carleton[45] was born in 1739, the eldest son of Francis Carleton, merchant, of Cork and Rebecca Lawton of Lake March in Co. Cork. He entered Kilkenny School in 1752 and the Middle Temple in 1758. He was admitted to the degree of barrister-at-law by King's Inns in 1764. He became king's counsel in 1768 and Recorder of Cork in 1769. He became MP for Tuam in 1772. He was appointed third serjeant in 1776[46] and second serjeant in 1777. He became solicitor general

36 Charles Cornwallis (1738–1805), 2nd Earl Cornwallis, 1st Marquess of Cornwallis, soldier and lord lieutenant of Ireland (1798–1801). James Quinn, 'Cornwallis, Charles' DIB; C. A. Bayly and Katherine Prior, 'Cornwallis, Charles, 1st Marquess Cornwallis (1738–1805)', ODNB online. [http://www.oxforddnb.com/view/article/6338], accessed 15 February 2011.

37 W. E. H. Lecky, *History of Ireland in the Eighteenth Century*. (London, 1898) v.303.

38 *ibid.*; Cokayne, *Complete Peerage*, ix. 641.

39 *ibid.*

40 Holdsworth, *HEL*, vol. 13; M. A. Thomson, *A Constitutional History of England 1642–1801* (London, 1938) p. 392.

41 His descendant, James Agar, was created Baron Somerton (U.K.) in 1873.

42 The primate of all Ireland, the Archbishop of Armagh, sat in the first session, the Archbishop of Dublin in the second session and the Archbishop of Cashel in the third, and the Archbishop of Tuam in the fourth session: see L. O. Pike, *A Constitutional History of the House of Lords* (London, 1894) p. 364–65.

43 (1795) 3 Ridg. PC 366 at 372, above, page 103.

44 (1581) 1 Co. Rep. 88b, 76 E.R. 199.

45 Ball, *Judges in Ireland*, ii.171, 187, 222-3; Cokayne, *Complete Peerage*; Patrick M. Geoghegan, 'Carleton, Hugh', DIB online. [http://dib.cambridge.org/viewReadPage.do?articleId=a1479], accessed 26 February 2013.

46 The serjeants at law had a different history in Ireland to those in England. In England there was an order of serjeants, with their own Inn of Court, Serjeants' Inn and the privilege of an exclusive right of audience before the Court of Common Pleas during term. In Ireland there was originally

in 1779 and MP for Naas in 1783. He was elected a member of the Royal Irish Academy in 1788. He became chief justice of the Common Pleas in January 1788. He was appointed keeper of the Great Seal on Lifford's death until FitzGibbon became Lord Chancellor.[47] He was created Baron Carleton and entered the lords in September 1789. He was created Viscount Carleton in 1797. He was appointed head of a special commission after the rebellion of 1798.

He voted for the Union and was a representative peer of Ireland in 1800. He was made DCL (*honoris causa*) by the University of Oxford in 1810 and died in 1826.

Hugh Carleton was the son of a well-to-do Cork merchant. He belonged to the small group of professional lawyers who took an active part in the work of the lords in its appellate jurisdiction. As chief justice of the Court of Common Pleas, he had no equity jurisdiction, but he clearly had equity experience as counsel, as *Boyle* v. *Lysaght*[48] illustrates. He appeared with FitzGibbon in the case, on opposing sides. Carleton successfully argued that the decree of a renewal on a lease for years with a covenant for perpetual renewal should have the benefit of the same relief in equity as a lease for lives perpetually renewable and that the decree should therefore be upheld.

Carleton came, like other members of the group, not from the landed gentry or aristocracy, but from the middle class who had made their money from trade and business. Also like the others of the group, he owed his position in the Irish Lords to a successful professional career and his peerage came as a result of his career and not from inheritance.

Carleton seems to have been given to melancholy and to hypochondria and he frequently complained of bad health. According to one anecdote, he came

only one serjeant, and even when more were added later, they did not have any exclusive right of audience before the Common Pleas in Dublin. See W. D. Ferguson, *A Treatise on the Practice of the Queen's Bench, Common Pleas and Exchequer of Pleas in Ireland, in Personal Actions and Ejectments* (Dublin, 1841); 'Serjeants at Law' in T. W. Moody, F. J. Byrne and F. X. Martin eds. *A New History of Ireland* vol. IX (Oxford, 1984), pp. 521–25. In 1627 the number of serjeants was increased to two, called the prime and second serjeant. A third serjeant was appointed in 1682. The appointment of third serjeants was apparently intermittent until 1726 when Mr (afterwards Lord Chancellor) Jocelyn was appointed. In 1805 the office of prime serjeant (then vacant) was abolished. The last prime serjeant, Arthur Browne, had died in 1803. The post of first serjeant was created. In England no more serjeants were created after the Judicature Acts of 1875–77 (Eng.) since the Court of Common Pleas disappeared with the creation of the High Court. In Ireland, where the office was not connected to the Common Pleas, it remained until 1922. Existing serjeants kept their titles and so the last serjeant, on either side of the Irish sea, was Serjeant Sullivan QC who was appointed in 1919 and died in 1959. In 1922 he took up practice in England and so also became the last serjeant to practise in England. He published a book entitled *The Last Serjeant* in 1952. See also D. Hogan and W. N. Osborough, eds., *Brehons, Serjeants and Attorneys* (Dublin, 1990).

47 The office was combined with lord chancellor, but it was customary to appoint lord keepers as a temporary measure pending the appointment of a new lord chancellor or during the temporary absence of the chancellor. More than one lord keeper was often appointed. In Ireland it appears to have been customary to appoint a cleric as one of the number: Carleton was appointed together with Robert Fowler, Archbishop of Dublin and Sir Samuel Bradstreet. See P. Brand, 'Chancellors and Keepers of the Great Seal, 1232–1922' in T. W. Moody, F. J. Byrne and F. X. Martin eds., *A New History of Ireland* vol. IX (Oxford, 1984), pp. 521–25.

48 See page 161 note 90.

into court one Nisi Prius day looking more gloomy than usual. He apologised to the bar for having to adjourn proceedings for the day and dismiss the jury. 'I am aware that an important issue stands for trial' he went on, 'but the fact is, I have met with a domestic misfortune, which has altogether deranged my nerves'. 'Poor Lady Carleton', he continued, in a low tone to the bar, 'has most unfortunately had a *fausse couche*', i.e. a miscarriage. John Phillpot Curran, who had been ready to present his case, exclaimed, 'Oh then my Lord, there was no necessity for your Lordship to make any apology; it now appears that your Lordship has no issue to try.' Curran's cruel gibe might have aroused the judge's anger, but Carleton merely smiled and thanked the bar for their consideration.[49] Carleton and his wife never had 'issue.'

Carleton initially resisted the idea of Union, but changed his mind later and voted for it in the end. He may have been holding out for more favourable retirement terms. When Lord Castlereagh sought his support Carleton replied that 'he saw many difficulties in the way.'[50] Nevertheless, he later expressed agreement with FitzGibbon's legal opinion that the Irish parliament was competent to legislate itself out of existence[51] and supported the Union. He retired, ostensibly on health grounds, with a large pension and settled in London where 'for twenty subsequent seasons he continued to enjoy its gaieties with hearty gusto.'[52]

Carleton's speciality was common law property and commercial law. Carleton contributed a number of judgments in the Irish House of Lords in the later period, 1793-96.[53]

In *Mandeville* v. *Lord Carrick*[54] his comment on Agar's intervention[55] shows a concern that the law of property should function in a predictable way. His pleadings in *Boyle* v. *Lysaght*,[56] as counsel in the case, seem to show a similar awareness of the importance of such a policy in the context of property pledged or mortgaged to creditors. The pleadings in the latter case are a lawyer's argument on behalf of his client and cannot, of course, be taken as indicating his own view on the matter. However, one can at least say that his work shows that he had a clear understanding of the requirements of a market economy at a time when it was just becoming a general feature of society. He seems therefore to have been relatively modern in his outlook. This suggests an interesting interpretation of the legal system at the end of the 18th century. Carleton, as chief justice of the Court of Common Pleas, presided over a court which had no equity jurisdiction. The conventional view has long been that equity jurisdiction, with

[49] W. J. Fitzpatrick, *Curious family history; : or, Ireland before the Union, including Lord Chief Justice Clonmell's unpublished diary; a sequel to the Sham squire and the informers of 1798* (Dublin, 1880). p. 164, quoted from Barrington, *Personal Sketches* i.379.

[50] Fitzpatrick, *Ireland before the Union*, p. 165.

[51] *ibid.*, p. 166.

[52] *ibid.*, p. 167.

[53] *Barton* v. *Massey* (1793) 2 Ridg. PC 553; *Blundell* v. *Macartney (No 3)* (1793) 2 Ridg. PC 557; *Mandeville* v. *Carrick (Lord)* (1795) 3 Ridg. PC 352; *Power* v. *Perse* (1796) 3 Ridg. PC 532; *Hayden* v. *Carroll* (1796) 3 Ridg. PC 545.

[54] (1795) 3 Ridg. PC 366.

[55] See page 104.

[56] See page 161 note 90.

its new doctrines and discretionary remedies, relieved the failings of the feudal common law which had become inflexible and rigid. If, however, certainty of result and predictability are requirements of a modern capitalist system, perhaps there is need to re-evaluate the contribution of the common law courts in this period. In the matters the common law courts dealt with, namely property and contract, their insistence on adherence to formality may not have been so old-fashioned as it might appear. There is also a corollary to this point, which is that equity did not always intervene to achieve greater flexibility or with a greater exercise of discretion in this period. The equity to renew leases for lives renewable forever, which is discussed in detail later, is a case in point. It became so extensive that it was granted in almost every case. The equity of redemption in mortgages is another example.

John FitzGibbon (1747–1802), Earl of Clare LC

John FitzGibbon[57] was born in 1747, the son of John FitzGibbon, barrister, of Mount Shannon Co. Limerick. His grandfather, Thomas FitzGibbon, was, according to Oliver Burke, an 'illiterate peasant.'[58] Neither Thomas, nor his wife, Owenney Quain, spoke English, although Owenney was apparently a remarkable woman, known and admired for her acts and sayings in her native Limerick. Thomas's son, John, the father of Lord Clare, had studied in France at St Omer's seminary, although it may not be true that he had become a Catholic priest. On his return he met his younger brother, Thomas, who was was about to go to France for the same reason. John persuaded him to abandon the idea, to conform to the Church of Ireland and to study for the bar. On being told of their intention, their father refused to receive them and was never reconciled to his sons. The local people shunned them and sarcastic verses were composed in Irish, one of which, translated into English, is as follows: 'There is no wrath that does not subside, but the wrath of God against the children of Gibbon.'

The future lord chancellor went to school in Dublin and graduated BA from Trinity College Dublin in 1767 and MA from Oxford, Christ Church, in 1770. He was admitted to the degree of barrister-at-law by King's Inns in 1772. Twenty-eight years later he was to lay the foundation stone of the new King's Inns building, by some irony, on the 1 August 1800, the same day that the Act of Union received the royal assent.[59] He was MP for Dublin University (Trinity

57 E. M. Johnston-Liik and James Quinn, 'FitzGibbon, John', DIB Online. [http://dib.cambridge.org/viewReadPage.do?articleId=a3209], accessed 26 February 2013; Anne Kavanaugh, *John FitzGibbon, Earl of Clare: Protestant Reaction and English Authority in Late Eighteenth-Century Ireland.* (Dublin, 1997) (a critical study of his political career). D. A. Fleming and A.P.W. Malcomson [eds.]. *'A Volley of Execrations': the letters and papers of John FitzGibbon, Earl of Clare 1772-1802* (Dublin, 2005), pp. 178–188. Anne Kavanaugh 'John FitzGibbon, Earl of Clare' in *The United Irishmen: Republicanism, Radicalism and Rebellion.* (Dublin, 1993); A. P. W. Malcomson, *John Foster: The Politics of the Anglo-Irish Ascendancy* (Oxford, 1978); W. N. Osborough 'FitzGibbon' in A. W. B. Simpson, *Biographical Dictionary of the Common Law* (London, 1984); E. FitzGibbon, *The Earl of Clare, Mainspring of the Union* (1960) (a hagiographical study by a relative).

58 O. Burke, *The History of the Lord Chancellors of Ireland*, p. 147.

59 Colum Kenny, *King's Inns and the Kingdom of Ireland: the Irish 'Inn of Court' 1541–1800.* Dublin, 1992, p. 261.

College Dublin), 1778-83 and for Kilmallock, 1783-89. He was made LLD (*honors causa*) by Trinity College Dublin in 1779. He became attorney general in 1783 and sworn of the Privy Council in the same year. He fought a duel with John Phillpot Curran in 1785.[60] He became lord chancellor in June 1789 and was created Baron FitzGibbon in the same month. He was sworn of the British Privy Council in 1790. He became speaker of the Irish House of Lords in 1790 and was vice-chancellor of Dublin University, 1791-1802. He was created Viscount FitzGibbon in 1793, and Earl of Clare in 1795. He was created Baron FitzGibbon (G.B.) in 1799. He lived at 6 Ely Place, Dublin.[61] which his father had bought and which was his boyhood home, and Mount Shannon, Co. Clare, which is now a ruin.[62] He died in 1802, following a fall from his horse. The fall occurred at Mount Shannon and FitzGibbon was to travel to England for treatment, but died at 6 Ely Place, Dublin and was buried in St Peter's, Dublin.

FitzGibbon's career is remarkable, in the context of the time, given that he was the son of a Catholic father who had conformed to the established church and grandson of a farmer. It was due without doubt to his intellectual gifts and abilities as a lawyer and his ruthless ambition. He rose to become not only lord chancellor but also effectively the leader of the Protestant ascendancy and the architect of the Union.

He was the key figure in the House of Lords at the end of the century and the most powerful figure in the government of Ireland before the Union. Although slight and small in stature, FitzGibbon was of strong and determined character and had outstanding intellectual gifts. He also demonstrated considerable moral courage. One instance of this was when he was attorney general. In 1784 Napper Tandy had directed sheriffs to summon meetings for the election of delegates to the proposed national convention demanding reform.[63] Reilly, the high sheriff of Dublin had summoned freeholders to meet to elect delegates. FitzGibbon wrote him accusing him of 'a most outrageous breach of duty' and threatening to prosecute him in the King's Bench. Reilly called the meeting anyway and was amusing the audience by reading FitzGibbon's letter, when the attorney general walked into the room and repeated his threat in front of the assembled company. Reilly was overawed by this and the meeting dispersed. It was a rare and perhaps unique example of an attorney general personally enforcing the law. FitzGibbon did not let the matter rest there, and moved in the King's Bench for for an attachment against Reilly as an officer who had abused his commission. The judges upheld FitzGibbon and were attacked for doing so in the House of Commons by Curran and others. Pitt thought the whole matter one of 'great delicacy and caution', but such were not FitzGibbon's methods. The 1790s saw the emergence of the United Irishmen into a mass

[60] Below, page 117.

[61] It is now occupied by commercial offices, but the interior, with its fine staircase and ceilings are intact and have been restored.

[62] Joe Carroll and Pat Touhy, *Village by Shannon: the Story of Castleconnell and its Hinterland* (Ireland, 1991)

[63] Edward Gibson, Lord Ashbourne, *Pitt: Some Chapters of his Life and Times* (London, 1898), pp. 251–252.

revolutionary organisation and FitzGibbon supported the most severe repressive measures to defeat it. In particular he earned the hatred of the radicals when he led a a visitation of Trinity College Dublin in April 1798 to question fellows and students about their political sympathies, and expelled nineteen students whom he suspected of being United men.[64]

FitzGibbon's great intellectual gifts were combined with an arrogant, ruthless and sometimes vengeful personality. As a rising lawyer and politician, FitzGibbon had vehemently opposed the granting of political power to Catholics and never altered his opinion. This may be attributed to cynical ambition, but probably also came from a deeper need to find acceptance in a class of contemporaries who were not inclined to trust him because of the Catholic roots of his family. It seems to have begun as a kind of over-compensation, a wish to prove himself, but it persisted long after he reached such a position of eminence that he could have safely moderated his attitude. His personality did not rise to the occasion of his eminence. He reluctantly accepted the reforms of 1782, probably because outright opposition would have harmed his career, but he opposed giving Catholics the right to sit in parliament and was able to speak without shame of the dangers of 'papist democracy'. He is also credited (or rather, debited,) with persuading George III not to agree to the enfranchisement of Catholics which Pitt had intended would coincide with the establishment of the Union. Pitt resigned over the issue[65] and so if FitzGibbon was instrumental in that, it must represent, second to his persuading the king as to the Union, one of the high points of his influence.

In other respects, FitzGibbon's political attitudes were not predictably reactionary. In 1791 the journeymen carpenters won a large pay increase. This so annoyed the building masters that they collaborated to produce a new combination bill which would impose severe penalties on attempts by workers to combine together to improve their conditions.[66] The obvious irony was that combining together is just what the building masters had done in order to produce the bill. The bill was passed by the House of Commons,[67] but FitzGibbon spoke against it in the House of Lords. He attacked it as representing a 'system of oppression and injustice' and said that it should have been called 'a bill for the encouragement of outlawries and highway robberies.'[68] He feared that it would encourage violence on buildings sites in Dublin. Journeymen carpenters organised marches and rallies in the Liberties and the Phoenix Park and the bill failed to pass the Lords.[69]

To what extent FitzGibbon's attitude to Catholics was a public stance, rather than a genuine and deeply–held opinion, is open to question. The experience of

64 C. J. Woods, 'FitzGibbon, John' in DIB online.

65 William Hague, *William Pitt The Younger*, pp. 464–477.

66 Brian Henry, *Dublin Hanged: Crime, Law Enforcement and Punishment in Late 18th-century Dublin* (1994), p. 75;

67 *ibid.*, p. 76; Mr Graydon and Mr Vandeleur, 'a bill to prevent unlawful combinations of journeymen artificers,' 10 March 1792, 15 *J. Ir. H.C.* Pt. 1 pp. 90, 93, 101, 103.

68 Henry (1994), p. 76.

69 *ibid.*

his father, whose admission as a barrister had met opposition, must have had some effect on the son. Wallace, in his study of the law reporters[70] includes a note on FitzGibbon's father, who had published a set of reports of English cases while still a student,[71] and which are reproduced in volume 94 of the *English Reports*. The reports were not well received in England, having been published without the permission of the judges.[72] In Ireland his admission to the bar in 1733 was 'violently opposed by a Protestant faction of King's Inn [*sic*], who having, probably, no better ground to oppose him, contended that the publication of his reports was a direct contempt against the judges of England.'[73] But there was a suspicion that the real reason was that the Protestant faction doubted the genuineness of his converison or at least that such doubts added to the vehemence of their opposition. At this time FitzGibbon could not have become a barrister under the Penal Laws without taking the oaths renouncing the Catholic faith.[74] O'Flanagan,[75] in his account of the incident, asserts that FitzGibbon senior had 'conformed to the religion then established by the State'. This is borne out by an entry in the Convert Rolls showing a John FitzGibbon of Dublin who is listed as having a certificate dated 20 November 1731 and enrolled on 23 November of the same year.[76] O'Flanagan further comments that the reports 'display great ability and accuracy, but not having the stamp of official fiat by the judges, were not recognised as entitled to the weight of authority; though Lord Hardwicke,[77] while regretting their want of authority, admitted their accuracy.' He added in a footnote[78] that the work:

> ...displays very great knowledge of common law and equity, for the points are stated with great clearness, and the judgments very lucidly and tersely given. The great objection was to their having been published by an unauthorised reporter, without the sanction of the judges, who complained very bitterly of having rank nonsense put into their mouths, and I suspect sent such representations to the Irish benches as nearly demolished FitzGibbon's chance of being admitted to the Irish Bar. It is clear that he would not have been allowed to practise in England.

Despite the opposition of some of the benchers of King's Inns, the lord chancellor, Wyndham, and the chief justice of the Common Pleas, Reynolds, supported FitzGibbon senior's admission on the ground that he had fulfilled all the legal requirements. The benchers yielded.

70 'FitzGibbon' in J. W. Wallace, *The Reporters: Arranged and Characterized with Incidental Remarks* (Boston, 1882), pp. 427–30.

71 1728–1733, King's Bench, Common Pleas, Exchequer and Chancery.

72 Wallace, *The Reporters*, p. 427; J. R. O'Flanagan, *Lives of the Lord Chancellors and Keepers of the Great Seal of Ireland* (London, 1870), ii.61-62, and see below.

73 Wallace, *The Reporters*, p. 428.

74 Above, page 8.

75 J. R. O'Flanagan, *Lives of the Lord Chancellors* 2 vols. (London, 1870), ii.61.

76 Eileen O'Byrne, ed., *The Convert Rolls*. (Dublin, 1981) p. 103.

77 Philip Yorke, 1st Earl of Hardwicke (1690–1764), LC (Eng.).

78 O'Flanagan, ii.61 n. 3.

The incident is more important for the present purpose in the effect it may have had on the son. It must surely have been related to him in his youth. It must have impressed upon him the force of sectarian suspicion even against converts and may therefore have contributed to his own later display of opposition to the Catholic interest as a response. The role of Wyndham and Reynolds, both Englishmen, may also have impressed him with the importance of adherence to the rule of law, both as a way forward for families in his position and also as a discipline to one whose mind tended towards discipline. It seems that there were malicious gibes by other members of the Ascendancy about FitzGibbon's origins and this must have had an impact on his attitudes. He may never have felt wholly secure as a member of the Protestant Ascendancy, even though at the height of his career he was paradoxically, its leading figure. His public opposition to Catholicism was often exaggerated, even by the standards of his own time and class. This suggests that there may have been an element of defensiveness, as if he constantly had to prove his loyalty. Outwardly, at least, he was an implacable enemy of Catholic emancipation and was the main force behind the movement for Union with Great Britain, which he saw as the only way of preventing the further emancipation of Catholics.

In *Redington* v. *Redington*[79] FitzGibbon gave judgment in a case on the Penal Laws affecting property. In the case itself he recognised as valid a conveyance which was intended as a device to avoid the Penal Laws, but the position was more complex than this might suggest. It is considered below.[80]

Although an able lawyer, his wit was no match for John Phillpot Curran. During legal argument FitzGibbon accused him of splitting verbal hairs. 'To me the words you seek to differentiate, "also" and "likewise", seem clearly synonymous', he said. 'No fanciful distinction, my lord,' Curran shot back. 'My lord, the great Lord Lifford for many years presided over this court. You also preside, but not *likewise*'.[81] Although Curran's gibe, which was wholly unjustified, won the verbal battle, the effect on his Chancery practice was disastrous. Attorneys wanted decisions in their favour and they believed that Curran would not get them before FitzGibbon. Curran lost the whole of his Chancery practice and, probably unfairly, never forgave FitzGibbon.

Curran and FitzGibbon had not always expressed their animosity in mere words. In 1785, while FitzGibbon was attorney general, he fought a duel with Curran. On that occasion also it was Curran's tongue which got him into trouble. Curran and FitzGibbon had clashed in the House of Commons on 12 August 1785 during the debate on the admission of the government's bill for reaching a commercial settlement with Great Britain.[82] They exchanged words and Curran, as later, got the better of the exchange. FitzGibbon then bitterly remarked that 'Curran was no lawyer and that the monstrous nonsense that came from him

79 (1794) 3 Ridg. PC 201.
80 See "Law and Politics: Penal Laws"
81 Leslie Hale, *John Philpot Curran* (London, 1958) p. 72.
82 Hale, *John Philpot Curran*, p. 71; James Kelly, *That Damn'd Thing Called Honour: Duelling in Ireland 1570-1860*. (Cork, 1995), pp. 137–38.

was fit only for Sadler's Wells.' This provoked the duel, but no injuries to either side resulted from it. It was arranged that both should fire on a signal. Curran did so, and missed. FitzGibbon took long and careful aim, but also missed, and stormed off the field. Curran shouted after him: 'It wasn't your fault, Mr Attorney; you were deliberate enough.'

A landowner might have accused Curran of not being a gentleman, and perhaps of being a bad horseman to boot. FitzGibbon accuses him of being a bad lawyer. This was the insult of a professional and a professional who valued the standards of his profession.

FitzGibbon as lord chancellor was the dominant figure in the later House of Lords as the final court of appeal in Ireland before the Union, first, in the number of judgments he delivered which was far in excess of that of the other members, and also through the force of his personality. He was intellectually the superior of most of those around him, but most of the time was polite and condescending, in the positive 18th century sense of the word. One exception seems to have been his attitude to the elderly Pery, whose opinions he dismissed abruptly and rather rudely on at least one occasion, probably due to Pery's support for a distinct Irish political identity.[83] It may also be that he deserved Hale's harsh description of him as 'warm in his friendship and implacable in his animosities, hating powerful talents because he feared them and trampling on modest merit because it was incapable of resistance.'[84]

FitzGibbon played a more major role in the work of the House of Lords than the other judges. Carleton, Scott (as Baron Earlsfort and later Earl of Clonmell) and Yelverton as heads of the other superior courts were occupied with the business of those courts, but they played a less active role in the Lords than Fitzgibbon who in addition was head of the Court of Chancery and so his contribution to the work of the Lords is all the more remarkable.

FitzGibbon displayed a considerable grasp of equity. In *Kenney* v. *Browne*[85] a case in which a tenant sought to establish an estoppel against a landlord, FitzGibbon, as Lord Clare LC, stated an equitable principle of estoppel in terms broad enough to foreshadow modern doctrine of proprietary estoppel. The case is considered in more detail below.[86]

A good example of his analytical skills is provided by *Deane* v. *Marquis of Waterford*[87] where he was called upon to interpret the test of reasonable period of time after a demand for renewal under the Tenantry Act. Rather than make general pronouncements, he developed a series of tests.[88] First, he proposed that one look at what the parties themselves regarded as a reasonable period in the conditions in the lease as to the time for renewal after a fall of one of the lives. The conditions were not dealing with a period after a demand, but seemed to

83 See below, page 128.

84 Hale, *John Philpot Curran*, p. 69.

85 (1796) 3 Ridg. PC 462, at 518, For the pleadings see 'House of Lords Appeals (Pleadings) 1787–90', vol. 47, King's Inns Library.

86 Below, page 166.

87 (1795) 1 Sch. & Lef. 451, reported as a note.

88 See page 155.

provide the most cogent analogy. He then drew on a more remote analogy: the statute laying down a period as to bringing ejectment for non-payment of rent. It was, nevertheless, drawn from a legal source and not merely his own subjective view of what was reasonable. Nor was he simply deciding what was reasonable on the facts: he was giving a guide to future judges as to how to proceed in such a case. Again, this was all subject to values of 'fairness' and equity which might provide an excuse for an otherwise excessive period.

FitzGibbon's record reveals a complex personality and a certain integrity and fearlessness. We refer below to the notion that, while law functioned to legitimate the rule of a relatively small class, the form of law required a degree of integrity.[89] The rule of law requires a distinction to be made between legal and political decisions, that individuals are equal before the law, etc. This produces a conflict of opposites, for such values, if they were fully realised, would transcend the mere legitimation of class rule. The Penal Laws were a major constraint on that integrity, but that is not to say that such values were entirely absent. There were elements of them in the legal system at the time and in the minds of those who operated it. It is also no doubt true that opinions as to the degree of integrity to be applied in maintaining the form of law varied between individuals in the 18th century, as it does today. FitzGibbon was among those who seems to have had a strong belief in the integrity of the legal system and the rule of law. One example was his wish to strengthen the law on champerty, expressed in his judgment in *Kenney* v. *Browne*:[90]

> It is a crime at common law to maintain a suit, in which the man maintaining is not interested, and the peculiar species of maintenance of which the appellant has been guilty is called champerty, – that is, maintaining a suit in consideration of having some part of the thing in dispute. The rule of the common law is, *Culpa est se immiscere rei ad se non pertinenti*,[91] – and, *pendente lite nihil innovetur*,[92] 2 Inst. 208...The most mischievous practice is further restrained by three several statutes, all of force in this kingdom...[93] These statutes, very much to the injury of society, have fallen so much into disuse, that, I believe, in the memory of man, there has not been an instance in which they have been executed according to the letter. In my judgment, their disuse has been essentially injurious to society, and I should wish to see some public examples of men prosecuted to justice for breach of these most salutary laws.

[89] Below, page 168.

[90] (1796) 3 Ridg. PC at 498–500 .

[91] It is a fault to meddle in a matters that do not concern one.

[92] During litigation nothing new should be introduced. Co. Litt. 344.

[93] 10 Cha. I, sess. 3, c. 15 (Ir.), 1634; 10 & 11 Cha. I, c. 11 (Ir.), 1635, s. 5. 10 Cha. I, sess. 3, c. 15, s. 2 provided that all statutes in force in England against maintenance, champerty and embracery were to be in force Ireland and therefore applied 32 Hen. VIII, c. 9, (Eng.), 1540. Embracery was the crime of attempting corruptly to influence a jury to find in favour of one side or other in a trial. Today, it would be charged as an attempt to pervert the course of justice.

He also drew a distinction between his political views and his legal function as a judge. His political opposition to Catholic emancipation is not reflected in any evident bias against Catholics in his legal opinions, while, on the other hand, his belief in legal equality did not translate into support for the emancipation of Catholics. It is the division in his mind between these two areas which is distinctively legal.

FitzGibbon did have at least one other redeeming feature. He was not a hypocrite. Many of his colleagues represented the movement for greater independence for the Ascendancy as a genuinely nationalist movement, although they had no intention of accepting the consequences, namely, full Catholic emancipation. FitzGibbon suffered from no such delusions and clearly perceived the dangers, from the Protestant perspective. His remarkable speech in 1789, noted above,[94] pointing out that the 'patriots' who called for independence derived the titles to their land from 'an act of violence, an act palpably subverting the first principles of the common law of England and Ireland', is testimony to that. The final irony of his life was that the achievement of the Union destroyed his own position of power. It could be said of him that he selflessly sacrificed himself on the altar of bigotry and oppression.

There is a portrait of Fitzgibbon by Gilbert Stuart,[95] an American, who is widely considered to be one of the foremost portrait painters of the 18th century. The original portrait now hangs in the Cleveland Museum of Art, in Cleveland, Ohio.[96] Copies are owned by King's Inns and Trinity College Dublin, although they do not quite capture the arrogant expression evident in the original. There is no indication that FitzGibbon disapproved of the portrait, however. Mount[97] recounts an anecdote which gives an insight into the characters of both Stuart and FitzGibbon:

[94] Above page 32.

[95] Gilbert Charles Stuart (1755 – 1828), David Rodgers, *Oxford Companion to Western Art*, [http://www.oxfordartonline.com:80/ subscriber/article/opr/t118/e2528], accessed 30 November 2009; John Wilson, Stuart, Gilbert Charles (1755–1828), ODNB online. [http://www.oxforddnb.com/view/article/26705], accessed 28 November 2009; John Coleman, 'Stuart, Gilbert Charles', DIB online 2010. Stuart took the last ship to leave Boston for England on the eve of Bunker Hill, 16 June 1775: Eleanor Pearson DeLorme, 'Gilbert Stuart: Portrait of an Artist', Winterthur Portfolio, Vol. 14, No. 4 (Winter, 1979), pp. 339–360. Stuart returned to what had become by then the United States in 1793, in order, as he told friends, to be able to paint the portrait of George Washington, the new president, and so establish his reputation there. His best-known work is the unfinished portrait of George Washington, known as *The Athenæum*. It was begun in 1796 and left incomplete at the time of Stuart's death in 1828. The image of Washington featured in the painting has appeared on the United States one-dollar bill for over a century.

[96] L. P., *Gilbert Stuart's Portrait of Lord FitzGibbon*, Bulletin of the Cleveland Museum of Art, Vol. 7, No. 1 (Jan., 1920), pp. 3–5 (Cleveland Museum of Art), Stable URL: [http://www.jstor.org/stable/25136337]. The portrait, on the death of the 3rd Earl in 1864, came into the possession of A. J. Beresford–Hope, of Bedgebury, Kent, a descendant of the 1st earl's sister. In May 1919 the Bedgebury estate was sold, and the painting bought by a New York dealer who took it to the United States. It was acquired by The Cleveland Museum of Art in May 1920.

[97] Charles Merrill Mount, *Gilbert Stuart: a biography* (Toronto, 1964), p. 135. The source is apparently James Dowling, an acquaintance of Stuart: J. D. Herbert [James Dowling], *Irish Varieties* (London, 1836). Mount, *Gilbert Stuart*, pp. 335, 344.

> Few invitations to FitzGibbon's home in Ely Place were refused, and Stuart appears to have been a frequent guest. To be among the associates of the all-powerful Lord Chancellor was advantageous, for this now was the centre of patronage and real power. Just as the cloth was removed after dinner one evening a gentleman came in, looking rather confused from not being on time. Lord FitzGibbon ordered a servant to place a small table on one side and provide him with dinner.
>
> 'You must try and make the best of it,' he explained. 'It was your own fault; we waited half an hour.'
>
> To the artist, seated beside him, Lord FitzGibbon said, 'Now, Stuart, you are so accustomed to look all men in the face who come before you; you must be a good judge of character. Do you know that gentleman at the side table?'
> 'No, my lord, I never saw him before.'
> 'Well, now tell me what sort of man he is in disposition.'
> 'Is he a friend?'
> 'No.'
> 'Then I may speak frankly?'
> 'Yes.'
> 'Why then, my lord, if the Almighty ever wrote a legible hand, he is the greatest rascal that ever disgraced society.'
> FitzGibbon laughed his immoderate appreciation and explained to Stuart how right he had been.

The man was apparently an attorney and had been accused of some impropriety in his affairs. FitzGibbon, as a barrister and judge, was no doubt conscious of the need to form an opinion of the character and truthfulness of witnesses, and it must have occurred to him that a portrait painter might have developed the same skill.

FitzGibbon's son and heir, John, the 2nd Earl of Clare, a friend of the poet Lord Byron from their school days, and later governor of Bombay (1830–34), died in 1851 without issue. FitzGibbon's second son, Richard Hobart FitzGibbon (1792–1851), became the 3rd Earl of Clare. Both of the first earl's sons supported Catholic emancipation. The 3rd earl's son, Lt John, Viscount FitzGibbon (1829–1854?)[98] was a lieutenant in the 8th Hussars and was wounded and reported missing in the Charge of the Light Brigade at Balaclava in 1854, when he was aged 25. His body was never found.[99] The 3rd earl died in 1864 without surviving issue and the title became extinct.

98 David Murphy, 'FitzGibbon, John Charles Henry' DIB online. [http://dib.cambridge.org/viewReadPage.do?articleId=a3210], accessed 28 February 2013; David Murphy, *Ireland and the Crimean War* (Portland, Oreg., 2002).

99 William M. Lummis and Kenneth G. Wynn, in their book, *Honour the Light Brigade* (J. B. Hayward, 1973), p. 74, which is a list of all those who took part in the Charge, records that Viscount FitzGibbon (which was his courtesy title) was made cornet, on 13 March 1850, and lieutenant on 27 June 1851. Witnesses of the Charge said he was hit in the chest by two bullets after Captain Nolan

James Hewitt (1715–1789), Viscount Lifford LC

James Hewitt[100] was born in 1714 or 1715,[101] the son of William Hewitt, a mercer and mayor of Coventry in 1744, and his wife Hannah. James was the pupil of a Warwickshire attorney but decided to become a barrister. He was called to the bar by Middle Temple in 1742. According to Oliver Burke[102] he came to prominence as a result of the riots following the introduction of the Gregorian calendar in 1752. The British statute 24 Geo. II, c. 23, 1750 (also known as Chesterfield's Act, after Philip Stanhope, 4th Earl of Chesterfield) changed the old Julian calendar to the Gregorian calendar promulgated by Pope Gregory XIII in 1582, since it was found that the old calendar was eleven days behind the actual or solar one, so that, for example, Easter no longer coincided with the spring equinox and Midsummer's Day no longer coincided with the actual longest day. The latter caused problems for agriculture, where it was essential to sow certain crops at certain times, and on certain traditional days, if they were to mature properly. The statute provided that 2 September 1752 (Julian) was to be followed by 14 September 1752 (Gregorian), thus omitting the eleven days, 3 to 13 September inclusive, and that the change was to apply 'throughout all His Majesty's dominions and countries in Europe, Asia, Africa and America, belonging or subject to the Crown of Great Britain'.[103] The statute also provided for a change in the 'supputation' of the year, namely that the civil (legal and ecclesiastical) year was to begin on 1 January, starting with 1 January 1752, and not 25 March, as had been the case since the 14th century.[104] A number of riots took place in 1753, although the extensive literature on riots in the 18th century has not shown that were any riots specifically on the absurd demand of 'Give us back our eleven days!'[105] Hewitt represented some of the rioters, in some cases

was killed. There is a story that he was captured, was held in Siberia and eventually returned to England about 1870, but despite appeals in newspapers to come forward, he never appeared. David Murphy, 'FitzGibbon, John Charles Henry' DIB.

100 WHP, MS 522; Andrew Lyall, 'Hewitt, James, 1st Viscount Lifford (d. 1789)', ODNB online. [http://www.oxforddnb.com/view/ article/13149], accessed 26 May 2009. W. N. Osborough, 'Hewitt, James 1st Viscount Lifford', DIB online. [http://dib.cambridge.org/viewReadPage.do?articleId=a3976], accessed 26 February 2013.

101 Cokayne, *Complete Peerage* gives his date of birth as 'probably' 1709: vii.651.

102 O. Burke, *The History of the Lord Chancellors of Ireland*, p. 140-2.

103 Section 1. Thus an example of the British parliament legislating for both Ireland and the North American colonies.

Section 2 of the Act, with remarkable prescience, provided that the century years 1800, 1900, 2100, 2200 and 2300 should be common years of 365 days and not leap years, while only every fourth century year should be a leap year of 366 days, namely 2000, 2400, and 2800, and so on.

104 *ibid.* The year 1752 therefore consisted of only 354 days. The historical or conventional year had long been treated as beginning on 1 January, and so for dates between 1 January and the 25 March before 1752, the practice was to put the legal year first followed by the historical year, e.g. '30 January 1648/9'. This is still followed by historians for dates before 1752. For dates from 1752 onwards only the latter year is required, and is known as 'modern style', i.e. the year beginning on the 1 January.

105 Robert Poole, ' "Give Us Our Eleven Days!": Calendar Reform in Eighteenth-Century England'. (1995) 149 *Past & Present*, pp. 95–139, [http://www.jstor.org/stable/651100], accessed: 1 November 2009. It may be that some ignorant people actually believed that they were being deprived of eleven days of their life, but the myth of specific 'eleven days' riots seemingly had its origin in a cartoon

successfully, and his appearance in the high profile cases benefited his career. The bar at least had no reason to deplore the adoption of the new calendar.[106]

Hewitt became serjeant in England in 1755 and king's serjeant in 1759. He was elected MP for Coventry in 1761 and became judge of King's Bench in England in 1766. He was appointed lord chancellor in Ireland on 24 November 1767[107] with the title of Baron Lifford. There is nothing to indicate whether he had any connection with the town of Lifford in Co. Donegal. It was not a popular appointment at the time, as it was thought that there were better qualified Irish candidates, particularly Anthony Malone, the attorney general, Philip Tisdall and the prime serjeant, Hely Hutchinson.[108] However, the 'English party' won, Hewitt owing his appointment to the influence of Lord Camden, the English lord chancellor[109] whose protégé he had been in England. Lord Mansfield had derided his appointment as justice of the King's Bench in England.[110] Lord Lifford nevertheless showed adaptability in his sympathy for the Irish position on the equity to renew leases for lives. Mansfield's low opinion of Lifford's professional qualities may also explain why, in the British House of Lords in *Kane* v. *Hamilton*,[111] he reversed Lifford's judgment on the issue. Mansfield mistook for an error, or excessive exercise of jurisdiction, what was in fact a genuine understanding of the Irish law on the subject, adopted by Lifford after he had consulted widely with experienced Irish practitioners,[112] and what was itself a response to conditions prevailing in Ireland. Lifford had to wait until the passing of the Tenantry Act 1780 and the decision in *O'Neil* v. *Jones*[113] and later cases to see his position vindicated. His decisions in the Irish Court of Chancery are reported in a volume edited by James Lyne from notes by John Wallis, known as *Wallis by Lyne*.[114]

Lifford dissented on a vote of thanks to the Volunteers. He was created Viscount Lifford in 1781. In 1784 on he presided over a committee to approve revised plans for the new Four Courts building.[115] Thomas Cooley (1740–1784)

by Hogarth, showing a riot in an election campaign with the slogan on a placard: William Hogarth, 'An Election Entertainment', print, 1755. Some people may have had genuine cause for complaint, although the Act itself provided that nothing in the Act should accelerate demands by landlords for rent, or accelerate other payments such as annuities, or attaining the age of majority: s. 6. It is possible, however, that some landlords ignored the section. The new calendar was also denounced, with equal absurdity, by some Protestants, as a 'Popish calendar' because it changed the date of Easter: O. Burke, *The History of the Lord Chancellors of Ireland*, p. 140.

106 *ibid.*

107 *The Scots Magazine*, James Boswell, ed. (Edinburgh) 1789 Vol 51. p. 258.

108 Ball, *Judges in Ireland*, ii.156. According to *The Scots Magazine* (Edinburgh) 1789 Vol 51. p. 258, the office had been offered to Baron Smythe, Judge Aston and Mr Sewell, the master of the rolls.

109 Peter D. G. Thomas, 'Pratt, Charles, first Earl Camden (1714–1794)', ODNB online. [http://www.oxforddnb.com/view/article/22699], accessed 30 June 2009.

110 Ball, *Judges in Ireland*, ii.157.

111 Below, page 152.

112 Below, page 153.

113 (1785) 1 Ridg. PC 175. See below, page 158.

114 See below, 'Bibliography', page 263.

115 C. P. Curran, 'Cooley, Gandon and the Four Courts' in Costello, Caroline, ed., *The Four Courts: 200 Years: Essays to commemorate the Bicentenary of the Four Courts*, p. 111. Dublin, 1996.

the original architect had died and James Gandon was commissioned to complete the design. Lifford died in office in April 1789 and was buried in Christ Church Cathedral, Dublin. He does not seem to have been particularly diligent in his duties and left a large backlog of cases at his death.

Lifford was the last English lord chancellor before the Union and preceded FitzGibbon as chancellor. He held the office for 21 years and six months,[116] longer than anyone since Edward I's time, and longer than anyone since the Conquest except two, namely Stephen Ridel in the reign of Richard I and Formund le Brun in that of Henry III.[117] His family remained in Ireland and a younger son, Joseph Hewitt, became a judge of the Irish King's Bench.[118]

William Hewitt (1719-1781), the younger brother of Lifford, had a more remarkable life, and death, than his brother. He was the owner of slave plantations in the West Indies. In 1767 he had been appointed, through his elder brother's intercession, a commissioner for the sale and disposal of lands in the ceded islands in the West Indies.[119] He was appointed commissioner 'for adjusting the differences that have arisen or may arise in respect to sales and leases of lands in the islands of Grenada, the Grenadines, St Vincent, Dominica, and Tobago'. He became an owner of plantations, and hence a slave owner, in his own right. The work of the commission ended in 1771 and William Hewitt returned to England in 1776 where he remained for some time. William lost his estates on Dominica when it fell to the French in 1778. This left considerable debts, especially as he was never paid his salary or expenses by the British treasury for the period 1776–1781. In an effort to retrieve the situation he returned to the West Indies but was 'driven from island to island by the French'.[120] While he was staying in Barbados his house was demolished by a hurricane and he was buried for a while among the ruins. He lay injured for some time but was rescued and went to St Eustatius to recover with the intention of returning to England, but died there on 16 May 1781, apparently from the injuries he had sustained.[121]

William's slave plantation, some 190 acres in the parish of St Andrew's, Dominica, was named the Lifford Estate, after the title of his brother, the lord chancellor of Ireland.[122] His affection for his brother's title and other names associated with the family did not end there. Like other slave owners he refused to recognise the original African names of his captives and imposed on them those of his own choice. A lease which he made of some of his slaves records that one of them, a woman, was called 'Lifford'. Eight other female slaves were

[116] Note, in 2 Ridg. PC 143.

[117] *The Scots Magazine* (Edinburgh) 1789 Vol 51. p. 258. Ridel held the office for thirty-three years and le Brun for twenty-four. According to Ball, *Judges in Ireland*, le Brun became chancellor in 1268, was removed from that office in 1273, but is mentioned as chancellor again in 1276. He died in 1283. Ball says le Brun became owner of Roebuck near Dublin in 1261. Roebuck Castle currently houses the School of Law, University College Dublin.

[118] In 1792. The appointment is noted in 2 Ridg. PC 445.

[119] WHP, MS 522.

[120] Letter, Lifford to Sir Grey Cooper, Bart, 31 December 1781, WHP, MS 522/466–507.

[121] *ibid.*, Handlist, 2nd deposit, Paul Kelly, London, 1972, p. 15 note re William's death.

[122] MS 522/505 map of Wm. Hewitt's estate.

leased 'to have and to hold to him the said Francis Powars his executors and administrators and assigns for and during the term of five years'.[123] Other deeds in his possession at his death include the grant of an annuity in exchange for slaves,[124] a sale of slaves,[125] and the hire of a slave.[126] He had also leased 42 slaves to Powars on mortgage.[127] One sale of slaves in favour of John Woodville, in exchange for an annuity, records that one of the slaves was called 'Coventry', no doubt named after the city of origin of the Hewitt family, and the grant was 'to have and to hold the said slaves and every of them with the future issue of the females'.[128]

William seems to have died intestate,[129] Lifford had not only been responsible for introducing his brother into the practice of slavery, but as the administrator of his estate, Lifford would have become himself, in that capacity, a slave owner. There seems a certain irony in that, given that the lord chancellor of Ireland was head of a court of conscience and equity.

James Hewitt (1751–1830), the eldest son of Lifford, succeeded his father as 2nd viscount in 1789, and had acted as clerk to William in the West Indies from 1777 to 1781. He took holy orders and was dean of Armagh from 1796 to 1830.

Barry Maxwell (1723–1800), Earl of Farnham

Barry Maxwell[130] was son of John Maxwell, 1st Baron Farnham and was the heir of Robert Maxwell, 2nd Baron Farnham. He was admitted to the degree of barrister-at-law by King's Inns in 1748. He became a master of the bench of King's Inns in 1757. He was MP for Cavan, 1756–60 (as his father had also been) and MP for Armagh, 1761–68. He was prothonotary of the Court of Common Pleas, 1741–1800. He inherited the barony in 1779 from his eldest brother, Robert, the second brother, John, having died young and unmarried in 1778, a year before their father. Barry was created Viscount Farnham in 1781 and Earl of Farnham in 1785. He was sworn of the Privy Council of Ireland in 1796. He died on 7 October 1800, in Dublin.

Barry Maxwell was on the borderline between lay and professional members. He owed his membership of the House to inheritance, rather than rising through the legal profession. He had never been made a judge of one of the lower courts, but nevertheless was a prothonotary of the Court of Common Pleas, a position which was analogous to a master and so had minor judicial functions attached to it, and indeed continued to hold that position while a member of the Lords until his death. His father, John Maxwell, had also been a prothonotary of the Court of Common Pleas, and MP for Cavan. John had married the daughter of

123 Lease of slaves. 1 August 1768. Dominica. WHP, MS 522/184.
124 WHP, MS 522/185.
125 WHP, MS 522/189.
126 WHP, MS 522/195.
127 WHP, MS 522/201.
128 Sale of slaves. 21 December 1769, WHP, MS 522/186.
129 MS 522/467, Letter, draft, 15 December 1781, unaddressed re death of Wm. Hewitt.
130 Cokayne, *Complete Peerage*, v. 258; Kidd, Charles, Williamson, David (eds). *Debrett's Peerage and Baronetage* (1990 edition).

another prothonotary, James Barry, so both Barry Maxwell's father and father-in-law were prothonotaries. It may be that Barry owed more than his title to inheritance.

As Lord Farnham, he spoke on three occasions in the lords.[131] Two of them were cases on leases for life renewable forever.[132]

Hervey Morres (c. 1743–1797), Viscount Mountmorres

Hervey Redmond Morres[133] delivered one speech as a lay member in *Magrath* v. *Lord Muskerry*[134] against the view that the Irish House of Lords should be able to re-hear an appeal. He published his speech in his *The history of the principal transactions of the Irish Parliament, from the year 1634 to 1666.*[135] The lords reached the same conclusion, although whether they were influenced by Morres's arguments is less clear. Ridgeway described his speech, interpreting the standing orders of the House, as 'extremely ingenious', and 'displaying profound parliamentary knowledge', but he was not himself convinced.[136] Morres also published *An historical dissertation upon the origin, suspension, and revival, of the judicature and independency of the Irish Parliament . . . With a narrative of the transactions in 1719, relative to the celebrated declaratory law*[137] and several other works, including *Impartial reflections upon the question, for equalizing the duties, upon the trade, between Great Britain and Ireland*[138] and *The prodigal: or, marriage a-la-mode. A comedy, in five acts.*[139]

Morres attended Oxford University and graduated MA in 1766 and was awarded the DCL in 1773.[140] He was elected FRS in 1793. Morres was the nephew of John Ponsonby, speaker of the Irish House of Commons. He took his seat in the lords in October 1767. In August 1785 he attended the Irish House of Lords in the uniform of the Volunteers, and was a supporter of the English radical and campaigner for liberties, John Wilkes. In February 1789 he spoke in support of Pitt's refusal to sanction an unrestricted regency, and his speech was published in 1790. It included an historical survey of regency in the English constitution since the Conquest.[141] Horace Walpole described him as 'a young Irish patriot, of a very slender estate' and, 'wrong-headed'.[142] Morres dedicated his

131 *Boyle* v. *Lysaght* (1787) 1 Ridg. PC 384; *Magrath* v. *Muskerry* (1787) 1 Ridg. PC, Vern. & Scr. 166, 481; *Blundell* v. *Macartney (No 3)* (1793) 2 Ridg. PC 557.

132 *Boyle* v. *Lysaght* (1787) 1 Ridg. PC 384; *Magrath* v. *Muskerry* (1787) 1 Ridg. PC, Vern. & Scr. 166, 481.

133 Cokayne, *Complete Peerage*, ix. 355; Patrick M. Geoghegan, 'Morres, Hervey Redmond 2nd Viscount Mountmorres'. DIB online. [http://dib.cambridge.org/viewReadPage. do?articleId=a5981], accessed 26 February 2013.

134 (1787) Vern. & Scr. 166 at 172.

135 2 vols. (London, T. Cadell, 1792), ii.201. Above, page 97.

136 Above, page 97.

137 (London, 1795).

138 (London, 1785).

139 (London, printed for the author by William Woodfall, 1794).

140 Cokayne, *Complete Peerage*, ix. 355.

141 *The Letters of Themistocles*, (London : printed for Hookham and Carpenter, 1795).

142 Cokayne, *Complete Peerage*, ix.355-6, n. (b).

study of the regency to Walpole. Morres also contributed generously to funds to relieve authors in distress.

Hervey Morres died unmarried, having committed suicide at the age of about 54 by shooting himself in the head, on 17 or 18 August 1797.[143] His obituary in the *Gentleman's Magazine* described him as a 'good-natured, intelligent man, fond of talking, but more from the prevalence of strong animal spirits than vanity.'

George Nugent (1760–1814), Earl of Westmeath

George Frederick Nugent[144] was born in 1760. He was styled Lord Delvin until 1792. He was MP for Fore from 1780 to 1792 and was Colonel of the Westmeath militia. He married (1) 1784 Marianne, daughter of James Jeffreys of Blarney Castle Co. Cork and of Arabella, sister of John FitzGibbon, 1st Earl of Clare. This marriage was dissolved by Act of parliament in October 1796.[145] He inherited the earldom in 1792. He married (2) in 1797 Elizabeth Emily, 1st daughetr of the 1st Marquess of Drogheda. He was a representative peer of Ireland from 1801 until his death. He died in Dublin in 1814.

George Nugent was a lay member but delivered a brief judgment in *Barton* v. *Massey*[146] in February 1793. His first wife was a niece of FitzGibbon, the lord chancellor, so that might possibly explain why he took part.

Edmond Sexten Pery (1719–1806), Viscount Pery

Edmond Sexten Pery[147] was born in Limerick in 1719, the son of the Rev. Stackpole Pery and grandson of Edmond Pery of Stackpole Court, Co. Clare. He was admitted to the degree of barrister-at-law by King's Inns in 1745.[148] He was MP for Wicklow in 1751 and for Limerick, 1760–1785. He supported Grattan's policy of legislative independence. He was Speaker of Irish House of Commons from 1771 to 1785. On his retirement from the Commons in 1785 he was granted a pension and the title of Viscount Pery of Newtown-Pery in the county of Limerick in recognition of long service. He opposed the Union with Great Britain and voted against the Act. In the 1799 session of parliament when the measure was introduced, those opposed to it met in Pery's house in Dublin. He died in 1806.

Although Edmond Pery was by training a lawyer, he does not belong to the group of lawyers promoted to be the professional members of the court. He is

143 Cokayne, *Complete Peerage*, ix.355.

144 Cokayne, *Complete Peerage*; C. J. Woods, 'Nugent, George Frederick 7th Earl of Westmeath'. DIB online [http://dib.cambridge.org/viewReadPage.do?article Id=a6249], accessed 26 February 2013; J. Darby, *The History of Delvin* (Westmeath Examiner, *c.* 1991).

145 The trial for adultery (hers) is reported in *Westmeath* v. *Bradshaw* (1797) 1 *New Collection of Trials for Adultery* 3; Lawrence Stone, *The Road to Divorce: England 1530-1987* (Oxford, 1990) p. 264.

146 (1793) 2 Ridg. PC 553, see page 101.

147 Patrick M. Geoghegan, 'Pery, Edmond Sexten 1st Viscount Pery'. DIB online. [http://dib.cambridge.org/viewReadPage.do? articleId=a7293]; David Huddleston, 'Pery, Edmond Sexton (*sic.*), Viscount Pery (1719–1806)', ODNB online. [http://www.oxforddnb.com/view/article/22004], accessed 21 June 2009.

148 E. Keane, P. B. Phair, and T. U. Sadleir, *King's Inns Admission Papers 1607–1867* (Dublin, 1982).

chiefly remembered as speaker of the Irish House of Commons. When Benjamin Franklin visited Dublin in 1772 Mr Speaker Pery suggested to the House that the remarkable privilege granted to members of the British parliament, of sitting inside the bar of the House on the benches occupied by members, should be extended to the distinguished American visitor. The House of Commons unanimously agreed.[149]

He delivered a number of judgments in the Lords on appeals, more in the early period. He delivered three judgments in 1787, one in 1788, one in 1793. He was present in 1795 in *Hamilton* v. *Marquess of Donegall*[150] and made an interjection during argument by counsel, which Ridgeway reports as a note, and which illustrates his sense of Irish independence. He questioned the validity of a grant of fisheries by James I under the great seal of England:[151]

> James was seized, in right of his Crown of Ireland, of those fisheries, and the patents granting them are under the seal of England. I do not know whether there has ever been a determination, that a grant under the seal of Great Britain can pass lands in Ireland... One question therefore, which should be determined, is whether a patent under the seal of Great Britain is sufficient to pass lands lying in Ireland?

Lord Clare LC, however, then said that he did not think the matter worth pursuing, and it was not. This rather blunt dismissal is evidence that Pery did not wield much influence in the Lords, at least under Lord Clare. It probably also indicates that the lord chancellor found Pery's nationalist sentiments somewhat embarrassing given his own increasing identification with Great Britain.

Some of Pery's later judgments seem to show a fractious or irritable quality which may have been caused by illness, or mental exhaustion. He delivered a rare dissenting judgment, some twelve pages long, in *Blundell* v. *Macartney (No 3)*[152] which may be an example of this, or perhaps an example of his independence of mind. He was in favour of an order by consent of the parties being set aside, to which all the other judges were resolutely opposed. It should be borne in mind that he had entered the Lords at the age of 66 after a long and demanding career.

John Scott (1739–1798), Earl of Clonmell CJKB

John Scott[153] was born in 1739, the son of Thomas Scott of Mohubber, Co. Tipperary. He graduated BA from Trinity College Dublin in 1758. He was admitted to the degree of barrister-at-law by King's Inns in 1765. He married

149 M. MacDonagh 'The Old Irish Parliament' (1916) 8 *Irish Ecclesiastical Record* 99 at p. 112.

150 (1795) 3 Ridg. PC 267.

151 (1795) 3 Ridg. PC at 289.

152 (1793) 2 Ridg. PC 557 at 600.

153 Ball, *Judges in Ireland*, ii.171–5, 180–1; Rosemary Richey, 'Scott, John 1st earl of Clonmell Baron Earlsfort Viscount Clonmell'. DIB online. [http://dib.cambridge.org/viewReadPage. do?article Id=a7949], accessed 26 February 2013. Charles Phillips, *Recollections of Curran and some of his his Contemporaries* (London, 1822); Fitzpatrick, *Ireland before the Union*; Cokayne, *Complete Peerage*.

Catherine, daughter of Thomas Matthew of Thomastown, Co. Tipperary. He was elected member for Mullingar in 1768. He was appointed king's counsel in 1770 and solicitor general 1774. He was made DCL (*honoris causa*) by Dublin University (Trinity College Dublin) in 1775. He became attorney general in 1777. He married as his second wife Margaret, daughter and heiress of Patrick Lawless of Dublin in 1779. He narrowly escaped a mob of rioters who attacked his house in the same year. He became MP for Portarlington in 1783. He became prime serjeant in 1783 and was appointed clerk of the pleas in Exchequer for life. He became chief justice of the King's Bench in 1784. He was created Baron Earlsfort in 1784. He acted as speaker of House of Lords occasionally in 1786. In 1789 he was created Viscount Clonmell and Earl of Clonmell in 1793. He died in 1798 and was buried in St Peter's Dublin. He lived in Dublin in William Street and at 17 Harcourt Street[154] and near Dublin at Neptune, now Temple Hill, Blackrock. He left issue.

Known as 'Copper-faced Jack' because of his large red face, John Scott made a reputation as an orator as well as a lawyer. Grattan described his parliamentary manner: 'He struck his breast, slapped his hat, appealed to his honour and laid his hand upon his sword'.[155] According to Hale,[156] on the bench 'he swaggered, and bullied, he was jealous and ambitious and overbearing but he was cheerful, possessed some coarse wit and considerable learning.'

Unfortunately for his reputation, Scott left an extraordinary diary,[157] extracts of which were published long after his death, and which revealed his true character and feelings. They provide a portrait of an unpleasant, deceitful man who carefully developed an apparently affable exterior which he presented to the world, while concealing a fierce ambition and harbouring resentment and envy against his contemporaries. It amply demonstrates his low opinion of almost everyone, except himself. Lifford[158] was 'a declining insincere trickster,' Carleton 'a worthless wretch', Yelverton 'rooted in faction, coarse and of obscure origin,' Henn J 'at best a fool, Bradstreet J 'able, double and dying'. Hale adds that 'Scott hated FitzGibbon, who despised both Scott and Yelverton'.

Scott's diary reveals the unpleasant truth. He recorded a number of sage maxims, evidently of his own invention: 'All men will injure or deceive you; watch the whole world, as at this moment your friends, the very next your enemies; offend none; serve others sparingly; conceal your dislikes universally. Flatter all through' are some choice examples. Later he adds: 'Make yourself pleasing by flattering all. Make every man your dupe by flattery'. Another revealing entry runs as follows: '16th July 1793 - Died Lord Mountgarrett, as wicked a malignant selfish monster as I ever knew; a victim to his brutal appetites and thirst for blood; a lesson in vice, and a caution to be civil to all, obliging to

154 Now known as Clonmell House, No. 17 is the earliest surviving house on Harcourt Street.

155 Hale, *John Philpot Curran*, Ch. 9, pp. 109–18.

156 *ibid.*, p. 109.

157 Fitzpatrick, *Ireland before the Union*; John Scott, *John Scott, Baron Earlsfort, chief justice of the Court of King's Bench, Ireland, afterwards Earl of Clonmell – His private diary, 1174–98*. privately printed. Trinity College Dublin. (Dublin, 1807).

158 Hale, *ibid.*, p. 109.

many, to serve few, and offend none, as the safest, wisest, pleasantest mode of going through life'. Many were taken in by Scott's outward affability. Charles Phillips[159] drew a critical portrait of Scott, but added that 'his companionable qualities were well seconded by the fidelity of his friendships; and it is true of him that he never made an insincere profession [of friendship].'

Scott's insincerity extended to his politics. On a number of occasions he publicly expressed opposition to the Penal Laws, which made him appear in advance of most of his class. In 1795 he wrote a letter declaring that the country would never be at peace until the Roman Catholics were emancipated and the penal statutes entirely repealed.[160] However, at the same time he was prepared to take advantage of them when it suited his interest. He wrote a letter threatening to invoke the Penal Laws against his own step-daughter who had conformed to the Church of Ireland but was showing signs of 'relapsing' to Catholicism.[161]

Walter Hussey Burgh,[162] a former chief baron of the Exchequer, was more perceptive than some of his contemporaries. In 1789, after his death, his 'portrait' of Scott in verse was published.[163] The style, if not the quality, imitated Pope's Dunciad:

> Hail! [Scott] while noise and impudence avail.
> Hail! fortune's foundling, blasted bravo hail!
> Hail full-blown face and wonder's rolling eye,
> That swells astonishment and looks a lie
> And fierce and monster breeding seems to roll
> Over a dark and subterraneous soul
> ...Now looks portentous, stubborn, vicious, mulish
> And now the b[aw]dy, pleasant, arch, and foolish...
> Now with uplifted arm for prostitution
> Stands bully bold 'gainst Law and Constitution...
> Whether in grave debate, obscure or gay,
> He takes the merry mould of blasphemy.
> Regales the senate with a b[aw]dy song,
> While Hadock's church inspires his recant tongue.
> Whether as foe to freedom and to laws,
> The hireling vindicates the tyrant's cause...
> Amazing man! who too abandoned are
> For Parliament - to clam'rous for the Bar,
> Of thy friend's cheated w[hore] thou false trustee -
> Of every dupe thou common legatee...

159 Charles Phillips, *Curran and his Contemporaries*.

160 Fitzpatrick, *Ireland before the Union*, p. 61.

161 *ibid.*, p. 61. The letter is reproduced at pp. 196–200. He was in fact threatening to invoke the proviso to the statute of 1778, which had the general object of relaxing the Penal Laws. Below, page 166.

162 James Quinn, 'Burgh, Walter Hussey'. DIB online. [http://dib.cambridge.org/viewReadPage.do?articleId=a1143], accessed 26 February 2013.

163 The ode appeared in the *Evening Post* of 3 November 1789, Fitzpatrick, *Ireland before the Union*, pp. 17–18, Hale, *John Philpot Curran*, pp. 109–10.

> Who never frolicked but with Knavish view
> Nor played the fool but played the rascal too.

Fitzpatrick[164] commented:

> To find a Chief Baron of the Exchequer assailing the Chief Justice of the King's Bench in such terms is quite a sensational novelty. But in now viewing these lines historically, it is perhaps right to say that the strength of their expressions may, to some extent, have been influenced by the angry politics of the time. Burgh had been a member of the Opposition; and Scott was brought up and stationed in the House for the express purpose of Bullying the Opposition. One might also note that the verse was published some six years after Burgh's death.[165]

The reference to the 'false trustee' is explained in a letter.[166] It is addressed to Scott and signed 'Lucius.' It accuses Scott of ingratiating himself with one Celia Robinson, the mistress of a Mr Mathew, so as 'to obtain for him her implicit confidence as trustee to a considerable legacy from her dying master of certain lands on his Tipperary estate.' Mr Mathew was Scott's brother-in-law. Scott's first wife was Catherine Mathew, daughter of Thomas Mathew, and sister of Francis, 1st Earl of Llandaff and of the Mr Mathew referred to in the letter. The letter went on to accuse Scott of having denied the trust in an answer to a bill in equity after her lover's death and 'by a prudent advantage of the Popery Laws secured the possession to himself, and thus acquired his first acres of landed property, which in this country has since swelled to such a magnitude by means equally meritorious.'[167] Fitzpatrick cites a rental account of the property of Thomas Mathew, including land at Bouliduffe, which refers to the latter as a lease taken on trust for Celia Robinson by Scott, but 'turned to his own advantage'.

Scott and Carleton were friends as students, but quarrelled later in life after they both became judges. Carleton persuaded his father, then a rich merchant, to help Scott financially. This enabled Scott to complete his studies and without it he would not have been able to start at the bar. Fitzpatrick[168] comments that it would have been 'a loss which, it is not too much to say, the bar would have had no cause to regret.' He does, however, note that Scott repaid the kindness some years later. Fitzpatrick quotes a Mr O'Flanagan of the Irish bar as saying:

> Whatever the amount of the obligation Lord Clonmell was under to Mr Carleton, he amply repaid it. In after years, when the once rich merchant experienced those reverses of fortune so common in the commercial world, the then prosperous barrister contributed largely

164 Fitzpatrick, *Ireland before the Union*, p. 17.
165 See Fitzpatrick, footnote 63 and Appendix A 'Hussey Burgh.'
166 Fitzpatrick, *Ireland before the Union*, p. 19.
167 *ibid.*
168 *ibid.*, p. 160.

> towards his relief, and by his attention to the son's interests, proved to the father he had a grateful heart.

Scott later commented in his diary: 'my three puisne judges are actually combined against me; and that ungrateful monster, Lord Carleton, has made a foolish quarrel with me.'

Scott appears in the the House of Lords in number of cases from 1784,[169] but in several of them as presenting the opinions of the common law judges. In *Boyle* v. *Lysaght*, despite the fact that he was a common law judge he spoke (as Baron Earlsfort) strongly in favour of the equity to renew leases for lives and the role of Gilbert CB in putting them on a firm footing:[170]

> His lordship observed, that this case afforded an opportunity to that house of priding themselves in the consideration, that if the appellate jurisdiction of this kingdom had remained in its original and constitutional situation, there would have been no occasion to pass the tenantry act. That from the determination of that great man, Lord Chief Baron Gilbert, the case of *Sweet* v. *Anderson*, down to the reversal of the decree in *Murray* v. *Bateman*, persons having such cases,[171] were considered to have perpetual interests, and not depending on the strict terms of the renewal clauses.

The fact that, as a common lawyer, he nevertheless spoke so forcefully in favour of the Irish doctrine of equity seems to illustrate the strength of feeling among the Irish judges of the time that not only was the system since 1720, of ultimate appeals lying to the English House of Lords, an affront to Irish dignity, but that the English House of Lords had indeed proved insensitive and disrespectful of Irish legal doctrine and the most important example of that was their refusal to recognise the extensive equity to renew leases for lives developed in the Irish courts. In legal terms, the grievances of the 'patriots' in the Irish parliament was crystalized in that issue.

Another significant contribution as a judge of the court was in *Kenney* v. *Browne* where he delivered a brief judgment concurring with those of FitzGibbon and Carleton, recognising the principle of what would now be called proprietary estoppel.

There is a fine portrait of Scott by Gilbert Stuart which only recently came on the market and was fortunately acquired by King's Inns in the summer of 2009. Stuart was notoriously careless about money and was imprisoned for debt while in Dublin. Such was his reputation, however, that prominent people were prepared to visit the prison in order to have their portraits painted. He soon obtained his release, and bought the estate at Stillorgan Park outside Dublin,

[169] *Haire* v. *Lloyd* (1787) 1 Ridg. PC 341; *Boyle* v. *Lysaght* (1787) 1 Ridg. PC 384; *Magrath* v. *Muskerry* (1787) 1 Ridg. PC 469 at 509, Vern & Scr. 166, 481; *Reeves* v. *Newenham* (1788) 2 Ridg. PC 11; *Fauconberg* v. *Kingsland* (1790) 2 Ridg. PC 147; *Foster* v. *Lynch* (1795) 3 Ridg. PC 329; *Kenney* v. *Browne* (1796) 3 Ridg. PC 462.

[170] (1787) 1 Ridg. PC at 417–418.

[171] The word appears to be a misprint for 'leases'.

where he again lived in some style with and this again led to period in debtor's prison in 1789. There is a story, unsubstantiated, that Scott was among those who visited the debtor's prison to have his portrait painted by Stuart, a considerable irony, since, as chief justice of the King's Bench, Scott would have consigned many debtors to that place.

Barry Yelverton (1736–1805), Viscount Avonmore CB

Barry Yelverton[172] was born in 1736, the son of Francis Yelverton of Kanturk, Co. Cork and Elizabeth Barry of Kilbren in the same county. He went to school in Charleville and graduated BA from Trinity College Dublin in 1757, LLB in 1761 and was awarded an LLD in 1774. He was admitted to the degree of barrister-at-law by King's Inns in 1764. He became king's counsel and a master of the bench in 1772. He was MP for Donegal borough from 1774 to 1776, and for Carrickfergus from 1776 to 1783. He supported Grattan's policy of legislative independence. He became attorney general in 1782 and was sworn of the Privy Council in the same year. He was appointed chief baron of the Exchequer in 1783. He was created Baron Avonmore in June 1795. He supported the Union and was created Viscount Avonmore of Derry Island in Co. Tipperary in December 1800. He lived in Dublin in Ely Place and Marlborough Street and near Dublin at Fortfield, Terenure.[173] He died in 1805 and was buried at Rathfarnham near Dublin. There are portraits in Trinity College Dublin and King's Inns.[174]

Yelverton gained a reputation as one of the most able advocates of his time and an outstanding orator.[175]

Yelverton was glad to take the job of chief baron of the Exchequer because it was well paid[176] but he remained chronically in debt due to a large family and improvident habits. According to Hale, towards the end of his life he suffered the extraordinary indignity of having his salary as chief baron assigned to his creditors by deeds enrolled in his own court.[177]

Yelverton was active in the politics of the time as the founder in 1779 of the patriotic social and political debating society, the Order of St Patrick, better known by its colloquial name, the 'order of the monks of the screw'.[178] He took part in the successful campaign in 1779–80 to repeal the restrictions imposed by the Navigation Acts, the mercantilist-inspired legislation which had restricted the freedom of Ireland to trade directly with British colonies, especially in North America and the West Indies.[179]

172 James Kelly, 'Yelverton, Barry, first Viscount Avonmore (1736–1805)', ODNB online. [http://www.oxforddnb.com/view/article/30212], accessed 26 May 2009; Gerard O'Brien, 'Yelverton, Barry 1st Viscount Avonmore'. DIB online. [http://dib.cambridge.org/viewReadPage. do?articleId=a9161], accessed 26 February 2013. Ball, *Judges in Ireland*, ii.166, 180, 181, 219–20.

173 Ball, *Judges in Ireland*; James Kelly, 'Yelverton, Barry, first Viscount Avonmore (1736–1805)', ODNB.

174 Wanda Ryan–Smolin, *King's Inns Portraits*, (Dublin: 1992), p. 75.

175 Ball, *Judges in Ireland*, ii.166.

176 Malcomson, *John Foster*, p. 395.

177 Hale, *John Philpot Curran*, pp. 248–49.

178 Ball, *Judges in Ireland* ii.220, n. 2; Kelly, ODNB.

179 Kelly, *ibid.*

In *Maingay* v. *Gahan*[180] the plaintiffs brought an action of trespass *vi et armis* challenging the seizure of a cargo of brandy and wine from a ship at Bandon, Co. Cork, by revenue officers. The commissioners of appeal had upheld the seizure and forfeiture of the goods. The Court of Exchequer, with Yelverton as chief baron and Hamilton and Metge BB concurring, held that the ruling of the commissioners was not a conclusive bar to the action, but they were overruled by FitzGibbon, Scott and Carleton in the Court of Exchequer Chamber. The Court of Exchequer had relied upon the authority of *Henshaw* v. *Pleasance*[181] but in the Exchequer Chamber FitzGibbon said that it was not good law and that Lifford LC had frequently held so. The jurisdiction on the revenue side of Exchequer, he also held, was exclusively to recover the king's revenue. The revenue commissioners had an exclusive jurisdiction as to seizure of goods and forfeiture. The only remedy was to petition the lord lieutenant and council or the commissioners of appeal.[182] An opinion was delivered by Carleton, who examined the revenue statutes in detail and pointed out that the seizure could only be challenged by the owner of the goods.[183] As to jurisdiction, *Henshaw* v. *Pleasance* concerned a differently worded statute to those applicable in the present case. Both Carleton and FitzGibbon seemed to have demonstrated a greater grasp of the revenue law than Yelverton on that occasion.

Yelverton's strength was as the constitutional lawyer among the 'patriots' and his principal achievement was legislative, in his successful sponsorship of what became known as Yelverton's Act, 1782,[184] which altered the operation of Poynings' Law, 1495, and gave the Irish parliament control over legislation.

Yelverton joined the Lords relatively late, in 1795. However, as chief baron he appears on several occasions as presenting the report of the common law judges on questions put to them.[185]

In *Mandeville* v. *Lord Carrick*[186] his report of the opinions of the common law judges seems to show a grasp of property law in the context of *Shelley's Case* in its application to wills and the artificial destruction of contingent remainders. How much these reports and the answers to the questions were due to his influence is matter of speculation.

As chief baron of the Exchequer he was the only other judge in the lords, besides the lord chancellor, who exercised equity jurisdiction. That is no doubt the

[180] (1793) Ir. Term Rep. 1 (judgment of Yelverton CB,); noted in 1 Ridg. PC at p. 43, and see also the advertisement at the beginning of 2 Ridg. PC.

[181] 2 Black. W. 1174, 96 E.R. 692.

[182] Ir. Ter. Rep. at p. 71.

[183] *ibid.*, at p. 49.

[184] 21 & 22 Geo.. III c. 47 (Ir.), 1782. Above, pages 34, 37.

[185] *Atkinson* v. *Pilsworth* (1787) 1 Ridg. PC 449, at 461 (construction of deeds); *Chandos (Duchess)* v. *Brownlow* (1791) 2 Ridg. PC 345, at 384 (registration of deeds: unregistered deed ineffective against registered deed), decision of Court of Exchequer affirmed; *Mandeville* v. *Lord Carrick* (1795) 3 Ridg. PC 352 at 363 (*Shelley's Case*), judgment of Court of King's Bench affirmed; *Inchquin* v. *Burnell* (1795) 3 Ridg. PC 376, at 418 (covenant, nature of a reservation), decree of Court of Chancery reversed, and see Francis Hargrave, 'Argument for the Earl of Inchquin on his Appeal to the Irish House of Lords', in *Juridical arguments* (London, 1797-99), i.438–480.

[186] (1795) 3 Ridg. PC 352 at 363.

reason why he delivered the other judgment in *Kenney* v. *Browne*[187] in addition to that of the lord chancellor. In a lengthy judgment he concurs with Lord Clare LC in the landmark case that was an early recognition of what today would be called proprietary estoppel.[188] It was his most significant contribution as a member of the lords.[189]

In *Hayden* v. *Carroll*[190] he concurred with Lord Clare LC in interpreting the Bankers' Act[191] as applying to all the debts of bankers and not merely those incurred in their business as bankers.

Conclusions

The members of the Irish House of Lords in its appellate role, especially in the later period, contained a core of professional lawyers. James Hewitt, Lord Lifford was the last English lord chancellor before the Union and belongs to the early period. Edmond Pery had been a member of the bar and Speaker of the Irish House of Commons. He did not became a member of the lords until his retirement, taking only a small part in the proceedings during the period of revived jurisdiction. Barry Maxwell, Lord Farnham, although he had legal experience, had never been made a judge of one of the lower courts and owed his membership of the House to inheritance, as did George Nugent, Earl of Westmeath. The remaining group, consisting of Carleton, FitzGibbon, Scott and Yelverton, all belong to the later period and had a great deal in common. They were all Irish-born professional lawyers. They were all, nominally at least, members of the Church of Ireland and could not have been members of the Irish House of Lords unless they were. They all acquired their peerages by grant, not by inheritance. They had all previously had successful careers at the bar and the bench. Most of them supported Grattan's policy of reform and legislative independence for Ireland, but voted for the Union after the Rebellion. Their background was not that of the landowning class. Although FitzGibbon inherited an estate estimated at £6,000 a year from his father in the 1780s,[192] his father had made his fortune at the bar and the estate passed to FitzGibbon after he had established himself in the legal profession. Carleton was the son of prosperous Cork merchant. Not all were rich, as the case of Yelverton shows.

The extent to which the Irish Lords functioned as a professional court was lessened to some extent by the fact that the 'professionals' who sat in the Lords also sat as judges in the lower courts. The lord chancellor was an *ex officio* member of the Lords as well as presiding over the Court of Chancery. John Scott was appointed chief justice of the King's Bench in 1784 and entered the Lords

187 (1796) 3 Ridg. PC 462 at 521. Below, pages 166–167.

188 Below, page 167.

189 His other judgments are in: *Power* v. *Perse* (1796) 3 Ridg. PC 532; *Hayden* v. *Carroll* (1796) 3 Ridg. PC 545.

190 3 Ridg. PC 545.

191 33 Geo. II, c. 14, 1759, s. 8.

192 Malcomson, *John Foster*, p. 14; another source says £5,000: E. M. Johnston-Liik, James Quinn. 'FitzGibbon, John 1st Earl of Clare'. DIB online, [http://dib.cambridge.org/ viewReadPage.do?articleId=a3209].

in the same year. Carleton was made chief justice of the Common Pleas in 1788, and entered the Lords the following year as Baron Carleton. Yelverton, who had been appointed chief baron of the Exchequer in 1783, had to wait twelve years before entering it 1795 as Baron Avonmore. Thus the professional members of the court held substantial judicial positions in the lower courts at the same time as being members of the Lords and functioning as judges there.

CHAPTER 8

The Later History of Exchequer Chamber

We have already mentioned the Irish Court of Exchequer Chamber. There are many instances of appeals to the Irish Lords directly from the Court of Exchequer from the equity side, in the same way that appeals from Chancery lay directly to the Lords. In *Hamilton* v. *Marquess of Donegall*[1] a writ of error was taken from the common law side of Exchequer, first to the Exchequer Chamber and then to the Irish Lords. The substance of the case is discussed later.[2]

The plaintiff marquess succeeded in the Exchequer. A writ of error was taken to the Exchequer Chamber in 1794. The court consisted of the chief justice of the King's Bench, Lord Clonmell (i.e. Scott), the chief justice of the Common Pleas, Lord Carleton, and the lord chancellor, FitzGibbon. The two common law judges held in favour of the plaintiff. FitzGibbon disagreed, but said he would not go against the opinion of the other two members of the court, since it was a common law matter.

In the Lords, the lord chancellor spoke on the appeal and so did Lord Pery. Lord Pery's powers may have been failing, because he is reported as objecting at length to the way counsel had argued the case, but his objections seems to have been ignored in the subsequent proceedings. FitzGibbon then stated his intention to ask the opinion of the judges. The assembly of the common law judges was also sometimes referred to as 'Exchequer Chamber'and so *two* courts called 'Exchequer Chamber' were involved in the case. The judges duly delivered a unanimous opinion and the Exchequer Chamber (Coucil Chamber) was upheld. All three judges who gave judgment in the Exchequer Chamber were also members of the House of Lords but the fact that they had sat as members of Exchequer Chamber was not the subject of any objection.

In 1800, at the eleventh hour before the Union, the Irish Parliament passed an Act which entirely reconstituted the Court of Exchequer Chamber.[3] The reconstituted court became a general court of appeal from all the common law courts. It replaced the two courts in Ireland from time to time referred to as 'Exchequer Chamber', the assembly of the common law judges, which was not really a court

1 (1795) 3 Ridg. PC 267.

2 See page 170.

3 40 Geo. III c. 39 (Ir.), 1800.

at all,[4] and the Court of Council Chamber, the old court for errors in the Exchequer.[5] The Act also provided that writs of error from the Court of Delegates in Ireland should no longer go to the delegates in England, but to the Irish Court of Exchequer Chamber.[6]

In Ireland there had never been a court for errors in the King's Bench, since writs of error had gone from the Irish King's Bench to the English King's Bench, and from 1782 to the Irish House of Lords[7] but now they were to go to the newly-constituted Exchequer Chamber in Ireland, together with writs of error from the common law side of the Court of Exchequer.

It is interesting to note that a statute of James II's Jacobite parliament had foreshadowed such a development in Ireland. The Jacobite statute (which of course was not valid according to British constitutional law, or in Ireland under William and Mary's reign or later), was mainly concerned with ending writs of error from the Irish King's Bench to the English King's Bench, but in doing so it provided that writs of error from the Irish King's Bench should go to the Exchequer Chamber in Ireland[8] It was thus the first 'measure' in Ireland to extend the jurisdiction of the Exchequer Chamber beyond hearing writs of error from the Court of Exchequer.

The statute of 1800 further provided that the Court of Common Pleas was enhanced in status and no longer inferior to the King's Bench, as writs of error from the Common Pleas were also to go to the new court. The new Exchequer Chamber consisted of the two common law chief justices, the chief baron of the Exchequer and all the puisne justices and barons, twelve judges in all, with a quorum of nine. Thus the new court, rather than being an amalgamation of the two old courts, resembled more the assembly of the common law judges given a formal structure, but was just as unwieldy. Nevertheless, the court established by the Act of 1800 constituted a separate court hearing writs of error from all the common law courts and as such presaged modern courts of appeal.[9] The lord chancellor's role in the old Court of Council Chamber was gone and decision was by the majority. The lord chancellor's presence had always been something of an anomaly, since the old court was a court of common law, hearing cases from the common law side of Exchequer.

The Irish Court of Exchequer Chamber of 1800, since it was instituted just before the Union, was no doubt made in anticipation of the Union and in anticipation, therefore, of the consequent replacement of the Irish Lords with the British House of Lords as the court of last resort for Ireland. Indeed, it seems that the intention was that the new Irish court would enable the Irish common law judges, after the Union, to retain control over appeals before they went to

[4] Above, page 74.

[5] Above, page 74.

[6] 40 Geo. III c. 39 (Ir.), 1800, s. 2.

[7] Above, page 77.

[8] Below, Appendix F, page 221.

[9] The Irish Court of Exchequer Chamber survived the Union and remained until its jurisdiction was transferred to the new Irish Court of Appeal by the Supreme Court of Judicature Act (Ireland), 1877, s. 23., although during the Union appeals and writs of error lay to the British House of Lords.

the British House of Lords, and therefore some control over Irish law. Lord Kilwarden in introducing the first reading of the bill in the Lords perhaps hinted at this, while stressing the convenience and reduction in expense to litigants:[10]

> His lordship observed that he had consulted with the noble earl on the woolsack, and the other great law authorities, and had their consent and assistance in preparing the bill, whose object was to have a Court of appeal in this country, which would, in most cases, preclude the delay and expense of resorting to the British peers, as *dernier resort*, and thus disappoint litigious persons, and expedite the ends and purposes of judicial proceedings.

The Earl of Farnham, on the other hand, 'approved the court of appeal in this kingdom, and thought it should have power of final decision in all cases'. Although this wish was not to be granted, the new court would at least act as a 'buffer' between courts of first instance in Ireland and the British House of Lords, and so might avoid, after the Union, the conflict which had arisen in the previous century in the case of the equity to renew leases for lives. This conflict is discussed below. A less worthy motive may well have been that it was a form of compensation for the diminution of practices that would result to the Irish bar from the loss of appeals to the Irish Lords.

It is interesting to note that in England after the Union a single English Court of Exchequer Chamber was similarly constituted as a general common law court of error in 1830.[11] In fact, a number of statutes of the British parliament between the Union and 1830 had been concerned with reforming the administration of the Irish Court of Exchequer Chamber[12] and so these measures may well have suggested to reformers that an English court based on the same plan as the Irish court would be a welcome development. This change in England no doubt occurred for different reasons from those which led to the establishment of the new Irish court. The reason in England probably had more to do with the pressure of business on the British Lords, a pressure which had been increased to some extent by the Union.[13] Nevertheless, it seems clear that the English took the Irish Court of 1800 as the model for a general court of error hearing writs of error from all the common law courts. The English Act introduced one refinement: the members of the court were to be judges from the courts other than that appealed from.[14] Indeed, this may have developed as a practice in Ireland before

[10] PIHL, iii.555, Wednesday, 11 June 1800.

[11] 11 Geo. IV & 1 Will. IV c. 70, s. 8, given the somewhat inaccurate short title of the Law Terms Act, 1830; Holdsworth, *HEL*, i.245; Baker, *Introduction to English Legal History* 4th ed. (London, 2002) pp. 137–138. W. Cornish & G. Clarke, *Law and Society in England 1750-1950*. (London, 1989), pp. 25.

[12] Exchequer Chamber (Ireland) Act, 1820, 1 Geo. IV, c. 68; Common Law Procedure (Ireland) Act, 1821, 1 & 2 Geo. IV, c. 53.

[13] See Robert Stevens, *Law and Politics: the House of Lords as a Judicial Body, 1800-1976*. London, 1979, p. 15 n. 46: by 1808 there were 27 Irish appeals pending.

[14] The Jacobite Act of 1689 had specified that writs of error from the King's Bench should be heard in the Exchequer Chamber by judges from the other common law courts, the Common Pleas and Exchequer: below, Appendix F, page 221.

1830. The refinement was extended to the Irish Court of Exchequer Chamber in 1857.[15]

In the light of these developments, the Irish Court of Exchequer Chamber of 1800 can be seen not only as having its origins in the Jacobite statute of 1689 but also as the precursor not only of the English Court of Exchequer Chamber of 1830, but also, both in Ireland and in England, of the later courts of appeal.

The establishment of the Irish Court of Exchequer Chamber did not eliminate conflicts between the Irish and British courts after the Union, as one instance illustrates. It had long been the practice in Ireland for absentee landlords to grant terms of years to their agents in Ireland and for the agents to grant the entire term to an agricultural tenant. This was intended to be a sublease so that the agent would be in the position of a landlord and hence be able to impose the remedies available to a landlord. The practice was based upon the opinion of property lawyers in Ireland that the grant of the entire term could, in the case of a leasehold, nevertheless take effect as a sublease, despite the lack of a reversion, and a leasehold rent service could be reserved. It seems that this was probably because (a) the practice as to leaseholds was developed, both in England and in Ireland, by analogy to freehold, (b) but in Ireland, unlike England, there were exceptions to *Quia Emptores* 1290 whereby a grant of a fee simple could nevertheless take effect as a subinfeudation, and so tenure would be created, but no reversion would remain in the grantor.[16] Alternatively, it may be that *Quia Emptores* 1290 was not regarded in Ireland as applying to leaseholds at all, even by analogy.

The Irish Court of Exchequer Chamber upheld the Irish practice in *Pluck* v. *Digges*.[17] However, when the appeal went to the British House of Lords they reversed the Irish court,[18] apparently regarding the Irish practice as heretical. The British House of Lords decision was followed in Ireland by the King's Bench in *Lessee of Fawcett* v. *Hall*,[19] Bushe CJ accepting that the principle of *Pluck* applied to ejectment and to replevin, and in Chancery in *Cremen* v. *Hawkes*,[20] a case of a lessee for years who leased for his own term reserving a rent. The Court of Exchequer, however, in *Lessee of Walsh* v. *Feely*[21] confined *Pluck* to the remedy of distress at common law and allowed an action in ejectment despite the absence of a reversion. This particular conflict was only resolved by Deasy's Act, 1860[22] which provided that a reversion was not necessary to constitute the relation of landlord and tenant in Ireland.

15 Court of Exchequer Chamber (Ireland) Act, 1857, 20 & 21 Vict. c. 6, s. 1. See also Common Law Procedure Amendment Act (Ireland), 1856, 19 & 20 Vict. c. 102 (Irish Court of Exchequer Chamber and British House of Lords to be courts of appeal under the Act).

16 See pages 145, 145, 151.

17 (1828) 2 Hud. & Br. 1.

18 (1832) 5 Bligh (n.s.) 31, 5 E.R. 219.

19 (1833) Alc. & Nap. 248.

20 (1846) 8 Ir. Eq. R. 153, affirmed on appeal at 503.

21 (1835) 1 Jo. 413, following *Lessee of Coyne* v. *Smith* (1826) Bat. 90, n.

22 Landlord and Tenant Law (Amendment) Act, 1860, s. 3.

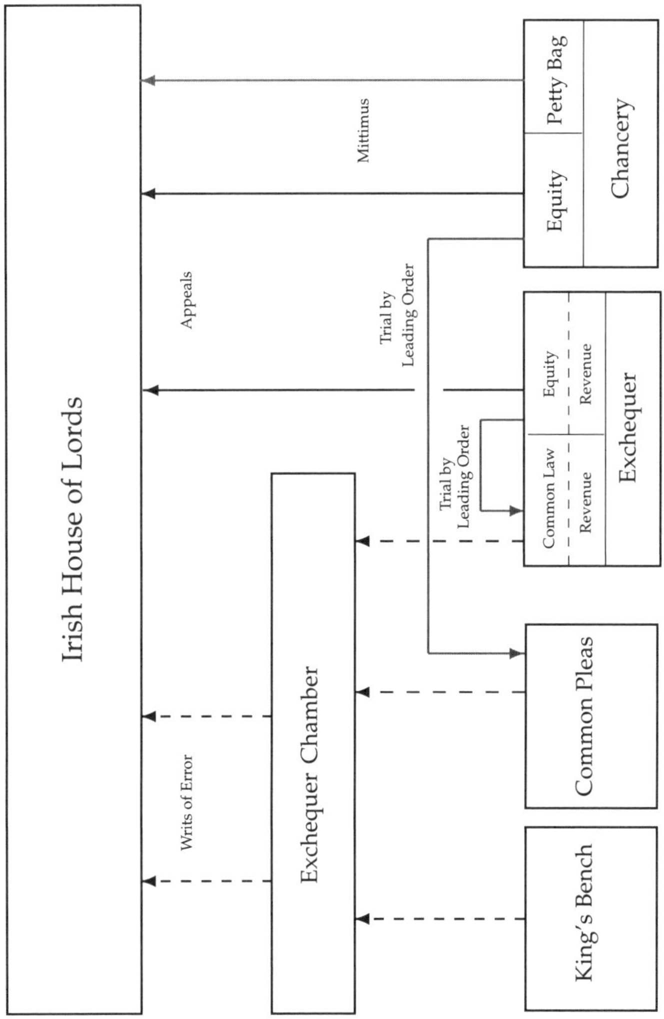

The Irish Legal System 1800–1801

CHAPTER 9

Substantive Law

This chapter examines some of the most important legal issues dealt with by the Irish House of Lords in its brief period as the final court of appeal in Ireland. Foremost among these was the question of the extent of the equity to renew leases for lives which, in the view of the Irish judges, was more extensive than that in England and which had considerable consequences for a large number of tenants in Ireland. Other cases concern the Penal Laws and the validity of a legal device to avoid their effect; the equitable doctrine of estoppel which in this context affected tenants and their right to improvements made to land; the extent to which testators could impose conditions as to marriage in leaving property by will; the distinction between actions of trespass and actions 'on the special case' which affected how the law could be developed; the issue of civil outlawry and its legal effect and finally a complex case on the system of registration of deeds which shows FitzGibbon at his best, in both his grasp of detail and at the same time never losing sight of the underlying principles of fairness in that context and in which he developed a new principle from existing legal materials.

Leases for lives renewable forever

The Nature of the Interest

Property issues are well represented in Ridgeway's reports, but one issue stands out as predominant. By the 18th century much of the land in Ireland was held by tenants from landlords in the peculiar form of 'leases for lives renewable forever.'[1] The essence of it was that L, a landlord, having the fee simple, would make a grant of land to T, the freehold tenant, for the lives of A, B and C at a rent. The estate was thus a freehold estate pur autre vie. A, B and C, who were known as 'cestuis que vie',[2] had no interest in the land. Their lives were simply used as measures of the duration of the estate granted to T. The lease would also contain a covenant to 'renew the lives', that is, appoint replacement lives, when each of the original ones died, on payment of a fine, meaning a lump sum, the renewal

[1] Lyall, *Land Law in Ireland*, 3rd edn. chapter 11, pp. 270–286; Wylie, *Irish Land Law*, 3rd. edn. paras. 4.160–67.

[2] Or, possibly more correctly, ceux que vie.

to be on the same terms as before, that is, including a covenant to renew the replacement lives in their turn. The interest was therefore virtually perpetual, so long as the tenant renewed the lives as required.

Although the interest was in theory freehold the interest was termed a 'lease' because it was a commercial, and not a family, arrangement, the tenant being charged a rent. In addition, the tenant would have to pay a 'fine', or lump sum, to renew any of the lives.

In the example just given, L, the landlord, would retain a fee simple reversion and is more accurately referred to as the 'reversioner in fee.' The tenants for lives would probably be described as landed gentry, either farming with hired hands themselves or in turn having tenants farmers under them, and possibly a mixture of both, if they sublet only a part of their land. Their tenants might also be smaller farming gentry or tenant farmers farming the land themselves. Available evidence suggests that the reversioners in fee tended to be the larger landowners, the kind of people who would have peerages and be lay members of the House of Lords. As such they had influence over the House of Commons, but not over the judiciary. The existence of the equity to renew shows this to be the case, because, insofar as the equity had any social effects in terms of class, it would tend to reduce the influence of the reversioners in fee, i.e. the larger landowners, and it hardly seems plausible that they would have tolerated this if they had had the power to prevent it. The equity therefore seems to validate the view that the judges of the House of Lords were independent of such influence and to support the view that the principle of the rule of law had taken root.

Sometimes the 'lease' would provide that renewals of the lives could only be obtained if they were applied for within a given period of time. A striking feature of equity jurisdiction in Ireland in the 18th century was the invention of the 'equity to renew.' Even if the lease itself provided for renewal within a given period, the Irish courts of equity would override the provision and allow the tenant under such a lease to renew on payment of fines. Although the Irish House of Lords did not invent the equity, its decisions in the period from 1782 to the Union strengthened and expanded it. The equity is further discussed below.

The Origin of the Tenure

The origin of the tenure is obscure. Edward Sugden, an Englishman who became lord chancellor of Ireland and later, as Lord St Leonards, of England, put forward the view in *Attorney General* v. *Hungerford*[3] that the tenure had been created to avoid the Penal Laws. This is certainly not so, since the first examples of such leases in the reports predate the Penal Laws. The first Penal Law affecting landed property was 2 Ann., c. 6 (Ir.), 1703. Smythe[4] lists known examples from cases, the earliest being that in *Boyle* v. *Lysaght*[5] which dated from 1660.[6] A pencilled

3 (1834) 2 Cl. & Fin. 357 at 371, 6 E.R. 1189 at 1196.

4 Hamilton Smythe, *The Law of Landlord and Tenant in Ireland* (Dublin 1842) pp. 229–232.

5 (1787) 1 Ridg. PC 384

6 *ibid.* The other examples he lists are: *Nangle* v. *Smith* 1 West 184, 1 Law Rec., 3rd ser., Eq. 119 (lease dated 1672); *Brown* v. *Tighe* (1834) 8 Bligh N S 272 (1663); *Inchquin* v. *Burnell* (1795) 3 Ridg. PC

note in the author's copy of Smythe reads 'Earl of Arran v. Quigley – 1609.'

In *Boyle* v. *Lysaght*[7] it is said that the tenure may have originated in the north of Ireland, but that 'the great Earl of Ormonde'[8] had introduced it in the south on his estate in order to encourage tenants to improve their holdings.

The origin of the tenure may in fact be much older than earlier commentators have thought. If one examines its actual effect, it was the grant to a tenant of a virtually perpetual freehold interest while at the same time reserving a rent to the grantor, and creating freehold tenure between grantor and grantee. The key word here is 'virtually'. The statute *Quia Emptores* 1290[9] had prohibited the obvious way of achieving this result, namely, by the grant of a fee simple estate while at the same time creating freehold tenure, which would normally include a rent service and covenants, between grantor and grantee. The clear implication of this is that leases for lives had been invented at some time in the past in order to avoid the effect of *Quia Emptores* 1290 in Ireland.[10] *Quia Emptores* 1290 had prohibited subinfeudation for a fee simple estate, that is, the creation of a new layer of freehold tenure in a grant in fee simple. Leases for lives thus created a form of tenure analogous to subinfeudation in fee simple, and therefore it seems probable that originally it was simply a device to avoid *Quia Emptores*. It was also a suitable form of property for 'plantations' or colonies of English and Scottish farmers. It created a structure with freeholders at the bottom who had potentially perpetual interests, giving them both an incentive to develop the land and a sense of permanence, but at the same time it was a hierarchical structure with the freeholders still to some extent dependent on the favourable opinion of the larger landowners who in turn owed allegiance to the British Crown. At a later period it would also have given tenants of sufficient property the right to vote.

But when did leases for lives renewable forever come into use? If they were a means of avoiding *Quia Emptores*, might they not be even older than the plantations? It seems that feudal lords on the Pale ignored the statute at first, because a special version of *Quia Emptores* was promulgated for Ireland. In 1293 Edward I 'sent' the statute 21 Edw. I c. 2 (Ir.), to Ireland. It validated subinfeudations in Ireland up to that time, required compliance with *Quia Emptores* 1290 from then on, but granted exemption to Irish lords on the 'marches' and

376 (lease dated 1668); *Ross (Earl)* v. *Worsop* (1740) 1 Bro. PC 281, 1 E.R. 568 (lease dated 1682).

7 (1787) 1 Ridg. PC 384 at 402.

8 James Butler, the 12th Earl of Ormonde, (1610–1688), had been created Marquess of Ormonde (Ir.), 1642, Duke of Ormonde (Ir.) 1661, (Eng.), 1682, Cokayne, *Complete Peerage*, x. 150. James Butler, the 13th Earl and 2nd Duke of Ormonde (1665–1745), succeeded his grandfather in 1688 and it is evidently he who obtained the private Act of parliament, 8 & 9 Will. III, c. 5 (Eng., private), 1697, enabling him to grant leases for lives binding on his successors in title, since he only held a life estate.

9 18 Edw. I cc. 1, 2 (Eng.).

10 H. F. Berry, ed., *Statutes, etc., Ireland: King John to Henry V* (The Irish Record Office Series of Early Statutes, vol. 1. Dublin, 1907), Preface xv; presumed that the statute had been transmitted to Ireland. Donaldson, 'The Application in Ireland of English and British Legislation made before 1801' (PhD. Queen's University, Belfast. 1952), pp. 80–81: The statute was referred to in a case before the justiciar and the Irish council in 1302: Cal. Just. Rolls Ir., 1295–1303, p. 384. The statute in any case applied to Ireland by Poynings' Law, 1495 (10 Hen. VII, c. 22 (Ir.)).

'lands of war' from the 1290 statute as to the future.[11] Such conditions would have lasted until the Battle of Kinsale in 1601, which saw the end of resistance to English rule. After that, there was a period in which the Crown made grants in fee simple *non obstante Quia Emptores*, i.e. giving a licence to grantees to further subinfeudate notwithstanding *Quia Emptores*. This was an exercise of the 'dispensing power' asserted by medieval kings to grant exemption to individuals from specific statutes. This continued until the end of James II's reign, when the dispensing power was prohibited in Great Britain by the Bill of Rights. No Bill of Rights was enacted for Ireland, although one was proposed,[12] but it is also the case that there are no examples of *non obstante* grants under William and Mary. However, even in this period not everyone would have had the influence with the Crown in order to obtain a *non obstante* grant. The earliest certain evidence is a grant from the time of Charles I[13] and there may have been earlier instances. Furthermore, from the beginning of the reign of William and Mary, leases for lives renewable forever would have been the *only* way that *Quia Emptores* could have been avoided.

The Rules of Occupancy

A peculiarity of a lease for lives was that, as an estate estate pur autre vie, it was not, in the eyes of the common law, an estate of inheritance. If A held land for the lives of X, Y and Z and A died while at least any one of X, Y and Z were still alive, the land did not pass to the common law heir by the rules of descent.[14] Instead, the land passed to the general or special occupant. If the grant had said simply 'to A' for the relevant lives, the common law took the view that on the death of A, if any remnant of the estate remained it belonged to no one. The common law solution was to treat it as if the property had been abandoned. Hence, the first person to take possession of the land took the remainder of the estate, in the same way as a finder of abandoned property. In the case of estates pur autre vie this person was known as the 'general occupant'. In theory the general occupant could be anyone at all, but in practice it would be a relative who would be the first to know of the death and might well already occupy the land as part of the household. If the grant had said 'to A and his heirs for the lives of X, Y and Z' the courts introduced a further refinement. There was still no 'heir' in the strict common law sense, but the person who would have fitted that description,

[11] H. F. Berry, ed., *Statutes, etc., Ireland: King John to Henry V.* (Dublin, 1907). *English Law in Ireland 1290–1324* (Cambridge, 1967), p. 162. In the original French: 'si il ne seyt en tere de gerre ou de marche e la eyent bien poer les seygnurs qe tengt del Rey a feffer autres a tenyr de eus…' In English: 'if it be not in land of war or in the marches [i.e. on the border beyond the Pale] and that there the lords that hold of the King have full power to enfeoff others to hold of them for the defence of the land…'.

[12] W. N. Osborough, 'The Failure to Enact an Irish Bill of Rights: a Gap in Irish Constitutional History' (1998) 33 *Irish Jurist (n.s.)* 392–416.

[13] *Delacherois* v. *Delacherois* (1862-64) 11 H.L.C. 62, a case from Ireland.

[14] There was a practical feudal reason for this. In the feudal period an heir taking by descent was liable to pay a relief to the lord of the tenure. But in this case it seemed unfair to make the next tenant pay a full relief for an interest which, might last only a short time - in the case of an ordinary life tenancy.

normally the eldest son,[15] was allowed to take as 'special occupant'. Leases for lives descended to the special occupant in the absence of a will.[16]

Leases for lives and the Penal Laws

Although the tenure could not be considered a device to avoid the Penal Laws, tenants of leases for lives suffered slightly less of a disability under them than those holding a fee simple, since the slight advantage applied only to leases for lives held at the time the first Penal Law as to property came into force.

If a Catholic tenant for lives died without leaving it by will, the son would take as special occupant and not under the common law rules of descent, strictly speaking.

The first Penal Law as to property, 'An act to prevent the further growth of popery'.[17] provided by section 3 that if the eldest son and heir of a Catholic became a Protestant, then the father became a mere tenant for life, and the reversion vested in the Protestant son. But that section applied only to the real property of which a '[Catholic] parent shall be then seized in fee tail or fee simple'. It did not apply to leases for lives: a tenant for lives was only a tenant pur autre vie. Moreover, the interest was not 'discoverable', that is, was not vulnerable to a claim by a Protestant discoveror under the second Penal Law,[18] again, so long as the tenant for lives did not attempt to leave it by will.

Section 6 of the 1703 Act made Catholics unable 'to buy and purchase' either in their own name or in trust for them 'any lands, tenements or hereditaments... or any leases or terms... other than any term of years' not exceeding 31 years. All other estates 'to be bought and purchased' in excess of that were made void. The section was held to include wills,[19] since 'purchaser' in the technical language of real property law meant, and means, a person who takes by act of parties as opposed to operation of law, and does not imply that consideration was paid.[20] A person taking under a will took by 'purchase'. But a person taking as special occupant did not.

In 1709 the second Penal Law, 'An Act for explaining and amending an act intituled, an Act to prevent the further growth of popery'[21] introduced the particularly draconian means of enforcement of the Protestant discoveror.[22] Any Protestant was given *locus standi* to challenge a 'purchase' in breach of the Acts,

[15] Under the rules of descent at common law, the rule of primogeniture meant that land held in fee simple or fee tail passed to the eldest son, or, failing sons, to the daughters in a form of co-ownership called coparcenary.

[16] *Stewart* v. *Lord Blaney* (1790) 2 Ridg. PC 204 at 206; Lyall, *Land Law in Ireland*, 3rd edn. (Dublin, 2010) p. 284 pp.; 2nd edn. p. 260.

[17] 2 Ann., c. 6 (Ir.), 1703.

[18] See below.

[19] *Farrell* v *Crosbie* (1773) How. Po. Cas. 256, at 263–264. See page 148.

[20] 'Bought and purchased' might have been thought to mean an inter vivos conveyance for value, but the phrase was interpreted to mean two separate instances.

[21] 8 Ann., c. 3 (Ir.), 1709.

[22] 8 Ann., c. 3 (Ir.), s. 27.

and if successful could keep the interest challenged.[23] Informers in the past had been rewarded by legislation under which the were awarded part of a penalty, but the Act of 1709 created an enormous incentive, far greater than anything before.

A person who took under an inter vivos conveyance was a 'purchaser'[24] and also a beneficiary under a will. But a son who took as special occupant was not a 'purchaser.' He took by operation of law, namely, the rules of occupancy. An heir who inherited a fee simple or fee tail by descent was not a purchaser either, but as will be discussed below, a fee simple was subject to the gavelkind clause, under which land was divided among the sons or daughters rather than pass under primogeniture to the first son.[25]

The argument that land held under a lease for lives acquired before the first Penal law came into force was not 'discoverable' was put forward against a Protestant discoveror in *Chaddick* v. *O'Hagherin*,[26] and was accepted by both sides, although the discoveror succeeded on other grounds. The case is poorly reported and only a few sentences outline what must have been a much more complex argument than they suggest. However, the case was explained in a later case, *Farrell* v *Crosbie*[27] The defendant's father, a Catholic, took a lease for lives under a lease granted before the first Penal law came into effect. He left it by will to his son, also a Catholic. Counsel for the defendant conceded that the will was made void by the first Penal Law, since the father had not converted within time after the Act, but argued that in that case 'the defendant was entitled as special occupant to the interest in the lands...' In other words, if the will was void, then the son took by operation of law, was not a 'purchaser' and so the Protestant discoveror had no *locus standi*. However, counsel for the plaintiff Protestant discoveror argued successfully that the effect of the second Penal law[28] was that the will was validated, or 'revived', for the purpose only of a claim by a discoveror,[29] and that being so, the defendant took under the will, was therefore a 'purchaser', and that 'the interest is discoverable on that account'. It both was, and was not, a will. The Penal Laws allowed the State to have it both ways, at the expense of logic and integrity. Both sides nevertheless accepted that someone who took as a special occupant would not be vulnerable to a Protestant discoveror. *Farrell* confirmed that this was the case.

One can therefore reach the following conclusion, which does not seem to have been noticed by commentators, at least since *Farrell* v *Crosbie*. A lease for lives *held by a Catholic when the first Penal Law came into force* could be kept within

[23] Section 27 applied where Catholics 'who have purchased several lands, tenements and hereditaments and taken leases contrary to the true intent and meaning of the said [1703] Act.'

[24] And so too was a person who took under an inter vivos gift, since 'purchase' technically did not imply valuable consideration, only an act of parties, or party.

[25] Page 163.

[26] (1736) How. Po. Cas. 76.

[27] (1773) How. Po. Cas. 256, at 263–264, in Chancery.

[28] 8 Ann., c. 3 (Ir.), 1709,.

[29] As to leases for lives. If the interest had been a fee simple or a fee tail it would not be discoverable, but go as gavelkind: *Farrell* v *Crosbie* How. Po. Cas. at 263.

a Catholic family, passing by special occupancy from one generation to another, provided the tenant for lives did not at any time leave it by will. So long as that was the case, it was not vulnerable to a Protestant discoveror, since there was no 'purchase' after the Acts, nor was it subject to the gavelkind clause, which only applied to fees simple and fees tail. The only argument that might have been made against this was that a renewal of the lives might be considered to be a 'purchase' and therefore discoverable, but Howard cites the case of *Moore* v. *Lynch*[30] which held that this was not so; that the covenant was held to be part of the 'acquisition and purchase which was precedent to those statutes [the Popery Acts]' and so a renewal was not discoverable.

Whether this was a deliberate result, or an unintended consequence of the definitions of the words in the Acts, is unclear. Presumably, if it had been noticed and thought to create a significant problem, legislation could have been passed to prevent it.

The Equity to Renew

The case which firmly established the extensive equity to renew lives was *Sweet* v. *Anderson*[31] in 1718. A lease was made to Arthur Anderson for his own life and that of his nephew, the colourfully-named John 'Black Jack' (or 'Black John') Anderson, with a covenant to renew the lives on payment of a fine within 12 months of the death of the life concerned. Arthur, the grantee, died in 1714 leaving his interest by will to the respondent. The respondent applied for a renewal, within 12 months of the death of Arthur, which was refused. Black Jack had left Ireland and not been heard of since 1697. The appellant refused, on the ground that Black Jack must be presumed, by statute, to have died after seven years from when he was last heard of, and no renewal had been applied for in accordance with the covenant within 12 months of that date. This was a reference to 7 Wm III, c 8, (Ir.).[32] An obvious problem with leases for lives was the question of what was to happen if one or more of the lives simply disappeared or had not been heard of for some time. The statute, passed by the Irish parliament, created a presumption that the cestui que vie had died where it is shown, by the lessor or a reversioner, that a cestui que vie of a lease for lives or other life estate had been 'absent or beyond the seas' for seven years or more with no proof that he or she was still alive. The appellant therefore maintained that any right to renew had been forfeited.

The respondent filed a bill in the Court of Exchequer in 1715, and it came before the court in February 1717. The court directed an issue to be tried before

[30] How. Po. Cas. 287, Exchequer, Hill. 1739, and Trin. 1740. In a note he also cites the case of *Broder* v. *Martin* How. Po. Cas. 288 in the same court as 'having received such a determination' but, in a note, that he had 'searched many years for this case, but ineffectually.'

[31] (1718) 2 Bro. PC 256, affirmed (1722) at 430; 1 E.R. 927. The case was reported in 1772, long after it was heard. The printed pleadings are at: HLRO, Hl/PO/JU/4/3/4, 'Appeal Cases and Writs of Error, series 3, 1721–24'. 16 Oct 1722. The parchment petition and appeal of Stephen Sweet is at: HLRO, large parchments, HL/PO/JO/10/3/214/46.

[32] The statute was based on the English Act 18 & 19 Cha. II, c. 11 (Ruffhead 19 Cha. II, c. 6). It was given a short title, the Life Estates Act, 1695 by the Short Titles Act, 1962 (RI).

a jury at the next assizes to be held in Kilkenny as to whether Black Jack was alive at the time the renewal was sought, and if not, when he had died. The issue was tried before Sir John St Leger, one of the barons of the Exchequer, at the Kilkenny assizes on 2 April 1718. The jury returned the verdict that: 'We find that Black John Anderson, son of Alexander Anderson, is the cestui que vie in the lease mentioned; but we do not find that he is dead.'

On 7 July 1718 the case came before the Irish Court of Exchequer. Gilbert CB hit upon a novel solution which made him temporarily very popular in Ireland, at least with tenants for lives.[33] The judge noted that Black Jack had been absent for 21 years. Since the cestui que vie would be presumed dead after seven years, under the statute, then if the respondent paid three fines, one fine for every seven years, he could have his renewal. There is a certain ingenious logic behind the decision. The implication is that one could not only presume the cestui que vie to be dead after seven years: one could also presume that the life had been replaced. Furthermore, since the presumed replacement 'life' had naturally not been heard of from the beginning, one could also presume that the replacement had been presumed dead after a further seven years, and so on. These cumulative payments became known as 'septennial fines.' The decision was upheld on appeal to the British House of Lords in 1722.[34]

It may be noticed that British House of Lords did not reverse the decision taken by the Irish court familiar with Irish conditions. Furthermore, the lease itself only provided for actual, not presumptive, death and so in allowing a renewal long after the fictional event the British Lords implicitly supported the notion, as the Irish Court of Exchequer had done, that an equity to renew existed long after an actual death, and after the death of both lives in this case and despite, also, the twelve month limitation which the deed attempted to impose on renewal. Lyne also reports a later case with almost the identical facts as *Sweet* in the Irish Court of Exchequer in 1766, *Shore* v. *Lord Darnley*[35] in which a renewal was ordered. One of the cestuis que vie, T. Shore, had died and another, H. Shore, had left Ireland several years before. On the death of T. Shore the tenant plaintiff applied for a renewal, saying he had no information as to H. Shore, offered to pay septennial fines from the time he left Ireland and tendering a fine on the death of T. Shore. The defendant refused a renewal on the ground that a condition in the lease stated that if the tenant failed to nominate a new life within 12 months of the death, the landlord could refuse a renewal, and cited the statute 7 Will. III, c 8, (Ir.) by which H. Shore should have been presumed dead, having been absent for more than seven years.

He submitted that he was entitled to refuse unless the plaintiff could prove that he had nominated a new life within 12 months of H. Shore's death. The Irish Court of Exchequer decreed a renewal of the lease on payment of the septennial fines, and without costs.

[33] His subsequent fall from favour has been mentioned above: See page 1.

[34] (1722) 2 Bro. PC 430; 1 E.R. 927. The case is reported long after the decision. Above, page 149 note 31.

[35] (1766) Wal. by L. 192.

It is open to question whether Gilbert actually invented the equity, or merely extended it by his ingenious remedy. Gilbert certainly invented septennial fines and extended the equity to cases where the cestui que vie had disappeared. But one suspects that the equity itself was of much older origin. If the theory is correct, that the lease for lives renewable forever was a device to avoid *Quia Emptores* 1290, then one would expect the equity to be older than the 18th century, and there is some evidence that this is so. The Irish Lord Chancellor, Lord Lifford, delivering judgment in the Irish Chancery in *Bateman* v. *Murray*,[36] apparently believed that the equity existed before Gilbert:

> Lord Chief Baron Gilbert only invented the mode of making satisfaction for lapse of time by the rule... adopted respecting septennial fines.[37]

and he repeated the view later in the Irish House of Lords in *Boyle* v. *Lysaght*:[38]

> Hence it happened that tenants neglected to make renewals upon the fall of the lives, and were guilty of great laches:– The landlords thereupon brought ejectments, and tenants resorted to courts of equity for relief; and courts of equity, where the breach was made up by an adequate compensation, thought they were entitled to relief:– But still considerable difficulties arose in estimating what should be a compensation, until that great man, Lord Chief Baron Gilbert, who presided in the Court of Exchequer in this kingdom, struck out the compensation of septennial fines; considering a life as equal to seven years, upon the idea of the act which says, that if a man is not heard of for seven years, he is presumed dead. That compensation is a fine for every seven years with interest.

Lifford clearly seemed to think that there had been cases before *Sweet* v. *Anderson* in which the equity had been recognised, but that there had been difficulties in fixing the amount of compensation. He does not say that these difficulties proved insurmountable. Charles Molyneux, 1st Earl of Sefton[39] in his pamphlet[40] addressed to Lifford, in support of the Tenantry Bill, gives the impression that before *Sweet*, the equity was satisfied by a single fine, plus interest over the period of delay, and that Gilbert's septennial fines were therefore highly

[36] (1779) 1 Ridg. PC 187 note; *Murray* v. *Bateman, Lady Rosse, his wife* (1776) Wal. by L. 181. The British House of Lords decision is reported in (1779) 5 Brown 20, 2 E.R. 506. See also above page 91 note 19 and page 92 note 22.

[37] *ibid.*, at p. 196.

[38] (1787) 1 Ridg. PC 384 at 403-4; Vern. & Scr. 135.

[39] Charles William Molyneux (1748–1795), 8th Viscount Molyneux (Ir.). He conformed to the Church of Ireland, 1769 and was created Earl of Sefton (Ir.) on the advice of Lord North. The title was a fiction: Sefton referred to Sefton in Lancaster, the manor of which had been in the family since at least 1212 when it was held by Richard de Molyneux. As an Irish peer (without a peerage in the peerage of Great Britain) he could sit in the British House of Commons, and did so as MP for Lancashire from 1771–74. Cokayne, *Complete Peerage*, xi.592.

[40] *Some thoughts on the Bill for the relief of tenants holding leases for lives, renewable for ever. Addressed to Lord Lifford, Lord Chancellor of Ireland* (Dublin, 1780).

favourable to the landlords.[41] He also pointed out that if the tenant lost the renewal, all the improvements went to the landlord. There was no compensation for improvements under the law at the time.

Lord Pery in the same case expressed the same opinion as Lifford as to Gilbert's part in the matter:[42]

> I concur with the noble Viscount in every point, except this, that the equity of the tenant is a *local equity*. It is a general principle of equity, to relieve against a mere lapse of time. But as the landlord suffered an injury by the tenant's neglect to renew in time, it was necessary to make him compensation. The only difficulty was in settling what that compensation should be. ... That of septennial fines, established by Lord Ch. B. Gilbert, was more than adequate; for at that time the price of an annuity for life was ten years purchase.

A clash between the British and Irish courts was to come later in the century. In that conflict the British lords were not simply concerned to prevent the further extension of the Irish equity, but to reverse to some extent the position that they had accepted in *Sweet* v. *Anderson*,[43] namely that an equity to renew could exist even after the time for renewal provided for in the lease had expired.

The first skirmishes were inconclusive. *Ross (Earl)* v. *Worsop*[44] was before the British House of Lords in 1740. A renewal was refused, but the landlord was absent from Ireland at the time and on his return consented to a renewal. In *Pendred* v. *Griffith*[45] the British House again refused a renewal on the ground of lapse of time, but as Ridgeway points out,[46] the tenant had concealed the death of the cestui que vie. No court of equity would grant a renewal in such a case, since the tenant did not come to equity 'with clean hands.'

The clash came to a head between 1720 and 1782 during the period when appeals lay to the British House of Lords in two cases. Lord Mansfield in *Kane* v. *Hamilton*[47] and Lord Thurlow in *Bateman* v. *Murray*,[48] in 1779 refused to recognise that the Irish equity was as extensive as the Irish courts had held it to be, or as extensive as they themselves had held it to be in *Sweet* v. *Anderson*.

41 It is interesting that Sefton supported the bill, but his main estate was in England. Cokayne adds that Georgiana, Duchess of Devonshire, described him in 1777 as 'the most disagreeable and noisy of fools' and that in the same year he sold a piece of land to Liverpool corporation for £2,500 which became the centre of the city and subsequently worth millions: Cokayne, *ibid.*, xi.593, n. a.

42 *ibid.*, at p. 417; Vern. & Scr. at 154.

43 (1772) 2 Bro. PC 256, affirmed 430; 1 E.R. 927.

44 (1740) 4 Bro. PC 411, 1 E.R. 568.

45 (1744) 4 Bro. PC 512, 1 E.R. 590.

46 1 Ridg. PC 185.

47 (1776), noted at 1 Ridg. PC 180 at 185; the printed pleadings are at: HLRO, HL/PO/JU/4/3/19, 'Appeal Cases and Writs of Error, series 3, 1775–76'. The proceedings in the Irish Court of Exchequer are reported as *Hamilton* v. *Kane* (1774) Wal. by L. 172.

48 (1779) noted at 1 Ridg. PC 187 at 201, reversing the Irish lord chancellor, Lord Lifford, 5 Bro. PC 20, 2 E.R. 506; the printed pleadings are at: HLRO, HL/PO/JU/4/3/21, 'Appeal Cases and Writs of Error, series 3, 1779–80'.

In *Murray* v. *Bateman*[49] in 1776 Lord Lifford in the Irish Chancery heard a case in which a tenant held for three lives with a covenant for perpetual renewal, the renewal to be within three months of the fall of any life. The tenant had not applied for a renewal until the fall of the last life, even though he was also bound by a covenant that required him to prove every year that the lives were in being, and in default the landlord was entitled to a fine. The lord chancellor nevertheless decreed a renewal.

In *Boyle* v *Lysaght*[50] later in the century Lifford LC recalled how he had arrived at his judgment upholding the renewal in *Murray* v. *Bateman*:

> I had a great number of those cases laid before me, besides those that had been cited at the bar. I directed a search to be made, and I found that they abounded in the courts. I also enquired of the judges, of the ablest men, and oldest practitioners in the hall, and they all agreed that the uniform practice was to decree renewals in all cases, except where there was fraud or dereliction[51] on the part of the tenant. Some of those persons are now dead, Lord Annaly[52], Mr Justice Robinson[53], Mr. Malone,[54] Chief Justice Patterson[55] [*sic*] and others, who were perfectly acquainted with the determinations that had been made, and they said moreover that the cases which had passed *sub silentio* were innumerable. In consequence of this general remonstrance, I formed my opinion, notwithstanding any ideas upon the subject that might have brought with me from England, where this kind of tenure is not known: accordingly I decreed a renewal. I did consider that there was a local equity, and as have I often heard it called, the old equity of the kingdom.

The British House of Lords on appeal[56] reversed the Lord Lifford. In particular the British House held, in this case and *Kane* v *Hamilton*, that equity did not

[49] The Irish Chancery judgment is reported at (1776) Wal. by L. 181, sub nom.

[50] (1787) 1 Ridg. PC 384.

[51] 'Dereliction' in the 18th century sense of complete abandonment: Dr Johnson defined 'dereliction' in the first edition of his *Dictionary* as 'an utter forsaking or leaving; an abandoning' and in the fourth edition as '1. the act of forsaking or leaving; abandonment, 2. the state of being forsaken' and not in the sense of mere neglect. The Oxford English Dictionary, while repeating Johnson's sense, as '1. The action of leaving or forsaking (with intention not to resume); abandonment', adding 'now rare, except in legal use', then adds '2. in the modern use implying a morally wrong or reprehensible abandonment, or neglect, chiefly in the phrase *dereliction of duty*'.

[52] John Gore, 1st Baron Annaly of Tenelick, (1718–1784), CJKB 1764, created Baron Annaly, 1766. Cokayne, *Complete Peerage*, i.163; Ball, *Judges in Ireland*, pp. 212–13.

[53] Christopher Robinson (1722–1788), KC 1745, JKB 1758–1788. Ball, Judges in Ireland, p. 144. Note: p. 210, *ibid.*, says he was JCP, but this is wrong. A portrait of Robinson, as KC, 1750 by Benjamin Wilson, discovered by Professor Colum Kenny in Leeds Museum and Galleries, is the frontispiece of Colum Kenny, *King's Inns and the Battle of the Books, 1972* (Dublin: Four Courts in association with The Irish Legal History Society, 2002).

[54] Edmund Malone (1704–1774), KC 1745, 2nd serjeant 1759, JCP 1766–1774. Ball, *Judges in Ireland*, p. 214.

[55] Marcus Paterson (1712–1787), CJCP 1770–1787. Ball, *Judges in Ireland*, pp. 216–17.

[56] *Bateman* v. *Murray*, (1779) noted at 1 Ridg. PC 187 at 201.

permit a renewal after an indefinite delay and contrary to limiting clauses in the lease itself, apart from cases of fraud or accident, against which even the English courts would give relief. Lord Thurlow stated his view of the equity in the following terms:[57]

> when the lessee has lost his legal right, he must prove some fraud on the part of the lessor, by which he was debarred the exercise of his right, or some accident or misfortune on his own part which he could not prevent, by means whereof he was disabled from applying at the stated times for a renewal according to the terms of his lease.

This went against a long series of cases in Ireland, and was contrary to the British House of Lords own decision in *Sweet* v. *Anderson*, as Lord Farnham pointed out in *Boyle* v. *Lysaght*[58] the British Lords, he said,

> had not the excuse to plead that they were ignorant of the established law of this kingdom in such cases, for they had themselves ratified and confirmed it in *Sweet* v. *Anderson* and many subsequent cases which had come before them.

Lord Pery in the same case agreed with Lifford's comments:[59]

> I cannot help expressing my surprise, that in the case of *Murray* v. *Bateman*, the lords of England should overturn the known settled law in such cases.– That decision made it necessary to pass the tenantry act, to prevent the confusion that was likely to arise in this kingdom from that determination. That court was a very proper one at the time, but as jurisdiction is now restored to this House, it is now unnecessary.

The decisions in the British House of Lords caused great concern in Ireland where the extensive equity had long been recognised. They also had some awkward practical results of which the British court seemed unaware or unconcerned about. Leases for lives renewable forever had been treated as equivalent to a fee simple in Ireland. They had been mortgaged by a conveyance of the lease as security. If the leases no longer existed or could not be renewed, mortgagees would lose their security.[60] Moreover, 'quasi-settlements' had been created out of the leases. Since they were regarded as the equivalent of fees simple, tenants had created 'entails' out of them and other interests, such as jointures, associated with 'real' settlements. The entails were not 'real' fees tail, because they had not been created out of a real fee simple, but were called 'quasi-entails'.[61] Again, if the lease could not be renewed, family members of the tenant would lose their income from the jointures charged on the lease.

57 (1779) 1 Ridg. PC 201.
58 (1787) 1 Ridg. PC 384 at 419.
59 1 Ridg. PC at 417.
60 'House of Lords Appeals' (Pleadings) 1787–90, Vol. 47, *Boyle* v. *Lysaght*, King's Inns.
61 Lyall, *Land Law in Ireland* 3rd edn. (Dublin, 2010), pp. 289–291.

Tenantry Act, 1780

When the Irish parliament began its course of legislative activity towards the end of the century it hastened to give statutory form to the Irish equity. In 1780 the Tenantry Act[62] was passed. It reasserted the Irish equity and gave it statutory form. This was even before Yelverton's Act, and the Act was passed through the Poynings' Law process, but it was clear that change was on the way to give the Irish parliament greater independence. There seem to have been an awareness that the British House of Lords had overstepped the mark.

The preamble recited that:[63]

> Whereas it has been for a long time a received opinion in this kingdom, to which some decisions in courts of equity and declarations of judges have given countenance, that courts of equity would in such cases relieve against lapse of time upon giving adequate compensation to the persons, to whom such fines were payable, or their representatives: and to the end that such interests may not be defeated by a mere neglect, where no fraud appears to have been intended, upon making full satisfaction to the lessors, or those deriving under them...

Section 1 of the Act recognised the 'old equity of the country':

> That courts of equity upon an adequate compensation being made shall relieve such tenants and their assigns against such lapse of time, if no circumstance of fraud be proved against such tenants or their assigns; unless it shall be proved to the satisfaction of such courts, that the landlords or lessors, or persons entitled to receive such fines, had demanded such fines from such tenants or their assigns, and that the same had been refused or neglected to be paid within reasonable time after such demand.

Before the landlord made such a demand, the equitable doctrine of laches[64] did not apply and the equity would be defeated only by fraud or other inequitable conduct, but not by delay alone. The effect of a demand was therefore to apply the equitable doctrine of laches and delay in itself, if of an unreasonable duration, would disentitled the tenant. The new concept of unreasonable delay, was addressed by Lord Clare LC (FitzGibbon) in the Court of Chancery in *Deane* v. *Marquis of Waterford*:[65]

> The act declares, that unless the tenant shall pay his renewal fines within a reasonable time after a demand made, he shall forfeit his right of renewal; and the single point in this case is, whether, under

62 19 & 20 Geo. III c. 30 (Ir.). The bill was before the Irish House of lords in August 1780 and received the royal assent on 7 September 1780.

63 See Appendix M, page 246.

64 LF. delay.

65 (1795) 1 Sch. & Lef. 451, reported as a note.

> all the circumstances which are in proof, the plaintiff has incurred such a forfeiture. It certainly appears he has been guilty of gross neglect, unaccounted for, in not renewing his lease: the first life fell in the year 1748, the second in 1754, and the third in 1761: no application whatever was made on his part for a renewal. But in February, 1793, an application appears to have been made to him on the part of the defendant: Mr. Jas. Glascock, the agent for the defendant, then informed him that all the lives in his lease had fallen, and called upon him to renew.

Lord Clare then went on to note that a genuine mistake had then been made on the part of the defendant's agent as to the calculation of the renewal fines. As a result of the mistake a much larger sum was demanded than was in fact due, and this led to negotiations between the defendant and the plaintiff before the mistake was identified, causing the delay in renewing the lease since 1793 for several months. The lord chancellor displayed his impressive analytical powers in refining the test of a reasonable delay in the section:

> Certainly however the plaintiff has, in this case, acted with so little vigilance or attention on his own part, in clearing up this mistake, and ascertaining the fines really due to his landlord, subsequent to the 10th of August, 1793, when a formal demand was made upon him, that he cannot be entitled to a decree in this cause, unless upon the fullest indemnification to the defendant from all the consequences of his negligence and inattention. ... if I were on the abstract question to declare that ought to be deemed a reasonable time within this clause of the act, I would say that it was no more than what was necessary to give the tenant full opportunity for ascertaining when the cestui que vie died, for computing the amount of the fines due, and for preparing leases and tendering them for execution. The precise time to be allowed the tenant cannot necessarily be defined; it must depend upon the difficulties which he may fairly have to encounter in complying with the demand: but I should incline strongly to determine that if a precise time for payment of the renewal fine was limited by the lease upon the fall of each life, that the tenant ought to be restricted to the same time after a demand made, unless he has a fair and reasonable excuse to assign for exceeding it. So if no time was limited by the lease, I should incline strongly to adopt the rule by analogy to the statutes giving the remedy by ejectment for non-payment of rent; and to determine that the tenant coming into a court of equity for a renewal, after six months from the demand made upon him ought to be able to account fairly for his neglect. In this case I think the error into which the tenant fell with respect to the identity of one of the lives comprized in his lease, is a sufficient ground for the interposition of a Court of equity, to relieve him from the forfeiture which otherwise, in my opinion, he must have

incurred; and upon this circumstance alone it is that I ground my decree for a renewal.

A number of cases came before the courts in Ireland between the reversal of the Irish Chancery by the British House of Lords in *Bateman* v. *Murray* and the passing of the Tenantry Act. *Freeman* v. *Boyle*[66] was before the Irish lord chancellor in June 1780 and he refused the renewal, considering himself bound by the decision of the British House in *Bateman* v. *Murray*. The Tenantry Act came into force in September 1780.

Freeman v. *Boyle* did not reach the Irish House of Lords, to whom jurisdiction had been restored in 1782, until 1788. The Irish House, applying the statute, allowed the tenant to renew on payment of septennial fines.[67]

Magrath v. *Lord Muskerry*,[68] in its actual decision, held, *inter alia*, that after the fall of all the lives the tenant no longer had a right of renewal, but the facts were governed by the law immediately before the Tenantry Act 1780, as represented by the British House of Lords case of *Murray* v. *Bateman*. Although *Magrath* did not reach the Irish lords until May 1787, by the time that the Tenantry Act came into force on 7 September 1780 the landlord had already brought ejectment on title at law and had obtained possession of the premises.[69] Lifford noted that the landlord was within the proviso to the Act, section 3, which provided that the Act would not apply to a suit commenced before 15 May 1780 and still pending.[70] Lifford LC, when he heard the case in 1780, had therefore felt bound to apply the law before the Act, as represented by *Murray* v. *Bateman*. In fact, although the lords took the same view of the law applicable on the facts of the case before them, they also took the opportunity to re-assert their view of the Irish equity, which was that it was, and apparently had always been, available after the fall of all the lives, and no matter how long the delay was, providing there was no evidence of fraud.

In so far as *Magrath* v. *Lord Muskerry* decided that the equity was not available after the death of all the lives, it was contrary to *Sweet* v. *Anderson*[71] and *in curiam*, for in *Sweet*, one life, Arthur Anderson, was certainly dead, and the other, Black Jack Anderson, was presumed to be dead under Gilbert CB's ruling. This had been upheld by the British House of Lords themselves. One wonders why the Irish Lords in *Magrath* did not point this out, as indeed Lord Farnham did in *Boyle* v. *Lysaght*[72] and, bound as they were by the British decisions on

[66] (1788) 2 Ridg. PC 69, 76.

[67] See also *Boyle* v. *Lysaght* (1787) 1 Ridg. PC 384. Both cases actually involved leases for 99 years and lives, both lives and the term being renewable. The equity, and the Act, were held to apply to such leases.

[68] (1787) 1 Ridg. PC 469, Vern. & Scr. 166.

[69] 1 Ridg. PC 483.

[70] Since the bill passed through its legislative stages before the amendment to Poynings Law, it had to be submitted to the Westminster for approval or amendment. The original draft had merely exempted suits in which a judgment or decree had actually been obtained before the Act came into force, but the amendment to the proviso, excluding pending suits, had been inserted by the British attorney general. See Appendix M, page 245.

[71] (1718) 2 Bro. P.C. 256, affirmed, 1722, 430.

[72] (1787) 1 Ridg. PC 384 at 419.

the facts, and faced with conflicting British House of Lords decisions, prefer the earlier decision in *Sweet* to the more recent one in *Murray*. There were, however, other grounds on which the tenant would have failed in any case in *Magrath*: the tenant had engaged in tedious and vexatious proceedings against the landlord and had ignored the interlocutory orders of the court.[73] Such conduct would have disentitled him to equitable relief quite apart from the rest of his case.

One further point: the fact that the respondent in *Magrath* had obtained judgment at law before the Tenantry Act came into force was material for the purpose of applying the proviso in the Act, but as to cases after the Act, it was irrelevant. Apart from the transitional provision, equity prevailed over the common law and the fact that one had obtained judgment at law did not prevent a court of equity from intervening.[74] Counsel for the plaintiff in the Irish Chancery in *Murray* v. *Bateman*[75] cites the case of *Kirkwood* v. *Lord Tyrone*[76] in which Lord Tyrone had brought ejectment and obtained possession, but the plaintiff in equity succeeded in a bill for renewal. The report states that this was 'affirmed by the Lords'. This evidently means the British House of Lords. The cases cited before and after in counsel's argument are from the 1750s and 1760s. The editor, Lyne, states in a footnote that he was not able to find the case[77] and Lifford LC in his judgment mentions that the case was not to be found in the Lords' printed cases.[78] Nevertheless, Lifford himself cited the case of *O'Hara* v. *Bourke*[79] in the Irish Court of Exchequer in which an ejectment had been brought at law, and yet the plaintiff obtained a renewal by the unanimous opinion of the Court of Exchequer.

In *O'Neil* v. *Jones*[80] the covenant expressly providing that the right to renew was to expire six months after the death of the life for which renewal was sought. Furthermore, all the cestuis que vie had died. The surviving life had died in 1769. The tenant had neglected to renew for twenty years from the death of the first life, nine years from the death of the second life, and six years from the death of the last life. The case did not come before the lord chancellor, however, until November 1782. The court held that a renewal would be granted even after the six months had expired and even though all the lives had died. The court thus reasserted its view of the Irish equity. The case was argued by counsel for the landlord on the basis that:

73 1 Ridg. PC 469

74 Lord Redesdale LC, after the Union in *Lennon* v. *Napper* (1802) 2 Sch. & Lef. 682, at 686, said that obtaining possession at law 'is only material as it changes the character of the landlord in respect to the land, when he takes possession as owner' and that he did not understand what Lord Lifford meant in *Ross (Lord)* v. *Worsop* (1740) 4 Bro. PC 411, 1 E.R. 568 by saying, *obiter* (there had been no change of possession in the case), 'as to there being a legal estate for the equity to attach upon. The equity arises from the contract; the change of possession is a circumstance, as it alters the condition of one of the parties materially; but in any other view, I do not understand this expression.' The landlord's obtaining possession at law would give him seisin at law, so long as he remained in possession, but that would not hinder the operation of equity.

75 (1776) Wal. by L. 181.

76 Wal. by L., at 188–9, no date given.

77 *ibid.*, p. 190.

78 Wal. by L. at 197.

79 (1756) Wal. by L. 201. The case is reported by Lyne in a note: Wal. by L. at 191.

80 (1785) 1 Ridg. PC 175.

> on the principles of the old equity, the tenant had been guilty of gross laches and neglect, sufficient to induce a forfeiture of his interest... it is a maxim in law that *crassa negligentia æquiparatur dolo*[81]

FitzGibbon and Carleton, as counsel, argued in support of the decree to renew:[82]

> all cases of leases for lives renewable forever, have been governed in this kingdom by an ancient and long established rule of equity, which was, that mere laches on the part of the tenant should never work a forfeiture of his lease, but that the landlord should be compelled to renew at any time, even after the fall of *all* the lives, upon receiving a full and adequate pecuniary compensation.

They then went on to point out that the Tenantry Act had been passed to re-establish the old equity. The report states that after hearing counsel, the court simply ordered that the appeal be dismissed and the decree of the Court of Chancery should be affirmed. FitzGibbon and Carleton's argument prevailed. Lyne[83] commenting on the argument that 'gross and inveterate neglect may amount to fraud', notes that although it was argued by counsel for the landlord in *O'Neil*, 'the courts, however, have never got so far as this in judgment', but that Lifford LC expressed the opinion (on the Tenantry Act) that 'wilful and contentious neglect, followed up by litigious conduct in the prosecution of the suit, is misconduct amounting to fraud.'[84] Lifford's exact words were:

> It [the Act] relieves in case of mere neglect, where there is no fraud, unless there has been a demand and refusal, which is made at the bar the definition of dereliction. But I think, gross, wilful, obstinate and contentious neglect on the part of the tenant, is the proper definition of dereliction.

Lifford notably required all four characteristics: 'gross, wilful, obstinate *and* contentious' neglect, before a demand by the landlord. It would clearly be wrong to say, as counsel argued, that the only form of 'dereliction' would be unreasonable delay after a demand, under the Act, by the landlord. Inequitable conduct, even before a demand, would disentitle the tenant from a renewal in a Court of equity. But at the same time, there is nothing to indicate in the case law that delay, however long, without more, would disentitle a tenant *before* a demand by the landlord. In fact the Irish case law supported the opposite. The factor which disentitled the tenant in *Magrath* was inequitable conduct in pursuing the suit. The requirement is some element of dishonesty which protracted the delay. It must also be taken into account that Lyne wrote his book after the Union, when appeals again went to the British House of Lords, and precedents in that period,

81 Gross neglect may amount to fraud.

82 1 Ridg. PC 177. This of course does not in itself indicate either FitzGibbon's or Carleton's personal view of the law, since they are arguing the case on behalf of their client. FitzGibbon's judgments as lord chancellor, however, indicate that it did accord with his own view.

83 James Lyne, *A Treatise on Leases for Lives, renewable for ever* (Dublin, 1837), p. 177.

84 *Magrath* v. *Lord Muskerry* 1 Ridg. PC 496, at 494.

some of which he cites, must be treated with caution.[85] If the issue ever arose in the Republic as to the extent of the Irish equity the best guides must be those of the Irish courts, excluding those in the period when appeals went to the British House of Lords in cases where the Irish court felt bound by those decisions, and more especially including those of the Irish House of Lords after it recovered its jurisdiction.

On the cases as a whole, if one takes judicial remarks at face value it would seem that the judges saw their role as giving effect to the intent of the parties, to the wish to create a virtually perpetual estate. The lord chancellor in *Boyle* v. *Lysaght*[86] expresses this notion when speaking of the reversal by the British lords of Irish decisions on the issue:

> I am satisfied that the principles of it were not understood there [i.e. in England]. They were unacquainted with that local equity, and that it was the intent of the original parties to convey a perpetuity: all this I say was unknown to them: they had no such tenures: no such determinations in that kingdom.

Since the equity overrode express conditions in the leases it cannot simply be explained as an attempt to give effect to the specific intent of the parties as recorded in the lease. The analogy may be more accurately to the old common law form of mortgage by conveyance of the fee simple, in which the deed lays down a legal date for redemption at six months from the date of the deed, but both parties take into account the equitable right to redeem and that the rights of the parties in the meantime were governed by principles of equity, as both were well aware. The equitable right to redeem is not lost because the legal date has passed. Moreover, any attempt by the clause in the mortgage to 'clog or fetter' the equitable right to redeem would be invalid. In this area the competing concepts are those of contract and property. Once the parties choose the form of mortgage, the actual conditions in the contract may be overridden if they are inconsistent with the property form. The same was true of the treatment of leases for lives renewable forever by the Irish courts. Intention of the parties was important in deciding whether they had intended the lease for lives to be renewable *perpetually*, but once that was established, the property form prevailed. The fact that all the lives had died meant that the *common law* right to renew had come to an end, but that did not affect the equitable right to renew, just as the equity to redeem a mortgage continues long after the common law right has gone. And, as with a mortgage, no 'clog or fetter' was allowed to restrict the equity to renew a lease for lives renewable forever. In their report on the Tenantry Bill, the British attorney general and solicitor general essentially accepted that such leases in Ireland were considered by all as perpetual interests:[87]

[85] e.g. *Mountnorris* v. *White* (1814) 2 Dow 459, in which the British House of Lords reversed the Irish Court of Exchequer which had upheld the tenant's right of renewal, Lyne, p. 178,

[86] (1787) 1 Ridg. PC 384, at 406.

[87] PRO PC 1/12/26. 17 July 1780. See Appendix L, below, page 241.

> But it is to be observed that from the nature of these Leases it is apparent that those who granted them had it not in their Contemplation that their Estates would ever return to them but intended only to obtain the payment of certain Fines and Rents, and if these can be by any other method secured without giving to the Lessors a right to resume their Estates they will enjoy all the fruits which they ever expected to derive from them.

Social Effects

The tenure had one important effect in the 18th century. We have seen that until 1793 the franchise in Ireland was confined to Protestant freeholders. Since there were no secret ballots at the time, Protestant landowners could not only vote themselves, but could influence the way their tenants voted. Catholic landowners, although not numerous and without the vote themselves, could nevertheless have influenced the way their Protestant tenants voted. Leases for lives gave a freehold interest to Protestants tenants and so qualified them to vote. The extensive equity to renew leases for lives would have had the effect of strengthening the legal position of tenants holding by that tenure vis-à-vis their landlords and therefore possibly making them rather more politically independent. It would therefore be tempting to reach the 'realist' conclusion that the judges were motivated by a desire to secure the political power of Protestant tenants, either from influence by landlords generally or vis-à-vis Catholic landlords. It might be tempting to conclude, in other words, that the judges of the House of Lords, who mostly had political careers themselves, had some political motivation behind their decisions. But this does not in fact seem to be the case. A less political but similarly 'realist' conclusion would be that they may have been concerned to protect the integrity of the franchise, but there is no evidence that this was their main concern either.

There is a more mundane explanation which may be the most important. Most of the land in Ireland at the end of the 18th century was held for leases for lives renewable forever[88] and, as we have seen, such interests were used as security for creditors and as the basis of family settlements.[89] Leases for lives renewable forever had always been treated in Ireland as perpetual interests equivalent to a fee simple. The extension of the equity increased the security of such interests, and protected family members of the tenant and mortgagees, as Carleton noted in his pleadings in *Boyle* v. *Lysaght*.[90] The lands, he asserted, were 'security for creditors and a fund for family settlements – circumstances in the contemplation of the legislature at the enacting of that salutary law [the Tenantry

88 Sir L. Parsons, 13 *Parliamentary Debates* 213: 'Almost all the lands of the country are let for lives, so that almost every peasant has a freehold tenure.' Ingram, *A History of the Legislative Union of Great Britain and Ireland* (1887) p, 23. The last part of the sentence may not be accurate. Middle ranking tenants held on leases for lives, but they may have let out to the cultivators on lesser forms of tenure. See also the preamble to the Tenantry Act, 1780.

89 For quasi-settlements, see Lyall, *Land Law in Ireland* 3rd edn. (Dublin, 2010), pp. 290–91.

90 'House of Lords Appeals' (Pleadings) 1787–90, Vol. 47, King's Inns.

Act, 1780].' The reason for the extensive Irish equity was simply a recognition of the empirical fact that in Ireland such interests had long been treated as if they were fees simple. Lord Lifford LC delivering judgment in *Boyle* v. *Lysaght*[91] accepted Carleton's argument on behalf of the tenant:

> These leases then were considered as perpetual interests, and upon that principle they gained ground, and became a fund for settlements of every kind, for mortgages and other securities for money. If a man had one of these leases, there would have been no more doubt of lending him money than if he had a fee.[92]

One effect of the equity was to reduce, to some extent, the political influence of all landlords. It seems unlikely, therefore, that a reduction in Catholic landowning influence, such as it was, was a motive for the equity, either on the part of the judges or the politicians. The reduction of the scope of the equity by the English judiciary met vehement opposition in the Irish parliament only a few years before the reforms which conferred the vote on Catholics. Protestant politicians, such as Henry Flood, both supported the extension of the franchise and supported the passing of the Tenantry Act to re-establish the full force of the equity.

As far as the judiciary were concerned, it seems unlikely that the detectable effects of the equity on social classes, which have just been described, formed a motive for the creation or extension of the equity. The existence of the equity shows, if anything, that the judges were independent of influence by the larger landowners who stood to lose by the interest of their tenants in the land being rendered more permanent. There is also little reason to suppose that the judges were acting as the conscious instruments of the freehold tenants. There is some evidence, which has already been noted, that the judges separated their judicial role from their political opinions, a separation made all the more remarkable for the fact that most of them had active political as well as legal careers. Their role in relation to the equity seems to be what they expressed it to be: to uphold a form of property on whom many had come to rely. If the leases were not renewable then mortgagees would lose their security family members would lose their income from jointures or rentcharges charged on the land. It should therefore be noted that the form of property which the judges were upholding was a peculiarly 18th-century form of property. It was both a commodity form, an alienable, in this case mortgageable, interest playing its role in the market, and, on the other hand, a form which was used to maintain dependent relatives of the landed class who themselves had no land and who were a form of rentier. The equity supported both aspects of this dual and contradictory form of property, although to the judges of the time there is no apparent awareness of this contradiction.

91 (1787) 1 Ridg. PC 384.
92 *ibid.*, at p. 403.

Penal Laws

The Penal Laws have already been considered in the context of leases for lives and the conclusion was that such leases could not be used as a device to avoid them. We now turn to examining devices to avoid them which may have been at least partially successful and the way these were treated by the House of Lords.

Recent work by historians suggests that the property aspect of the Penal Laws either was not enforced in the late 18th century to the extent that was once thought, or was circumvented by legal devices.[93] A number of lawyers, including Speaker Connolly and FitzGibbon's father,[94] made fortunes out of the Penal Laws. If there was money to be made, it seems likely that it might be made partly at least by inventing or refining devices whereby Catholic clients might avoid the laws. Again, there would not have been money to be made by lawyers if all such devices had been unsuccessful. There is some evidence from Ridgeway's reports that some judges, FitzGibbon included, were prepared to countenance such devices if they complied with the letter of the law.

The 'Gavelkind Clause'

Under the 'gavelkind clause', section 10 of 2 Ann., c. 6 (Ir.), 1703,[95] land held by a Catholic in fee simple or fee tail was considered to be 'in the nature of gavelkind' and was to be divided among the sons of the landowner on the landowner's death. A fee simple which passed in this way was not therefore 'discoverable'. A conveyance *inter vivos* in fee simple to a Catholic was void and 'discoverable', but inheritance by gavelkind was not discoverable.[96] 'Discovery' and gavelkind were mutually exclusive.[97]

'Gavelkind' was the name which the English used for the Irish law of inheritance under the Brehon laws, according to which land was divided equally among the sons of the deceased. The name was chosen because it reminded them of English gavelkind, a Saxon custom in Kent which had survived the Norman Conquest and under which land was also divided between the sons. The Act had the effect of taking away freedom of testation from Catholics as to real property, since the provisions of the Act overrode a gift in a will of real property.[98] There was nevertheless a proviso to the section whereby, if the eldest son of the Catholic landowner conformed to the Church of Ireland, he could take as heir. The policy was carried forward by section 3 of the same Act. If the eldest

93 L. Cullen, 'Catholics under the Penal Laws' (1986) 1 *Eighteenth-Century Ireland* 23, and see below.

94 Malcomson op. cit. footnote 199 188, p. 14.

95 Above, page 147. On the Penal Laws as to property generally, see W. N. Osborough, 'Catholics, Land and the Popery Acts of Anne' in Wheelan and Power eds., *Endurance and Emergence: Catholics in Ireland in the Eighteenth Century.*

96 If a Catholic attempted to leave a fee simple by will, the will was void and under the first Penal Law the fee simple passed to the sons by gavelkind.

97 *Farrell* v *Crosbie* (1773) How. Po. Cas. at 264, above, page 148 held, in relation to a lease for lives, that the effect of the second Penal Law was to 'revive' the will for the purpose of discovery, but this was not so if the interest had been a fee simple or a fee tail, in which case the property would go as gavelkind: How. Po. Cas. at p. 263.

98 *Burke* v. *Morgan* (1717) 5 Bro. PC 365; 2 E.R. 734.

son of a Catholic became a member of the Church of Ireland during his father's lifetime, then any land of which the Catholic parent had been seized in fee tail or fee simple would from then on vest in the parent for a life estate only, the reversion vesting in interest in the son. Under section 7 of the Act any Catholic who became entitled 'to enter, or take' property by devise, descent, gift, remainder or trust, which the Protestant held in fee simple or fee tail, had six months within which to conform to the established church. If he or she did not do so, then he only took a life estate and the remainder vested in his son or nearest Protestant relative.

Avoidance

We have already seen that under section 6 of the 1703 Act a Catholic could not purchase land other than for a lease of 31 years. It was not unknown for Protestant neighbours or friends to hold land on behalf of Catholics, but such arrangements must have been based upon a high degree of moral trust since an express trust in favour of a Catholic would have been void.[99]

The introduction of the Protestant discoveror[100] in turn produced a device for avoidance, the false Protestant discoveror. The son or daughter, of the Catholic landowner, or perhaps another relative, would outwardly conform and then bring an action as discoverer, claiming the land. This would have the beneficial effect, so far as the family were concerned, of preventing a real Protestant discoveror making a claim. The courts in the early part of the 18th century in turn reacted to this by developing, or adopting, the concept of the 'constructive papist'[101] and might refuse to accept the genuineness of the son's or daughter's conversion.[102]

The assumption behind the main provisions seems to have been that not only would the eldest son become a Protestant, but his family from then onwards would probably be Protestant. It is known that in some parts of Ireland it became the practice in Catholic landowning families for the eldest son in each generation to conform to the Church of Ireland for the purpose of retaining the land, but he would bring up his own children as Catholics, either with the exception of the

[99] The Act also only applied to buying and purchasing of land. Sales could therefore have been disguised under other forms, provided the judiciary was prepared to look at the form and ignore the content. Mortgages may have been used. A Protestant might mortgage his land by conveyance of the fee simple with covenant to reconvey on redemption. The real purpose of the transaction would be to convey the fee simple in the land to the Catholic. Hence the loan would need to be equal to the value of the land. The Protestant would not repay the loan. The mortgagor could then execute a release of the equity of redemption. This would operate to destroy the equity rather than convey it, and in any case would not on the face of it be for any consideration. Thus the transaction would not infringe the literal meaning of the words in the Act. However, courts do not always feel disposed to use the literal meaning of words and so a certain indulgence on the part of the judges has to be assumed if the device were to be effective. It is known that the O'Connor family of Clonalis House used mortgages to avoid the effect of the Penal Laws. A list of the papers is available in G. W. and J. E. Dunleavy, *The O'Connor Papers* (Wisconsin, 1977).

[100] Above, page 147; 8 Ann., c. 3 (Ir.), 1709, s. 27.

[101] Perhaps invented by West LC, above, page 64.

[102] *Irish Exchequer Reports 1716–1734* 125 Seld. Soc. (for 2008) p. cxxxvi–cxxxvii.

eldest son, or even including the eldest son, who could conform when the need arose. This complied with the letter of the law while avoiding its intended result.

This practice was mentioned in *Redington* v. *Redington*.[103] A Catholic father purchased land in Galway in the name of his eldest son who had 'conformed to the Protestant religion at the desire of his father'. The father also purchased land for another son who had also conformed and this was said 'to protect this purchase against popery laws'. The father could not have taken a fee simple estate in the land himself in either case because of the ban in the Penal Laws on Catholics acquiring more than a lease for 31 years. Furthermore, the normal presumption of law when X purchases land in the name of Y, i.e. the conveyance is to Y, but X pays the purchase price, is that Y is to hold the legal estate on an implied trust for X. It is presumed that X had some motive other than to make a gift to Y unless there is evidence to rebut the presumption. One should notice in the present context that if this presumption applied and were not rebutted, the conveyance would fall within section 6 of 2 Ann., c 6. However, there are situations in which this presumption is replaced by an opposite presumption, that it is a gift to Y. This is the presumption of advancement. One such instance is where X is the father of Y. In such a case the law recognised that X owes an natural obligation, that is, an obligation derived from natural law, to provide materially for Y. If X then purchases property in the name of Y, it is presumed to be in discharge of the obligation: it is an 'advancement'. The House of Lords held that the gift was an advancement to the son. The son did not hold it on trust for the father. The only reported judgment is a lengthy one by FitzGibbon in which he reviewed the law on advancement.[104] The purchase may have been a intended as a device, whereby the father would acquire bare possession, or it may have been intended as a gift to the son, in which case it achieved its object, but at the price of the son conforming to the Church of Ireland. No issue was raised as to the genuineness of the son's conformity and FitzGibbon does not raise it himself.

In recognising the gift as an advancement, was the court turning a blind eye to a device to avoid the Penal Laws? Were the judges at the end of the century quietly abandoning the notion of the 'constructive papist'? Or were they just applying a well-recognised doctrine of equity? In either event, the result was that the land went to the (supposedly) Protestant son.

The 'device' of course would only be effective if younger sons in each generation secretly remained Catholics. However, once a son became a Protestant, and his son did likewise, there was the danger that what had been a matter of expediency would become a matter of habit or conviction. It has also been seen that a Catholic father, as in *Redington*, could only give land to a younger son if that son also became a Protestant. The 'device' might well turn out to have the effect that the Penal Law intended: the conversion of the family to

[103] (1794) 3 Ridg. PC 106.

[104] 3 Ridg. PC at 160–201. FitzGibbon's speech is ALSO reproduced in D. A. Fleming and A. P. W. Malcomson [eds.]. *'A Volley of Execrations': the letters and papers of John FitzGibbon, Earl of Clare 1772-1802* (Dublin, 2005), pp. 178–188.

Protestantism. In apparently supporting the device, the judges may have been giving effect to the policy of the statute.

Relaxation

The property provisions of the Penal Laws were relaxed to some extent by the Catholic Relief Act, 1778.[105] Section 1 provided that after the 1 August 1778 Catholics could acquire, notwithstanding the statutes of 2 and 8 Anne, leases not exceeding 999 years or for any term of years determinable on not more than five lives. This was subject to taking an oath of allegiance.[106] Section 2 provided that the 'Gavelkind Act' would no longer apply to land held by a Catholic in fee simple or fee tail and they would thereafter descend according to the general law. Section 6 provided that if an eldest son conformed to the Church of Ireland the conformity would, after 1 November 1788, no longer have the effect reducing the estate of his Catholic father to a life estate and vest the reversion in the son. Section 8 provided something of an amnesty in that titles which had not been litigated before 1 November 1778 could not thereafter be impugned. Section 10, however, contained a sting in the tail. A Catholic who had conformed to the Church of Ireland could not take any benefit under the Act if he or she reconverted to Catholicism. It was this provision which Scott used to threaten his step-daughter.[107]

By a further Act of 1782[108] Catholics, provided they took the oaths, were finally enabled to purchase or hold any interest in land.[109]

Estoppel in Equity

In *Kenney* v. *Browne*[110] an attorney[111] had fraudulently obtained a lease of his client's property and then made improvements to the land. The attorney argued *inter alia* that the improvements gave rise to an estoppel against the client/landlord preventing him from challenging the lease. FitzGibbon, after a detailed review of the facts, set out a broad principle which shows his grasp of equity. It foreshadowed proprietary estoppel and Lord Kingsdown's much quoted speech in *Ramsden* v. *Dyson*:[112]

> As to the equity arising from lasting and valuable improvements, I do not consider a man, who is conscious of a defect in his title and with that conviction in his mind expends a sum of money in

105 17 & 18 Geo. III c. 49 (Ir).

106 Section 3. The oaths were provided for by 13 & 14 Geo. III, c. 35 (Ir.), 1773–74.

107 Above, page 130.

108 21 & 22 Geo. III, c. 24 (Ir.).

109 Except advowsons or boroughs returning members of parliament: Parnell, *History of the Penal Laws*, p. 119.

110 (1796) 3 Ridg. PC 462, at 518. For the pleadings see 'House of Lords Appeals (Pleadings) 1787–90', vol. 47, King's Inns Library.

111 Thomas Kenney, or Kenny, transferred from the Court of King's Bench to the Court of Exchequer in 1788: Edward Keane, P. Beryl Phair and Thomas U. Sadleir eds., *King's Inns Admissions Papers 1607–1867* (Dublin, 1982), p. 265; PIHL, iii.17.

112 (1866) L.R. 1 H.L. 129.

> improvements, as entitled in any sort to avail himself of it. If the person really entitled to the estate will encourage the possessor of it to expend his money in improvements, or if he will look on and suffer such an expenditure, without apprising the party of his intention to dispute his title, and will afterwards endeavour to avail himself of such fraud; upon the ground of fraud the jurisdiction of a Court of Equity will clearly attach upon the case. But does it follow from thence, that if a man has acquired an estate by rank and abominable fraud, and shall afterwards expend his money in improving the estate, that therefore he shall retain it in his hands against the lawful proprietor? If such a rule should prevail, it will certainly fully justify a proposition, which I once heard stated at the bar of the Court of Chancery, that the common equity of this country was, to improve the right owner out of the possession of his estate.[113]

Encouragement by the owner of the legal title is clearly identified as an important factor on the facts in FitzGibbon's judgment. It distinguishes the facts set out from the case of fraud which FitzGibbon describes by contrast in the second part of the passage. The phrase 'without apprising the party of his intention to dispute his title' implies, although it does not make explicit, the element now identified as reliance. The improver relies on the encouragement by the person 'really entitled', namely, at common law, in the belief that he, the improver, is to have a renewal of his lease, or has a valid grant of some interest in the land. Nevertheless, FitzGibbon also saw that acquiescence might be an alternative to active encouragment: of looking on and saying nothing, knowing that the improver proceeds on a misapprehension of his rights.

From the point of view of the improver, FitzGibbon's statement impressively encompasses both the mistake type of case, where the improver believes he or she has a title, and the type of case where the improver is under no such misapprehension, but the improver believes that he has, or will acquire, an interest in the land. Later judgments have sometimes failed to perceive that both these situations may give rise to the equity based upon encouragement, reliance and detriment and this had led to difficulties in developing equitable estoppel.[114] There is also an awareness of the social context, of the need, while excluding fraudulent claims, to design a principle in such a way as not to exclude the bona fide improving tenant who contributes to the development of agriculture.

In the same case Lord Yelverton stated the principle in similar terms:

113 (1796) 3 Ridg. PC at 519. For a discussion of estoppels in the 18th century see *Hume* v. *Burton* (1785) 1 Ridg. PC 204 at 246–47.

114 See for example the five probanda of Fry J in *Willmott* v. *Barber* (1880) 15 Ch D 96 at 105f, which were cast in terms limited to the mistake situation and did not refer to active encouragement. The probanda 'had the perhaps unintended effect of imposing a strait-jacket on the development of proprietary estoppel during the following hundred years' (Gray, *Elements of Land Law* 2nd edn. p. 321). Gray notes that the limitation of the principle to the mistake situation was not fully-overcome in England until *Taylor Fashions Limited.* v. *Liverpool Victoria Trustees Co. Ltd.* [1982] QB 133; (1981) *LQR* 513.

> Improvements are also relied upon; but I know of no case where they have assisted a man in a defence of this kind, except where a party having the deeds or title in his pocket, and knowing they would avoid the tenant's interest, stands by, sees the improvements going on, encourages them, and then seeks to recover possession of the land, with those improvements upon it. There is no case where improvements have protected the party making them, but where he was a bona fide possessor of the land. I leave it to your Lordships to determine, whether under all the circumstances, Kenney is a such a possessor of land in question.[115]

There is a slight difference in approach: Yelverton treats 'stands by' and 'encourages' as pertaining to the same situation, whereas the first is usually used to describe the position of the legal owner where the improver, or relior, has made a mistake as to his or her rights, and encouragement implies an active role by the legal owner in inducing the improver or relior to believe he or she will be given an interest in future. FitzGibbon's formulation seems to perceive already that the two are distinct branches of the estoppel doctrine.

The principle also meant that tenants could sometimes win in court against landlords. All of this calls to mind E. P. Thompson's comment on the rule of law in the 18th century in England[116] to the effect that while law functioned to legitimate class rule, it was also paradoxically true that since that rule was legitimated through the form of law, law had to maintain a degree of autonomy. Law, in Thompson's phrase, 'has its own characteristics, its own independent history and logic of evolution.'[117] It is in the nature of law as an ideal form that it should treat parties as equal before the court, decide on the evidence and not on the class, religion or race of the parties, etc. This must lead to the conclusion that law had within itself the possibility of transcending the legitimating of class rule. Integrity was a quality of content, not merely of form. We have already noted that FitzGibbon was among those who seems to have had a strong belief in integrity in the legal sense, although he did not favour equality in a political sense.

Conditions on Marriage: Landowners and Professionals

A case which reveals something of the relations between professionals and landowners is *Keily* v. *Monck*.[118] In that case the testator devised real property to his daughters on condition that should any of them marry someone who was not, at the time of the marriage, seized of a freehold estate of the clear yearly value of £500 sterling over and above every charge and incumbrance, then the legacy to such a daughter was to be forfeited. The proviso would have been

[115] (1796) 3 Ridg. PC at 529-30.

[116] E. P. Thompson, 'The Rule of Law', Chapter 10 part iv in *Whigs and Hunters: The Origin of the Black Act* (Harmondsworth, 1977).

[117] *ibid.*

[118] (1795) 3 Ridg. PC 205.

satisfied only by a very rich man indeed, and only by a man whose wealth was in land. Judgment was delivered by the lord chancellor, FitzGibbon, now the Earl of Clare. He held that the condition amounted virtually to a total restraint on marriage, and was void.

It is interesting, in view of his record, to see that the lord chancellor was capable of indignation at the injustice of it all:

> What man of the profession of the law has set out with a clear unincumbered real estate of £500 a year, or has acquired such an estate for years after entering into the profession? How many men of the other learned professions can come within this condition? It will in effect exclude ninety-nine men in one hundred of every profession whether civil, military, or ecclesiastical. It in effect excludes nearly every mercantile man in the kingdom, for, let his personal estate be never so great, unless he is seized of a real estate of the ascertained description, he is excluded... In a word, the condition which this weak old man would impose upon his daughters, as the price of their portions, does, to my judgment clearly and unquestionably lead to a total prohibition of their marriage, and as such ought to be condemned in every court of justice.

FitzGibbon's characterisation of the testator as a 'weak old man' seems to betray a certain animosity. The mask of judicial impartiality seems to slip for a moment. Perhaps it was present to the mind of the lord chancellor that he himself, at least in his younger years, would not have qualified to marry the old man's daughter. Indeed, his specific reference to 'a man of the profession of the law' suggests that that was exactly what was present to his mind. The passage is a rather startling example of hypocrisy, given FitzGibbon's support for discrimination against Catholics, but it is more significant for what it tells us, or suggests, about the relationship between landowners and professionals at the end of the century. Although the Irish House of Lords as a legislative body was dominated by landowners, the case does seem to illustrate that the Irish House of Lords with its more restricted membership as a court of law was not the landowners' poodle. Since the subject matter of most cases concerned land, it could be said to reflect the landed interest in that sense, but only because of the nature of society at the time. We also refer to this point below in the section on the criminal jurisdiction. The Irish House of Lords in its role as a court in the 'professional period' was staffed by those who had come up through the professions. Indeed, FitzGibbon's list of the men of the learned professions 'civil, military, or ecclesiastical' and 'mercantile men' is a partial list of what might be termed the bourgeoisie, in contrast to landed proprietors.

Francis Hargrave wrote an opinion on the case, in favour of the legality of the condition, although it is unclear on whose behalf the opinion was written.[119] He took the view that 'a condition, absolutely enjoining celibacy, or being tantamount to a prohibition on marriage, would I presume be extremely questionable;

[119] Hargrave, *Jurisconsult Exercitations.* (London, 1811-1813), ii.255–57.

though no express authority condemning such a condition as a void one occurs to me at present in writing of our own [English] lawyers.' He went on:

> After that age of twenty-one, our law, except in the case of the royal family, leaves both male and female at full liberty to marry without asking for leave from any one. Yet if *real* estate be devised or given on condition not to marry *at any time* without consent, I apprehend, that the condition is effectual... As also I cannot consider the condition in the present case as intended to prohibit marriage, or as nearly equal to producing such an effect, but merely as a guard against an imprudent match, it follows, that, according to my notions of the law of England, the condition is legal... I am personally no friend to conditions requiring women to marry for the sake of fortune... but yet if I had the honour to sit in judicature, I should, according to my present impressions, be forced to confess, that the condition was (a)[120] lawful; and therefore that, however harsh, it must prevail.

The characterisation of the condition as a guard against an 'imprudent match' seems odd. Presumably the young lady could make many matches which were 'prudent', in the sense that her husband had not only a sufficient but ample income, but still fall far short of satisfying the condition. A law that upheld the absolute right of a person to marry whom they wished, but at the cost of foregoing a large fortune, would not only be 'harsh'. It would have placed a far greater value on the freedom, or, as FitzGibbon might put have put it, on the avarice, of testators rather than on the 'full liberty to marry' of the daughters.

Trespass and Case

In *Hamilton* v. *Marquess of Donegall*[121] the original action was brought by the marquess, who owned a fishery in the upper part of the River Bann and Lough Neagh. The defendant was Lady Hamilton, who owned the fishery in the lower part of the river.

The respective titles had arisen in the following way. King James I in 1613 created a body corporate, the 'Governor and Assistants, London, of the new plantation in Ulster within the kingdom of Ireland' and granted to them and their successors the creek and river Bann from the sea as far as Lough Neagh, including the soil of the river and all fisheries as well as salmon and eels and other fish. King James died in 1625, seized of the residue, which became vested in King Charles I. In 1637 a writ of *scire facias* issued in England by which the grant of 1613 was revoked and the premises became re-vested in Charles I. On his death they passed to King Charles II. In 1660 by letters patent he granted Arthur, the then Earl of Donegall, his heirs and assigns, under the great seal of Ireland the part of the river from the Lough to 'the rock, or fall of water, called

120 Hargrave's footnote (a) at this point reads: 'See further, as to the legality of the condition, in the answer to the 2d question.'

121 (1795) 3 Ridg. PC 267. Above, page 128

the salmon leap' and the fishery in that part. The letters were enrolled in the Court of Chancery in Ireland. The plaintiff was the heir at law of the earl.

In 1662 Charles II reconstituted the Society of Governors and Assistants and made a new grant by letters patent in their favour of the lower part of the river as far as and including the salmon leap, the soil of the river and the right to take salmon and other fish in those parts. In 1620 the Society constructed a number of traps on the salmon leap to catch the fish at that point. The Society made a lease of their fishery in favour of Sir Henry Hamilton, the original plaintiff. Sir Henry died in 1782 and Lady (or Dame) Marianne Hamilton, the plaintiff in error in the House of Lords, was the successor in title to the heir of Sir Henry.

The marquess[122] alleged that Lady Hamilton's maintenance of the traps on the river prevented salmon from leaping and reaching the fishery belonging to the marquess and so causing him loss.

The action was framed as an action on the case.[123] It was not brought in trespass, since trespass only lay for an act directly causing an invasion of the defendant rights. If Lady Hamilton had entered onto the marquess's land, that would clearly be trespass. But she did not. The action of maintaining the traps on her own land was not illegal in itself: it was part of her natural rights as owner of her land, or fishery. The problem was that it caused consequential loss to the marquess. The courts therefore had to decide whether proof of those facts was a sufficient to found an action on the case, and therefore whether the law would give a remedy in such circumstances. In developing the law in this area the courts had regard to a number of policy issues.[124] Certain activities which admittedly caused consequential loss were socially beneficial. To restrain them would restrain competition and damage the free market. One example was the provision of schools. FitzGibbon mentions a case of grammar schools in Gloucester.[125] The Prior of 'Lanton' (Llanthony)[126] had from 'time out of memory' the right to appoint a master to hold and teach a grammar school in Gloucester, and had appointed the plaintiff. The defendant set up a school in the city, causing the income of the plaintiff to be sharply reduced. It was held that the action would not lie. The provision of schools was socially beneficial and the law would not restrain competition just because it caused loss to someone else.

[122] Arthur Chichester (1739–1799), 5th Earl of Donegall (Ir.), created Baron Fisherwick (G.B.) in 1790 and the next year Earl of Belfast and Marquess of Donegall (Ir.). He had sought British peerages as a price of his support for the government. The lord lieutenant, Westmorland, wrote to W. W. Grenville on 5 May 1790: 'You must decide in England whether Lord Donegal's [*sic*] weight generally calculated is worth the the price he asks, an Irish Marquisate and English [*sic*] Barony... agreeable as the assistance of 4 Members might be to the Irish Government, I can by no means recommend that an English [*sic*] peerage should be made often the price of Irish support.' Cokayne *Complete Peerage* iv.391.

[123] Above, page 56.

[124] Baker, *Introduction*, pp. 429–30.

[125] Y.B. Hil. 11 Hen. IV f. 47a-47b pl.21, Seipp No. 1410.021; 3 Ridg. PC at 319; J.H. Baker & S.F.C. Milsom, *Sources of English Legal History* (London, 1986) p. 613 ('Case of Gloucester School'); A.K.R. Kiralfy, *A Source Book of English Law* (London, 1957), p. 126 (*Hamlyn* v. *More*). Baker, *Introduction*, p. 429.

[126] The priory of Llanthony, now ruined, was a former Augustinian priory in the Vale of Ewyas, in Monmouthshire, seven miles north of Abergavenny at Llanthony.

In the Court of Exchequer the jury found the facts as alleged by the marquess and the court gave judgment in his favour. Yelverton CB and barons Hamilton and Metge agreed that the facts amounted to a good cause of action.[127] Power B dissented.

Lady Hamilton then brought a writ of error in the Exchequer Chamber. This time, Lord Clonmell CJKB and Lord Carleton CJCP gave their opinion in favour of the marquess. The lord chancellor was not bound by their opinion, since the chief justices were only assisting the lord chancellor in Exchequer Chamber,[128] and the report states that he did not agree with it, but he said that he would not decide against the opinions of the two common law chief justices, and so gave judgment for the marquess.[129] Lady Hamilton then brought a writ of error in the House of Lords.[130] In the Lords, the lord chancellor first moved that three questions should be put to the judges,[131] which are here paraphrased:

1. Was the keeping and maintaining of the traps, as found by the jury, sufficient (on its own) to maintain an action on the case?

2. Was the injury complained of by the marquess (the original plaintiff), as found by the jury, sufficient to maintain an action on the case?

3. On the record as a whole, did it appear that the marquess had a good cause of action?

Crookshank J delivered the unanimous opinion of the judges,[132] that 1. the keeping and maintaining of the traps was not sufficient, independent of the injury, to found a cause of action, but on 2. and 3. they answered in the affirmative, that is, that the record disclosed a good cause of action.

The lord chancellor then gave his opinion at some length. He considered the distinction between trespass and case:[133]

> And the clear legal distinction is, that where the *immediate* act itself occasions a prejudice, or is an injury to the plaintiff's person, house, land or other property, there trespass generally is the proper remedy, and not trespass upon the case.
>
> But where the act in itself is not an injury, but a *consequence* resulting from it is prejudicial to his person, or property, there an action of trespass upon the case is the proper remedy.

Thus, if any action lay, it would be in case and not trespass. The next question was: what kind of consequential injury was a good ground for an action on

127 3 Ridg. PC at 281.
128 Above, page 75.
129 In Hilary term, 1794; 3 Ridg. PC 282.
130 Hence, in the name of the case in the Lords, her name came first as the 'plaintiff in error'.
131 16 February 1795; 3 Ridg. PC 314.
132 2 March 1795; 3 Ridg. PC 315.
133 3 Ridg. PC at pp. 316–17.

the case? He then goes on to cite the case on the Gloucester grammar schools, mentioned above, and continues:[134]

> So if I have a mill, and another will erect a mill in the neighbourhood, whereby the profits of my mill are lessened, no action will lie. But it is otherwise, if by the erection of such a mill, the water is prevented from flowing to my mill.

He cites other cases where there was damage, but no action, such as a person erecting a house which blocks the view from an adjoining house. Mere inconvenience was not enough. In his view the test was that even though the act was indirect in an action on the case, the injury nevertheless had to be direct:

> To maintain this action therefore, in my judgment, there must be direct substantial, solid injury to the plaintiff's person, or property, directly laid by him, and directly found by the jury... A mere ideal, or fantastical injury will not maintain this action...

He noted that both plaintiff and defendant derived their title from grants by the Crown, and that, in his view, the grant of the marquess (original plaintiff) was prior to that of Lady Hamilton (original defendant). It was also clear on the record that there had been uninterrupted possession of both parties for more than a century, and an action on the case could be founded on possession alone.[135] Although he put the issue in substantive terms, he did not see it entirely freed from procedural issues, since he said that the question was whether the jury found such a substantial injury by its verdict. The marquess in his view was entitled to the possession of the water of his fishery and the free passage of fish from the sea and to catch as many fish as he could 'by his industry and art'. And Lady Hamilton had essentially the same right. She could not alter the state of the water. Nor could she obstruct the passage of fish from the sea into the marquess's fishery 'in any manner not essentially necessary to enable her to exercise her right of catching fish, in their passage up the river.' The jury only found that the traps prevented large quantities of fish from passing into the marquess's fishery, but not that it had thereby been injured or lessened in value. This is then FitzGibbon's point: there was nothing, in his view, to stop Lady Hamilton taking as many fish as she liked from her fishery using any other means, such a nets or rods or any 'ordinary or accustomed method'. It was this point on which the lord chancellor disagreed with the judges in the Exchequer and the Exchequer Chamber. He notes that the jury, by way of explanation, found there was another injury, namely that the speed of the water was increased which contributed to the inability of the fish to pass into the marquess's fishery. If this had been alleged, he would have had no hesitation that that would found an action on the case, but it was not alleged by the marquess in pleadings and was not on the face of the record. Nevertheless, FitzGibbon again accepted that

134 *ibid.*, at pp. 319–20.
135 *ibid.*, at p. 323.

the majority of the judges took a different view, and would allow the action on the substantive point, that the traps caused indirect injury in substantially reducing the number of fish reaching the marquess's fishery. It is unfortunate that we do not have the arguments of the judges, either in Exchequer Chamber or in the Lords. The report ends with the order that the judgment of the Exchequer Chamber be affirmed and so the marquess succeeded.

It is notable that FitzGibbon saw the issue as simply the meaning of the words in the grant to Lady Hamilton, her rights under it and their strictly logical consequences. He does not treat the issue as one of reasonableness in the use of resources as between neighbours. This may have been a particular trait of FitzGibbon, or reflects his training as an equity lawyer, but it cannot be taken as characteristic of the age or of judges at the time, since the common law judges disagreed with him and he accepted their view in the end.

Court of Exchequer, Outlawries and Custodiam Leases

In *Dillon* v. *Burton*[136] William Blood, deceased, was during his life seized of a life estate in certain lands in County Clare. He was indebted to Michael McNamara for £200, which debt was secured by a bond and warrant.[137] In 1781 McNamara sued Blood on the bond and obtained an outlawry against him. McNamara also obtained an inquisition to ascertain the extent of Blood's lands and, on the estreat of the lands to the Crown, was subsequently granted a *custodiam* lease of the lands by the Court of Exchequer.

In 1782 the appellants sued Blood on other debts in two civil actions and obtained two outlawries against him. The inquisitions on those outlawries found that some of the lands comprised in the former inquisition to be the estate of Blood and the appellants also obtained *custodiam* leases of the lands. The Crown, not having any interest in the direct management of estreated land, would let it out on a *custodiam* lease.[138]

In 1783 Blood was also outlawed in a civil action at the suit of the respondent, who also obtained a *custodiam* lease. Lord Clare LC then continued:[139]

> It may be necessary to state shortly what the course of the Exchequer is upon these *custodiam* leases. An injunction goes to the sheriff to put the custodee in possession, and immediately after an order is made upon the tenants of the lands granted *in custodiam*, to pay their rents to the custodee. So that in fact all money received under these grants in *custodiam* are received by authority of, and pursuant to, the order of the Court of Exchequer. And where the custodees are more in number than one, the Court of Exchequer alone, as court of revenue, determines in what order they shall be paid.

136 (1794) 3 Ridg. PC 80.

137 i.e. a bond with a warrant of attorney.

138 See Gorges Edmond Howard, *A Treatise of the Exchequer and Revenue of Ireland*. (Dublin, 1776), ch. 30; Conroy's *Custodiam Reports*, 1652–1788. The practice of granting *custodiam* leases was ended in Ireland in 1835, 5 & 6 Will. 4, c. 55 (Ir.), s. 31.

139 3 Ridg. PC 97.

It appeared that in 1784 the appellants, as second custodees, paid McNamara, the first custodee, the balance owing to him by Blood, and took an assignment of his *custodiam* lease and in the same year obtained an order of the Court of Exchequer giving them liberty to proceed, as assignees of McNamara, in their own names. Burton, the respondent, was the last custodee. Complaints were made by the appellants, on the revenue side of the Exchequer, that Burton had continued to receive rents from the tenants, and in 1787 they applied for an attachment against him. The court of Exchequer, after hearing Burton, made an order for attachment, but directed that it should not be delivered to the pursuivant,[140] that is, brought into effect, until further order. A further year went by and then the appellants applied again to the Court of Exchequer, which ordered that an attachment should not issue for a month, the solicitor undertaking to pay the costs, which he did. Nothing then happened until 1790 when the appellants filed an original bill on the equity side of Exchequer claiming a review of the proceedings by the same judges on the revenue side, and an account for the rents. Lord Clare LC then made the point that they should again apply to the Exchequer, revenue side, and indeed that was the only course open to them. He also pointed out that if the equity side of Exchequer could entertain such a bill, there would be no reason why the same bill could not have been brought in the court of Chancery to review the order of the Exchequer exercising its revenue jurisdiction, but its revenue jurisdiction was exclusive to the Exchequer, so the appeal to the Lords on the refusal of the Exchequer equity side to hear the bill would necessarily fail. The lord chancellor gave the only speech on the appeal. He recognised that there might be circumstances in which one custodee might seek relief in a court of equity, however:[141]

> I will not say that a case may not arise, where one custodee might come into a court of equity for relief against another. If after a *custodiam* had been dissolved and the King's hands removed, it appeared that by fraud one custodee had prevented another from receiving his debt, there the jurisdiction of equity would properly attach...

While the *custodiam* lease existed, the matter was within the direct jurisdiction of the Crown and that is what gave the revenue side of the Exchequer its exclusive jurisdiction.

Equity and the Registration of Deeds

In *Chandos (Duchess)* v. *Brownlow*[142] a number of questions arose on the interpretation of the statute 6 Ann., c. 2 (Ir.), 1707, known as The Registry Act, which provided for the system of registration of deeds. This Act continued to be in force until very recent times in both parts of Ireland when it was replaced with modern Acts. These Acts of 1970 and 2006 are couched in similar terms,[143]

140 Or poursuivant, a king's messenger: Jacob, *Law Dictionary*.
141 3 Ridg. PC at 102.
142 (1791) 2 Ridg. PC 345.
143 Registration of Deeds and Title Act 2006 (R.I.); Registration of Deeds Act, 1970 (N.I).

and so the principles considered in the Chandos case are still of some relevance today.

The case concerned an extremely complex series of family settlements and deeds, but the material facts were as follows.[144] The manor of Villars was held in fee simple by George Rodney Bridges (G.R.B.). In 1712 he executed a settlement on the marriage of his son, George Bridges (G.B., or Mr B), whereby the manor was limited to G.B. for life, remainder to his intended wife (Mrs B) for life, remainder to his first and other sons in tail male, remainder to G.B. in tail male. The reversion in fee simple remained in G.R.B. A limited power of leasing was reserved to persons who took estates for life under the settlement, when they should be in possession of the land. G.R.B. died before 1718 and the reversion in fee simple descended to his son, G.B.

In 1718 G.B. entered an agreement with Earl of Caernarvon, the appellant's great-grandfather, for a grant of his (G.B.'s) reversion. G.B., a relative of the then Earl of Caernarvon, had no issue of his own and the agreement was made in consideration of 'natural love and affection' for his near relative, the earl.

In 1719 the then Earl of Caernarvon was created Duke of Chandos.[145] In view of this, the agreement of 1718 was relinquished and in February 1728 a grant of the reversion was made to the earl, now duke, by G.B. in consideration of £7000 which was paid. The duke was therefore a purchaser for value of the reversion.[146]

In November 1729 the lease which was central to the dispute was executed by G.B. and Ann his wife. G.B. at that time had only a life estate, and his wife a life estate in remainder. The lease was for three lives, with a covenant on the part of G.B., his wife and their heirs, executors and assigns for perpetual renewal. The lease was registered under the Registry Act, but the deed granting the reversion to the earl/duke was not. Nor were the settlements of 1718 and 1728. One renewal was executed by Mrs B.

In 1735, to complicate matters further, a bill of discovery under the Penal Laws was brought in the court of Exchequer by John Taylor, a Protestant discoveror, against the original lessees under the lease of 1729, claiming the lease as forfeit to him under those laws. He obtained a decree to that effect in June 1740. The respondent lessees were successors in title to Taylor.

[144] What follows is taken partly from Ridgeway's report of the case and also from Francis Hargrave's opinion on behalf of the duke published in *Juridical arguments and collections* (London, 1797–99), i.111–318.

[145] 2 Ridg. PC at 350; James Brydges (1674–1744), created Duke of Chandos, 29 April 1719. Cokayne, *Complete Peerage*, iii.129. The surname is spelled 'Bridges' in Ridgeway's report and that spelling is retained in the text above. The duke used the considerable fortune he made in the lucrative office of paymaster general of the forces abroad to build a palace at Canons, Stanmore, Middlesex. Handel spent two years there writing what became known as the Chandos Anthems for performance in the chapel and his first English oratorio *Esther*. The chapel is now a church and the only part of the palace still remaining. The duke lost his considerable fortune in speculative investments and the palace, except for the chapel, was demolished on his death and sold for its materials. Dean Swift commented that 'all he got by fraud is lost by stocks': Cokayne iii.130 f.

[146] 2 Ridg. PC at 348, 350, 362.

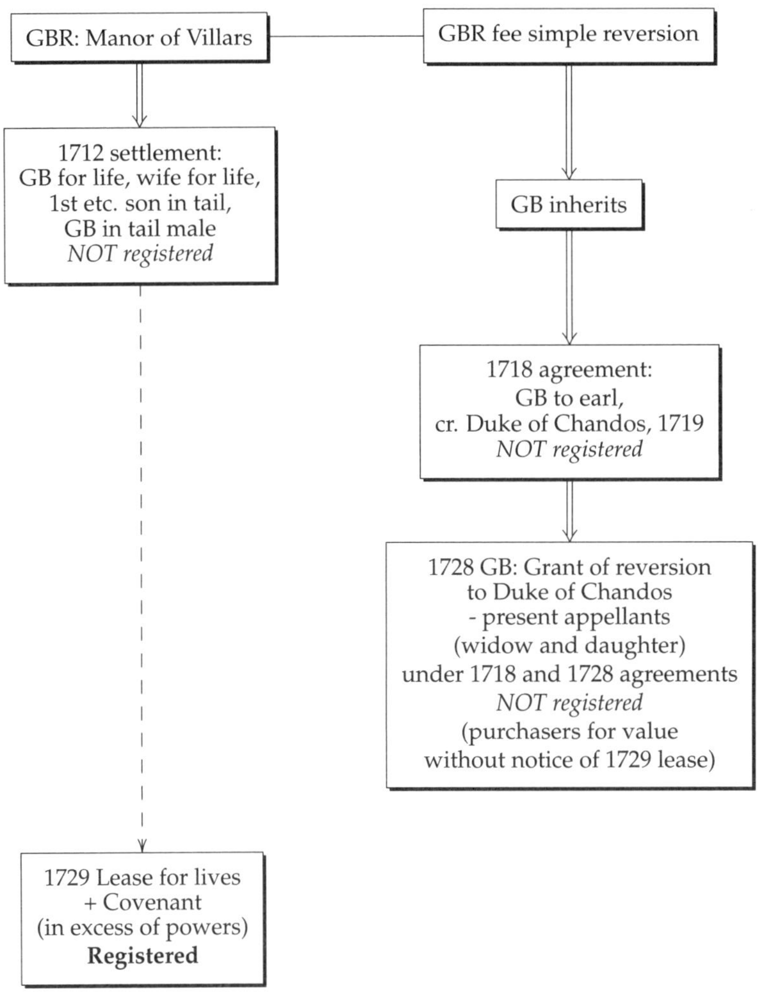

Transactions in *Chandos (Duchess)* v. *Brownlow* (1791)

The respondents (we shall continue to refer to them as that, for the sake of clarity) filed a bill, several times amended, in the equity side of the court of Exchequer, against the Duke of Chandos, to compel him to renew the lease. The duke put in an answer that alleged that the lease was invalid as granted by Mr. Bridges. The Court of Exchequer granted an interlocutory order, that the parties should proceed to trial at the next assizes, on the factual issue as to whether the respondents (lessees) had notice of the settlements of 1718 and 1728 at or before the time of execution of the lease of 1729. The duke then brought an action for ejectment at common law, and the respondents took defence to it in the King's Bench.

The original bill in 1769[147] in the present proceedings was filed by the lessees against Henry, 2nd Duke of Chandos,[148] to have the covenant for renewal attached to the decree of the equity side of the court on the reversion purchased by the then earl, prior to the execution of the lease.

The appellants (technically 'plaintiffs in error') in the present proceedings were Anna Eliza, dowager Duchess of Chandos, and her daughter, Lady Eliza Bridges, who was under age and who was represented by the duchess, as her mother and guardian. They claimed the freehold reversion under the grant of 1728 and descent from the duke.

The appellants alleged that the bill should be dismissed, *inter alia* on the ground that:

1. the lease was obtained by fraud.
2. since the execution of the lease the lessees had been guilty of fraud and neglect, by which they have forfeited their right of renewal.
3. the covenant did not bind the duke/earl, or persons deriving the reversion from him, at law, and that consequently a court of equity could not grant specific performance against the appellants, as a purchaser for value without notice of the lease and covenant.

In reply, it was argued that notice was irrelevant, and in the alternative, if it was material, notice had been established by proof. The issues before the Lords were:

1. Was notice, actual or constructive, material to the case, i.e. (a) if it were proved that the duke was a purchaser for value of the reversion without notice of the lease? and (b) that the agent of the original lessees in negotiating the lease had notice of the settlements of 1718 and 1728?
2. Was the covenant in the lease binding on the duke or on the assignees of the reversion at common law, so as to make them liable for breach of covenant, the only remedy for which at common law was damages?

147 2 Ridg. PC 362.
148 Cokayne, *Complete Peerage*, iii.131.

3. If the covenant was binding, would a court of equity give the remedy of specific performance?

4. If the covenant was not binding on the reversion at common law, did the Registry Act enlarge the effect of the covenant so as to give the right to maintain an action at common law for breach of covenant against assignees of the reversion, the the lease of 1729 having been registered, as against the appellants, who claimed as assignees of the reversion under the unregistered settlement?

FitzGibbon in his speech accepted that a registered deed took priority over any unregistered deed, regardless of time. The main purpose of the Registry Act was to replace priority based on time with priority of registration. But covenants were a different matter. He was strongly of the view that the covenant did not bind at common law, on the tests applied to the running of covenants, and that the Registry Act did not give a right of action to enforce what was not binding at common law.

First, the judges were asked for their opinions. Yelverton CB reported that they were unanimous.[149] They said in their view there was no express provision in the Registry Act which permitted, in itself, an action for breach of covenant at common law. They declined to give any opinion as to whether an action of covenant could, or could not, be brought at common law 'with the aid of the statute.' They nevertheless rejected the notion that the duke's unregistered deed could, in view of the statute, defeat the registered lease. They agreed that the unregistered settlement of 1728 was, in the words of the Act, 'fraudulent and void' as against the registered lease. The common law judges therefore accepted the principle of the Act, that registration was decisive. FitzGibbon, giving the only speech in the Lords, on the other hand, spoke strongly in favour of the equitable principle of coming to the aid of a purchaser for value without notice, even though that might undermine the principle of the Registry Act.

Before discussing the judgment of FitzGibbon, it may be noted that the Lords divided on the issue to reverse the interlocutory order of the court of Exchequer, contents - 3, not-contents - 6, so the order was affirmed, without prejudice to any application by the appellants to have the issue tried by a jury outside the county in which the land lay. The result was therefore ultimately inconclusive at the time as a precedent binding on lower courts on the Registry Act and notice, but remains valuable and persuasive today on the law of registration of deeds, namely, for the lord chancellor's reasoning that the Registry Act could not be used by a party who had no claim at common law to assert, in a court of equity, rights by virtue of the Act alone, against a purchaser for value of an unregistered deed without notice of a registered one.

FitzGibbon, giving the only speech in the Lords, dealt first with the issue as to whether the lessees were affected by notice of the unregistered deed of 1728.

As to actual notice, he said the original lessees had actual notice of the unregistered deed of 1728. That had been established both by a credible witness and

149 2 Ridg. PC 384.

by features of the original lease indicating notice of the settlement. But there was no evidence that the present lessees had actual notice. He also found that there was constructive notice on the part of the present lessees.[150] He therefore concluded there was neither actual nor constructive notice on the part of the present lessees.

The issues were narrowed to two questions:

> First, whether the registration of the lease of 1729 let in the covenant for renewal on the reversion granted by Mr B. to the earl by the deed of 1728 so as to enable the respondents to demand a renewal as against Lady Anna Eliza at law.
>
> Secondly, whether Lady Anna Eliza was entitled to a remedy in equity.

If the covenant was not binding on her at law then, in FitzGibbon's view, the respondents could not obtain specific performance of the covenant in a court of equity. If it was binding at law, the issue was whether, consistently with principles of equity, the respondents were entitled to specific performance.

As to the first question, FitzGibbon believed he saw an inconsistency in the argument. The respondents claimed that under the Registry Act the appellants' deed of 1728, being unregistered, was 'fraudulent and void', in the words of the Act, as against their lease and the covenant for renewal. But they also argued that the Act made the same deed effectual in that they had a right to a renewal effective against the deed of 1728 and Lady Anna Eliza. Or to put it in other words, that Lady Anna Eliza both was, and was not, an assignee of the reversion of the manor of Villars. The respondents were trying to have it both ways. 'This species of legal magic, I confess, goes beyond my powers of comprehension' FitzGibbon said.[151] The original lessees by registering the deed of 1729, did, so far as that deed conveyed them an estate in the land, acquire 'a legal right of estate' against the assignee of the reversion, claiming under the unregistered deed of 1728. But the original estate granted by the 1729 deed was spent,[152] and the question was as to the effect of the covenant for renewal. The covenant did not enlarge the estate granted under the lease of 1729. Confirmation of that was the judgment of the King's Bench on the appellant's title, based on the special verdict in ejectment, which established that the legal estate was then in the appellant, and that 'legal priority originally acquired by the registration of the 1729 deed is at an end.'[153]

He then went on to examine whether the covenant for renewal was binding at law and launched into a consideration of the rules at common law as modified

150 The evidence was that the lessees had placed no confidence in William Pescod as their agent in negotiating the lease. Although he had notice of the settlement, it could not be imputed to them. Therefore, FitzGibbon concluded that the lessees were not affected by notice of the 1728 settlement. He distinguished *Le Neve* v. *Le Neve* 1 Ves. 64, 3 Atk. 646, 26 E.R. 1172. and the cases cited therein by Lord Hardwicke, in which the notice of the agent was imputed to the principal, who confidentially employed the agent.

151 2 Ridg. PC 404.

152 Because the original lives had died.

153 *ibid.*, p. 405.

by statute. It is perhaps odd that he felt this necessary, as there seems to have been an obvious objection to the covenant for renewal being binding on anyone except the parties to it and that is that the lease, and therefore the covenant for renewal, were granted by GB in excess of the powers contained in the settlement of 1712. Nevertheless, FitzGibbon discussed the rule in order to dispose of the notion that the covenant 'ran with the land' no matter into whose hand it came. His remarks are an important contribution to the subject, particularly his point that covenants ran with the estate, not with 'the land' as is commonly stated. The respondents, in order to charge the appellants at law with the covenant, therefore had to trace into their possession the estate, or part of it, which the lessor had when he made the lease.

What was the situation of the parties at the time of the execution of the lease of 1729? Mr B. was tenant for life of the land, with remainder to his first and every other son in tail male, and the reversion in fee simple was in the earl, who had purchased it for valuable consideration. So when Mr B. made the lease he could bind only the assignee of his life estate, unless the subsequent registration of the lease extended the covenant for renewal beyond its original effect at common law.

An objection to this in argument was that a covenant for renewal ran with the land and bound the land 'let it come into the possession of whom it may.' FitzGibbon found that the objection was based on a 'strange misconception'. Covenants were said to run with the land under the statute 10 Cha. I, sess. 2, c. 4 (Ir.), 1634.[154]

> But can any man seriously assert that because a covenant for renewal is said to run with the land, it is in the power of a person seized of a limited estate in the land, to charge it by such a covenant, in the hands of the remainderman or reversioner, claiming by deed paramount to the lease and covenant? The covenant runs, not with the land, but with the estate of the lessor in the land:– a covenant, which runs with the land, attends the estate which the lessor had in the lands when he made the lease, but the moment that estate is spent, the covenant is at an end, as against the possessor of the land. He is not personally chargeable in respect of the covenant, unless his possession is derived under the estate of the lessor.

FitzGibbon went on to say that he did not ask the judges whether, independent of the Registration Act, the appellant could be charged on the covenant at law, because he thought that the answer was obvious, that she could not be. So he merely asked them whether *the Act* had enabled the respondents to charge the appellant at law for breach of the covenant. They answered in the negative. He

[154] If the subject matter was in existence at the time of the demise, the assignee was bound, even though not named. If the subject matter was not in existence at the time of the demise, the assignee was not bound, unless he was named. But if a person covenanted for himself and his assigns to do something collateral which did not concern the land, the covenant did not bind the assignee even though he was named: *Spencer's Case* (1583) 5 Co. Rep. 16a, 77 E.R. 72, 2 Ridg. PC, FitzGibbon at 410.

concluded that the covenant for renewal was not binding on the appellant at law or in equity.

He had already pointed out, he says, that by registering the lease, the original lessees acquired a legal right against the earl and every person claiming under him. But in FitzGibbon's view the Registry Act had no further effect. It did not extend the effect of the covenant for renewal. As to the covenant itself, it was 'a contract for himself, his heirs and executors, and *his assigns claiming from him subsequent to the lease*'; if respondents were to bring an action against the heir of Mr B. or his executor for breach of covenant for refusal to renew the lease, they could not do so, because the original contract by the covenantor extended only to the assignees of the covenantor claiming from him subsequent to the lease: *Target* v. *Lloyd*.[155] The Registry Act did not displace the reversion which was vested in the earl by a deed prior to the lease. The respondents acknowledged that by filing the present bill, because they called upon the appellant, as deriving the fee simple under the unregistered deed of 1728, to execute them a new lease.

Having concluded that the covenant did not bind the reversioner at common law, FitzGibbon then considered, even if it had done, whether the reversioner would be relieved in equity.[156] Fitzgibbon here seems to consider this in order to persuade the other lords, who may have taken the view that it was binding at common law, that, even if it was, and he was wring as to that, that equity still would not give a remedy unavailable at common law.

He noted that the appellant's father, the late Duke of Chandos, in the original bill, had stated that the Earl of Caernarvon, his grandfather, was a purchaser of the reversion for valuable consideration, without notice of the lease of 1729, or the covenant for renewal. The purchaser of the reversion was a bona fide purchaser of a legal estate without notice of the lease and in FitzGibbon's view, that was decisive. Registration of deeds did not entirely displace the role of equity:[157]

> The principle is admitted, that if a man acquires a legal title under the registry act, with notice of a prior unregistered title in another to the same land, that a court of equity may control him in the exercise and assertion of his legal title, notwithstanding the words of the registry act.

This seems to be one of the earliest reported statements of that principle in Ireland, and clearly one of the most authoritative. The earliest authority was *Forbes* v. *Deniston*[158] in 1722 in which the British House of Lords reversed the Irish court of Chancery.[159] The principle cited above has since been reiterated

155 (1726) 2 Vent. 277, 86 E.R. 439. 2 Ridg. PC 413.

156 2 Ridg. PC 421.

157 2 Ridg. PC 429.

158 (1722) 4 Bro. PC 189, (1722) 2 Bro. PC 425, 2 E.R. 129,

159 FitzGibbon does not cite *Forbes*, which was first reported in Brown's *Parliamentary Cases*, the first edition of which was only published in 1779. However, FitzGibbon does cite Lord Hardwicke in *Le Neve* v. *Le Neve* (1748) 3 Atk. 646, 26 E.R. 1172 on the later English registration of deeds

several times.[160]

By the same token, FitzGibbon argued, equity could intervene to prevent the creation or revival of a legal title by virtue of the Act as against a purchaser for value without notice:[161]

> upon the same principle, the same court will not be warranted in its interposition under the authority of the same act, to create or revive a legal title not in existence, and which can exist only by the aid of a court of equity against a purchaser for valuable consideration without notice, who certainly has as strong claims to the protection and assistance of a court of equity as any other person whatever.

Chandos v. *Brownlow* shows FitzGibbon, the dominant figure in the Irish House of Lords as an appellate court, at his brilliant best. He displays in this case his great intellectual gifts as a lawyer and as an equity judge. First, from a complex set of facts he isolated the facts relevant in terms of legal principle; then he stated the novel legal issue they raised, saw an analogy to an established rule in the same area of equity intervention, and then used it to formulate a new rule of equity to solve the problem at hand, based nevertheless on the same underlying principles of equity jurisdiction. The principle he arrives at in *Chandos* v. *Brownlow* is one of equal standing with that in *Forbes* v. *Deniston*, *Agra Bank* v. *Barry*, and *Re Fuller* mentioned earlier.[162] FitzGibbon here shows his confidence and his mastery of equity. His judgment in *Chandos* v. *Brownlow* is a *tour de force*.

One might also note here that the case is further testimony to FitzGibbon's integrity in matters of law. He applies principles of equity even though the conclusion is to reject the claim of successors in title to a Protestant discoveror.

Act, 7 Ann. c. 20 (Eng.), applying the system to the county of Middlesex, and Harwicke in *Le Neve* cited *Forbes*. He recognised it to be the first authority on the principle, so it is a little odd that FitzGibbon does not himself cite *Forbes*. Perhaps he had no report or primary source of the British House of Lords judgments available to him, and perhaps did not wish to cite the case second-hand from Hardwicke. Nevertheless, Brown's *Parliamentary Cases* had been published several years before FitzGibbon delivered judgment in *Chandos* v. *Brownlow* in March 1791. Perhaps a copy had not found its way to Ireland, but it remains something of a mystery. It may be noted that Mr Calaghan in *Blennerhasset* v. *Babington* (1733) *Ir. Exch. Rep.* 223 (Seld. Soc. vol 125 for 2008) on the same point did not refer to *Forbes* either.

[160] *Delacour* v. *Freeman* (1854) 2 Ir. Ch. R. 633; *Montgomery* v. *McEvoy* (1857) 5 Ir. Ch. R. 126; *Clarke* v. *Armstrong* (1861) 10 Ir. Ch. R. 263; *Re Floods Estate* (1863) Ir. Ch. R. 312; *Agra Bank* v. *Barry* (1874) L.R. 7 H.L. 135; *Re Fuller* [1982] I.R. 161, HC.

[161] 2 Ridg. PC 429.

[162] Above, note 160.

CHAPTER 10

Criminal Jurisdiction

Writs of Error

One of the features of Ridgeway's *Reports of Cases in Parliament* is that they contain no instance of a criminal writ of error to the House. There were many capital offences at the time and the hangman was regularly employed, but their lordships were more concerned with property issues such as *Shelley's Case* and leases for lives.

Henry,[1] in a recent study of the death penalty in 18th century Ireland, states that between 1780 and 1795 there were a total of 390 homicides reported in the city and country of Dublin. Of these, 189 were 'murders', presumably meaning apparently deliberate killings, an average of about twelve a year. In the same period there were 199 verified hangings of convicted felons - murder was not the only capital offence at the time. Furthermore, a number of those hanged were probably innocent. Henry estimates at least eight were innocent, one example being Hugh Feeney and John Murphy who were hanged on 20 March 1784 just minutes before the hangman received word that the lord lieutenant had reprieved them.[2]

The absence of criminal writs of error is odd given that the standing orders of 1692 [3] seem to contemplate an extensive criminal jurisdiction.[4] It is true that there was no substantive appeal on the merits in 'common law' cases, but writs of error were available. Until 1836[5] a defendant in felony had no right to have counsel address the jury on his behalf,[6] although it was allowed informally before then. He could, nevertheless, address the court on matters of law.

[1] Brian Henry, *Dublin Hanged: Crime, Law Enforcement and Punishment in Late 18th-century Dublin* (Dublin, 1994), p. 77.

[2] Henry (1994), p. 27.

[3] See Ireland, Parliament, House of Lords, *Rules and Orders to be Observed in the Upper House of Parliament of Ireland.* (Dublin, printed by W. Sleater, MDCCXC. [1790]). The dates of the orders are noted in the margin.

[4] The Orders of 1692 are evidently not the first standing orders adopted. There is reference from 1640 to a rule as to the immunity of peers from legal process within 40 days of a sitting of parliament: *Cal. St. P. Ir.*, 1633–47, vol. 258, p. 237. Letter from Sir George Radcliffe to Lord Lieutenant, re the Bishop of Killala. The rule is also contained in the 1692 Orders.

[5] 6 & 7 Will. IV, c. 114 (Eng., Ir.) (defendants in felony).

[6] Allyson N. May, *The Bar and the Old Bailey, 1750–1850* (Chapel Hill, N. Carolina, 2003).

Another factor may have been that the judge's summing up to the jury was not recorded in writing. Writs of error could only be brought on errors on the face of the (written) record, but a bill of exceptions could supplement that, for example, with objections to oral rulings of the judge.[7] Criminal trials took place at assizes or in the King's Bench and writs of error in the Irish King's Bench had lain to the English King's Bench, but that had changed in 1782, with such writs going in theory to the Irish House of Lords.[8] So none of these factors provides an explanation. The only other possibility seems to be that a writ of error in felony was not regarded as of right in Ireland in the 18th century, particularly as murder was treated as treason until 1791,[9] and writs were refused, but there is no indication as to that.

Original Criminal Jurisdiction

The Irish Lords, like their British counterpart, asserted the right to try peers accused of crimes. The origin was said to be the provision of Magna Carta whereby no freeman was to be imprisoned or disseised except by the lawful judgment of his 'peers' or by the law of the land. 'Peers' in this context meant 'equals' but implied a privilege for those later accorded the rank of peer.[10]

Magna Carta Hiberniæ

The right to trial by ones 'peers' derived from *Magna Carta* and that was the basis of the privilege claimed by Irish peers to be tried by the Irish House of Lords.

Magna Carta had been sent to Ireland in 1217. A version of the Great Charter existed in the Red Book of the Irish Exchequer with minor adaptations for Ireland, known as *Magna Carta Hiberniæ*[11] but whether the adaptations had any official sanction is doubted by some historians.[12] The Red Book was destroyed

7 Above, page 71.

8 Above, page 77.

9 Under the statute 10 Hen. VII, c. 21 (Ir.), 1495: below, Appendix J, repealed by 31 Geo. III, c. 17 (Ir.), 1791.

10 The privilege was only extended to female peers by 20 Hen. VI c. 9 (Eng.), 1442. The last trial of a peer by the House of Lords in the United Kingdom took place in December 1935. Lord de Clifford was tried for the manslaughter of Douglas George Hopkins who had been killed in a motor car accident. The verdict of the peers was 'not guilty.' Trial of peers by the British House of Lords was abolished by the Criminal Justice Act, 1948, s. 30. The privilege included the doubtful advantage, if found guilty of a capital crime, of being hanged with a silken rope instead of the usual hemp.

11 1 Hen. III, 1216; H. F. Berry, ed., *Statutes and Ordinances, and Acts of the Parliament of Ireland: King John to Henry V*, (Dublin, 1907), pp. 5–19.

12 R. Dudley Edwards, '*Magna Carta Hiberniæ*' in J. Ryan, ed., *Essays and Studies Presented to Professor Eoin MacNeill*, (Dublin, 1940), pp. 307–318; H. G. Richardson, 'Magna Carta Hiberniæ' (1942–43) 3 *Irish Historical Studies* 31–33; Richardson wrote: 'granted that the authentic charter of 1216 was law in Ireland, this crude substitution of names could not be justified on any principle of interpretation known to medieval (or modern) lawyers'. Certainly not modern lawyers, but what the 13th century theory of statutory interpretation was, if indeed there was one, would seem to be far from clear. He also wrote (note 2): 'The language of the letter (for text see Cal. pat. rolls, 1216–25, p. 31) seems plainly to bear only one construction, that the charter of 12 November 1216 was sent unaltered. It is the liberties granted to England that are reduced to writing and sealed: they

with the public records in the Four Courts in 1922, but the charter is reproduced in H. F. Berry, ed., *Statutes and Ordinances, and Acts of the Parliament of Ireland: King John to Henry V*, (Dublin, 1907).[13] In the Republic, the charter is one of the retained statutes in the Statute Law Revision Act 2007.[14]

Although historians have expressed doubts as to whether there was a distinct *Magna Carta Hiberniæ*[15] there is nevertheless no doubt that the Charter was intended to be applied to Ireland and to give rise to the same rights. *Magna Carta Hiberniæ* cannot be traced further back than the early 14th century when it was copied into the Red Book. Apart from minor variations it follows the charter issued by Henry III on 12 November 1216. The differences are in clauses in which 'Ireland' is substituted for 'England' (in reference to the Church), 'Dublin' for 'London', 'the Liffey' for 'the Thames and Medway', the standard measures of wine, corn, cloth, etc., by 'the quarter of Dublin' instead of 'the quarter of London' and references to the Cinque Ports and Wales are omitted. Oddly, the reference to the honors of Wallingford, Nottingham, Boulogne and Lancaster were left unaltered.

There seems no doubt that the charter sent to Ireland in 1217 was that granted to England. Nevertheless, those clauses, if they were to have any meaning in Ireland, would necessarily have been construed by courts in the same way in which they were amended. Today, in the case of private documents 'construction' in law would allow a court to 'read' a word in a document that is not there, or to give a word a special meaning rather than its literal one, in order to give some meaning to an otherwise meaningless clause or to carry out the intention of a testator. No such liberty is allowed in the interpretation of statutes. But it is doubtful whether such a distinction was drawn in 1217. Since the intention of the king, or the king in council, was that the Charter should apply in Ireland, then it could be said that any adaptations made by royal authorities in Ireland and made necessary by the failure or inattention of the English authorities to adapt it expressly, were in pursuance of that will. Arguably, all that the clerks in Ireland did was to write in the words as they would have been construed. Also, if the Charter had been 'given' to Ireland, which was a separate jurisdiction to that of England, then, adapted or not, in law it would constitute a separate legal document with a separate identity. In interpreting the charter, had they been called upon to do so, judges in Ireland would be interpreting a distinct document from the English charter. It is therefore legitimate to speak of *Magna Carta Hiberniæ* even if the text was identical to the English Charter. It would follow that trial by one's 'peers' applied in Ireland and, again by necessary construction, to peers of the *Irish* parliament. In fact it was assumed in the past that such

are extended to Ireland by the king's grace and gift.' But if the words 'the English church' were not construed in Ireland to mean 'the Irish church' then those liberties would not have been extended to Ireland and the king's will would not have been carried out.

13 1 St. Realm 14 (1235-1377) 'Charter of Liberties' reproduces the charter with collation of variations, including the Irish ones.

14 Section 2 and Sch., listed as '1216 (1 Hen. 3) [PRO vol. 1] the Great Charter of Ireland' and given the official short title, *Magna Carta Hiberniæ*.

15 Above, note 12.

a jurisdiction existed and so, by implication, that there was a distinct *Magna Carta Hiberniæ*. Historians have perhaps not appreciated these points.

Early Examples

The original criminal jurisdiction of the Irish House of Lords over its own members was therefore clearly of ancient origin and quite distinct from the appellate jurisdiction. It does not seem to have had a continuous history, no doubt due to the confused state of the country and its institutions from time to time. In June 1628 Lord Dunboyne[16] was tried for manslaughter by a number of peers, including Viscount Netterville of Dowth.[17] Although one source asserts that the trial took place 'in the King's Bench',[18] this seems to refer to the venue rather than the nature of the court. Cokayne says that Lord Dunboyne was indicted by a grand jury of Tipperary for the manslaughter of one James Prendergast, tried by his peers and acquitted on 11 June 1628.[19]

Oddly, the standing orders of the Irish Lords adopted in 1692 contemplate the House having an original criminal jurisdiction, and one not expressly confined to peers. Order 102 is headed 'Trial of such Persons as shall be brought before the Lords' and recites that:

> As this court is the highest, from whence others ought to draw their Light, so the proceedings thereof should be the most clear and equal, as well on the side of finding out Offences where there is just ground, as on the side of affording all just means of Defence to such as shall be questioned and therefore in all cases of Moment the defendant shall have copies of all Depositions, pro et contra, after publication, a convenient time before the Hearing, to prepare themselves.

This clearly seems to contemplate a trial at first instance, as does order 104 which concerns the right of defendants to counsel. The order states that:

> This is to be done, because in all causes, as well civil as criminal and capital, all lawful Helps cannot before just Judges make any one that is guilty to avoid Justice; and on the other side, God forbid that the innocent shall be condemned!

To what trials or crimes these noble sentiments were addressed is something of a mystery. The order does not expressly limit the jurisdiction to the trial of peers, although it may include trials on impeachment. Order 104 in fact repeats the phrase in the 1641 resolution.[20] At that time it may have been contemplated that trials for treason or for other offences would take place by way of impeachment. The orders do refer to 'privilege of peerage' but it is clear that the phrase

16 Edmund Butler, 3rd Baron Dunboyne (d. 1640). Cokayne, *Complete Peerage* iv. 517. Below, page 193 and note 47.

17 Cokayne, *Complete Peerage*, ix. 472.

18 HMC, Hodgkin MSS, p. 292; Cokayne, *Complete Peerage*, ix. 472 n. f.

19 Cokayne, *Complete Peerage* iv. 517.

20 Below, page 191.

indicates immunity from legal process of the Lords and their immediate retinue while parliament was in session, or within 40 days of a session.[21] Exceptions were liability to answer a writ of habeas corpus[22] and liability as a trustee.[23] Order 53, on the other hand, is headed 'Imprisonment' and provides that:

> the privilege of this House is that no lord of parliament sitting in the parliament, or within the usual time of privilege of parliament, is to be imprisoned or restrained without sentence or order of the House unless for Treason, Felony, or refusing to give security for the Peace.

This, however, only refers to imprisonment, as perhaps after arrest, and not to trials. The only criminal proceedings in the Irish House were trials of peers and they are discussed in the next section.

The original criminal jurisdiction of the Irish House was recognised in England in 1577. In that year the chancellor of Ireland, Sir William Gerard,[24] put a question to the Queen's Council in England as to trial of Irish peers for treason. The answer was that an Irish peer was not triable in England, either by the English peers or by jury, because he or she was not a subject of England but of Ireland and should be tried in Ireland.[25] The legal opinion is noted in Dyer's Reports as follows:

> Gerrarde, Chancellor of Ireland moved this question to the Queen's Counsel: Whether an earl or Lord of Ireland, who commits treason in Ireland by open rebellion, shall be arraigned and put to his trial in England for the offence, by the statute of 26 H. 8 c. 13.[26] 32 H. 8 c. 4. 35 H. 8 c. 2[27] or 5 Ed. 6 c. 11.[28] And it was holden by Wray, Dyer, and Gerrarde Attorney General, that he cannot; for he cannot have his trial here by his peers, nor by any jury of twelve, because he is not a subject of England, but of Ireland; and therefore his trial shall be there. And it is said, that the usage there of attainting a peer is by Parliament, and not by peers.

In *O'Rorke's Case*[29] in 1591 the English King's Bench held that treasons committed

[21] Orders 53, 44. Order 44 had been amended by 11 & 12 Geo. III, c. 12 (Ir.), 1771. The statute recites that Lawrence Tathe brought the assize of novel disseisin against John Barnewall, knight of the county of Dublin (i.e. a member of parliament) for two water mills in Athirde in Co. Lowth with the intent of recovering them by default, since Barnewall was attending parliament. The writ was declared null and void.

[22] Order 48.

[23] Order 51.

[24] Appointed, 1576, died, 1581. He was being succeeded by archbishop Adam Loftus, who was appointed lord keeper. Ball, *Judges in Ireland*, i.137-9, 217-18. Ball (i.137) says Gerard was a cousin of Queen Elizabeth's attorney general, Sir Gilbert Gerard, but at i.217 says Sir Gilbert was master of the rolls in England.

[25] 'Treason committed in Ireland, by an Irish peer, cannot be tried in England', 3 Dyer 360b, 73 E.R. 807; *Reports from the Lost Notebooks of Sir James Dyer. Vol. I.* (J. H. Baker, ed.) 109 Seld. Soc. (for 1993), p. lxxxvi; Madden & Fieldhouse, *The Empire of the Bretaignes* (Connecticut, 1985), p. 73.

[26] 26 Hen. VIII, c. 13 (Eng.), 1534 (treason, England and dominions).

[27] 35 Hen. VIII, c. 2 (Eng.), 1543 (treason, outside dominions).

[28] 5 & 6 Edw. VI, c. 11 (Eng.), 1551 (treason).

[29] 1 And. 262, 123 E.R. 463.

on foreign land were triable in England, 'Ireland excepted':[30]

> Un Irishman, nome Orork, commit divers Treasons en Ireland encounter le Roign; le question fuit, si il poit estre trye icy en Anglitеr̃ pur ceux Treasons nient esteant un baron ou Pere... A que fuit respond, & agree, per touts les Juges, que touts treasons faits en forrein terrs (Ireland excepted) serra tries icy en Angliterre. Per Statute 35 H. 8 c. 13 [*sic*]. Et pur ascun treasons per le Statute de 26 H. 8.
>
> An Irishman, named O'Rorke, committed various treasons in Ireland against the King: the question was, if he could be tried here in England for his treasons, not being a lord or peer... To which the judges answered and agreed, that all treasons committed in foreign lands (Ireland excepted) are to be tried here in England. By Statute 35 Hen. VIII, c. 13 [*sic*].[31] And for other treasons by the statute 26 Hen. VIII.[32]

The exception appears in Anderson's report, although there is some doubt as to its authenticity, since it appears in parenthesis and in English rather than in the Law French of the rest of the report. This suggests it may have been added later as an afterthought. Ireland was not really 'foreign' for this purpose, or not regarded as so at this time. Irish courts might be expected to have jurisdiction, including, in the case of an Irish peer, the Irish House of Lords. The first statute referred to, 35 Hen. VIII, c. 2 (Eng.), 1543, concerned treasons committed outside the king's dominions, and provided that they were triable in England. It clearly would not refer to Ireland. However, the last statute mentioned, 26 Hen. VIII, c. 13 (Eng.), 1534, concerned treasons committed in England *and the king's other dominions*, which would have included Ireland. The effect of the two statutes taken together would seem to have been that treasons committed *anywhere* within the king's dominions were triable in England. It would therefore appear that what the judges were being asked was not whether an Irishman was triable in England or not, but merely under what statute was he triable in England. The judges' answers, or the report of them, are far from clear on the point. Did they mean he was triable under 26 Hen. VIII, c. 13 and not 35 Hen. VIII, c. 2, or that he was not triable in England at all, but in Ireland, which had the king's courts also?

The next precedent occurred in the 1640s. The Earl of Strafford at his trial in 1641 argued that he should have been tried by the Irish House of Lords since his alleged crimes had been committed in Ireland.[33] One might notice that this might have been thought to involve two different points. First, should an English peer be tried by the Irish House of Lords for crimes committed in Ireland? The answer to this would seem obvious: the Irish House, like its English counterpart, only had jurisdiction over its own members, and Strafford was

30 1 And. 262, 123 E.R. 463.

31 The error is in Anderson's report. The reference seems to refer to 35 Hen. VIII, c. 2 (Eng.), 1543–4 (treason, outside dominions), above.

32 i.e. 26 Hen. VIII, c. 13 (Eng.), 1534 (treason, England and dominions), above.

33 (1641) 3 St. Tr. 1382.

not an Irish peer. Strafford's claim could have been rejected on this narrow ground. Secondly, could anyone, peer or commoner, be tried in England for offences, specifically treason, committed abroad, and was Ireland 'abroad' for this purpose? One might expect an English court to decide that it did have jurisdiction to try treasons committed abroad, treason being a particularly dangerous crime. Furthermore, even if treasons committed in Ireland were held to be triable in England, that would not in itself call into question the jurisdiction of the Irish courts or the Irish House of Lords in the case of peers. Nevertheless, the English court decided the issue on a much wider ground than either of the two just mentioned. It was resolved that the 'parliament of England has power of judicature for things done in Ireland'.[34] The principle announced threw doubt on the Irish House of Lords' jurisdiction as a court of law of any kind and also, by implication, on its status as an independent institution. The earlier law was cast aside. Earlier precedents seem to have been ignored.

This seems to be a clear indication that the British authorities no longer trusted the Irish House to convict Irish peers of treason. This novel assertion of jurisdiction produced in May 1641 a joint resolution by both Houses of the Irish parliament in the following terms:[35]

> ...For the avoiding of any Doubt or Ambiguity which might be moved or stirred up against the Power of Judicature of the high court of Parliament in this Realm, and to manifest and declare a most clear, undoubted, and undeniable Truth to all Posterity, the Lords spiritual and temporal and Commons, in Parliament assembled, do hereby declare and protest, that the said Court of Parliament of this Kingdom hath always had and ought to have full power and authority to hear and determine all treasons and other offences...as well capital as criminal...and that the said Court of Parliament is the supreme Judicatory in the said Realm.

This express claim to supreme judicial power was a reaction to a novel assertion of supremacy by the English parliament. Then in 1645 Lord Connor Maguire,[36] an Irish peer, claimed trial by his peers by the House of Lords in Ireland in accordance with Magna Carta. Lord Maguire took part in the rebellion of 1641. He was arrested in the same year and sent to England by the lords justices in 1642 to stand trial in London.[37] He was arraigned before the English King's Bench. His case was argued by Sir Matthew Hale.[38] The claim was denied by the English King's Bench which held that 'a baron of Ireland was triable by a jury

[34] 3 Dyer 360b, 73 E.R. 807 n. 6; Madden & Fieldhouse, *The Empire of the Bretaignes* (Connecticut, 1985), p. 73. Sir Matthew Hale repeated this opinion in *Pleas of the Crown*, i.155.

[35] *Cal. St. P. Ir.*, 1633–1647, pp. 296–7; 1 *J. Ir. H.C.* 213, 24 May 1641.

[36] *Lord Connor Maguire* (1645) 4 St. Tr. 654; Cokayne, *Complete Peerage*, viii.356. Although called Lord Connor Maguire in Ireland, he was more correctly Connor or Connor Roe, Lord Maguire, 2nd Baron of Enniskillen, son of Bryan Roe Maguire, 1st Baron Maguire. He was born in or before 1612.

[37] Cokayne, *Complete Peerage*, viii.356.

[38] Cokayne, *Complete Peerage*, viii.356 n. e.

in this kingdom', the Lords and Commons approving.[39] He was convicted and hanged, drawn and quartered at Tyburn, 20 February 1644/5. As Cokayne notes, he was disembowelled while still alive 'in circumstances of ghastly barbarity.'[40] Peers guilty of treason were liable to be executed by beheading, so he was not granted the privilege of peerage in that respect either.

This showed not only that the joint resolution of 1641 had fallen on deaf ears, but that the English courts were prepared to depart from the earlier law in the aftermath of the 1641 rebellion.

Sir Matthew Hale in the 1660s claimed that a final appeal lay on a writ of error to the English House of Lords from a 'judgement given in the lords' House of Parliament in Ireland.'[41] Despite this, the Irish Lords had recovered their jurisdiction to try peers for criminal offences by the early 18th century and continued to exercise it throughout the century. It was no coincidence that by that time Catholics had been excluded from sitting in either House of the Irish parliament.

The procedure of the Irish Lords in its original criminal jurisdiction remained quite distinct from the House in its appellate capacity. While the procedure and composition of the Irish House of Lords in its appellate capacity developed in the period before the Union from that of a legislative body towards that of a professional court, the procedure of the House exercising its original criminal jurisdiction in the trial of peers changed little, and remained similar to that of a deliberative body. This was largely because the peers functioned as the jury. Hence, lay peers, as well as those legally qualified, took part in the trial and decided the guilt or innocence of the accused.

Eighteenth-Century Trials

There were three trials of peers before the Irish House of Lords in the 18th century. All were for murder. Lord Barry of Santry was convicted and condemned to death but obtained a pardon, but only as to his life. His estates were forfeited. Lord Netterville was acquitted and so was the Earl of Kingston.

Lord Barry of Santry

Lord Barry of Santry,[42] commonly known in Ireland as Lord Santry, was tried and convicted of the murder of Laughlin Murphy, whom he had stabbed in 'a fit of passion' in an incident on 9 August 1738.[43] Murphy did not die until seven weeks later, but at the inquest the coroner's jury returned a verdict of 'wilful murder' and named Santry as the killer.[44] At a friend's urging, Santry surrendered himself to Lord Chief Justice Rogerson of the King's Bench and was

39 *ibid.*, (1645) 4 St. Tr. at p. 665.
40 *Complete Peerage*, viii.357 n. a.
41 Madden & Fieldhouse (1985), p. 74.
42 Henry Barry, 4th Baron Barry of Santry (1710–1751). Cokayne, *Complete Peerage*, i.448.
43 *ibid.*
44 See Neal Garnham, 'The Trials of James Cotter and Henry, Baron Barry of Santry: two case studies in the administration of criminal justice in early eighteenth-century Ireland' (1998–9) 31 *Irish Historical Studies* 328–342. The following account is taken from that source, Cokayne, *Complete Peerage* and Sir John Strange's 'Notes on Lord Netterville's Trial', Appendix J, page 233.

placed in the custody of one of the Dublin city sheriffs. There followed a flurry of consultation as to the procedure to be followed. On 20 November 1738 the lords justices, who carried out the functions of the lord lieutenant in his absence, wrote to the prime serjeant, the attorney general and the solicitor general asking them for their opinions as to how to proceed. They also informed the lord lieutenant, the Duke of Devonshire,[45] who asked Lord Hardwicke, the English lord chancellor, for his views.

Hardwicke recommended that although 'murder is deemed high treason in the law of Ireland' (by the statute 10 Hen. VII, c. 21 (Ir.), 1495)[46] Devonshire should offer no advice until the records of the King's Bench had been searched for precedents. In the meantime, the lords justices sent Devonshire the opinions of the Irish law officers. Santry would have to be tried by his peers, but in their opinion a letter from the king was necessary first. They also asked that 'his Majesty's learned council in England' should be consulted as to the procedure. In Dublin, the authorities had researched the cases of Sir James Ware and Sir Richard Cox and found that Lord Dunboyne had been tried for manslaughter by his peers in 1626.[47] The lords justices recommended to Devonshire that the lord chancellor, Lord Wyndham[48] would be the best candidate to act as lord high steward, the officer who would preside over the trial. Finally the king's letter arrived, authorising a commission appointing Wyndham to the office.

Santry came to trial on 27 April 1739. Wyndham had decided that the chamber of the House of Commons would be more suitable as a venue, given the public interest that had been generated. The public galleries were in fact crammed with onlookers. Wyndham address the assembled Lords, stressing that despite the public interest, it was their duty to decide on the evidence alone.

The prosecution then presented its case with a string of witnesses. They attested that Santry and a group of friends had spent most of the day drinking in the kitchen of Patrick Corrigan's tavern in Palmerstown. At one point, Murphy, who knew Santry and may formerly have been his footman, passed by the kitchen door and Santry had invited him to join the company. As the night wore on, the group began to disperse, until by half past ten that night, only Santry, Murphy and a Mr Humphreys remained. For some reason, Santry and Humphreys began to quarrel. Santry became angry and twice attempted to draw his sword, but being incapacitated by drink, was unable to draw it from the scabbard. In a rage, he then stormed out of the room, but before he reached the street, he collided with Murphy. He pushed Murphy back into the kitchen, swearing he

45 William Cavendish, 3rd Duke of Devonshire, KG, PC (1698–1755).

46 Appendix J, page 233.

47 A grand jury in Tipperary had indicted him for the manslaughter of one James Prendergast. He was ordered to be tried by his peers in 1628, and was acquitted. Cokayne, *Complete Peerage*, iv. 517.

48 Andrew Lyall, 'Wyndham, Thomas, Baron Wyndham (1681–1745)', ODNB online ed., [http://www.oxforddnb.com/view/article/30147], accessed 3 June 2008; John Cronin, Patrick A. Walsh, 'Wyndham, Thomas Baron Wyndham of Finglas', [http://dib.cambridge.org/ viewReadPage.do?articleId=a9146.] His grandfather, Sir Wadham Wyndham, one of the justices of the English King's Bench (1660–68), was the grandson of John Wyndham and Florence, sister of Nicholas Wadham, founder of Wadham College, Oxford. Edward Foss, *Judges of England*, vii.198.

would run through the next man to speak. Murphy, with fatally ill-judged courtesy, then said he wished no one would offend his lordship. According to the witnesses, true to his word, Santry then plunged his sword into Murphy's side. Murphy fled into the next room, but then returned, bleeding profusely from the wound and collapsed on the kitchen floor. Santry then dashed out of the tavern, mounted his horse, and made off into the night. It was to be another six weeks before Murphy died, and much of the trial was taken up with accounting for what had caused his death. Santry had not only paid money to the innkeeper at Palmerstown, but had sent a surgeon from Dublin to tend him and a carriage to take him home. Murphy had not been prepared to let the matter drop and after an unxsuccessful attempt to persuade a magistrate to initiate a prosecution for assault, finally persuaded the lord mayor to take his statement. It seemed he had also attempted to obtain a medical opinion as to his injury, allegedly in an attempt to claim money from Santry. Murphy died a month and half after the incident. Dr Bradford, the surgeon who had been originally called by Santry, arranged for a number of his apprentices to clean and sew up Murphy's body, shortly before the inquest. The coroner expressed disapproval of this and moved to adjourn the inquest, but Bradford said he could confirm that Murphy had died of 'an inflammation of the lungs', possibly pneumonia. No other surgeon could be found who was willing to examine the body. The coroner found that he could not determine the cause of death, but the jury returned a verdict of 'wilful murder'.

In his defence, Santry's lawyers first tried to make a case that Murphy had been the aggressor, and attempted to discredit the prosecution witnesses. But their main claim was that Murphy had died of 'spotted fever' and not as a result of the wound. Witnesses were called to show that Murphy had not spent the six weeks languishing from his wound, but had been seen daily going about his business and had even been seen staggering around in Dublin's Ormond Market, apparently drunk and apparently happy. The claim perhaps had some plausibility, since it was agreed that the wound would not on its own have caused his death, although why this should be so is not stated. However, the issue was then whether an infection had set in and caused Murphy's death, in which case it would have been a proximate cause of death for which Santry would be liable.

The prosecution in cross-examination effectively demolished the defence case, Dr Bradford admitting that he had left Murphy untreated for three days, because Santry had underpaid him. Even after he had been paid in full, Bradford himself had not treated Murphy, but had delegated it to one of his apprentices. The other defence witnesses also became less sure of their initial testimony that Murphy had seemed well in the intervening six weeks. The defence case was not helped either when one of its witnesses, John Creag, swore he had seen Murphy alive in December, three months after the inquest on his body!

Bowes,[49] the third serjeant, in summing up for the prosecution, gave a speech

[49] John Bowes (1691–1767), later attorney general, appointed chief baron of the Exchequer, 1741 and lord chancellor, 1757. Created Baron Bowes of Clonlyon in the same year. Ball, *Judges in Ireland*, ii.206; Cokayne, *Complete Peerage*, ii.259.

which one observer described as 'his most masterly performance'. After eight hours of evidence and legal argument, the peers retired to consider their verdict. After a short time they returned and the foreman stood and gave the verdict, 'guilty, upon my honour'. This account suggests that the usual procedure had been modified, for in the House of Lords each peer would have stood up in turn to deliver verdict, as on a vote of the House.

Wyndham had no choice but to pronounce sentence of death. Under the draconian statute 10 Hen. VII, c. 21 (Ir.), 1495, murder in Ireland was to be treated as treason, for which the mode of execution in the case of commoners, was hanging drawing and quartering, but in the case of peers, beheading with an axe. The statute of 1495 was repealed in 1791.[50]

Santry was condemned to death on 27 April 1739 and also attainted, so that his estates were forefited. The effect of attainder on his peerage was that it was forfeited for his own life.[51] The peerage descended in the same way as an entail and under the statute *De Donis*, as interpreted, the forfeiture did not affect the heirs. He obtained a pardon, as to his life, in June 1740 and so survived his attainder. In the meantime, it was reputed that the government had ordered an axe to be made for the purpose of his execution, but it was not needed and the public funds spent on its production were therefore wasted. The axe was said to be laid up in a neighbour's house.[52] His estates were restored but not his title. If he had had issue the title would have remained in abeyance until his death. As it was, he died without issue and so the title probably became extinct.

Lord Netterville

Lord Netterville[53] was indicted in August 1743 for the murder of Michael Walsh of County Meath and tried on 3 February 1743/4. He was acquitted.[54] Two principal witnesses had died since making their depositions, and their depositions could not be read in evidence. The lord high steward put the question, 'Whether Nicholas, Lord Viscount Netterville, is guilty of the felony whereof he stands indicted, or not guilty?' Each peer being called in turn, beginning with the last created Baron, declared, upon his honour, standing in his place uncovered and laying his right hand on his breast, that 'Lord Netterville is not guilty.' The lord high steward then broke his white wand, and adjourned the proceedings of the House.

The Earl of Kingston

The Earl of Kingston[55] and his second son, Robert Edward, afterwards Viscount Lorton, were tried for murder and acquitted, the former by the Irish House of

[50] By 31 Geo. III, c. 17 (Ir.), 1791.

[51] *ibid.*, note c.

[52] B. W. Adams, *The History and Description of Santry and Clougher Parishes, County Dublin* (London, 1883), p. 109; Garnham, *ibid.*, at p. 336. I am grateful to Prof. W. N. Osborough for reference to this source.

[53] Nicholas Netterville, 5th Viscount Netterville (1709–1751).

[54] Cokayne, *Complete Peerage*, ix. 474.

[55] Robert King, 2nd Earl of Kingston (1754–1799). Cokayne, *Complete Peerage*, vii.299.

Lords on 18 May 1798,[56] the latter at Cork Assizes in April 1798. Hale[57] gives an interesting account of the facts and the subsequent proceedings. The accused, at the time the facts occurred, held the courtesy title of Lord Kingsborough, his father still being alive. It was alleged that the earl shot Colonel Henry Fitzgerald, a natural son of his wife's brother. The accused had a town House in London by the Thames. One day his daughter Mary disappeared, leaving a note saying she intended to drown herself in the river. She had shown no previous sign of anxiety and Lord Kingsborough was convinced she was still alive. He advertised extensively for his daughter. No one appeared more concerned than Colonel Fitzgerald, who had been brought up as one of the family. A woman responded to the advertisement, saying that a girl answering Mary's description had taken lodgings with her in London. When the woman saw Colonel Fitzgerald she said 'Why, that's the man who brought the young lady to us.' Fitzgerald turned and ran. He was later challenged to a duel by Kingsborough's son, and, although no one would act as his second, a meeting took place at which six shots were fired at a distance of ten paces without injury on either side. The Kingsboroughs took their daughter back to County Cork. Colonel Fitzgerald, who was infatuated with Mary, soon followed. Kingsborough and his son heard a rumour that a stranger, acting somewhat mysteriously, was staying at a local inn. They went to his room in the inn but found the door locked. They forced the door. Colonel Fitzgerald tried to defend himself, or at least so it was claimed by Kingsborough, who shot and killed him, in order, so he also claimed, to defend his son. The grand jury of County Cork returned true bills of murder and Kingsborough, who had by then succeeded to the title on his father's death, claimed trial by his peers.

The Irish peers assembled in the Commons chamber, because the Lords chamber was too small to accommodate all those who were to attend.[58] The masters in Chancery and the judges led a procession into the chamber, followed by the eldest sons of peers, who were allowed to attend sittings,[59] and those peers who were under age and could not vote. Then came the peers, 57 in all, three archbishops and thirteen bishops. Last came FitzGibbon, as lord high steward of the court carrying his white wand of office. Sir Fortescue Chichester, Ulster King of Arms,[60] then entered, carrying the armorial bearings of the accused on a shield, and stood at the left of the bar. Next Lord Kingston himself entered, dressed in mourning. Further drama was added to the proceedings by the executioner, who stood on the other side of the bar, , bearing a large hatchet with a broad blade. The procedure prescribed that the blade was to be averted from the accused until the verdict was delivered. If the accused was convicted the blade would then

[56] *ibid.*, vii.299, note e.

[57] Leslie Hale, *John Philpot Curran*, pp. 169–71; Jonah Barrington, *Personal Sketches of His Own Times* (London, 1869). 3rd edn. pp. 108–9

[58] Jonah Barrington, *Personal Sketches*, 3rd edn. pp. 108–9.

[59] This is to be distinguished from attendance under a writ of acceleration which would give the right to participate in debate and vote: see above, note 51 page 11.

[60] The office of Ulster King of Arms was instituted by Edward VI in 1552 and the heraldic authority of the office extended to the whole of Ireland.

be turned towards him, indicating the sentence. The roll was then called, which showed that two-thirds of the peers were absent. The royal commission was read, the bill of indictment presented and the clerk of the Crown directed the serjeant-at-arms to make proclamation to the constable of Dublin Castle to bring the accused to the Bar. The accused was then escorted in by the constable and his deputy. The accused bowed to the lord high steward and fell on his knees at the Bar. FitzGibbon commanded the prisoner to rise. The indictment was read again and the Clerk asked the accused to answer it. The accused pleaded not guilty. The Clerk then asked how he would be tried to which the answer was 'By God and my peers.' The serjeant-at-arms then called on the witnesses to come forward and be heard. None appeared. It seemed that the relatives of Colonel Fitzgerald did not want to pursue the matter. The elaborate ritual had been for nothing. The Lords were called upon to pronounce their verdict in the absence of evidence. Each peer stood up in turn, the most junior first, and each declared 'Not guilty, upon my honour!' The bishops were precluded from voting in criminal trials. The lord chancellor then rose and declared the opinion of the peers 'that Robert, Earl of Kingston, was not guilty of the charge against him. 'He then broke his wand, descended from his chair and the trial ended. Five days later, as Hale notes, the rebellion of the United Irishmen began and one effect of that, as Hale puts it, was the murder of the Irish parliament.

An Act of Pains and Penalties

The case of *Hume* v. *Burton*[61] has already been discussed, but an incident during the House of Lords proceedings gave rise to a bill of pains and penalties against Viscount Strangford.[62] The incident also raised the constitutional issue as to whether that was the correct course, or whether he should have been impeached first by the House of Commons, or tried by the ordinary courts.

Strangford had written a letter to George Rochfort, a party in the case, soliciting a bribe in return for his favourable vote in the House of Lords. Of course, Strangford did not put it quite so crudely, but the House of Lords was in no doubt as to his meaning. Indeed, the letter is set out in the journals of the House:[63]

> Dear Sir,
> As a busy scene is likely to open after the recess, which will bring on momentous transactions to individuals, I could wish, by regular attendance, to frame a right judgment on the different cases [which] will be brought forward, but as distressed circumstances deprive me

[61] (1784) 1 Ridg. PC 16, above, pages 50, 71, 88, 96, 96. On 24 November 1783 Annaly CJKB, Robinson J and Henn J attended the House of Lords and acknowledged their seals to the bill of exceptions to the writ of error in the case: 5 *J. Ir. H.L.* 399.

[62] Philip Smythe, 4th Viscount Strangford (1715–1787). His second wife, Hannah, was the daughter of the Rt. Hon. John Rogerson CJKB. Cokayne, *Complete Peerage*, xii.360–61; 5 *J. Ir. H.L.* 494-97; 3 *J. Ir. H.C.* 187–200, 225; *Proceedings against Philip Lord Viscount Strangford for acting criminally and corruptly as a Lord of Parliament in Ireland* (1784) 22 St. Tr. 161, Addenda 1253.

[63] 5 *J. Ir. H.L.* 497, 10 April 1784.

> of means to appear, shall I be deemed too presumptuous in looking up, once more, to that friendship I experienced early in life? I am conscious, that on a former application, you assigned such reasons for a denial as silenced all reply; but as probably, since that time, rents have been more punctually paid, I am encouraged, from that consideration, to hope forgiveness, by renewing a request productive of too many advantages to enumerate: £200 would fix me in the most enviable situation, and one hundred would surmount some pressing difficulties, and enable me, by daily appearance, to express my gratitude, by doing justice, where I flatter myself to see success crown the undertaking. Be so good to favor with a line one who you may be assured, is with sincerest regard,
>
> D[ea]r Sir,
> Your very faithful
> and most humble serv[an]t
> Strangford.
> South-Hill
> 10th Jan. [1784]

Rochfort sent the letter to the clerk of the House. The House ordered Strangford to attend. At first he pleaded by letter that he was suffering from 'gout in the stomach' and that any attempt to travel might produce 'most fatal consequences to the short remainder of a very declining life'.[64] The Lords examined his doctor who attested to his condition, but they finally lost patience and ordered Black Rod to take him into custody for contempt.[65] He duly appeared, evidently having survived the rigours of the journey.[66] He admitted writing the letter, but claimed he had no corrupt motive or intention. The Lords then discharged him from custody, and he retired from the sitting. The letter was then read. A resolution was passed unanimously declaring that Strangford had acted 'criminally and corruptly' in writing the letter, and the House again ordered Black Rod to take him into custody. They then adjourned the matter until the following Monday, when Strangford was to be brought in custody to the House. On the next Monday, the House unanimously resolved that Viscount Strangford should be disabled from sitting in parliament, or making a proxy and that the judges should be instructed to prepare a bill to that effect. Strangford was then brought in and the lord chancellor informed him of the resolutions as to his conduct. He was then again released from custody.[67] The next mention in the journals was on Tuesday, 13 April 1784, when the clerk of the parliaments (the chief clerk of the House of Lords) was ordered to inform Robinson J and Hellen J that they were

64 5 *J. Ir. H.L.* 493.

65 *ibid.*, p. 494.

66 5 *J. Ir. H.L.* 497, Saturday, 10 April 1784. His address of 'South Hill' and the fact that he died in Palmerston: Cokayne, *Complete Peerage*, xii.361, indicates that he lived on the outskirts of Dublin.

67 5 *J. Ir. H.L.* 500, Monday, 12 April 1784.

to expedite the preparation of the bill.[68] Lord Carysfort presented the bill on the following day and it was given a first and second reading on the following day, without any indication of a debate.[69] It was also ordered that a copy of the bill be sent to Lord Strangford. The long title was *An Act for disabling Philip Lord Visc. Strangford from sitting in Parliament or making any Proxy therein, and also from sitting and voting on the Trial of any Peer*, and so the inclusion of the provision as to trials of peers was presumably inserted by the judges.

The bill was then sent to the Commons.[70] On the second reading, the speaker, not unreasonably, said he thought that before proceeding further, the House ought to have some evidence before them of Lord Strangford's guilt. He then examined, at the bar of the House, 'an officer of the House of Lords' who recited the facts and the circumstances and also a messenger who declared that he had served Lord Strangford with a copy of the proceedings against him, and his answer was that 'it was very well.' The provost of Trinity College Dublin, John Hely-Hutchinson[71] then gave a lengthy speech in which he said that he applauded the intention of the Lords in upholding the 'purity of the final judicature', but wondered whether the means to achieve it was the right one:

> My decided opinion is, that it is contrary to the established principles of the constitution, to proceed against any man by a bill of pains and penalties, when justice can be obtained by the due course of law. . . and that it is for this reason the high court relieves only such as can have no remedy but in Parliament, and for matters determinable at common law, remits the parties to their legal remedy.

He went on to quote Magna Carta and the right of trial by one's peers and to note that Strangford's peers were those in the Lords, and he doubted whether in the circumstances the House of Lords should have acted in their legislative capacity:

> Bills of pains and penalties are laws *ex post facto*, made to punish one man by a rule not applicable to the rest of his fellow-subjects, and which did not exist when his offence was committed. Such a bill is therefore to be justified by necessity only.

Corruption by a peer in a matter of judicature had been punished before and the proper mode of redress was by impeachment. He went on to cite precedents, including that in 1620 of Sir Francis Bacon, Viscount St Alban,[72] in 1624 of the

68 *ibid.*, p. 503, Tuesday, 13 April 1784.

69 *ibid.*, p. 507, Wednesday, 14 April 1784.

70 3 *J. Ir. H.C.* 187–196. Friday, 23 April 1784.

71 (*c.* 1723–94), provost, 1774–1794. James Kelly, 'Hutchinson, John Hely-' DIB online, [http:// dib.cambridge.org/ viewReadPage.do?articleId=a4179], accessed 6 March 2013. After several unsuccessful attempts to buy a seat in the Commons, Hely-Hutchinson finally secured a seat in 1759 for the borough of Lanesborough, Co. Longford, in return for the payment of 500 to Luke Dillon, who controlled the borough.

72 Markku Peltonen, 'Bacon, Francis, Viscount St Alban (1561–1626)', ODNB online. [[http:// www.oxforddnb.com/view/ article/990], accessed 26 July 2009. The title seems to have been 'St Alban' not ' St Albans': Cokayne, *Complete Peerage*, xi.283 n. d.

Earl of Middlesex[73] and in 1725 that of Lord Macclesfield.

Bacon had been impeached as lord chancellor, being accused of taking bribes. He had accepted two gifts from litigants who had cases pending, but denied a corrupt motive. Several other bribes were alleged but the evidence was dubious, and underlying the whole impeachment was the attack against patents and monopolies and the beginnings of the larger struggle between king and parliament. Bacon was fined £40,000, which was never collected, and imprisoned in the Tower of London at the king's pleasure, although he was released after only three days. He was also barred from any office or employment in the state and forbidden to sit in parliament or come within the verge (12 miles) of the court. In order to prosecute Bacon the English parliament of 1621 revived the procedure of impeachment, which had become obsolete by then.[74] The Commons acted in the nature of a grand jury, deciding on whether a charge should be brought, and if so, the trial took place in the House of Lords, peers acting in the manner of a jury.

The Earl of Middlesex was accused of corruption in misusing the stamp of the Court of Wards and in accepting bribes.[75] He was fined £50,000, excluded from public office, and exiled from the (king's) court. He lobbied successfully to have the fine reduced, first to £30,000 and then to £20,000.[76] He was pardoned in 1627.

Lord Macclesfield[77] was impeached as lord chancellor and his only punishment was a fine. He was accused not only of selling vacant Chancery masterships, which had been done before, but of maximising his gain by selling to the highest bidders. Selling them was one thing, but conducting an auction was going too far. Macclesfield's counsel denied that the lord chancellor had acted criminally in taking 'presents' of cash during these transactions, on the ground that he had merely conformed with what he took to be the usual practices of his office. However, his defence failed to establish that the sale of masterships under his two immediate predecessors had been as regular a practice as he claimed and had not, therefore, as he also claimed, been 'legitimised by prescription.'[78]

The Hely-Hutchinson went on to mention impeachments in Ireland in 1641, those of Bolton LC, the Bishop of Derry, Sir Gerald Lowther CJCP, and Sir George Radcliffe.[79] The procedure was then novel and the lords justices had sent a message to the Commons asking for precedents for the right of judicature in

[73] Michael J. Braddick, 'Cranfield, Lionel, 1st Earl of Middlesex (1575–1645)', ODNB online, [http://www.oxforddnb.com/view/ article/6609], accessed 26 July 2009.

[74] Peltonen, *ibid.*

[75] Braddick, *ibid.*

[76] *ibid.*

[77] A. A. Hanham, 'Parker, Thomas, 1st Earl of Macclesfield (1667–1732)', ODNB online. [http:// www.oxforddnb.com/ view/article/ 21341,], accessed 26 July 2009.

[78] Hanham, *ibid.*

[79] See John McCafferty, 'To follow the late precedents of England': the Irish impeachment proceedings of 1641' in D. S. Greer and N. M. Dawson, eds., *Mysteries and Solutions in Irish Legal History, Irish Legal History Society discourses and other papers, 1996-1999*, (Dublin, Four Courts, in association with The Irish Legal History Society, 2001).

parliament.[80] After that year, the lords justices were attended by the speaker and most of the members of the Commons 'at the council table' and asked that the Commons would not proceed with impeachments until they received advice from England on the issue of the judicature 'in capital cases'. Charles I had then sent a letter, requiring both Houses to supply precedents of the right of judicature. Both Houses, in their address to the king, declined to supply precedents, in case it should call their jurisdiction into question. The provost admitted that there were, in fact, no precedents to produce. Nevertheless, he argued that 'the jurisdiction of the Lords in criminal cases, was never at any time questioned.'

In 1695 supporters of Lord Deputy Capell's[81] attempted to impeach Lord Chancellor Porter[82] on the dubious grounds of undue favouritism to Catholics and Jacobites. An odd procedure took place in the Irish House of Commons. The lord chancellor was called before the Commons. He made a speech in his own defence, the prosecuting members then offered proof, and the House voted that the case had not been proved and rejected the articles of impeachment, by 121 votes to 77. The Porter incident was part of a broader political conflict between Whigs and Tories at the time, and between Catholic and Protestant influences in Europe.

The Hely-Hutchinson concluded that:

> These are our only precedents. The two first, not in favour of the power of impeaching, and that which we are about to make, directly against it. And though, in the impeachment in the year 1640, the Lords and Commons declare, that the Lords spiritual and temporal in Parliament assembled, have full power and authority to hear and determine all treasons and other offences perpetrated within this kingdom, yet there is no instance upon the journals of our Houses of Parliament, where any judgment has been given on an impeachment; and clear as our right is to impeach, I have known many rights of this kingdom, equally unquestioned, heretofore disputed.

He further cited Lord Cowper[83] as giving his opinion that bills of pains and penalties 'can only be justified where the offender is in open rebellion, or has fled from the justice of his country.' This seems to be a reference to Cowper's opposition to the bill of pains and penalties against Bishop Atterbury in 1723.[84] Atterbury was heard in the House of Lords, but the bill was passed, depriving him of all his preferments and imposing perpetual exile. He died in Montpelier in 1732.

80 3 *J. Ir. H.C.* 191.

81 Henry Capell, 1st Baron Capell of Tewkesbury, appointed lord deputy by William III in 1695, above, page 19.

82 Ball, *Judges in Ireland*, ii.12–14.

83 Geoffrey Treasure, 'Cowper, William, first Earl Cowper (1665–1723)', ODNB, Oxford University Press, Sept. 2004; online edn., Jan. 2009 [http://www.oxforddnb.com/view/article/6511], accessed 26 July 2009.

84 *ibid.* Francis Atterbury (1663–1732), Bishop of Rochester, politician, and Jacobite conspirator.

Hely-Hutchinson's view found no support in the Commons, Dennis Daly describing the bill as 'a fair and honourable effort of the Peers to expel corruption from amongst them'. He rejected the Irish instances of impeachment cited by the provost. Both were 'judges of inferior courts' [to the House of Lords] impeached for bribery and corrupt practices. But there was, he said, no instance where a lord of parliament had disgraced himself in that manner. Therefore, since it was 'new case' it could be remedied by Act of parliament.[85] The prime serjeant also expressed a view in favour of the bill. The question was put to consider the bill the next day, and carried with one dissent, presumably that of Hely-Hutchinson.

On 24 April 1784 the Commons resolved itself into a committee of the whole House to consider the bill. John Foster moved to amend the bill by reciting the circumstances in the preamble, and Hely-Hutchinson spoke in support. It would do justice to the peer's heir, a young man who 'promised to be an ornament to his country.'[86] He had not changed his former opinion, he said, that impeachment was the proper procedure, but did not wish it to be thought that he was seeking to delay action, or to impose a more severe penalty. There was evidently some concern the a bill merely setting out the penalties would not appear oppressive and would not satisfy wider opinion. Strangford's letter was in fact included in the preamble to the Act as published. The duly-amended bill was passed by the House, without dissent. The Lords signified their agreement to the bill on 11 May 1784[87] and on the 14 May it received the royal assent.[88]

The adoption of the procedure of a bill of pains and penalties was certainly curious. It could be seen as putting the Irish parliament in a bad light, of acting in a summary manner when an ordinary citizen would have had the benefit of a trial. It is also odd in a period when the Irish parliament and the Lords in particular were concerned to assert their rights and privileges, especially after the Renunciation Act, and might therefore have been inclined to proceed by impeachment. On the other hand, Strangford could have claimed his privilege of a trial, but did not so so. The evidence, consisting of the letter alone, was convincing and the result was a foregone conclusion. There was also no doubt some embarrassment on the part of the Lords that one of their number could act in such a way and a concern to act swiftly to dispose of the matter. They might also have been reluctant to invoke the powers of the Commons, rather than deal with the matter themselves. It is also the case that Strangford got off lightly. The Act and its sanction was the extent of the proceedings against him. He was neither fined nor imprisoned, except briefly by Black Rod, penalties which an ordinary citizen might well have faced.

[85] 3 *J. Ir. H.C.* 195.

[86] Lionel, 5th Viscount Strangford (1753–1801), the second but first surviving son and heir, Capt., 23rd Regiment of Foot, served in many campaigns in the American War of Independence. He retired in 1784 and took holy orders.

[87] 3 *J. Ir. H.C.* 199.

[88] 3 *J. Ir. H.C.* 225; 23 & 24 Geo. III, c. 59 (Ir.), 1783–84.

Committal for Contempt

On 1 March 1793 Simon Butler[89] and Oliver Bond, as chairman and secretary respectively of the Dublin Society of United Irishmen, were summoned before the Irish House of Lords in respect of a printed sheet which had been issued by the group. A committee of secrecy had been set up by the House to inquire into the causes of unrest in the country. The sheet had criticised the committee for compelling witnesses to answer questions on oath. Butler and Bond admitted its publication but submitted that it contained nothing illegal or contrary to the constitution. The Lords nevertheless voted it a 'false, scandalous, and seditious libel; a high breach of the privileges of this house, tending to disturb the public peace, and questioning the authority of this high court of parliament'. It ordered the defendants to be imprisoned in Newgate gaol for six months and to pay a fine of £500 each. Francis Hargrave's opinion had been sought as to whether the proceedings in the House of Lords were proper and whether they could be challenged. He gave his opinion that the proper way to challenge them was by writ of habeas corpus, but this course of action does not seem to have adopted.[90]

The incident has an interesting sequel. It seems to be the only instance, in Ireland at least, of a sitting lord chancellor being challenged to a duel. Butler was a barrister and was the third son of Edmund Butler, 10th Viscount Mountgarret (d. 1779) and his wife, Charlotte (d. 1778), daughter of Sir Simon Bradstreet and his wife, Ellen. He was admitted to the Irish bar in Michaelmas term 1778 and was made a king's counsel and a bencher of the King's Inns, Dublin, in Trinity term 1784. The lord chancellor, as speaker of the House of Lords, in pronouncing the sentence had, addressed Butler and said 'he could not plead ignorance, as his noble birth, and his professional rank at the bar, to which he was a disgrace, had aggravated the crime.' Butler resented the insult and as soon as he was released, sent his friend Archibald Hamilton Rowan, another prominent United Irishman, as his second, to demand satisfaction. He called upon FitzGibbon to retract his remarks, but FitzGibbon refused. Rowan said that in his and Butler's opinion the sentence of the House of Lords had not authorised such language and if it had been said between 'two private gentlemen', his course would have been easy, but the lord chancellor's situation embarrassed him. He then took his leave, saying that the the lord chancellor's position prevented him acting 'as he would have done with a private gentleman'. FitzGibbon was not averse to fighting a duel and had done so before, but may nevertheless have been conscious of being open to the charge of cowardice if he refused. He therefore invited a military friend, Colonel Murray, to breakfast the following morning and asked his advice. Murray considered that he should not be held personally responsible for words spoken in his official capacity. Murray then went to see Rowan who was somewhat surprised that he knew what had passed between himself and the lord chancellor, but accepted Murray's view on behalf of Butler.

[89] Liam Chambers, 'Butler, Simon (1757–1797)', ODNB, 2004 [http://www.oxforddnb.com/view/article/4206], accessed 1 Nov 2009. James Quinn, 'Butler, Simon', DIB online. [http://dib.cambridge.org/ viewReadPage.do?articleId=a1289] accessed 19 February 2011.

[90] Hargrave, *Juridical Arguments and Collections*. vol. 1. London, 1797–99, pp. 1–21. *Eighteenth Century Collections Online* [ECCO]. Gale. 1 November 2009.

CHAPTER 11

Conclusion

The life of the Irish House of Lords as the final court of appeal in Ireland at the end of the 18th century was a brief one, being some seventeen years in all. It may therefore seem little more than a curiosity at the present time. Nevertheless, the great constitutional debate which took place at the end of the 18th century, and the demand in Ireland for recognition and respect for its institutions, contributed to the Irish House of Lords becoming in substance what it had claimed to be in form for over a century: a court where law ruled. The procedure and composition of the court at the beginning of the period was that of the legislative body, a body composed largely of landowners, with all members voting, often without stated reasons. At the end of the period the procedure and composition resembled that of a modern appeal court, being composed of professional lawyers with previous judicial experience. An important element in this procedural transformation was the adoption of the convention that only legally qualified members gave judgment on appeals, a convention which was finally established by its British counterpart only some fifty years later. The later Irish House of Lords was a court of considerable professional competence and produced some precedents of lasting value. The later court at least approached the ideals of a legal system, with a concern for the rule of law and decisions based on legal principles. Hence, although the work of the appeal court was mainly concerned with property issues, which reflected the dominance of the landed interest of the time, in actually dealing with those issues the court seems to have functioned in a relatively autonomous way.

The demise of the court with the Union also produced one significant development in the legal system. The establishment just before the Union of the Irish court of Exchequer Chamber, as a court hearing appeals from all the common law courts, formed the model in 1830 for the British court of the same name, and so was the precursor of the modern courts of appeal in England and Ireland.

Appendices

APPENDIX A

Statutes of the Parliament of Drogheda, 1460

38 Hen. VI, c. 6 (Ir.)[1]

Legislative Independence and against Appeals to England

VI. Also at the request of the Commons: That whereas the land of Ireland is and at all times has been corporate of itself, by the ancient laws and customs used in the same, freed from the burthen of any special law of the realm of England, save only such laws which by the lords spiritual and temporal and the commons of the said land had in the Great Council or Parliament there held, admitted, accepted, affirmed and proclaimed, according to sundry ancient statutes thereof made. And whereas also of ancient custom, privilege and franchise of the said land, there is and at all times has been the seal of the King current, by which the laws there and also the King's subjects of the same land are guided and directed, which seal is called the seal of the said land, to which all the said subjects ought to do loyal obedience. And it has not been seen or heard that any person or persons inhabiting or resident in any other Christian land so corporate of itself ought to obey any mandate within the same land given or made under any other seal than the proper seal of the same, by which any person should be had or compelled to go by any such mandate out of the said land. And if such mandate were obeyed in the said land of Ireland, very great prejudice and derogation and very perilous inconveniences would result to the same, contrary to the franchises, liberties and ancient customs thereof, and to the very great and immeasurable vexations of the said subjects of the same, of which many instances have been in late days seen and experienced. And moreover whereas in no realm or land which has within itself a constable and marshal of the same, ought any person of that realm or land to sue or prosecute any appeal or other matter determinable before the said constable and marshal, before the constable and marshal of any other land where such appeal or matter took no foundation or effect. And this notwithstanding, that although there are in the said land and of ancient custom have been a constable and marshal, yet divers persons of the same land have oftentimes heretofore sued and procured, of great malice, many of the King's subjects of the same to be sent for, to come into England by colour of such appeals, in great derogation and prejudice of the said liberty and franchise. Whereupon the premises considered: It is ordained, enacted and established in the said Parliament and by authority thereof, that henceforth no person or persons being in the said land of Ireland, be by any command given or made under

[1] Henry F. Berry, ed., *Statute Rolls of the Parliament of Ireland, reign of King Henry VI*. Irish Record Office series of early Statutes, ii.645, 647. Translated from the French. The statute is not reproduced in the *Statutes at Large* (Dublin, 1786–1804).

any other seal than the said seal of the same land, compelled to answer to any appeal or any other matter out of the said land. And that no officer or minister of the same land to whom any such command comes, put that command or any proclamation or any other thing contrary or prejudicial to the said ancient custom privilege or franchise in execution, on pain of the forfeiture of all the lands and goods which he or any other to his use has in the said land; and moreover of a thousand marks, the one moiety to the King and the other moiety to the party who will sue in this case against the said officer or minister by writ of *Scire facias*, or by any other action at the law proper in this behalf. It is also ordained by the said authority that any appeal of treason taken in this land be determined before the constable and the marshal of the said land for the time being, and within the said land, and in no other place. And if any person shall hereafter appeal any other person in the said land, and the matter of said appeal be found and proved not true, that then such person taking or commencing such appeal for the same be adjudged to death, and that no pardon shall serve him in such case.

38 Hen. VI, c. 12 (Ir.)[2]

Against Writs of Capias in the Exchequer

XII. Also at the request of the Commons: That whereas heretofore a writ of Edward the Third, formerly King of England, was directed to his treasurer and barons of his Exchequer of Dublin, the tenor whereof follows in this form:

> Edward by the grace of God, King of England and France and lord of Ireland, to his treasurer and barons of his Exchequer of Dublin greeting. Whereas according to the law and custom of our land of Ireland, common pleas ought not to be pleaded before you at the Exchequer, unless those pleas especially touch us or any of our officers of the same Exchequer. And now on behalf of the men of the liberty of Meath in the aforesaid land, on grievous complaint, it is shown to us, that you, at the suit of certain persons asserting themselves to be valets of the officers of said Exchequer, who are not our officers, serving in the Exchequer aforesaid, cause the said men to be distrained to answer before you in the said Exchequer in pleas of trespasses, contracts, debts and accounts, contrary to the law and custom abovementioned; We unwilling that the said men should be unduly oppressed, command you that you in no wise compel or cause to be compelled, contrary to the law and custom abovementioned, men of the said liberty, or other men of our land aforesaid, to answer before you in the Exchequer aforesaid concerning such trespasses, agreements, contracts, debts or accounts, unless they touch us or some of

[2] Reproduced in the *Statutes at Large* (Dublin, 1786–1804), i.23; Berry, ed., *Statute Rolls of the Parliament or Ireland*, ii.667, 669. Reproduced here from Berry.

> our officers of the Exchequer aforesaid who shall be serving in the said Exchequer.
>
> Witness myself at Westminster the twentieth day of October in the thirtieth year of our reign of England, and of our reign of France the seventeenth [1356].

The which writ and the mandate of the King therein openly expressed notwithstanding, still the men of the liberty of Meath specified in the said writ are continually distrained by writs of *Capias* and distress coming out of the King's Exchequer of this land, at the suits of such person and persons as are named in the same writs, valets or officers of the said Exchequer, where they are not valets or officers, to answer there in pleas of trespass, contracts, debts and accounts, contrary to the tenor of the said writ and the due execution of the same in former times, and to the extreme and intolerable damage of the said men. Whereupon the premises considered: It is ordained by authority of the said Parliament, that whosoever sues any action in the Exchequer of the King in Ireland, unless the plaintiff be officer to the said Exchequer or servant to any officer of record of the said Exchequer, shall lose ten pounds, one moiety to the King, and the other moiety to the party that will sue, as often as he sues any such action.

APPENDIX B

Poynings' Law, 1495 (English Statutes)

An Act confirming all the Statutes made in England

10 Hen. VII, c. 22 (Ir.), 1495

ITEM, prayen the commons, that forasmuch as there been many diverse good and profitable statutes late made within the realm of England by great labour, studie and policie, as well as in the time of our sovereign lord the King, as in the time of his full noble and royal projenitors, the late Kings of England, by the advise of his and their discreet counsail, whereby the said realm is ordered and brought to great wealth and prosperitie and by all likelyhood so would this land, if the said estatutes were used and executed in the same: wherefore be it ordeyned and established by authority of this present Parliament by the assent of the lords spirituall and temporall, and commons assembled in the same, That all estatutes, late made within the said realm of England, concerning or belonging to the common and publique weal of the same, from henceforth be deemed good and effectuall in the law, and over that be acceptyd, used, and executed within this land of Ireland in all points at all times requisite according to the tenor and effect of the same; and over that by authority aforesaid, that they and every of them be authorized, proved, and confirmed in this said land of Ireland. And if any estatute or estatutes have been made within this said land, hereafter to the contrary, they and every of them by authority aforesaid be adnulled, revoked, voyd and of none effect in the law.

APPENDIX C

Poynings' Law, 1495 (Parliaments)

An Act that no Parliament be holden in this Land until the Acts be certified into England.

10 Hen. VII, c. 4 (Ir.)

ITEM, at the request of the commons of the land of Ireland bee it ordeyned, enacted, and established, That at the next Parliament, that there shall be holden by the King's commaundment and licence, wherein amongst other the King's Grace intendeth to have a generall resumption of his whole revenue sith the last day of the raigne of King Edward the second, no Parliament bee holden hereafter in the said land but at such season as the King's lieutenant and counsaile there furst doe certifie the King, under the great seal of that land, the causes and considerations of all such acts, as them seemeth should passe in the same Parliament; and such causes, considerations and acts affirmed by the King and his counsaile to be good and expedient for that land, and his license thereupon, as well in affirmation of the said causes and acts, as to summon the said Parliament under his great seal of England had and obtained, that done, a Parliament to bee had and holden after the form and effect aforesaid: and if any Parliament be holden in that land hereafter contrary to the forme and provision aforesaid, it bee deemed void and of none effect in the law.

APPENDIX D

Poynings' Law (Parliaments) Amendment, 1556

An Act declaring how Poynings Acte shall be exponed and taken.

3 & 4 Ph. & Mar., c. 4 (Ir.)

WHEREAS at a Parliament holden at Drogheda the Monday next after the feast of saint Andrew the Apostle in the tenth yeare of the raign of the late King of famous memory Henry the seventhe, graundfather unto our soveraign Lady the Queen, before Sir Edward Ponings, knight, then lord deputie of this realm of Ireland, an act among other things was enacted and made for and concerning the order, manner, and forme of Parliament to bee from henceforth holden and kept in this realm of Ireland, in forme following:
[recites Poynings' Act, 1495];
and by the said act more at large doth appeare: for as much as sithence the making of the said act diverse and sundrie ambiguities and doubts have been made and risen upon the true understanding and meaning of the same; for the avoyding of the which doubts and ambiguities, and for a full and plain declaration of the true meaning and understanding of the said act, be it ordayned, enacted, and established by authority of this present Parliament assembled, That the said act, and every clause and article therein conteyned, shall from the first day of September last past be expounded, understanded, and taken as hereafter followeth; that is to say, That no Parliament be summoned and holden within this realm of Ireland until such time as the lieutenant, lord deputie, lord justice, lords justices, chiefe governour or governours, or any of them, and the counsaile of the said realme of Ireland, for the time being, shall have certified the King and Queen's majesties, her heyres and successours, under the great seale of this said realme of Ireland, the considerations, causes, and articles of such acts provisions, and ordinances, as by them shall be then thought meet and necessary to be enacted and passed here by Parliament, and shall have also received again their Majesties answer, under their great seale of England, declaring their pleasure, eyther for the passing of the said acts, provisions, and ordinances, in such form and tenour as they shall be sent into England, or else for the change or alterations of them, or any part of the same.

II. And be it further enacted by the authority aforsaid, That after such return made and after licence and authority to summon a Parliament within the said realm of Ireland, graunted under the great seale of England unto the said lieutenant or lord deputie, or other lord justice, lords justices, chief governour or governours of the same realm of Ireland, for the time being, and not before the same lieutenant, lord deputie, lord justice, lords justices, chief governour or governours, shall and may summon and hold a Parliament within this realm of Ireland, for passing and agreeing upon such acts, and no other, as shall be so retorned under the said great seale of England.

III. And forasmuch as manie events and occasions may happen during the time of the Parliament, the which shall be thought meet and necessary to be provided for, and yet at; therefore be it further enacted and established by authority of this Parliament, That as well after every such authority and licence sent into this realm of Ireland, as also at all times after the summons, and during the time of every Parliament to be hereafter holden within the said realm of Ireland, according to the tenor and form of this act, the lieutenant, lord deputie, lord justice, lords justices chiefe governour or chiefe governours and counsaile of the same realm of Ireland for the time being, shall and may certifie all such other considerations, causes, tenours, provisions, and ordinances, as they shall further then think good to be enacted and established, at and in the same Parliament within the same realm of Ireland, to the King and Queen's Majesties, her heyres and successors, under the great seal of this said realm of Ireland, and such considerations, causes tenours, provisions, and ordinances, or any of them, as shall be thereupon certified and returned into the said realm, under the great seal of England, and no others, shall and may pass and be enacted here in every such Parliament within this said realm of Ireland, in case the same considerations, causes, tenours, provisions, and ordinances, or any of them, be agreed and resolved upon by the three estates of the said Parliament; any thing contayned in this present act, or in the aforesaid act at Drogheda to the contrarie notwithstanding.

IV. Provided alwayes, and be it further enacted by the authority of this present Parliament, That all and every Parliament and Parliaments summoned, kept and holden within this realm of Ireland, since the making of the said former act, in the said tenth yeare of the reigne of the said late King Henry the seventh, and all and every act, acts, ordinances, an provisions, made, passed, ordeyned, and enacted in the same, shall be and remaine in such and the same force, strength, validitie and effect, to all intents, constructions, and purposes, as if this act had never been made: this act, or any thing therein contained to the contrary notwithstanding.

V. Provided also, that this act, or any thing therein conteyned, shall not extend or be meant, to the defeating or hindrance of any the provisoes made this cession of this present Parliament.

APPENDIX E

Precedents Extracted from the Records of Ireland

Precedents Extracted from the Records of Ireland to Prove the Jurisdiction of the Parliament of this Kingdom to Hear and Adjudge All Cases. [Marsh's Library MS, undated, Z 3.2.5 p. 1.]

1. Case of Michael Ar[ch]b[isho]p of Dub. 5 Edw 4. [1465]
2. Case of John Ar[ch]b[isho]p of Dub. 16 Edw 4. [1476]
3. Case of Nicholas Husse, Baron of Galtrym[3] imprisoned in Dublin Castle by the Earl of Shrewsbury. 26 Hen. 6. [1447]
4. A Judgment of the Lords to quiet John Kennock in the possession of the Treasurership of Limerick being collated thereto by the Bishop. 27 Hen 6. [1448]
5. To discharge Rich. Chambers [?] of a fine of 12 layd upon him by the Barons of the Exchequer of the Liberty of Rich. Duke of [blank] in Meath. 36 Hen 6. [1458]
6. To discharge the Exec[utor]s of Sir Wm [?] Welles ag[ains]t a demand of a bond debt claimed by the executors of William Whitby. 7 Edw 4. [1467]
7. Proceedings & Judgment of the H. of Lords in 1634, in favour of Art Bagnall [or Bagnale] Esq about Lands in Mourne claimed by Pat. Gough.
8. Many other Orders about Privileges this year - also upon Complaints between Party & Party.
9. Orders of the H. of Commons, as to Grievances in the Govt. of the College & that the Students be at Liberty to exhibit their Complaints to the Committee appointed for that Purpose. 27 February 1640.

An Order 8 June 1641 inhibiting their Election of Fellows & Scholars of the House on Trinity Monday this year.

Ordered, that the Committee do view their Statements & select such as are fit to be observed [?]. 2d Aug 1641. Various Orders & Resolutions of the Commons this Year.

[The above reproduces the single MS page. The catalogue in Marsh's Library lists a total of 89 records.]

[3] i.e. Galtrim, Co. Meath.

APPENDIX F

The Jacobite Declaratory Act

An Act Declaring that the Parliaments of England *cannot binde* Ireland, *and against Writs of Error and Appeals, to be brought for Removing Judgments, Decrees and Sentences given in* Ireland *into* England.

5 Jas. II c. 10[4] (Dublin, 1689)

Whereas this his Majesties Realm of *Ireland* is and hath been always a distinct Kingdom from that of his Majesties Realm of *England*, always Governed by His Majesty and his Predecessors according to the Ancient Customs, Laws, and Statutes thereof, and as the People of this Kingdom, did never send Members to any Parliament ever held in *England*, but had their Laws continually made and Established by their own Parliaments, so no Acts passed in any Parliament held in *England* were ever binding here, excepting such of them as by Acts of Parliament passed in this Kingdom, were made into Laws here, yet of late times and especially in the times of distractions) some have pretended that Acts of Parliament passed in *England* mentioning *Ireland* were binding in *Ireland*.

And as these late opinions are against Justice and natural Equity, so they tend to the great oppression of the people here, and to the overthrow of the Fundamentall Constitutions of this Realm: And to the end that by these modern and late opinions no person may be further deluded;

[s.1] Be it therefore Enacted by the Kings most Excellent Majesty, by the advice and consent of the Lords Spiritual and Temporal, and the Commons in this present Parliament assembled, and by Authority of the same, and it is so hereby declared, that no Act of Parliament past, or to be past, in the Parliament

[4] Source: Ireland, *Anno V. Jacobi II. Regis...* [Dublin?, 1689?], British Library, G.6022 (122), pp. 41–5. Transcribed by Dr John Bergin. Numbered '3' in Ebenezer Rider, *An Appendix to the late King James's Acts; containing an exact list of the Lords Spiritual and Temporal and Commons who sate in the Parliament held in Dublin, in 1689. To which is added, A Catalogue of the Titles of all the Acts passed in the said Session, and the preamble to the Act for restoring the old Proprietors to their Estates, &c., as it passed the House of Commons.* (Dublin, published by Ebenezer Rider, 1740) which was subsequently followed by Davis. Section numbers have been inserted by the present author. Other contemporary copies (with minor differences) are: MS copy in Marsh's Library; *A List... with the True and Authentick Copies of several of the Acts of the said pretended Parliament...* (London, 1690), pp. 5–8. Also printed, with minor variations from *Anno V. Jacobi*, in: *The Acts of that Short Session of Parliament, held in Dublin, May 7, 1689* (Dublin, 1740), pp. 1–9; *The Hibernian Mirror... II. The acts of that short session of parliament held in Dublin, May 7, 1689* (Dublin, 1751), pp. 1–9; *The Acts of that Short Session of Parliament, held in Dublin, May 7, 1689* (Dublin, 1756), pp. 1–7; [Thomas Davis], 'Irish state papers: no. 1. Statutes of 1689', in *The Dublin Magazine* (Jan. 1843), pp. 30–32; Thomas Davis, *The Patriot Parliament of 1689*, ed. by Charles Gavan Duffy (London, 1893), pp. 43–8. A new transcription of the surviving statutes of James II's parliament in Dublin is currently in preparation by the author and Dr John Bergin for the Irish Manuscripts Commission.

of *England* tho *Ireland* should be therein mentioned, can be, or shall be any way binding in *Ireland*, excepting such Acts past, or to be past in *England*, as are, or shall be made into Law by the Parliament of *Ireland*.

[s.2] And whereas several Writs of Error, were formerly sued out and Returnable into the Kings Bench in *England* in order to Reverse Judgments given in His Majesties Court of Kings Bench in *Ireland*; And whereas most of the said Writs of Error have been brought for delay, and thereby many of his Majesties Subjects of this Realm were greatly hindred from recovering their just Rights, and put to vast Charges in attending such Suits in *England*; for the prevention whereof, Be it hereby Enacted by the Authority aforesaid, that no Writ of Error shall be hereafter brought out of *England* in order to Remove any Record, or Transcript of Record out of his Majesties Court of Kings-Bench in *Ireland*, or out of any other Court of Record here, into *England*, in order to Reverse any such Judgments.

[s.3] But in regard Judgments to be given in his Majesties Court of Kings Bench in *Ireland* may happen sometimes to be erroneous, Be it Enacted, by the Authority aforesaid, that where any Judgment shall at any time hereafter be given in the said Court of Kings-Bench in *Ireland* in any Suit or Action of Debt, Detinue, Covenant Accompt, Action upon the Case, *Ejectione firmae*, or Trespass, first Commenced, or to be first Commenced there, other than where the Kings Majesty shall be Partie, the Plaintiff, or Defendant, or other person or persons against whom any such Judgment shall be given, may at his Election sue forth of the High Court of Chancery in *Ireland*, a special Writ of Error to be Devised in the said Court of Chancery directed to the Chief Justice of the said Court of Kings-Bench in *Ireland* for the time being, Commanding him to cause the said Record, and all things concerning the said Judgments to be brought before the Justices of the Common-Pleas, and the Barons of the Exchequer here into the Exchequer Chamber in *Ireland*, there to be Examined by the said Justices of the Common-Pleas, and the Barons of the Exchequer; which said Justices of the Common-Pleas, and Barons of the Exchequer, or any four, or more of them, by vertue of this present Act, shall thereupon have full Power and Authority to Examine all such Errors as shall be assigned or found in or upon any such Judgment as the Law shall require, other than for Errors to be assigned, or found for, or concerning the Jurisdiction of the said Court of Kings-Bench in *Ireland*, or for any want of form in any Writ, Return Plaint, Bill, Declaration, or other Pleadings, Process, Verdict, or Proceeding whatsoever, and other than for such Mistakes, Errors, or Failings, as are now supplyed, or helped by some Statute or Statutes in force within this Realm.

And that any one or more of the said Justices and Barons in the absence of the rest, shall have Power to Adjourn the said Court, and continue the Proceedings of the said Writ of Error from time to time; and that after that the said Judgment shall be Affirmed, or Reversed; the said Record, and all things concerning the same shall be Removed, and brought back into the said Court of Kings-Bench, that such further Proceedings may be thereupon, as well for Execution as otherwise, as shall appertain.

[s.4] And be it further Enacted by the Authority aforesaid, that such Reversal, or Affirmation of any such former Judgment shall not be so final, but that the Party who findeth himself grieved therewith, shall and may sue in the High Court of Parliament in *Ireland*, for the further and due Examination of the said Judgment, any thing herein contained to the contrary notwithstanding.

[s.5] And be it further Enacted by the Authority aforesaid, that from the end of this present Session of Parliament no Execution shall be stayed in the said Court of Kings-Bench, by Writ of Error, or Supersedeas thereupon, after Verdict and Judgment thereupon in any Action personal whatsoever, unless a Recognizance with Condition, according the Statute made in the tenth year of the Raign of our late Soveraign Lord King *Charles* the First, shall be first acknowledged in the said Court of Kings-Bench.

[s.6] And further, that in Writs of Error to be brought upon any Judgment after Verdict in any Action of *Ejectione firmae*, no Execution shall be thereupon, or thereby stayed, unless the Plaintiff or Plaintiffs in such Writs of Error, shall be bound unto the Defendant in such Action of *Ejectione firmae* in such reasonable Summe as the said Court of Kings-Bench shall think fit, with condition, that if the Judgment shall be affirmed in the said Writ of Error, or that the said Writ of Error be discontinued in default of the Plaintiff or Plaintiffs therein, or that the Plaintiff or Plaintiffs be Non-suited in such Writs of Error, that then the said Plaintiff or Plaintiffs shall pay such Costs, Damages, summe and summs of Money as shall be Awarded upon, or after such Judgment affirmed, Discontinuance or Non-suit had; And to the end that the same summe and summs, and damages may be ascertained; Be it further Enacted by the Authority aforesaid, that the said Court of *Kings-Bench*, upon such affirmation, discontinuance, or Non-suit, shall issue a Writ to Inquire as well of the Measne profits, as of the Damages by any waste committed after the first Judgment in *Ejectione firmae*; and upon the Return thereof Judgment shall be given, and Execution awarded for such Measne Profits, and Damages and also for the Costs of Suit.

[s.7] And whereas of late times several persons have brought Appeals before the House of Lords in *England*, in Order to Reverse Decrees granted in the High Court of Chancery in *Ireland*, which tend to the great charge, trouble, and vexation of such of his Majesties Subjects as have obtaind such decrees, and is an apparent new Encroachment upon the fundamental Constitutions of this Realm, and also Appeals before Delegats in *England*: Be it therefore Enacted by the Authority aforesaid, that no person or persons whatsoever, do hereafter presume to sue out any such Appeals, or to tender, or produce any such Appeal to the Lord Chancellor, or Lord Keeper of *Ireland*, or to any of the Officers of the said Court of Chancery, and that such Appeals shall be void, and that no Appeal whatsoever to Reverse any Decree or Sentence past, or to be past in *Ireland*, shall be brought into *England*, either before the House of Lords there, or any Commissioners or Delegats of Appeal, and that all such Appeals shall be disallowed.

[s.8] And for rendering this present Act the more Effectual; Be it hereby Enacted by the Authority aforesaid, that it shall be a High Misdemeanor in any person or persons whatsoever, that shall in drawing of Pleadings either in Law or Equity, or in any Bill of Exception to be Filed in any Court in *Ireland*, or that at any Tryal, before any Court within this Realm, shall deliberately Insist that any Act of Parliament made or to be made in *England*, wherein *Ireland* is or shall be mentioned, is or can be binding in *Ireland*, though it should not be made into a Law here by any Act made, or to be made, in a Parliament held or to be held here; And also that it shall be a high Misdemeanor in any person or persons whatsoever, who within this Realm shall tender or produce any Writ or Writs of Error out of *England* in his Majesties Court of Kings Bench in *Ireland*, or to all or any the Judges of the said Court for the time being, Returnable to the Court of Kings Bench in *England*, or that shall tender or produce any Appeal to the Lord Chancellor, or Lord Keeper, of *Ireland* for the time being, or to any of the Officers of the said Court of Chancery, or to the Chancellor, Treasurer and Barons of the Exchequer from the House of Lords in *England*, or that shall tender any Appeal out of *England* to any Spiritual Judge or Spiritual Court, or Delegats within this Realm, in Order to Reverse any sentence given in *Ireland*, by any Court of Delegats in *England*; And that if any person or persons shall Offend herein, he shall be Fined and Imprisoned according to the Discretion of the court where he shall be prosecuted for the same.

APPENDIX G

Order of English House of Lords, 24 May 1698

in the Bishop of Derry's Case

WHEREAS a Petition and Appeal was offered to the House on the 7th of January last, of the Society of the Governor and Assistants of London, of the new Plantation in Ulster, in the Kingdom of Ireland, against a judgment given by the Lords Spiritual and Temporal of Ireland in Parliament there assembled, on the 24th day of September last, upon the Petition and Appeal of William, Lord Bishop of Derry, against the Decree or Order made in the said Cause in the Court of Chancery there: Whereupon a Committee was appointed to consider of the proper method of appealing from the decrees made in the Court of Chancery in Ireland, and that pursuant to the Order of the said Committee, and a Letter sent to the Lords Justices of Ireland, by order of this House: several precedents have been transmitted by the Lords Justices to this House, copies whereof were ordered to be delivered to either side: after hearing counsel upon the Petition of the Society, London, presented to this House the 20th of April last, praying that they might be heard, as to the jurisdiction as to the House of Lords in Ireland, in receiving and judging Appeals from the Chancery there, as also counsel for the Bishop of Derry: After due consideration of the precedents, and of what was offered by Counsel thereupon. It is this day ordered, adjudged and declared, by the Lords Spiritual and Temporal in Parliament assembled, that the said Appeal by the Bishop of Derry, to the House of Lords in Ireland, from the Decree or Order of the Court of Chancery there made, in the cause wherein the said Bishop of Derry was Plaintiff, and the said Society of the Governor and Assistants London, of the new Plantation in Ulster, in Ireland were Defendants was *coram non judice*, and that all the proceedings thereupon are null and void, and that the Court of Chancery in Ireland ought to proceed in the said Cause, as if no such Appeal had been made to the House of Lords there, and if either of the said Parties do find themselves aggrieved by the said decree or Order of Chancery, they are at liberty to pursue their proper remedy by way of Appeal to this House.

Ordered, that the Lord Chancellor do write to the Lord Justices of Ireland. MAL. JOHNSON. Cler. Parli.

APPENDIX H

Reasons Against the Foregoing Order by William Molyneux, Esq.[5]

1st. Because upon the Conquest of Ireland by Henry II he introduced the laws of England in that Kingdom, and sent over the *Modus Tenendi Parliamentum in Terminis*, the same with that of England, in which record it is said that such things may be examined and corrected, *in Pleno Parliamento et non alibi*:[6]

2dly. Because in the 20th year of Henry the Third, it was provided that all laws and customs which are enjoyed in England, shall be also in Ireland, and that the land shall be subject thereunto and governed thereby *sicut Dominus Johannes Rex cum ultimo esset in Hibernia statuit et fieri mandavit et quod Breva de communi jure quæ currunt in Anglia similiter currunt in Hibernia.*[7]

3rdly. Because King Edward III. in the 29th year of his reign, ordained for the quiet and good government of the people in Ireland, that in all cases whatsoever, errors in judgment, in records, and proceedings in the Courts of Ireland, shall be corrected and amended in Parliament in Ireland.

4thly. Because it appears by other ancient records, *quod terra Hiberniæ intra se omnes et omnimodas habet curias prout in Anglia.*[8]

5thly. Because a conqueror, by the laws of England and of nations, having power to introduce what laws he will in the conquered country, and King Henry II. pursuant to that power, having introduced the laws of England, and particularly that of holding Parliaments in Ireland, the House of Lords in Parliament in Ireland, may proceed to hear and determine judicially, such matters as shall be brought before them, in the same manner as the Lords in Parliament in England.

6thly. Because pursuant to the many concessions made by King Henry II, King John, King Henry III, and other Kings of England, the Lords in Parliament in Ireland have proceeded to correct and amend errors in judgments and decrees in the courts of Ireland [as appears by the several precedents certified over to your Lordships], and their judgments never before this called in question, many

[5] Above, Appendix G. The edition of *The Case of Ireland's being bound by Acts of Parliament in England, Stated* by William Molyneux published in Dublin in 1782 contained at page 62 the following statement which the editor of the 1782 edition obtained through the Rev. Thomas Brooke Clarke, from William Johnson of Dublin who copied it from the original manuscript in the handwriting of the author written on blank leaves of one of his printed cases, which he sent to the then Bishop of Meath.

[6] In full parliament, and not elsewhere.

[7] i.e. just as King John commanded that the same writs should run in Ireland as in England.

[8] i.e. that Ireland has the same courts and in the same manner as in England.

of them being very irregular, it is therefore presumed to have been by a good and lawful jurisdiction, otherwise they would have been by our ancestors [who were zealous assertors of their rights] long before this called in question.

7thly. The order declaring the appeal was coram non judice, and null and void, will call all other judgments and decrees in question, under which many estates have been purchased, settled and enjoyed, which will be of fatal consequences to many families, and create great discontent and dissatisfaction in that Kingdom.

8thly. Because the declaring the said appeal to be coram non judice and null and void, strikes at and tends to the destruction of the jurisdiction of this House; for Ireland having *omnes et omnimodes curias prout in Anglia*, must include the high court of Parliament, and if their high court of Parliament, being an exact picture of the high court of Parliament in England, cannot judicially hear and determine appeals, writs of error, and impeachments, it may from thence be alleged that this here cannot

9thly. Because this resolution strikes at, and tends to abridge, the King's prerogative in Ireland; all appeals and writs of error in Parliament, being *coram rege in Parliamento*, and, therefore, these words, coram non judice, takes from the King the judicial power which is given to him there.

10thly. Because the Peers of Ireland have little else left them beside their judicature, which if taken away, they will be of little esteem there, and many of the Peers of England have some of their titles of honour from that Kingdom.

11thly. Because it is the glory of the English laws, and the blessing attending Englishmen, that they have justice administered at their doors, and not to be drawn, as formerly to Rome, by appeals which greatly impoverished the nation, and by this order, the people of Ireland must be drawn from Ireland hither, whensoever they receive any injustice from the Chancery there, by which means poor men must be trampled upon, not being able to come over to seek for justice.

12thly. The danger of altering, changing, or lessening a constitution, for above 500 years unshaken, or so much as called in question in any one thing, (the custom and usage of Courts being the law of Courts) may occasion the destruction of the whole, for the judicial power of the House of Peers in Ireland, in criminal causes by way of impeachment or otherwise, may by the same reason be called in question, as their judicature in civil causes, which will encourage evil disposed men, especially those in employment in that Kingdom [who are generally very arbitrary] to act wickedly; and the better we preserve the constitution of Ireland and of those plantations dependant on England, the better we shall preserve our own and they will be barriers to ours, to prevent any invasion of theirs, and since the Kings of England have in all times in matters relating to their revenue, their grants by letters patent, and their Ministers, not only empowered the Parliament of Ireland to hear, correct, reform and amend them, but also acquiesced in their judgment, it ought not now to be questioned.

13thly. Because this taking away the jurisdiction of the Lords' House in Ireland, may be a means to disquiet the Lords there, and disappoint the King's affairs.

14thly. Because the judicial power of the House of Peers in Ireland is in no respect altered by an act of Parliament, the statute of the 10th of Hen. 7 c 4 called Poyning's [*sic*] Law, only directs a new form of passing bills into laws, but alters nothing of the judicial power and their argument of their having the interpretation of all laws by a judicial power being allowed them, will enable them to make the laws what they please, will as well hold against the jurisdiction of this House, which ought not to be suffered.

APPENDIX I

Declaratory Act, 1720

6 Geo. I c. 5. (G.B.)

An Act for the better securing the Dependency of the Kingdom of Ireland upon the Crown of Great Britain.

WHEREAS the House of Lords of Ireland have of late, against law, assumed to themselves a power and jurisdiction to examine, correct and amend the judgments and decrees of the Courts of Justice in the Kingdom of Ireland, therefore for the better securing the dependency of Ireland upon the Crown of Great Britain, may it please your most excellent Majesty that it be declared by and with the advice and consent of the Lords spiritual and temporal and Commons in this present Parliament assembled and by the authority of the same, that the said Kingdom of Ireland hath been, is, and of right ought to be subordinate unto, and dependent upon the Imperial Crown of Great Britain, as being inseparably united and annexed thereto, and that the King's Majesty by and with the advice and consent of the Lords spiritual and temporal and Commons of Great Britain in Parliament assembled, had, hath, and of right ought to have, full power and authority to make laws and statutes of sufficient force and validity to bind the Kingdom and people of Ireland.

APPENDIX J

Queries relating to Lord Netterville's trial in Ireland

and who was tried by his peers in Ireland 3 February 1743[9]

By the Statute 10 H. 7 c. 21[10] in Ireland it is enacted as follows:

> That if any person of malice prepense do slay or murder, or of the said malice do provoke – or procure any other person to slay or murder etc [?] be deemed traitor attainted of high treason, likewise as it should extend to our sovereign Lord's person, and to his Royal Majesty.

A. together with B, C etc. [?] stands indicted for the murder of J.S. and the indictment charges "that A B etc at such a time and place and feloniously traitorously and made an assault upon J. S. – that B then and there gave J.S. a mortal wound with a gun-shot whereof he died – and that A. C. etc were then and there present aiding abetting and comforting and assisting the said B. to commit the said felony treason and murder. – J.N. gives evidence against A. before the coroner duly holding his inquest, which evidence is by the coroner duly reduced into writing signed by the coroner & J.N. and certified to the next justices of gaol delivery together with the recognisance of J.N. to appear & prosecute, pursuant to the Irish statute 10 Car. 1 sess. — c. 18[11] which statute extends to treason as well as felony and comprehends the English statutes 1 & 2 P. & M. c. 13[12] and 2 & 3 P. & M. c. 10.[13]

J. N. cannot be produced upon the trial of A., either absconding or being out of the kingdom, but there is no evidence that A. is instrumental to either. J. W. After the fact committed gave an information before a justice of the peace who certified the same to the next justices of gaol delivery - J. W. - likewise absconds or is out of the kingdom, but there is no evidence that A is instrumental to either. T. P. gave informations before a justice etc but is dead - It is apprehended that

[9] Notes by Sir John Strange, (bap. 1696, d. 1754), judge, from a manuscript in the Collection of Chief Baron Parker now in Harvard Law School Library HLS MS 1011, p. 101-105. Baker, *English Legal Manuscripts in the United States of America. A descriptive list, Part II: 1558-1902.* Cambridge, Selden Society, 1990, no. 549.

In his early career Strange studied in the practice of Charles Salkeld, a solicitor of Brook Street, Holborn, where Thomas Parker (later Chief Baron of the Exchequer), Philip Yorke (later Lord Chancellor Hardwicke), and Robert Jocelyn (later lord chancellor of Ireland) had also all trained. A. A. Hanham, 'Strange, Sir John (bap. 1696, d. 1754)', ODNB online. [http://www.oxforddnb.com/view/article/26635], accessed 9 March 2013; Sir Thomas Parker, (c. 1695-1784), a nephew of Thomas Parker, 1st Earl of Macclesfield LC, was appointed chief baron of the English Exchequer in 1742.

[10] 10 Hen. VII, c. 21 (Ir.), 1495.

[11] 10 Car. I, sess. 2, c. 18 (Ir.): 'An Act appointing an Order to Justices of Peace, touching the bailment, committing and taking examination of prisoners, &c.'

[12] 1 & 2 Ph. & Mar., c. 13 (Eng.), 1554.

[13] 2 & 3 Ph. & Mar., c. 10 (Eng.), 1555.

the Stat. of P. & M. in England and though Stat. 10 Car. 1 in Ireland impowers justices of the peace to take informations upon oath, only when the offender is brought before them, and that in order either for the bailment or commitment of such offender: (and justices of the peace in Ireland have no other jurisdiction in cases of treason than the justices of the peace in England). But in the present case A was never brought before any magistrate, neither was he present before the coroner or either of the said Justices whom the said informations were so taken by them resp[?] but surrendered himself long after to prevent his being outlawed.

A. was not present at the time of the of the fact committed nor went he with B.C. et or any of them in order to commit the same. 1st question - Can all or any and which of the informations so as aforesaid taken be read in evidence against A upon his trial. 2nd question - Will evidence of A's directing or advising B.C. etc. or any of them to slay JS [?] maintain this indictment which charges A to be present at the time the murder was committed in manner above-mentioned? **[102]** Vide *Rex* v. *Pain* in Comb. 358[14] and compare with S.C. in Salk. 281,[15] 1 Ld. Raym. 729[16] and 5 Mod. 164.[17] *Rex* v. *Thatcher and Weller* 2 Jones 53.[18] 4 Inst. 177. 3 Inst 129. 130. Brook *faux Imprisonment* pl. 8. Peare [?] pl. 6. 10 Co. 76b. Kel. 19.[19] 55 H.P.C. 263.[20] *Harrison's Case* State Trials[21] 4 Vol. 492.[22] 2 Ro. A. Tryal 686. 1. Salk. 290.[23] 291. 4 Mod. 146[24] 147. 1. H.P.C. 305.[25] 306. 2 D . 284. 285.

[*There follows a passage which is crossed through and repeated in substance below, from 'The next question...' to 'brought home to the prisoner'.*]

The two points stated are:

1. Whether as A. is charged to be present aiding and abetting and assisting when in fact he was not there, whether evidence of his directing or advising B or C or any of them to slay J.S. will be sufficient to maintain such an indictment.

2. Whether the ex[am]i[n]at[i]on before the coroner or those before justices of the peace under the circumstances stated in your [letter] can be read in evidence or either of them.

As to the first of these I think there would be no doubt, if the case arose in England and was tried there, but that the evidence of directing and advising B and C to slay JS would not maintain the indictment, for murder (with us) is but

14 *R* v. *Pain* (1724) Comb. 358, 90 E.R. 527.

15 *R* v. *Pain* (1795) 1 Salk. 281, 91 E.R. 246.

16 *R* v. *Payne* (1792) 1 Ld. Raym. 729, 91 E.R. 1387.

17 *The King* v. *Paine* (1794) 5 Mod. 163, 87 E.R. 584.

18 *Thatcher and Waller's Case* (1729) T. Jones 53, 84 E.R. 1143.

19 Kelyng J. 19, 84 E.R. 1063 (text).

20 Hale's *Pleas of the Crown*.

21 *Harrison's Case* (1660) 5 St. Tr. 998, 1008, 1230 (a regicide).

22 1730 edition edited by Sollum Emlyn, 4 St. Tr. 484 at 492.

23 *Brown* v. *Hedges* (1795) 1 Salk. 290, 91 E.R. 257 (declaration of trover in Middlesex, proof of one in Ireland, good).

24 *Howard* v. *Tremain* (1793) 4 Mod. 146, 87 E.R. 314.

25 Hale's *Pleas of the Crown*.

a species of felony where there may be accessories before the fact, and in such case the indictment must not charge A as a principal present aiding and abetting, but must describe his offence as being accessory before the fact. If therefore A was to be tried here, I should have no doubt but he ought to be acquitted of this indictment. **[103]** But as murder is not barely a felony with you, but is made high treason by the Stat. 10 Hen. 7 c. 21 and it is clear law that in high treason there are no such things as accessories, but all are principals, it may perhaps be said that the indictment could not have been drawn otherwise than it is in order to charge A as a principal, and that the words, "then and there present" are only form, the substance being the abetting; this however (upon the best cons[truction] I can give it) does not satisfy me that A is properly indicted. The statute makes 2 distinct treasons 1. To slay or murder of malice prepense 2. To provoke this or procure any other person of the said malice prepense to slay or murder, and in either of these cases, I think the fact should be described so as to tally with the words outlining [?] the offence. - The proper indictment therefore in my opinion would have been to have described the murder by B and then to have charged A that he did of malice prepense and traitorously et[c] provoke this[?] and procure B. to slay and murder J.S., and as it is not so laid to tally with the first words of slaying and murdering, I should apprehend the evidence does not maintain the present indictment and it is in effect charging one sort of treason and proving another.

Upon this occasion I have been looking in the precedents which were settled by Mr Attorney General and myself upon the Stat. 9 G. 2[26] against enlisting soldiers for foreign service, and I find we always thought it necessary to consider how our fact [?] would best tally with one or other of the provisions of the Act and lay the indictment accordingly.

The next question is whether the examination before the coroner or either of those before justices of the peace can be read under the circumstances in which they appear.

And my opinion (which I submit to your judgment) is that neither of the 3 can be read.

And as to the first (the deposition before the coroner) there are but 3 instances that I know of which can introduce it, neither of which occur in the present case, i.e. the witness is not dead and there is no evidence of his being unable to travel, nor of his being kept out of the way by the procurement of the prisoner, for not being able to find him is not enough, and the opinion of the judges in *Lord Morley's Case*[27] is now further established by my Lord Hale in his *History of Pleas of the Crown* 1 vol. 305. 306 and 2 vol. 284, 285. There is indeed in the printed trial of *Harrison*[28] a sort of a different opinion of Holt's who let the deposition be read though the evidence of practice in keeping away the witness is not brought home **[104]** to the prisoner, but I rather think from the Chief Justice's manner of summing it up, and the practice ever since to require that strictness of evidence,

[26] 9 Geo. II, c. 30 (G.B.) (foreign enlistment).

[27] *Thomas, Lord Morley and Mounteagle* (1666) 6 St. Tr. 770 (murder).

[28] *Harrison* (1660) 5 S.T. 998, 1008, 1230 (a regicide).

that it is either a mistake in the note taken or at least not a designed information of the general rule of evidence.

The examinations before justices of the peace under the statute, can (I think) neither of them be read, for the circumstance to give them jurisdiction viz. having the offender before them, fails, whereby the benefit of a cross-examination is taken from the prisoner and perhaps by design of the prosecutor. And the danger of the attempts upon a witness or to keep him out of the way does not does not seem very great in the case of a private ex parte examination, the contents whereof are unknown to the prisoner. I must add that this circumstance of the prisoner not being present does not weight with me in the case of the deposition before the coroner, where it seldom happens that the guilty person appears before the inquest.

J Strange
January 1743

...

My Lord,

Leighton Grange 11 January 1743

I had yesterday the honour of your Lordship's letter of the 3rd instant proposing a doubt in what manner the execution of Lord Netterville is to be awarded in case he shall be found guilty, in answer to which and the reasons contained in your letter, I shall submit what occurs to me at present, because as the trial is to be the 18 inst. it would be inconvenient to take a longer time. However, if I see occasion to vary my opinion I intend to trouble you again.

As my Lord is to be tried by his peers and the constituting a Lord High Steward is necessary for the purpose of such trial only. It seems to be to be very right for the High Steward to dissolve his commission the moment the verdict of the peers and the sentence are given; and if you look into the commission itself (which is printed in *Lord Mohun's*[29] and *Derwentwater's*[30] trials) you will find there is no power given to award execution; it must be done by virtue of the King's writ and the precedent for that purpose in *Lord Stafford's Case*[31] is certainly right and what (I believe) has been followed ever since, except in the case of *Layer*,[32] where the place several times appointed for his execution was

[29] (1692) 12 St. Tr. 950, No. 371, trial for murder of William Mountford. He was found not guilty. 13 St. Tr. 1034, No. 403, 1699, trial for the murder of Richard Coote. He was found not guilty unanimously.

[30] James Radcliffe, styled 3rd Earl of Derwentwater (1689-1716), Jacobite army officer. He was beheaded on Tower Hill on 24 February 1716. (1716) 15 S.T. 762 (and Lord Kenmure).

[31] (1680) 7 S.T. 1294, and see the writs at p. 1562.

[32] 16 St. Tr. 94 and see p. 321 and also *The Whole Proceeding Upon the Arraignment, Tryal, Conviction, and Attainder of Christopher Layer, Esq. for High Treason in Compassing and Imagining the Death of the King: in the Court of King's-Bench at Westminster... in the Ninth Year of the Reign of Our Soveraign Lord*

ordered by a rule of the King's Bench, the reason of which I take to be, because that court had power so to do in its ordinary jurisdiction and was not dissolved at the close of the trial, as the authority of a High Steward is.

[105] Your Lordship makes two observations upon *Lord Stafford's Case*; the first is, that you apprehend the issuing those writs to have been necessary as the execution was totally varied from the judgment; but I submit it to your further consideration whether that be so or not; for upon looking into the judgment you will find beheading to be a part of it, and as the King could dispense with the whole sentence or nay part of it, the appointment of the execution by beheading only operates as the King's pardon of all the rest. It is not an altering of the judgment, but a carrying a part of it only into execution.

The other observation you make is upon the words, *'aliquo – judicio, lege, ordinantione, seu mandate preautea habit fact[.] ordinat[.] seu dat in contrar[.] non obstante*; which you seem to think suppose a prior order to have been given, though that does not appear, but I take it those words do not import a prior award of execution to have been made, but are only a command that execution should be done solely by beheading, 'any judgment law or order to the contrary referring to the common judgment for high treason, which had been pronounced by the High Steward in the same terms as in the case of a commoner (as by law it should) and if you cast you eye upon the petition of the sheriffs to the Lords and Commons upon receiving the King's writ, you will find their scruple to be grounded on that only.

I have not directed any search to be made into the records of *Lord Derwentwater's Case* those particulars not being to be got at without a formal application (which I imagine you would not at present care to have made). But I verily believe he and *Lord Kenmure*[33] were executed upon the same sort of writs as the Lord Stafford.

I suggest your Lordship has no doubt of the power of the Crown to put to death by beheading only, whatever the sentence of death may import. If you have you will find it settled upon cons[ideration] of precedents in *Lady Lisle's Case*[34] in the State trials, who was sentenced to be burnt, and yet beheaded, and in *Lord Audley's Case*[35] whose head was taken off, though the judgment was only to be hanged.

J. S.

George. London: Printed by S. Buckley, 1722/3.

33 15 St. Tr. 762. William Gordon, 6th Viscount Kenmure and Jacobite Marquess of Kenmure (d. 1716), Jacobite conspirator. On 24 February 1716 he was beheaded with Lord Derwentwater on Tower Hill.

34 (1685) 11 St. Tr. 298, No. 331. It is one of Judge Jeffreys' most notorious cases. The husband of Lady Alice Lisle had been a regicide. She was a woman of great piety and disapproved of her husband's involvement. A preacher who had been with Monmouth had come to her house and she let him in. She did not ask him from where he had come. The jury found her not guilty. Jeffreys was furious and sent them back. They found her not guilty again. Jeffreys threatened them with attaint of jury. They then found her guilty. James II only changed burning to beheading and she was executed. Her husband was 'one of Cromwell's lords' and was known as Lord Lisle.

35 *Mervin, Lord Audley* (1631) 3 St. Tr. 402 (for rape and sodomy).

APPENDIX K

Report on the Tenure of Judges Bill, 1776

[f1] To the Right Honourable the Lords of a Committee of His Majesty's most honourable Privy Council appointed to consider the Irish bills.[36]

May it please your Lordships

In humble obedience to His Majesty's Order in Council of the third day of November last; we have considered and examined a bill lately transmitted from Ireland intitled. 'An Act for making the commissions of judges to continue *quam diu se bene gesserint*.'

In England judges anciently held their commissions during life, or pleasure as the crown thought fit to grant them. Now their **[f2]**[37] commissions must be made *quamdiu se bene gesserint;*[38] but revocable at the pleasure of the three estates of Parliament.

In Ireland it is a fundamental part of their constitution (for such Poynings' Law hath been always and deservedly thought) that all judicial offices, and offices of accompt, should be holden during His Majesty's pleasure; in consideration (as the Law declares) of the great and manifest inconveniences, attempted there, contrary to all natural allegiance, and to the King's grievous displeasure, by such persons, holding their offices by patent for term of life.

At the end of above two hundred years, without any complaint, or special cause assigned, the Lord Lieutenant and Council of Ireland have proposed an Act to alter the law in this respect, and make the commissions of judges revocable only at the joint pleasure of His Majesty, and the two Houses of Parliament in Ireland.

Besides the general objection to altering the constitution without serious and urgent occasion and the difference above **[f3]**[39] alluded to between the two cases, there is still another difference. In England the law is to be repealed, in the particular instance, by the Act of the whole legislature, though done in a more summary manner than the ordinary form of making laws. In Ireland the same thing is proposed to be affected, not only more summarily in the manner, but wholly omitting the certificate under the Great Seal of Ireland by the Lord Lieutenant and Privy Council there, and the return thereof under the Great Seal

[36] PRO PC 1/11/9.
[37] Incorrectly numbered 1 in original.
[38] L. During good behaviour.
[39] Incorrectly numbered 2 in original.

of Great Britain by His Majesty with the advice of His Privy Council thereto.

The last Articles are also made a fundamental part of their constitution, by the same Poynings' Law, which, after being twice dispensed with, was at length by the eleventh of Elizabeth sect. the third Chapter the eighth[40] fixed, with a provision, that it should never be altered or suspended in the ordinary course of legislation.

All which is humbly submitted to Your Lordships consideration.

E. Thurlow[41]

Al. Wedderburn[42]

28 February 1776.

40 11 Eliz. sess. 3 c. 8 (Ir.) s. 3.

41 Edward Thurlow, 1st Baron Thurlow (1731–1806). He became solicitor general in March 1770 and attorney general in January 1771. On 3 June 1778 Thurlow was created Baron Thurlow of Ashfield, Suffolk, and became lord chancellor.

42 Alexander Wedderburn, 1st Earl of Rosslyn (1733–1805). He became solicitor general in 1770 and lord chancellor at the end of January 1793.

APPENDIX L

Report on the Tenantry Bill

Report of Mr Attorney General and Mr Mansfield upon the Petitions against and in support of the Bill for the Relief of Tenants holding under Leases for Lives.[43]

R 18th July 1780
Read - Counsel
Heard thereupon -
Bill referred back
to Mr Attorney General -

[f5a] To the Right Honourable The Lords of the Committee of Council to consider of the Irish Bills

May it please Your Lordships

In Obedience to your Lordships Order of the 13th instant referring to us the annexed Petition of the Right Honourable Arthur Sanders Gore Earl of Arran and others praying to be heard by counsel against a Bill lately transmitted for from Ireland intitled 'An Act for the relief of Tenants holding under Leases for Lives containing Covenants for perpetual Renewals,' to hear the Petitioners upon the subject matter of the said Petition and report our opinion thereupon to your Lordships which Petition sets forth[:]

'That the Petitioners find that Heads of a Bill have been lately transmitted from Ireland and are now before your Majesty's most Honourable Privy Council intitled "An Act for the relief of Tenants holding under Leases for Lives containing Covenants for perpetual Renewals" **[f5b]** which if passed into a Law will as your Petitioners apprehend not only be attended with the greatest Injury and damage to your Petitioners and to many other proprietors of Lands within that Kingdom but also tend to involve every person who is interested in those Tenants tedious and troublesome suits'

'That the Petitioners humbly conceive that the Courts of Equity are invested at present with full and sufficient powers to relieve any Tenant who may by any accident or unavoidable Fatality become an Object proper for such relief without the Aid of An Act of Parliament' and also of another order of Your Lordships of the same date referring to us the annexed Memorial of several

[43] PRO PC 1/12/26. 17 July 1780.

Tenants in Ireland holding under Leases for Lives containing Covenants for perpetual Renewals praying to be heard by their counsel in support of the Bill to hear the Memorialists upon the subject matter of the said Memorial and report our to your Lordships which Memorial sets forth 'That the **[f6a]** Memorialists have been informed that a Petition hath lately been presented to Your Majesty by the Earl of Arran and others, praying to be heard by Counsel before the Attorney and Solicitor General in opposition to a Bill lately transmitted from Ireland entitled 'An Act for the relief of Tenants holding under Leases for Lives containing Covenants for perpetual Renewals'

'That the Memorialists conceiving it extremely material for the Tenantry and occupiers of Lands in general in the said Kingdom of Ireland that the said Bill should pass into a Law.'

It appears to us that a very considerable part of the Lands in Ireland hath for a great number of years past been held under Leases granted by the Owner to Tenants for three Lives containing Covenants on the part of the Grantor for renewals of the Leases within a limited time after the dropping of the respective Lives upon the payment of a certain sum under the name of a Fine. **[f6b]**

The Leases made by different Landowners vary not only the limitations of the renewal and the sums payable but in the form of the Stipulation for renewal. In some of the Leases there is only a simple Covenant that the Lessor and his Heirs will upon payment of a certain sum within a specified time after the dropping of each Life grant a new Lease for an additional Life with a like Covenant for renewal; in others It is declared that if the Tenant does not pay the Fine within the time limited, that the Lessor and his Heirs shall not be obliged to renew the Lease but shall be discharged from the Covenant in that respect. In others there is contained a proviso or condition that if the Tenant fail in payment of the Fine according to the Terms of the Lease the Lessor and his Heirs may re-enter into the possession of the Estate demised to hold the same discharged of the Lease.

Where from the fraud or improper conduct of the Landlord or from accident or Misfortune, the Tenants have omitted to apply for renewals and pay their Fines within the respective time limited by their Leases, Courts **[f7a]** of Equity in Ireland have compelled Renewals upon compensation being made to the Lessors or their Heirs without any regard to the different modes of the Stipulation for Renewals contained in the Leases and in instances of Appeals to the House of Lords here the decrees have been affirmed.

The Compensation to the Lessor and his Heirs where the Application is made recently after the expiration of the time limited is the Fine with interest from the time the same ought to have been paid according to the Covenant; but where a long period of time had elapsed the Compensation became difficult to ascertain for if the renewal had been in due time the person whose name might have been inserted in the renewed lease might have died, and therefore that chance ought to be taken into the Calculation.

A Rule of Compensation upon such chances was laid down by the Court of Exchequer in Ireland on the 2d December 1720 in a cause *Anderson* and *Sweet* and was adopted by the House of Lords upon the Appeal, and has ever since been practised in cases where a Court of Equity ought to relieve the Tenant. **[f7b]** A life is estimated at seven Years only, and therefore at the end of seven Years from the decease of one of the Lives in the Lease the life which ought to have been inserted in his room is supposed to drop and another Fine is considered to become due and Interest is computed upon that Fine and so from seven years to seven years – this mode of computing the Compensation will not as we conceive be found unfavourable to the Lessors and their Heirs – the Idea seems to have been taken from An Act of Parliament passed in England in the 19th year of the reign of King Charles the 2d[44] and enacted in Ireland the 7th year of the reign of King William the third [45] upon the subject of Leases for Lives whereby a person for whose Life any Estate is held is beyond [the] Seas or absenteth himself within the Realm for seven Years and no sufficient and evident proof be made of his being alive is presumed to be dead.

The object of the present Bill is to authorise and require Courts of Equity to oblige the Lessors and their Heirs to renew Leases containing Covenants for the perpetual Renewals where the omissions to renew in due time is to be imputed to the inattention or negligence of the **[f8a]** Tenant in the same manner and upon the same Terms of Compensation as in cases of Accident or misfortune where Courts of Equity in the ordinary exercise of their Judicature constantly give relief.

It has been suggested to us that an opinion has generally prevailed in Ireland that a Lessee's right of renewal was not lost by such inattention and negligence and that the Lessors have been accustomed to renew Leases notwithstanding any such Negligence in their Lessees; That it has lately become publick in consequence of some judicial decisions founded on a true and just interpretation of these Leases that the opinion which had so prevailed was erroneous and that great unease and Alarm had arisen among the persons interested in Leases of this kind least [*sic*] by the Lessors taking advantage of the inattention of their Lessees the latter should be deprived of that property which they had considered as permanent and secure. That the present Bill was framed with a view to remove all such Apprehensions[.] This effect it will certainly have as it will secure to the Lessees and those who have purchased their titles, a Stable and certain Interest in their Estates and in this view it appears to us to be a beneficial Law - The principal objection to the Bill is the supposed injury which it does to the Lessors, by **[f8b]** altering the engagement between them and their Lessees and depriving them of the most effectual method to enforce the payment of their fines which was, their right to take back their estates where the Lessees omitted to pay their fines within the time stipulated and this objection appears to us to have great weight: But it is to be observed that from the nature of these Leases it is apparent that those who granted them had it not in their Contemplation that their Estates would ever return to them but intended only to obtain the payment of certain Fines and Rents, and if these can be by any other method secured without giving to the Lessors a right to resume their Estates they will

[44] Cestui que Vie Act, 1665 , 19 Chas. II c. 6.
[45] Life Estates Act, 1695, 7 Wm. III c. 8 (Ir.).

enjoy all the fruits which they ever expected to derive from them. The present Bill has made some provision for this purpose, but it is probable that others may be found necessary which may be with more propriety be made by the Irish Parliament in some future Bill, than by any Attempt here to amend the present and We humbly conceive it may be proper and expedient for Your Lordships to return the present Bill.

Ja. Wallace[46]

James Mansfield[47]

17 July 1780

[46] James Wallace (bap. 1729, d. 1783), appointed solicitor general by Lord North in 1778, attorney general in 1780.

[47] Sir James Mansfield [formerly Manfield], (bap. 1734, d. 1821), appointed solicitor general on 1 September 1780, following Wallace's promotion to attorney general. He was appointed chief justice of the Common Pleas on 24 April 1804.

APPENDIX M

Amendments to the Tenantry Bill 1780

[PRO PC/125, Council Register, 1 March 1780 to 31 December 1780:]

[p. 287]

As to the Bill Entitled,

> An Act for the Relief of Tenants holding under Leases for Lives containing Covenants for Perpetual Renewal.

The Lords of the committee having taken the Opinion of Your Majestys Attorney General thereupon and have also heard counsel on a petition of the Right Honourable Arthur Sanders Gore Earl of Arran and others against the Bill, as likewise upon the petition of several tenants in Ireland holding under leases for lives containing covenants for perpetual renewals in support of the Bill, and their lordships do thereupon agree humbly to report to your majesty as their opinion, that the said Bill is proper to be passed with some amendments viz.

[p. 288]

After the word [Equity] insert [upon an adequate compensation being made].

After the word [Act] leave out [provided always that such landlords or Lessors or persons entitled to such Fines respectively shall have full satisfaction made to them for all such fines and the interest of the same according to the usual practice of courts of equity in cases of such nature and shall also receive the full costs out of pocket in such suits as shall be instituted against them respectively for the purpose of enforcing a specific execution of such covenants.]

After the word [made] insert [or any suit commenced before the fifteenth day of May one thousand seven hundred and eighty and now depending for the recovery of the possession of any manors messuages lands tenements or hereditaments on account of nay lease or leases not having been renewed according to the covenants for perpetual renewals therein contained.]

. . .

[p. 295]

At the Court at St Jamess 28th of July 1780

Present

The King's Most Excellent Majesty

Lord President
Viscount Stormont
Lord Chamberlain
Viscount Falmouth
Lord George Germain
Lord Amherst

Whereas the Bills hereunder mentioned which were lately transmitted from Ireland in due form by the Lord Lieutenant and privy Council of that kingdom have been examined and considered by His Majestys Attorney and Solicitor General who have made their Report thereupon to a Committee of His Majestys most Honourable Privy Council appointed to consider the same; And Whereas the said Committee have this day reported to His Majesty at this Board, that the said Bills are proper to be passed with the following amendments, viz.

An Act for the Relief of Tenants holding under Leases for Lives containing Covenants for Perpetual Renewal.

Vide the amendments to these Bills entered in the committee report Page 285 &tc.

...

The Tenantry Bill as Amended

[*Reconstruction based on the above documents. Words to be deleted in the draft are represented as struck through, words to be inserted are represented as underlined.*]

19 & 20 Geo. III c. 30 (Ir.)

[Preamble] Whereas great parts of the lands in this kingdom are held under leases for lives with covenants for perpetual renewals upon payment of certain fines at the times therein respectively mentioned for each renewal... and whereas it has been for a long time a received opinion in this kingdom, to which some decisions in courts of equity and declarations of judges have given countenance, that courts of equity would in such cases relieve against lapse of time upon giving adequate compensation to the persons, to whom such fines were payable, or their representatives: and to the end that such interests may not be defeated by a mere neglect, where no fraud appears to have been intended, upon making full satisfaction to the lessors, or those deriving under them; be it declared and enacted by the Kings most excellent Majesty, by and with the advice and consent of the lords spiritual and temporal and commons in this present Parliament assembled, and by the authority of the same,

[I] That courts of equity upon an adequate compensation being made shall relieve such tenants and their assigns against such lapse of time, if no circumstance of fraud be proved against such tenants or their assigns; unless it shall be proved to the satisfaction of such courts, that the landlords or lessors, or persons entitled to receive such fines, had demanded such fines from such tenants or their assigns, and that the same had been refused or neglected to be paid within reasonable time after such demand.

II. Provided always, and be it enacted by the authority aforesaid, That in case the landlord shall find any difficulty in discovering his tenant or the assignee of such tenant, so as to make a demand on such tenant or assignee, that then and in every such case a demand made of the said on the lands from the principal occupier of the same, together with a notice of such demand, to be inserted for the space of two months in the London and Dublin gazettes, shall be considered to all intents and purposes a demand within this act.

~~III. Provided always that such landlords or Lessors or persons entitled to such Fines respectively shall have full satisfaction made to them for all such fines and the interest of the same according to the usual practice of courts of equity in cases of such nature and shall also receive the full costs out of pocket in such suits as shall be instituted against them respectively for the purpose of enforcing a specific execution of such covenants.~~

III. Provided always, and be it enacted by the authority aforesaid, That nothing herein contained shall in any sort affect any judgment or decree already given and made, or any suit commenced before the fifteenth day of May one thousand seven hundred and eighty, and now depending for the recovery of the possession of any manors, messuages, lands, tenements, or hereditaments on account of any lease or leases not having been renewed according to the covenants for perpetual renewals therein contained.

APPENDIX N

The Repealing Act, 1782

An Act to repeal an Act, made in the Sixth Year of the Reign of His late Majesty King George the First, intituled An Act for the better securing the Dependency of the Kingdom of Ireland upon the Crown of Great Britain.

22 Geo. III c. 53 (G.B.)

Whereas an Act was passed in the Sixth Year of the Reign of His late Majesty King George the First, intituled An Act for the better securing the Dependency of the Kingdom of Ireland upon the Crown of Great Britain; May it please Your Most Excellent Majesty that it may be enacted; and be it enacted by the King's Most Excellent Majesty, by and with the Advice and Consent of the Lords Spiritual and Temporal, and Commons, in this present Parliament assembled, and by the authority of the same, That from and after the passing of this Act, the above mentioned Act, and the several Matters and Things therein contained, shall be, and is and are hereby repealed.

APPENDIX O

Yelverton's Act, 1782

An Act to regulate the Manner passing of Bills, and to prevent Delays in summoning Parliament.

21 & 22 Geo. III c. 47 (Ir.)

WHEREAS it expedient to regulate the manner of passing bills in this kingdom, be it enacted by the King's most excellent Majesty, by and with the consent of the lords spiritual and temporal and commons in this present Parliament assembled, and by the authority of the same, That the lord lieutenant, or other chief governor or governors and council of this kingdom, for the time being, do and shall certify all such bills, and none other, as both Houses of Parliament shall judge expedient to be enacted in this kingdom, to his Majesty, his heirs and successors, under the great seal of this kingdom, without addition, diminution, or alteration.

II. And be it further enacted by the authority aforesaid, That such bills as shall be so certified to his Majesty, his heirs and successors, under the great seal of this kingdom, returned into the same under the great seal of Great Britain, without addition, diminution, or alteration, and none other shall pass in the Parliament of this kingdom; and former law, statute or usage to the contrary thereof in any wise notwithstanding.

III. And be it further enacted, That no bill shall be certified into Great Britain as a cause or consideration for holding a Parliament in this kingdom, but that Parliaments may be holden in this kingdom, although no such bill shall have been certified previous to the meeting thereof.

IV. Provided always, That no Parliament shall be holden in this kingdom until a licence for that purpose shall be first had and obtained from his Majesty, his heirs and successors, under the great seal of Great Britain.

APPENDIX P

Appeals and Writs of Error to Parliament, 1782

An Act for Redress of erroneous Judgments, Orders, and Decrees.

21 & 22 Geo. III c. 49 (Ir.) 1781–82

Whereas erroneous judgments, orders, and decrees, ought only to be reformed finally in the high court of Parliament in this kingdom; be it declared and enacted by the King's most excellent Majesty, by and with the advice and consent of the lords spiritual and temporal and commons, in this present Parliament assembled, and by the authority of the same, [I] That from henceforth all such judgments, orders, and decrees, shall be finally examined and reformed in the high court of Parliament in this kingdom only; and any law, statute, or practice to the contrary thereof, in any wise notwithstanding.

II. Provided always, and be it enacted by the authority aforesaid, That nothing herein contained shall invalidate or affect any judgment, order, or decree which has been given or made on Great Britain, previous to the first day of June, one thousand seven hundred and eighty two, but that the same shall remain in full force; any thing herein contained to the contrary thereof in any wise notwithstanding.

III. And be it enacted by the authority aforesaid, That it shall and may be lawful to and for the lord lieutenant or other chief governor or chief governors of this kingdom for the time being, to grant warrants for sealing writs of error returnable into Parliament, and that the sum of three pounds shall be paid to the cursitor for every such writ of error by the party applying for the same, to be distributed in such manner as the lord high chancellor shall direct.

APPENDIX Q

The Renunciation Act, 1783

An Act for removing and preventing all doubts which may have arisen or might arise concerning the exclusive rights of the Parliament and Courts of Ireland in matters of legislation and judicature.

23 Geo. III c. 28 (G.B.)

WHEREAS, by an Act of the last session of this present Parliament entitled 'An Act to Repeal an Act Made in the Sixth Year of... George I...'[48] it was enacted that the last-mentioned act and all matters and things therein contained should be repealed... for removing all doubts respecting the same... be it declared and enacted... that the... right claimed by the people of Ireland to be bound only by laws enacted by His Majesty and the Parliament of that kingdom in all cases whatever, and to have all actions and suits at law or in equity which may be instituted in that kingdom decided in His Majesty's courts therein finally and without appeal from thence, shall be and it is hereby declared to be established and ascertained forever, and shall at no time hereafter be questioned or questionable.

II. And be it further enacted by the authority aforesaid that no writ of error or appeal shall be received or adjudged, or any other proceeding be had, by or in any of his Majesty's courts in this kingdom in any action or suit at law or in equity instituted in any of his Majesty's courts in the kingdom of Ireland...

[48] 6 Geo. I c. 5. Above, page 231.

APPENDIX R

Irish Court of Exchequer Chamber, 1800

An Act for the more speedy Correction of Erroneous Judgments given in the Courts of Law in this Kingdom.

40 Geo. III, c. 39, (Ir.)

WHEREAS the present course of examining and correcting erroneous judgments given in the superior courts of law in this kingdom is inconvenient and it would tend to the case of the suitor, and the dispatch of business, if one court composed of the twelve judges of the land were created to which writs of error should lie directly from the four superior courts, and from whose judgments writs error might be brought before the king in Parliament; it therefore enacted by the kings most excellent Majesty by and with the advice and consent of the lords spiritual and temporal, and commons in this present Parliament assembled, and by the authority of the same, that it shall not be lawful from and after the passing of this act, to sue forth any writ of error to the Court of King's Bench to reverse judgment of the court of law before the king in Chancery,[49] or to reverse any judgment of the Court of Common Pleas or to sue forth any writ of error to the court now held before the chancellor or treasurer, commonly called the Exchequer Chamber, to reverse any judgment of the Court of Exchequer, or to sue any writ of error returnable directly to Parliament to reverse any judgment of the Court of King's Bench.

II. And be it further enacted, That where judgment hath been given for the reversal whereof a writ of error may now by law be brought and where judgments shall be given in any of the said courts of King's Bench in law before the king in Chancery, of Common Pleas, and of Exchequer respectively, writs of error may be sued forth of the Chancery, commanding transcripts of the records of such judgments respectively, to be brought before the chief justice of the Court of King's Bench, the chief justice of the Court of Common Pleas, the chief baron of the Court of Exchequer, the other justices of the said courts of King's Bench, Common Pleas, and the other barons of the Court of Exchequer, into a chamber to be appointed by the chief governor or governors of Ireland for that purposes and to be called the Exchequer Chamber, and that the said chief justices, chief baron, and other justices and barons, or any nine of them shall have power and authority to examine such judgments respectively, and to reverse or affirm the same, or to award such judgment as to law and justice shall pertain, and to send writs as the case may require to the courts from which such transcripts shall be respectively brought, directing such courts to cause execution to be done,

[49] i.e. the Court of Delegates hearing appeals in ecclesiastical cases under 25 Hen. VIII, c. 19 (Eng.), 1533. Above, page 65.

as if the judgment had been originally awarded therein; and further that the said chief justices, chief baron, justices and barons shall and may in all cases depending, award such costs moderate, reasonable, or exemplary, as to them shall appear just.

III. And be it enacted, That writs of error may be sued in the High Court of Parliament, by any party aggrieved by any judgment of the said chief justices, chief baron, justices and barons for the further and due examination thereof; provided always, that it shall and may be lawful for the Court of King's Bench, and the said court, commonly called the Exchequer Chamber, to proceed to judgment in cases now depending before them upon writs of error, and that all judgments thereon to be given, may be removed by writ of error to Parliament, in the same manner as if this act had not passed; provided always, that nothing herein contained shall be construed to give a right to any person to sue forth a writ to reverse a judgment in which the king, is a party, other than as by law the same is now allowable.

IV. And be it further enacted, That the said chief justices, chief baron, justices and barons shall assemble and hold their first sitting on the first sitting-day of the term next ensuing the passing of this act, and shall and may adjourn, and hold their future sittings to and in term, or out of term, being within twenty days of the last day of every term as to them shall seem most convenient for the dispatch of suits depending before them, and that it shall be lawful for any one or more of the said chief justices, chief baron, justices and barons, when nine shall not be present, to adjourn the said court, and that it shall and may be lawful for his Majesty to appoint a clerk of the said Court of error, to continue during pleasure, with a salary not exceeding three hundred pounds by the year to be paid by quarterly payments out of the consolidated fund.

Bibliography & Indexes

Bibliography

STATUTES

Ireland, *The Statutes at Large, 1310–1800*. 22 vols. Dublin, 1786–1804. Eighteenth Century Collections Online, Gale Databases.

Ireland. Henry F. Berry, ed., *Statutes and ordinances, and acts of the Parliament of Ireland: King John to Henry V*. Dublin, HMSO. 1907.

Ireland. Henry F. Berry, ed., *Statute Rolls of the Parliament or Ireland: reign of King Henry VI*. Irish Record Office series of early Statutes, vol. 2.

Ireland, Philomena Connolly, ed., *Statute rolls of the Irish Parliament: Richard III – Henry VIII* Dublin, 2002.

Ireland, *The Irish Statutes: Revised Edition, 3 Edward II to the Union AD 1310–1800*, 1885, reprint 1995.

Ireland, *Anno V. Jacobi II. Regis...* [Statutes of James II's parliament in Dublin] [Dublin?, 1689?], British Library, G.6022.(122.) [Only known copy. No title page and all pages after p. 56 missing.]

Davis, Thomas, *The Patriot Parliament of 1689*, ed. by Charles Gavan Duffy. London, 1893.

JOURNALS, etc.

Ireland, Parliament, House of Lords, *Journals of the House of Lords*. 1634–1800. 8 vols. Dublin, 1800.

Ireland, Parliament, House of Commons, *Journals of the House of Commons of the Kingdom of Ireland*. [Fourth Series] 1613–1800. 19 vols. Dublin, 1800.

Ireland, Parliament, *The Parliamentary Register of Ireland: history of the proceedings and debates of the House of Commons of Ireland*. 17 vol. Dublin, 1784–1801. Facsimile reprint, Bristol, 1999.

Ireland, Parliament, House of Lords, James Kelly, ed. *Proceedings of the Irish House of Lords 1771–1800*. 3 vols. Dublin, 2008.

Routledge, F. T., 'Journal of the Irish House of Lords in Sir John Perrot's Parliament' (3 May 1585–13 May 1586) (1914) 29 *English Historical Review* 104–117, Appendix.

ARCHIVES

Anonymous, 'Precedents Extracted from the Records of Ireland to prove the jurisdiction of the Parliament of this kingdom to hear and adjudge all cases.' Marsh's Library, Dublin. Z 3.2.5 p. 1.

Anonymous, 'The Report of the Committee of the Privy Council, Judges and others appointed by the Lords Justices and Privy Council to inspect the Journals of the House of Lords, Records and other Papers in order to find out what precedents there are relating to the methods which have been practised in appealing from decrees in the court of Chancery in Ireland, in pursuance of an order of the H. of Lords in England signified to the Lords Justices of Ireland, by a letter from the Lord Chancellor of England.' Marsh's Library, Dublin. Z 3.2.5 (75) pp. 277–87.

Anonymous, 'Some Reasons why an Appeale or Writ of Error does not lie in the H. of Lords in England to reverse a judgment, order or decree made by the House of Lords in Ireland.' Marsh's Library, Dublin. Z 3.2.5 (76).

Anonymous, 'The humble Petition of the Peers of Parliament in Ireland whose Names are hereunto Subscribed. Against a Bill entitled an Act for the better securing the Dependence of the Kingdom of Ireland upon the Crown of G. Britain. Marsh's Library, Dublin, Z 3.2.5 (82).

Anonymous, 'Case of Theobald, Viscount Mayo, against Lord Viscount Dillon, etc. [circa 1680]. Marsh's Library, Dublin. Z 3.2.6 (6).

Anonymous, 'Proceedings in the House of Lords, in the impeachment of the Lord Chancellor, John Bramhall, B'p of Derry, Sir Gerard Lowther, Chief Justice of the Common Pleas, and Sir George Radcliffe, Knight, for High Treason.' 27 February 1640. Marsh's Library, Dublin. Z 3.2.6 (115). Same as Z 3.2.5 (40).

Anonymous, 'Order of House of Lords in favour of Henry Steward, his wife and daughters and James Gray, who were fined and imprisoned by sentence of the Castle Chamber in the year 1639 for refusing to take an unlawful oath. 9 Sept 1642. Marsh's Library, Dublin, Z 3.2.6 (117).

Anonymous, 'Trial of Henry, Baron Barry of Santry. 1739' MS King's Inns Archives, Dublin. No number.

Anonymous, 'Proceedings in the Chancery side of the Exchequer'. KI MS 82.

Leeds, Duke of, 'The Duke of Leeds Reasons for Protesting Against a Vote made in the House of Lords in England, which declared a certain tryall before the House of Lords in Ireland to be *coram non judice*'. Marsh's Library, Dublin. Z 3.2.5 (83) pp. 323-24.

O'Byrne, Eileen. ed. *The Convert Rolls.* Dublin, Stationery Office for the IMC. 1981.

RULES

Ireland, Parliament, House of Lords, *Rules and Orders to be Observed in the Upper House of Parliament upon Writs of Error and Appeals*, Dublin, Printed by W. Sleater, 1784. Reproduced in 1 Ridg. PC xix.

PRINTED PLEADINGS

King's Inns, Dublin, Library, 'House of Lords Appeals', vol. 1 (1699) – vol. 51 (1801) (English, British and Irish HL).

National Library of Ireland, 'Appeals: Printed statements of cases of appellants, respondents, etc., in cases to be heard before the House of Lords.' 1710–1800. (British and Irish HL)

Lincoln's Inn, 'House of Lords Printed Cases, Judgments and Appeal Documents.' 1664 onwards. (English and British HL).

House of Lords Record Office, London, Main Papers (printed and unprinted). 1499–. Appeal Cases (printed) 1702 onwards. English and British HL)

Trinity College Dublin, 'Appeals to the House of Lords brought by various persons mostly residents of Ireland'. 1710–1739, 1729–1739, Index of appellants, typescript, 1956.

LAW REPORTS

Bryson, W. H., ed., *Robert Paynell's Reports (1627–1631)*. Tempe, Arizona, 2009.

Ridgeway, William, William Lapp and John Schoales, *Irish Term Reports, or Reports of Cases determined in the King's Courts, Dublin, from Easter Term, 34 Geo. III to Hilary Ter, 35 Geo. III inclusive* [1793–95]. 'vol. I' (no further volumes were published).

Ridgeway, William, *Reports of Cases upon Appeals and Writs of Error in the High Court of Parliament in Ireland, since the Restoration of Appellate Jurisdiction*. 3 vols. Dublin, 1795.

Vernon, G. W. (George William) and J. B. Scriven, *Irish Reports; or, reports of cases determined in the King's courts, Dublin; with select cases in the House of Lords of Ireland*. vol. 1. Dublin, 1790.

Wallis, John, [James Lyne, ed.], *Reports of Select Cases argued and determined in the High Court of Chancery in Ireland, principally in the time of Lord Lifford*. Dublin, 1839.

OPINIONS

Hargrave, Francis, *A Collection of Tracts relative to the Law of England, from Manuscripts, now first edited, by Francis Hargrave*. Dublin, 1787.

Hargrave, Francis, 'Irish case of marriage condition in 1791 and 1795' [*Kiely* v *Monck* 3 Ridg. PC 205] in *Jurisconsult Exercitations*.

Hargrave, Francis, ed. *Collectanea Juridica: Consisting of tracts relative to the law and constitution of England*. London, 1791–92.

Hargrave, Francis, *Juridical Arguments and Collections*. 2 vols. London, 1797–99.

Hargrave, Francis, *Jurisconsult Exercitations*. 3 vols. London, 1811–1813.

THESES ETC.

Donaldson, Alfred Gaston, 'The Application in Ireland of English and British Legislation made before 1801'. PhD, 2 vols. Appendix of statutes. Queen's University, Belfast. 1952.

Kavanaugh, Anne, 'John FitzGibbon' PhD, Trinity College Dublin (and see published book below).

McCabe, Patricia, 'Images of Law and Order: accoutrements, carriage, portraits and memorials of Lords Chancellor [*sic*] of Ireland 1660 – c. 1860.' PhD. 3 vols. Dublin, University College Dublin, 2002.

Ní Chúlacháin, Siobhán, 'Wardship of Adults in Ireland', LLM, University College Dublin, 1997.

Victory, Isolde L., 'Colonial Nationalism in Ireland, 1692–1725: From Common Law to Natural Right', PhD, Trinity College, Dublin, 1984.

BIOGRAPHICAL SOURCES

Ball, F. E., *The Judges in Ireland 1221–1921*. 2 vols. (London, 1927; reprint, Dublin, 1993)

Cokayne, G.E., *The Complete Peerage*. 14 vols. London, 1926. CD (pdf) version by ABC Publications, UK.

McGuire, James and James Quinn, eds., *Dictionary of Irish Biography*. Cambridge, 2009.

Matthew, H. C. G. and Brian Harrison, eds., *Oxford Dictionary of National Biography: from the earliest times to the year 2000*. Oxford, 2004.

Simpson, A. W. B., ed., *Biographical Dictionary of the Common Law*. London, 1984.

BOOKS & ARTICLES

Atwood, W., *The History, and Reasons, of the Dependency of Ireland upon the Imperial Crown of the Kingdom of England, Rectifying Mr. Molineux's State of the Case of Ireland's Being Bound by Acts of Parliament in England*. London, 1698

Baker, J. H., *English legal manuscripts in the United States of America: a descriptive list*. London, 1985–1990.

Baker, J. H. & S. F. C. Milsom, *Sources of English Legal History*. London, 1986.

Baker, J. H., ed., *Reports from the Lost Notebooks of Sir James Dyer. Vol. I.*. 109 Seld. Soc. London, 1993.

Baker, J. H., *An Introduction to Legal History*. London, 4th edition, 2002.

Baker, Sir John, *The Oxford History of the Laws of England. vol. 6. 1483–1558* Oxford, 2003.

Ball, F. Elrington, *The Judges in Ireland 1221–1921*. 2 vols. New York, 1927; reprint Dublin, 1993.

Ball, J. T. *Historical Review of the Legislative Systems Operative in Ireland from the Invasion of Henry the Second to the Union (1179–1800)*. London, 1889.

Ball, R. M., 'Exchequer of Pleas, Bills and Writs' (1988) *Journal of Legal History* 308.

Ballow, Henry (1792) *A Treatise of Equity...* Dublin, H. Watts. (edited by, but attributed to, Chief Baron Gilbert).

Bank of Ireland, Publications Department, *The Irish Parliament House*. Dublin, 1978.

Barrington, Sir Jonah, *Personal Sketches of his Own Times*. 3rd edn. London, 1869.

Beckett, J. C., *The Making of Modern Ireland, 1603–1923*. London, 1966.

Bergin, John, 'The Irish Catholic interest at the London Inns of Court, 1674–1800' (2009) 24 *Eighteenth-Century Ireland* 37–62.

Bicheno, Hugh, *Rebels and Redcoats*. London, 2004.

Black, Barbara A., *The Constitution of Empire: The Case for the Colonists* (1976) 124 *U. Pa. L. Rev.* 1157.

Bolton, G. C., *The Passing of the Irish Act of Union: a study in parliamentary politics*. London, 1966.

Bolton, Sir Richard, *Questions Propounded in Parliament and Declarations of the Law thereupon in Parliament*. Dublin, c. 1640. UCD special collections, bound with Patrick Darcy, *An argument delivered by Patricke Darcy, Esquire; by the expresse order of the House of Commons in the Parliament of Ireland, 9. Iunii, 1641*. Waterford, 1643.

Bryson, W. H., *The Equity Side of Exchequer* Cambridge, 1975.

Burke, Oliver J., *The history of the lord chancellors of Ireland from AD 1186 to AD 1874* Dublin, 1879.

Campbell, John, Lord, *Lives of the Chief Justices of England*. London, 1858.

Carroll, Joe and Pat Touhy, *Village by Shannon: the Story of Castleconnell and its Hinterland* Ireland, 1991.

Cary, John, *A Vindication of the Parliament of England, &c.* London, 1698.

Clarkson, Thomas, *The History of the Rise, Progress and Accomplishment of the Abolition of the African Slave–Trade by the British Parliament* London, 1839.

Cornish, William. & G. Clarke, *Law and Society in England 1750–1950*. London, 1989.

Costello, Caroline, ed., *The Four Courts: 200 Years: Essays to commemorate the Bicentenary of the Four Courts*. Dublin, 1996.

Costello, Kevin, *The Law of Habeas Corpus in Ireland*. Dublin, 2006.

Coxe, William, *Memoirs of the Life and Administration of Sir Robert Walpole...* (3 vols., London, 1798).

Cromartie, Alan, *Sir Matthew Hale 1609 – 1676: Law, Religion and Natural Philosophy*. Cambridge, 1995.

Curran, C. P., 'Cooley, Gandon and the Four Courts' in Costello, Caroline, ed., *The Four Courts*.

Curran, C. P., 'The Architecture of the Bank: 1. The Parliament House 1728–1800' chapter in F. G. Hall, *The Bank of Ireland 1783–1946*. Dublin, 1949.

Darcy, Patrick, *An Argument Delivered by Patricke Darcy Esq, by The Express Order of The House Of Commons in The Parliament of Ireland 9 June 1641*. Waterford, 1641.

Davis, Thomas Osborne, *The Patriot Parliament of 1689. With its statutes, votes and proceedings...* Edited with an introduction by the Hon. Sir Charles Gavan Duffy. London, Dublin, New York, 1893.

DeLorme, Eleanor Pearson, 'Gilbert Stuart: Portrait of an Artist', Winterthur Portfolio, Vol. 14, No. 4 (Winter, 1979).

Duncan, G. I. O., *The High Court of Delegates*. Cambridge, 1971.

Dunleavy, G. W. and J. E., *The O'Connor Papers*. Wisconsin, 1977.

Edwards, R. Dudley, '*Magna Carta Hiberniæ*' in J. Ryan, ed., *Essays and Studies Presented to Professor Eoin MacNeill*

Englefield, Dermot J. T., *The Printed Records of the Parliament of Ireland, 1613–1800: a survey and bibliographical guide*. London, 1978.

Falkiner, C. Litton, *Essays relating to Ireland* London, 1909.

Fisher, Joseph R., *The End of the Irish Parliament*. London, 1911.

Falkiner, C. Litton, *Essays relating to Ireland*. London, 1909.

Ferguson, William Dwyer, *A Treatise on the Practice of the Queen's Bench, Common Pleas, and Exchequer of Pleas, in Ireland, in Personal Actions and Ejectments*. Dublin, 1841.

FitzGibbon, E., *The Earl of Clare, Mainspring of the Union*. London, 1960.

Fitzpatrick, W. J., *Ireland before the Union, with extracts from the Diary of John Scott, LLD, Earl of Clonmell, Chief Justice of the King's Bench, (1774–1798). A Sequel to the Sham Squire and the Informers of 1798*. Dublin, 1867.

Flaherty, M. S., 'The Empire Strikes Back: Annesley v Sherlock and the Triumph of Imperial Parliamentary Supremacy' (1987) 87 *Colum. L. Rev.* 593.

Fleming, D.A., and A.P.W. Malcomson [eds.]. *'A Volley of Execrations': the letters and papers of John FitzGibbon, Earl of Clare 1772–1802* Dublin, 2005.

Foss, Edward, *Judges of England,...from the time of the Conquest*. London, 1864, reprint 2003, Making of Modern Law, Gale online.

Gadd, R. P., 'A Short Account of the Peerage of Ireland' [1986] *Coat of Arms* 42, 62.

Gadd, R. P., *Peerage Law*. London, 1985.

Galloway, Peter, *The Most Illustrious Order of St. Patrick 1783–1983*. Chichester, 1983.

Garnham, Neal, 'The Trials of James Cotter and Henry, Baron Barry of Santry: two case studies in the administration of criminal justice in early eighteenth-century Ireland' (1998–9) 31 *Irish Historical Studies* 328–342.

Greene, *From the Perspective of Law: Context and Legitimacy in the Origins of the American Revolution* (1986) 85 *S. Atl. Q.* 56.

Greer, D. S. and N. M. Dawson, eds., *Mysteries and Solutions in Irish Legal History, Irish Legal History Society discourses and other papers, 1996–1999*. Dublin, 2001.

Grey, T. C., 'Origins of the Unwritten Constitution: Fundamental Law in American Revolutionary Thought' (1978) 30 *Stan. L. Rev.* 843.

Gibson, Edward, Lord Ashbourne, *Pitt: Some Chapters of his Life and Times*. London, 1898.

Hague, William, *William Pitt The Younger*. London, 2005.

Hague, William, *William Wilberforce: the Life of the Great Anti-Slave Trade Campaigner* London, 2007.

Hale, Leslie, *John Philpot Curran*. London, 1958.

Hand, G. J., *English Law in Ireland 1290–1324* Cambridge, 1967.

Hale, Sir Matthew, *The jurisdiction of the Lords House, or Parliament, considered according to antient records*. London, 1796.

Hayes, Richard J., *Manuscript Materials for Irish Civilisation*. Boston, 1965.

Hayton, D. W., 'The Stanhope/Sunderland Ministry and the Repudiation of Irish Parliamentary Independence'. *English Historical Review* (1998) 113 No. 452, 610–636.

Hayton, D.W., ed. *The Irish Parliament in the Eighteenth Century: the long apprenticeship* Edinburgh, 2001.

Helmholz, R.H., *The Canon Law and Ecclesiastical Jurisdiction from 597 to the 1640s*. OHLE, vol. 1. Oxford, 2004.

Hemmant, M., ed. *Select Cases in the Exchequer Chamber before all the Justices of England*. 51 Seld. Soc. London, 1933.

Henry, Brian, *Dublin Hanged: Crime, Law Enforcement and Punishment in Late 18th-century Dublin*. Dublin, 1994.

Herbert, J. D. [James Dowling], *Irish Varieties*. London, 1836.

Holdsworth, Sir William, *Some Makers of English Law*. Cambridge, 1966.

Holdsworth, William Searle, Sir, *A History of English Law* (continued under the general editorship of A. L. Goodhart and H. G. Hanbury. vol. 17, General Index, by John Burke.) Seventh edition. With an introductory essay and editions by S. B. Chrimes. 17 vols. London, 1903–72.

Hargrave, Francis, *Juridical arguments and collections*. London, 1797. 2 vols.

Hawles, Sir John, *The English-man's Right. A dialogue between a Barrister at Law, and a Jury-man ... setting forth the antiquity ... use ... office, and ... priviledges of Juries by the laws of England*. London, 1680.

Hawtrey, E. C. (ed.), *The Private Diary of William, First Earl Cowper* Eton, 1833.

Hogan, D. and W. N. Osborough, eds., *Brehons, Serjeants and Attorneys*. Dublin, 1990.

House of Lords (Ireland) *Report of the Committee of Secrecy*. 6th September 1798.

House of Lords (Ireland) *Report of the Committee of Secrecy*. 30th August, 1798.

Howard, Gorges Edmond, *A Compendious Treatise of the Rules and Practice of the Pleas Side of the Exchequer in Ireland As It Now Stands Between Party and Party, With the Rules of the Said Court, and an Abridgment Under Each Head of Practice, of the Several Acts of Parliament Now in Force Relating Thereto*. Dublin, 1759. 2d ed., 1793.

Howard, Gorges Edmond, *A Treatise of the Exchequer and Revenue of Ireland*. Dublin, 1776.

Howard, Gorges Edmond, *A Treatise on the rules and practice of the Equity Side of the Exchequer in Ireland*. Dublin, 1760.

Hughes, J. L. T., *Patentee Officers in Ireland 1173–1826: including high sheriffs, 1661–1684 and 1761–1816*. Dublin, 1960.

Ingram, T. D., *A History of the Legislative Union of Great Britain and Ireland*. London, 1887.

Jacob, Giles and Thomas Edlyne Tomlins, *The Law-Dictionary*. London, 1811.

James, Francis, *Lords of the Ascendancy*. Dublin, 1995.

James, F. G., *Ireland in the Empire, 1688–1770*. Cambridge, 1973.

Johnston-Liik, Edith Mary, ed., *History of the Irish Parliament 1692–1800*. 6 vols. Belfast, 2002.

Johnston, E. M., *State of the Irish House of Commons, 1791*. Dublin, P.R.I.A. Sect. c V.59 N.1. 1957.

Johnston, E. M., *Great Britain and Ireland 1760–1800*. Edinburgh, 1963.

Johnston, E. M., *State of the Irish Parliament, 1784–87*. Dublin, P.R.I.A. Sect c V.71 N5. 1971.

Jupp, Peter, 'Earl Temple's Viceroyalty and the Question of Renunciation, 1782–3'. 17 *Irish Historical Studies* 499.

Kavanaugh, Anne, 'John FitzGibbon, Earl of Clare' in *The United Irishmen: Republicanism, Radicalism and Rebellion*. Dublin, 1993.

Kavanaugh, Anne, *John FitzGibbon, Earl of Clare: Protestant Reaction and English Authority in Late Eighteenth-Century Ireland*. Dublin, 1997.

Kearney, Hugh F., *Strafford in Ireland 1633–41: A Study in Absolutism*. Manchester, 1959.

Keane, E., P. B. Phair, and T. U. Sadleir, *King's Inns Admission Papers 1607–1867*. (Dublin, 1982).

Kelly, James, *Poynings' Law and the Making of Law in Ireland, 1660–1800* Dublin, 2007.

Kelly, James, 'The Origins of the Act of Union: an Examination of Unionist Opinion in Britain and Ireland, 1650–1800'. (1987) 25 *Irish Hist. Studies* 236–63.

Kelly, James, *Prelude to Union: Anglo-Irish Politics in the 1780s*. Cork, 1992

Kelly, James, *That Damn'd Thing Called Honour: Duelling in Ireland 1570–1860*. Cork, 1995.

Kelly, James, *Henry Flood: Patriots and Politics in Eighteenth-century Ireland*. Dublin, 1998.

Kenny, Colum, 'The Exclusion of Catholics from the Legal Profession in Ireland, 1537–1829', (1987) 25 *Irish Historical Studies*, 337–57.

Kenny, Colum, *King's Inns and the Kingdom of Ireland: the Irish 'Inn of Court' 1541–1800*. Dublin, 1992.

Kenny, Colum, *King's Inns and the Battle of the Books, 1972*. Dublin, 2002.

Kenyon, J. P., *The Stuart Constitution, 1603–1688: Documents and Commentary*. Cambridge, 1986.

Kiralfy, A.K.R., *A Source Book of English Law*. London, 1957.

Knafla, L. A., *Law and Politics in Jacobean England: the Tracts of Lord Chancellor Ellesmere*. Cambridge, 1977.

Large, D., *Wealth of the Great Irish Landowners 1750–1815*. Dublin, 1966.

Lecky, W. E. H., *History of Ireland in the Eighteenth Century*. London, 1898.

Lemmings, 'The Independence of the Judiciary in Eighteenth-Century England' in P. Birks, ed., *Life of the Law: Proceedings of the Tenth British Legal History Conference*. London, 1993.

Lyall, Andrew B., 'Human Rights and Conditional and Determinable Interests in Freeholds.' (1987) 22 *Irish Jurist* 250–284.

Lyall, Andrew B., 'The Irish House of Lords as a Judicial Body 1783–1800.' (1993–95) 28–30 *Irish Jurist* 314–360.

Lyall, Andrew B., *Land Law in Ireland*. 2nd. edition, Dublin, 2000, 3rd edition (with Albert Power), Dublin, 2010.

Lyall, Andrew B., 'Quia emptores in Ireland' in O. Breen, J. Casey, A. Kerr, eds., *Liber memorialis: Professor James C. Brady*, Dublin, 2001.

Lyall, Andrew, ed., *Irish Exchequer Reports 1716–1734*. 125 Seld. Soc. London, 2008.

Lyne, James, *A Treatise on Leases for Lives Renewable for Ever*. Dublin, 1837.

McCafferty, John, 'To follow the late precedents of England': the Irish impeachment proceedings of 1641' in Greer and Dawson, eds., *Mysteries and Solutions in Irish Legal History*

McCracken, John Leslie, *The Irish parliament in the eighteenth century*. Dundalk, 1971.

MacDonagh, M., 'Catholics under the Irish Parliament' (1914) 4 *Irish Ecclesiastical Record* 5th series 344.

MacDonagh, M., 'The Old Irish Parliament' (1916) 8 *Irish Ecclesiastical Record* 5th series 99.

McDowell, R. B., *Ireland in the Age of Imperialism and Revolution, 1760–1801*. Oxford, 1979.

MacIlwain, Charles, *The American Revolution: A Constitutional Interpretation*. Cornell, 1924.

Madden, F. & D. Fieldhouse, eds. *Empire of the Bretaignes, 1175–1688: the foundations of a colonial system of government*. Select Documents on the Constitutional History of the British Empire and Commonwealth. Vol.1, Connecticut, 1985.

Maguire, W. A., *Downshire Estates in Ireland 1801–1845: the management of Irish landed estates in the early nineteenth century*. Oxford, 1972.

Maitland, F. W., *The Forms of Action at Common Law*. Cambridge, 1st edition, 1909, reprint 1968.

Malcomson, A. P. W., *John Foster: Politics of the Anglo-Irish Ascendancy, 1740–1828.* Oxford, 1978.

Malcomson, A. P. W., *Archbishop Charles Agar: churchmanship and politics in Ireland, 1760–1810* Dublin, 2002.

Maxwell, C., *Country and Town in Ireland under the Georges.* Dublin, 1949.

May, Allyson N., *The Bar and the Old Bailey, 1750–1850.* Chapel Hill, N. Carolina, 2003.

Megarry, R.E., 'Lay Peers in Appeals to the House of Lords' (1949) 65 *LQR* 22

Mervin, Audley, *Speech of Mr Audley Mervin Upon Impeachment of Sir Richard Bolton &c &c.* March 4th 1640. Reprint Dublin, 1764. [See Darcy, Patrick, 1641]

Molyneux, Charles William, Earl of Sefton, *Some thoughts on the Bill for the relief of tenants holding leases for lives, renewable for ever. Addressed to Lord Lifford, Lord Chancellor of Ireland.* Dublin, 1780.

Molyneux, William, *The Case of Ireland's Being Bound by Acts of Parliament in England, Stated.* London, 1698, reprinted, 1720; 1892, with a life of the author by Very Rev. John Canon O'Hanlon.

Moody, T. W., W.E. Vaughan (eds.) *New History of Ireland*, vol. IV. Oxford, 1986.

Moody, T. W., F. J. Byrne and F. X. Martin (eds.) *A New History of Ireland* vol. 9. Oxford, 1984.

Morres, Hervey Redmond, Viscount Mountmorres, *The History of the Principal Transactions of the Irish Parliament, from the year 1634 to 1666.* vol. 2. 1st ed. reprinted. Introduction by Dermot Englefield. Shannon, 1971.

Morres, Hervey Redmond, Viscount Mountmorres, *Historical Dissertation upon the Origin Suspension and Revival of the Judicature and Independence of the Irish Parliament to which is annexed the standing orders of the House of Lords.* London, 1795.

Mount, Charles Merrill , *Gilbert Stuart: a biography* Toronto, 1964.

Murphy, David, *Ireland and the Crimean War.* Portland, Oreg., 2002.

Newark, F. H., 'Notes on Irish Legal History' in *Elegantia Juris.*

Newark, F. H., *Elegantia Juris: selected writings of Francis Headon Newark.* ed. by F.J. McIvor. Belfast, 1973.

O'Brien, Gerard, ed., *Parliament, Politics and People: Essays in Eighteenth-Century Irish History* Dublin, 1989.

O'Brien, J. and G. Guinness, *Dublin: A Grand Tour.* London, 1994.

O'Byrne, Eileen, ed., *The Convert Rolls.* Dublin, 1981.

O'Connell, M. *Irish Politics and Social Conflict in the Age of the American Revolution.* 1965.

O'Flanagan, J. R., *Lives of the Lord Chancellors and Keepers of the Great Seal of Ireland.* 2 vols. London, 1870.

O'Higgins, Paul, 'A Select Bibliography of Irish Legal History' (1960) 4 *Am. J. Legal Hist.* 173–80.

O'Higgins, Paul, 'William Ridgeway (1765-1817) - Law Reporter' (1967) 18 NILQ 208–22.

Osborough, W. N. 'Catholics, Land and the Popery Acts of Anne' in Wheelan and Power eds. *Endurance & Emergence: Catholics in Ireland in the Eighteenth Century*. Dublin, 1990.

Parry, Clive, *Nationality and Citizenship Laws of the Commonwealth and of the Republic of Ireland*. London, 1957–60.

Pawlisch, Hans S., *Sir John Davies and the Conquest of Ireland*. Cambridge, 2002.

Phillips, Charles, *Recollections of Curran and some of his his Contemporaries*. London, 1822.

Pike, L. O., *A Constitutional History of the House of Lords*. London, 1894.

Pollard, A. F., *The Evolution of Parliament*. London, 1920.

Poole, Robert , ' "Give Us Our Eleven Days!": Calendar Reform in Eighteenth-Century England'. (1995) 149 *Past & Present*, pp. 95–139

Quinn, D. B., 'The Early Interpretation of Poynings' Law, 1494–1534' (1941) 2:7 *Irish Historical Studies* 241–254;

Reid, J. P. 'In Legitimate Stirps: The Concept of "Arbitrary," the Supremacy of Parliament, and the Coming of the American Revolution'. (1977) 5 *Hofstra L. Rev.* 459.

Richardson, H. G., 'Magna Carta Hiberniæ' (1942–43) 3 *Irish Historical Studies* 31–33.

Rider, Ebenezer, *An Appendix to the late King James's Acts; containing an exact list of the Lords Spiritual and Temporal and Commons who sate in the Parliament held in Dublin, in 1689. To which is added, A Catalogue of the Titles of all the Acts passed in the said Session, and the preamble to the Act for restoring the old Proprietors to their Estates, &c., as it passed the House of Commons.*. Dublin, 1740.

Rogers, Nini, 'Ireland and the Black Atlantic in the eighteenth century.' (2000) 32 *Irish Historical Studies* 174–192.

Ryan, J., ed., *Essays and Studies Presented to Professor Eoin MacNeill*, Dublin, 1940.

Ryan-Smolin, Wanda, *King's Inns Portraits*. Dublin, 1992.

Sayles, C. O. *Contemporary Sketches of Members of the Irish Parliament in 1782*. PRIA V. 56 No. 3 sect C. 1954.

Schuyler, R. L., *Parliament and the British Empire: Some Constitutional Controversies Concerning Imperial Legislative Jurisdiction*. New York, 1929.

Scott, John, *John Scott, Baron Earlsfort, chief justice of the Court of King's Bench, Ireland, afterwards Earl of Clonmell – His private diary, 1774–98*. privately printed. Trinity College Dublin. Dublin, 1807.

Sheridan, Charles Francis, *Observations on the Doctrine laid down by Sir William Blackstone, respecting the extent of power of the British Parliament, particularly with relation to Ireland*. London, 1779.

Simms, J. G., *The Jacobite Parliament of 1689*. Pamphlet, Irish History Series, No. 6. Dundalk, 1974.

Smyth, C. J., *Chronicle of the Law Officers of Ireland from the earliest period to the present time*. London, 1839.

Smythe, Hamilton, *The Law of Landlord and Tenant in Ireland*. Dublin, 1842.

Stephen, H. J., *A Treatise on the Principles of Pleading in Civil Actions*. London, 1824.

Stevens, Robert, *Law and Politics: the House of Lords as a Judicial Body, 1800–1976*. London, 1979.

Sullivan, Alexander Martin, *The Last Serjeant; the memoires of Serjeant A.M. Sullivan Q.C.* London, 1952.

Swift, Jonathan, *The Correspondence of Jonathan Swift*. Williams, ed. Oxford, 1963.

Swift Macneill, J. G. *The Irish Parliament: What it Was and What it Did*. London, 1985.

Thompson, E. P. 'The Rule of Law', chapter 10 part iv in *Whigs and Hunters: The Origin of the Black Act*. Harmondsworth, 1977.

Twiss, H., *The Public and Private Life of Lord Chancellor Eldon*. London, 1844.

Victory, Isolde L., 'The Making of the 1720 Declaratory Act', in Gerard O'Brien ed., *Parliament, Politics and People: Essays in Eighteenth Century Irish History*. Dublin, 1989.

Victory, Isolde L., 'Colonial Nationalism in Ireland, 1692–1725: From Common Law to Natural Right'. (Trinity College, Dublin, Ph.D. thesis, 1984).

Walker, D. M., *The Scottish Legal System*. Edinburgh, 1981.

Wallace, J. W., *The Reporters: Arranged And Characterized With Incidental Remarks*. Boston, 1882.

West, Richard, *A Discourse Concerning Treasons, and Bills of Attainder*. London, 1716, reprinted 2008, Lawbook Exchange Ltd.

Whyte, J. H., *Landlord Influence in Elections in Ireland*. EHR LXXV. 1960.

Wylie, J. C. W., *Irish Land Law*, 4th. edition, London, 2010.

Wurzel, Harold, 'The Origin and Development of Quo Minus' (1939) 49 *Yale Law Journal* 39–64.

Yale, D. E. C., ed., *Sir Matthew Hale's Prerogatives of the King*. 92 Seld. Soc. London, 1975.

INDEX OF PEOPLE, PLACES & THINGS

INDEX OF SUBJECTS